BY TRUST BETRAYED

BY TRUST BETRAYED

Patients, Physicians, and the License
to Kill in the Third Reich

Hugh Gregory Gallagher

HENRY HOLT AND COMPANY
New York

Library of Congress Cataloging-in-Publication Data
Gallagher, Hugh Gregory.
By trust betrayed : patients, physicians, and the license to kill in the Third Reich / by Hugh Gregory Gallagher.—1st ed.
    p.   cm.
Bibliography: p.
Includes index.
ISBN 0-8050-0749-0
1. Euthanasia—Government policy—Germany—History—20th century.
2. Medical ethics—Germany—History—20th century.   3. World War, 1939–1945—Atrocities.   I. Title.
R726.G35   1990
174'.24'094309044—dc20   89–11136
                                                                  CIP

Henry Holt books are available at special discounts for bulk purchases for sales promotions, premiums, fund-raising, or educational use. Special editions or book excerpts can also be created to specification.

For details contact:
Special Sales Director
Henry Holt and Company, Inc.
115 West 18th Street
New York, New York 10011

First Edition

Designed by Susan Hood
Printed in the United States of America
10 9 8 7 6 5 4 3 2 1

Dedicated to the late
Dr. Alexander Mitscherlich,
a psychiatrist of courage and wisdom

In memory of Roland Marcotte
who is greatly missed by his friends

With special gratitude to Helga Roth, whose help
and enthusiasm made this a better book

Contents

Acknowledgments   ix

Introduction   1

1. Aktion T-4 at Hadamar   9

2. The Handicapped in Other Times and Places   24

3. Aktion T-4 Begins   45

4. Aktion T-4 Origins   74

5. Aktion T-4 in Action   96

6. The Children's Program   120

7. Aktion T-4 at Absberg   137

8. Aktion T-4 in Trouble   146

9. Aktion T-4 and the Doctors   178

10. Aktion T-4 and the Lawyers   205

11. Aktion T-4 and the Church   219

12. Aktion T-4 Sequelae: 1945–88   247

Afterword: A Conversation   275

Appendix A. Report of Pastor P. Braune   282
Appendix B. Sermon of Clemens August Graf von Galen, Bishop of Münster   294

Appendix C. Final Plea for Defendant Karl Brandt
                   by Dr. Servatius   298
Appendix D. Final Statement of Defendant
                   Karl Brandt   302

Notes   305
Bibliography   322
Index   331

Illustrations follow page 156.

Acknowledgments

With thanks to Paul Waggaman, Steven Sanders, Nestor Cordova, Mike Jarboe, Frederick Sollock.

With deep appreciation to Dr. Edmund Pellegrino, members and particularly the librarians of the Kennedy Institute of Ethics, Georgetown University, for their help and interest as I was writing this book.

With thanks to the following who helped me with translations: Robert Burns, Pete Moore, Ulrich Werner, Vivien Rubin, and the infallible Ron Grimes, reference librarian, Montgomery County Library System.

With special thanks to the World Institute on Disability, the Rehabilitation Institute, and the World Rehabilitation Fund; to Judy Heumann and Barbara Duncan, for continuing help and assistance; and for the travel grant, under the IDEAS program, which allowed me to spend a month in Germany in the spring of 1988.

And thanks to my agent Athos Demetriou and my editor at Henry Holt, Peter Bejger.

With thanks for the support and suggestions of Adelaide Blomfield, Evan Kemp, Janine Bertram, Bob Bernstein, Frank McArdle, Leonard Rubin, Marsha Dubrow, and, as always, Lorenzo Milam, Lauro Halstead, and John M. Dluhy.

And lastly with gratitude for the patience, good cheer, intelligence, and organizational skill of my editor Cherry Glazer.

In *Illness as Metaphor* Susan Sontag writes, "Everyone who is born holds dual citizenship in the kingdom of the well and in the kingdom of the sick."

There is a third kingdom—the land of the crippled. This place is no democracy; it is a dictatorship. The usual rights and privileges of citizenship do not apply here. A great wall surrounds this place, and most of what goes on within the wall is unknown to those outside it.

What follows is a message from over the wall.

Introduction

There's something happening here,
What it is ain't exactly clear.

"For What It's Worth,"
Buffalo Springfield, 1967

An attack of poliomyelitis in 1952, when I was nineteen, left me severely paralyzed. As a result I have lived with a wheelchair throughout my adult life. Wherever I go—and I have traveled a good deal—I go by wheelchair. My paralysis has become part of me; and, inescapably, it has had an impact upon how I see myself and how I am seen by others.

Before I had polio, I remember I was frightened by disabled people. They made me feel ill at ease, embarrassed. I would cross the street to avoid walking past a man in a wheelchair. Now, I find myself *in* a wheelchair, and it feels quite ordinary. My friends do not seem to pay much attention to it, one way or another. Certainly, they are not repelled, as I once was.

It was different in the 1950s. People would stare, avoid eye contact, overreact to my presence—not all the time, but often enough. This would cause the cords in my neck to tighten up.

I was reminded of this when I was doing research in Germany on this book. Several times I found my neck tightening up in the old way. Why would this be? I examined what was going on, and I found out something: the people I was passing were clearly made awkward by my presence. The Germans of today do, indeed, seem less comfortable with the disabled than are Americans.

As I get older, I find myself more and more interested in such things. How do other people react to their disability? How have disabled persons fared in other times, in other societies?

I wrote *FDR's Splendid Deception*, a psychological study of the crippled President, because I wanted to understand how, as a paraplegic, he was able to function at a time of much prejudice against such disabilities.[1] What I found was a strong personality struggling at great emotional cost to maintain the posture of denial which made his political career possible. It was my conclusion that this denial served to isolate the man from his loved ones, and that the struggle to maintain it ultimately killed him.

The FDR I found was a great President, but no role model for disabled people. He lived lonely and died relatively young.

Traditionally, or at least in recent centuries, Western society has thought of the disabled in the medical mode. They are seen as sick people who somehow never get well. This, of course, causes all sorts of difficulties in the relations between the disabled and the medical community. What *do* you do with "refractory cases," as the German physicians of the thirties called those of us who refuse to respond to therapy?

However, disabled people are not sick, most of them. They are disabled. If you stop looking at them as medical cases and instead see them as a minority group in the civil rights sense, certain things become clear. The disabled are a minority, functioning in a non-disabled society; and for a long time and in many ways they have been denied the civil rights which others take for granted.

Unlike most minorities, the disabled have no cultural unity, no shared heritage or history. The disabled are not all one color or race or social class. They are drawn from *all* races and classes. They often lead isolated lives, and it is only most recently in America that they have even begun to perceive of themselves as having shared resentments and common needs.

Almost every family has a crippled member; almost everyone has a friend or loved one with a crippling condition. Disability is, after all, a common condition of life. Most people, sooner or later, become disabled in one manner or another.

This is what makes a society's discrimination and cruelty toward the disabled such an intriguing business. The perpetrators are victimizing not some alien religious or ethnic group, but rather their fellow citizens, their own friends and family members, and in due course, themselves. Discrimination in any form is destructive. Discrimination toward disabled people is destructive, not just of others but, in a real sense, of our own family and oneself.

I have become convinced that the place of the disabled in society needs study. Anthropologists, sociologists, and historians need to investigate the origins and the development of social attitudes and behavior toward the disabled. Where did this behavior come from? What is its cause? How has it changed over the years? Very little work has been done on such matters.

And yet such matters are important. If the disabled are to obtain their rightful, useful status in society, they must understand their present position and the precedents upon which it is based. If society is to deal fairly and honorably with its disabled brothers and sisters, there must be a general understanding and awareness of what should constitute fairness and of how society has failed to be fair in the past.

I spent the past three years as a visiting adjunct fellow of the Kennedy Institute of Ethics at Georgetown University, researching and reading what little material is available on the social history of the disabled. Over the course of this reading, I became interested in the so-called euthanasia program of Nazi Germany. I found that the medical events which transpired over the life of the Third Reich present in sharp and high relief the hostility and the fear which portions of society have always experienced toward the disabled. The physicians of Germany *acted out* these feelings in ways so grotesque and clear that there can be no doubt what was going on.

Physicians are no worse and—although they may feel otherwise—perhaps not much better than any other profession as a group. The German nation, in all, is as good or bad as any other. However, what happened in Germany in the 1930s and 1940s, what German physicians did to their disabled patients, is of great importance to the struggle for disability rights, not just in Germany but everywhere. The feelings that drove the German doctors to do what they did are, in fact, everywhere. Such things as the profound fear of those who may be different; the loathing of the vulnerability of the sick and disabled; the demented drive for perfect health, perfect bodies, perfect happiness—these are universal. They must be seen for what they are—unreal and unworthy.

This book tells the story of the German physicians' private war upon their chronic patients, the patients' brave resistance, and ultimately the outrage of much of society when it learned of what was going on. This is an important part of the twentieth-century history of the disabled—important not just for the disabled, but for all who have an interest in justice and fair play.

Undoubtedly, present-day feelings about the crippled and the insane are governed, tempered by human concern for their well-being and a sense of fair play. There is, however, an underside to these feelings: the chronically disabled are seen as "other"; as beyond the pale; as being, somehow, a threatening enemy. This is the dark side, which was laid bare by Nazi Germany.

Every man has a dark side. Within it are strong, even violent, feelings of anger, fear, and hate. As a daily matter, these emotions are kept in check by a governor, an inner sense of appropriate response and behavior. In a breakdown this governor is lost. At such a time these dark feelings swell and expand until they fill the soul. Sometimes these feelings are more than experienced—they are acted upon. A crazy man, a man overwhelmed by his emotions, may do terrible things. And so may a crazy nation. Germany did such terrible things in the years of the Nazi Reich.

Nations, like persons, are capable of a nervous breakdown. How else may the Reich of Adolf Hitler be understood? Like the individual in a manic frenzy, the entire German nation seethed with madness. Hidden hates and fears surged forth in a paroxysm of self-destructive fury. It has been said that the madness of Adolf Hitler produced Nazi Germany, but it is as true, surely, to say that it was the madness of the Germany of the twenties and thirties which found its expression in Hitler. Hitler was crazy, certainly, but in this he was the very embodiment of the Germany of his times.

The physicians of Hitler's Reich participated in a program designed to kill their chronic patients. Systematically and efficiently, a good many more than 200,000 German citizens were killed by their physicians. The killed were citizens in good standing with the state. They were not, in most cases, terminally ill; neither were they often in pain or unusual distress. They were the institutionalized insane, the severely disabled, the tubercular, the retarded. They were those whose lives—in the eyes of their doctors—were "not worth living."

Although this program was authorized by Hitler and carried out under the auspices of the National Socialist government of the Third Reich, it would be a mistake to call it a Nazi program. It was not. The program was conceived by physicians and operated by them. They did the killing. While many of these physicians were Nazis, many more were not. The program's sponsors and senior participants were the leading medical professors and psychiatrists of Germany, men of international reputation.

The program did not just happen. The concept had been discussed and debated for more than fifty years. It was no more than a logical application of the principles of Social Darwinism and the budding science of eugenics. The program was based upon supposed scientific principles which were then in wide acceptance, not only in Germany but elsewhere in Europe and the United States. Eugenics, genetics, and biology were used to provide the rationale for killing.

It has been said that physicians are often frustrated by their inability to cure their chronic patients. If this is so, in the Germany of the thirties physicians sought to eliminate this frustration by eliminating the source—their patients.

Analysis of the behavior and thought of the participating physicians—as revealed in the correspondence and records of the time—illuminates this frustration dynamic that exists, felt and unfelt, in the relationship between a physician and his chronic patients. This is a dynamic that needs to be better understood—by doctors and patients alike.

The world has largely ignored the issue of what the German physicians did to their patients during World War II. After the war the German medical profession simply opened again for business, as though none of this had happened. It is true that some of the physician leaders of the program committed suicide, but others merely changed their names and resumed their practices. A part of one of the trials at Nuremberg examined the issue; several additional trials of specific individuals have occurred over the years, but that is all. Those trials which have been held have been unsatisfactory—largely because physicians, as always, are reluctant to testify as one peer against another. The courts themselves have participated in this denial—dismissing some cases, allowing decades-long delays in others; and in one memorable decision actually finding the physician defendant not guilty because of the general *Zeitgeist*, the "spirit of the time."

In fact, the patient-killing program was a major contributor to the *Zeitgeist*, serving as it did as the precursor of the Holocaust. It was, in fact, a grave collapse of medical ethics. It was a betrayal of the trust that exists between a patient and his physician. It was the ultimate abnegation of the Hippocratic Oath.

There can be no doubt that the questions the Nazis sought to address—right to life, right to death—are still here to be addressed. Today's medical technology, of course, makes them even more pressing and difficult. But they are the same questions. For this reason it is instructive to see what happens when a central government—in this instance, Nazi Germany—attempts to resolve as a matter of general policy the particular question of who shall live and who shall die; and, even more particularly, who shall make that decision? The experience of the German physicians in enforcing this policy revealed feelings, behavior, and relationships with a profound clarity.

Mad dogs are no problem for any sensible society: they must not be allowed to run wild. When they do they cause havoc. This is what happened in Germany.

There were "mad-dog" killers in the euthanasia program. Such psychotic acts are not relevant to the purpose of this book. These "mad dogs" and the acts they committed are as appalling, preposterous, even entertaining, as a grisly horror movie. But like a horror movie these acts are so remote from daily experience, so distant, that like cannibalism in Borneo or the Black Death of Europe the reader is quite untouched.

I believe it is a mistake to focus on these monstrous doctors doing their monstrous things. They divert attention from the real story. What is interesting *and* important about the killing program is not the mad-dog killers, but rather the careful, orderly, and quite methodical manner by which the full German medical and scientific establishment proceeded to kill its patients over a period of years.

These men believed they were acting as scientists, concerned with the welfare of their patients and the cleansing of the corporate body of the German *Volk*. They believed that modern science and technology presented medicine with the opportunity for a major breakthrough—a radicalization of therapeutic activity to rehabilitate those among the physically and mentally disabled who could be rehabilitated and the elimination of the remaining "refractory cases."

No doubt they meant well. But, no doubt about it, they were murderers, blinded by their own arrogance. This arrogance, bred of a confidence in science and the prestige of the medical profession, is by no means exclusively a German trait. It is universal and, as such, universally dangerous. And endlessly fascinating.

For as Goetz Aly and Heinz Roth say, behind the bestialities of the Nazi extermination excesses lingers a still more gruesome dimension: the mechanistic belief that the pursuit of "progress" can serve as justification for mass killings. This dimension must be exposed from the repression and secrecy with which it has been hidden. [2]

More gruesome than mad dogs—and as prevalent as ever—are the beliefs that the desire to perfect the human race justifies killing, and that arrogant professionals find it acceptable to interfere with the rights and lives of others.

1

Aktion T-4 at Hadamar

O man: respect mankind!

Memorial at Hadamar

I n my research of the literature of the Third Reich killing program, I found the name of the psychiatric institute at Hadamar appearing time and time again.

Hadamar seems to have been the very capital of medical killing in Germany. It had been one of the six official killing centers. After the end of the centralized program, the doctors of Hadamar had continued with their killing, using their own methods and criteria. Hadamar had participated in the "wild" euthanasia in the 14 f 13 program, which extended euthanasia to the concentration camps, and by the end of the war was killing even healthy laborers brought from Poland.

It became important to me that I see the place. Perhaps I could then understand how it happened, *why* it happened. In October 1987 I had the opportunity to make the trip.

We drove up one morning from Heidelberg on the autobahn. It was a cool day in early fall; and although there was not a cloud in the sky, the countryside was covered with a light and gentle haze. This gave the landscape an expressionistic look, as though an artist had used only a few broad brushstrokes to suggest the narrow valleys, the gentle rolling hills, the villages in the distance.

At Wiesbaden we turned north, along the Cologne road. After some thirty kilometers through what was clearly rich farm country, we could see the cathedral town of Limburg, coming up on the left. The cathedral itself, a church with an excessive number of spires, towers over the old parts of the city from its site on top of a rocky crag. The bishop's palace sits at the base of the hill in the midst of old half-timbered houses. Turning off the main road, we drove through the narrow streets of old Limburg on our way to Hadamar.

We had a hard time finding Hadamar on the road map: it was only a tiny dot, a mere eight kilometers northwest of Limburg. We were there in just a moment. Hadamar is a small farming town on the Elbbach River; its houses rise upon the hillside on both sides of the stream. The town boasts an impressive *Schloss*, now being restored, plus an abbey and several churches. It was a Saturday; stalls had been set up in the marketplace. Some sort of a local festival was under way, and there were a good many people on the streets.

We drove about searching for the psychiatric hospital, not knowing where to look. I had seen a snapshot of the place, taken some forty years before. I should be able to recognize the place *if* it were still standing, if it had not been substantially rebuilt. We followed the signs to the *Krankenhaus*, the local hospital. This turned out to be a warehouse-like building, on a street corner in the middle of town. This could not possibly be the place. I knew the hospital we were looking for was on the crest of a hill, set back from the road, well-landscaped: I had seen it in a wartime photograph. We combed the town, went back and forth along the main street, the *only* through street. We were about to give up the search when we spotted a small sign pointing the way to the "Psychiatrisches Institut."

The midday sun had burned off the morning haze. The sky was a bright blue, the air crisp and clean, and the autumn sun was hot, with sharp, intense rays. The small road gently wound its way up the hill. Back in the town the houses were built side by side, flush with the sidewalk. Here, the houses were single dwellings, with nice gardens and wide lawns. And at the end of the road was the Hadamar Psychiatric Institute. I recognized it at once.

The main building has been restuccoed and painted a bright off-white. A new front porch has been added. The building has new wings and, about the grounds, even newer, quite modern patient residences have been built. The great dark pines I remembered from the photograph were still there, but softened by the lighter greens of beech and oak trees. The sweeping lawns were bright green in the sharp full sun.

And everywhere there were flowers, great banks of flowers. The Germans have a way with geraniums. They bloom so thickly that the eye sees only a great swath of red. And German marigolds bloom right through the summer into the fall—weeks and weeks after American marigolds have given up the ghost. That afternoon the grounds of Hadamar Institute were alive, awash with the orange-gold of marigolds, the yellow of chrysanthemums, and the red of geraniums.

Benches have been placed in front of the main building, and patients were sitting about, soaking up the sun's rays, enjoying the flowers. A couple were strolling the grounds, chatting. To the side and behind the building young people were playing a game of volleyball, and their shouts and cheers carried over the campus in the clear air.

At that moment, in that sunlight, it was hard to believe that during World War II more than ten thousand—nobody knows how many *more* than ten thousand—mentally ill German citizens were killed by their psychiatrists in the basement of this building in front of me—this main building of the Hadamar Psychiatric Institute.

I had read the evidence presented at Nuremberg and at the other trials. It was hard to believe, but it was so.

Hadamar looked different back then—it was not so spruced up. The stucco needed painting. The pine trees were severe and dark. "The building itself resembled a morgue, gloomy and forbidding," said a visitor not long after the war. "Most of the rooms were small, cold, and bleak. There was little furniture other than beds, and these, without exception, were old and uncomfortable."[1]

Back then, a walled fence surmounted by barbed wire enclosed the grounds. SS guards patrolled the boundary; and no unauthorized personnel, including state officials from Wiesbaden, were allowed to enter. Many of the staff—the doctors and nurses, attendants and clerks—were local people who had worked for years at the hospital, but they had been forced to sign written oaths to the effect that they would never tell anyone what was going on within the barbed-wire fence.

The patients scheduled for killing were transported to the hospital in the big gray buses of the Gemeinnützige Krankentransportgesellschaft, the "General Patient Transport Company." No effort was made to hide the function of these buses—the logo of the company was painted clearly on the sides—although the windows of the vehicle were smoked so that passersby could not see in. Soon enough, the buses became well-known in the narrow streets of Limburg, and it was not long before the townsfolk, both in Limburg and in Hadamar, knew the destination of the buses' passengers. "There goes the murder box," children would shout when a gray bus drove by.

Several times a week one of the buses would take the winding road, past the beautiful houses, up to Hadamar. The buses were comfortably outfitted. Upholstered seats were two by two, and each bus could carry seventy or so patients. The buses were staffed by male nurses, recruited from the ranks of the SS by the program organizers at their Berlin headquarters. These nurses wore the white uniforms of a nurse and the black boots of the SS. This rather bizarre outfit was noted by the hospital staff, who referred to them as the "white coat–black boots."

These men might have come from the SS Corps, but they treated their patients kindly enough. They gave them physical assistance onto and off the buses, if this was needed. If the trip was a long one, they made sure their patients had thermoses of hot coffee and sandwiches to see them through. The nurses looked after the patients' few personal effects—they had been discouraged from taking much more than toiletries—and the nurses were responsible for the patients' medical charts and personal histories. Upon arrival at Hadamar, these were presented to the senior attending physician, Dr. Adolf Wahlmann.

Before boarding the bus at their home institution, patients had to be labeled, just as nowadays hospital patients are required to wear plastic identification bracelets. All items of clothing had to be similarly labeled. Various other cards—property information, defrayer-of-expenses information—and lists (in duplicate) had to be filled out and compiled, according to regulation. Today, it would be very difficult and complicated to move an entire ward of chronic patients from one hospital to another. There would be billing and insurance problems; medical, pharmaceutical, and procedural matters to be dealt with; and, of course, with the mentally incompetent, legal and custodial issues to confront. Such a move was no less complex or difficult in the Germany of the Third Reich. In Hitler's

Germany, the authorities operating his killing program were making a mockery of the traditions of German medicine and the principles and formalities of German law. They did not, however, mock the regulations. They followed the established administrative procedures to the letter.

The bus would move up the drive in front of the hospital and swing around to unload its passengers in the private area under the hillside, behind the main building. According to the testimony received at the Heyde trial, care was taken to see that the patients were unloaded at the killing hospitals in a place where their screams could not be heard.[2] Here at Hadamar, a special wooden garage, large enough to house two of the patient-transport buses, was constructed in the courtyard behind the main building. A covered walkway linked this garage with the hospital proper. Most of the patients were physically fit and able to walk into the hospital. Wheelchairs and stretchers were available for those who needed special assistance.

The patients were gathered from the various medical institutions of central west Germany. They had a variety of complaints— schizophrenia, depression, mental retardation, tuberculosis, dwarfism, paralysis, epilepsy—even, upon occasion, such things as delinquency, perversion, alcoholism, and "antisocial" behavior.

All these people would be herded into the front hall where tables had been set up, and Dr. Wahlmann, administrator Alfons Klein, and head nurse Irmgard Huber were waiting to admit them. Patients were matched with their medical charts; their temperatures and pulse rates would be taken and, as necessary, they would have a short word with the doctor.

The hospital had been informed of the expected arrival time of the new patients. Already, Nurse Huber would have readied the large ward and small rooms on the ground floor reserved for the temporary patients. The more permanent patients were housed on the upper two floors of the Institution. Beds were made with fresh linen and warm blankets, and all was done to make welcome the patients after their tiring journey. Hot coffee and rolls might be passed out, and aspirin or a sedative would be available if needed. If it was late in the day, the nurses would help the patients undress and see them to bed.

Different killing procedures were developed over time at the euthanasia centers. At Hadamar, during the period of the official euthanasia program, killing was done by the administration of carbon monoxide gas. This method had been selected as the most *humane* of the various methods tested.[3]

At the conclusion of the official patient-killing program, the Hadamar carbon monoxide equipment was crated up and shipped to Lublin, Poland, to be used in the killing of Jews.[4] This did not mean that the killing ended at Hadamar. Not at all. After the official phase, responsibility for selecting patients to be killed, as well as for the killing itself, was decentralized; and at Hadamar it rested in the able hands of the medical director. In this phase the killing was done through hypodermic injection of a mixture of morphine and scopolamine by Nurse Huber and chief male nurse Ruoff, under the direction, of course, of Dr. Wahlmann.

The Hadamar gas chamber was set up in the basement, in a room about ten by sixteen feet, with a ceiling eight feet high. The chamber was rigged up to look like a shower room with nozzles out of which—at the touch of a button—would flow carbon monoxide rather than water. About the perimeter of the room were ranged chairs and benches for the use of the patients. Some twenty to thirty patients could be accommodated comfortably. "There was plenty of room," said a defendant, Viktor Brack, later at the trial.[5]

At the conclusion of the admissions procedures the nurses would tell the patients they were to have a nice shower to rest and cleanse them after their journey. The unsuspecting patients would have no objection to such a suggestion. Even if they should object, of course, no exceptions were allowed. Led by a nurse, small groups of patients would file down the stairs to the "showers." There, the patients would carefully remove their clothes—again with the help of a nurse, if necessary—and enter the gas chamber. Once all were inside, the nurse would close the door and lock it.

This was not always as smooth a procedure as it sounds. Some of the patients were paralyzed and had to be carried down the stairs. Others were ill and weak, and they also needed major assistance.

Killing, "final medical assistance," was a medical procedure and could be done only under the authority and at the direction of a physician. At Hadamar the physician was Dr. Wahlmann. When the chamber door was locked and sealed, it was he who pushed the button which caused the poisonous gas to pour through the shower nozzles. He would watch this through a peephole in the door. According to testimony received at Nuremberg, "A few minutes after the gas was let in, the patients became sleepy and tired and died after a few minutes. They simply went to sleep without even knowing that they were going to sleep."[6] Elsewhere it was claimed that it took only twenty-two seconds for the patients to die.[7] However long it took, the normal procedure was to leave the gas in the chamber for some twenty minutes, with the doctor watching closely through his little window. By this time, when the patients were clearly dead, the gas would be evacuated from the chamber. Dr. Wahlmann would then enter the chamber to certify that all were dead.

The bodies were removed by patient-laborers who normally worked on the Hadamar hospital farm. Using stretchers, they would carry them to the crematorium which had been installed, also in the basement of the building. Smoke from the burning of the bodies became a well-known sight in the neighborhood.

> . . . the citizens of Hadamar watch the smoke rise out of the chimney and are tortured with the ever-present thought of the poor sufferers, especially when the nauseating odors carried by the wind offend their nostrils.
>
> The effect of the principles at work here is that the local children call each other names and say, "You're crazy, you'll be sent to the baking oven in Hadamar."
>
> —From a letter of the Bishop of Limburg, Aug. 13, 1941, to the Reich Minister of Justice[8]

In the fall of 1941 when the Hadamar gas chamber was removed, the crematorium was shut down also. From then until the end of the war, those who were killed at Hadamar were buried in a hospital graveyard about sixty yards behind the main building. This contained mass graves, including a children's section. The caretaker of the cemetery during most of this time was Philipp Blum, who was the nephew of Alfons Klein, the hospital administrator. Blum's duties were varied: he served as doorman and telephone switch-board operator as well as chief of burials. According to testimony, it was Blum's practice to "walk around in the ward" before the patients were killed, presumably sizing up his soon-to-be clients.[9]

At first, care was taken with the dead. The body was placed with respect in a coffin and taken out for burial to a nearby field set aside for the purpose. But the bodies began to pile up. Soon they were being buried in mass graves, without ceremony. A curious coffin with a trap door was devised for the purpose. The body was placed in the coffin; the coffin was carried to the gravesite, placed on a framework over the hole, and the trap door sprung. In this way the coffin could be used over and over.[10]

It cannot have been easy carrying all those bodies by stretcher out to the burying ground. Blum had the help of Friedrich Dickmann, a former patient who served as handyman about the hospital. Throughout the war there were more than one hundred long-term patients resident at Hadamar. They worked the farm, maintained the grounds, and helped in the kitchen. The resident patients would help in the grave digging, as needed.

The killed patients' records and medical histories would then be given by the nursing staff to a Mr. Adolf Merkle, the hospital book-keeper. He carefully entered the fact of each patient's death into his record book and filled out a death certificate accordingly. There was a meeting each morning of Dr. Wahlmann; the administrator, Klein; and the chief nurse, Huber. At this meeting, Wahlmann would go over the list of the newly dead and assign a suitable cause of death to each. He always made an attempt to find a cause of death that would be appropriate to the medical history of the deceased. Pneumonia and tuberculosis were popular in the last years of the war. With the causes of death filled in, it was the duty of Blum, telephone operator and grave digger and general factotum, to take the certificates round to City Hall, where they were duly recorded.

Mr. Merkle felt it would arouse suspicions if a large number of patients died on the same day. Therefore, he took to spacing out the dates of death on the certificates so that instead of reporting a great number of deaths over a short period of time, the institution reported a steady number, spread over a lengthy period. Mr. Merkle, how-ever, was an orderly man. He kept his patient lists in alphabetical fashion. This meant that Merkle had his Hadamar patients dying in the order of the alphabet—A's and B's today, C's and D's tomorrow, and so forth. [11]

There seems to have been considerable trouble with the staff stealing valuables from the deceased: wristwatches, jewelry, even the goldwork from teeth. This was upsetting to the management. After all, such items were supposed to be collected, recorded, and forwarded to Berlin to be used for the war effort. No attempt was made to forward the effects of the dead person to his family or heirs. After the war, bundles of old clothes, the last vestiges of the victims, were found in the attics of Hadamar. [12]

After the official end of the euthanasia program, the rate of killing slowed, but it did not cease. Word was passed, apparently, that it was all right for doctors to kill disabled patients, but no longer would the state direct the victim-selection process. It was up to each physician, each institution, to act on its own.

On April 15, 1943, Hadamar began to function as something of a killing center for children. Not just infants, but children—even teenagers—were killed. And not just the disabled and retarded were selected. The inmates of orphan asylums, juvenile homes, and foster care were appraised; and many healthy children who were thought to be troublemakers went to their death. So did children of mixed races, children with adolescent pimples, and even those who may have annoyed a staff member for one reason or another.

On May 15, 1943, a letter was sent from Hadamar to all the juvenile homes in Hesse. It set the criteria for children who should be transferred to Hadamar, so as to benefit from its new therapy. The letter assured the homes' personnel that the young patients would receive "correct treatment for their well-being," in addition to receiving "good and sufficient education," with time for healthy play activities. The letter said that Hadamar had teachers on the staff to handle the nonmedical side of the program. This, of course, was a lie; the whole program was a hoax. The children were going to their deaths.

▬

As I got back in my car after a tour of the grounds, I felt a cold wind rising. The sun's rays were still warm but I noticed a cloud bank building to the west. I was deeply puzzled by what had gone on at Hadamar.

Originally, I suppose, the idea had been to kill the severely retarded, the violently, chronically insane, and the desperately and painfully disabled. The idea was to put them out of their misery in much the same way society shoots horses or puts down a suffering dog. There was a scientific rationale, of course: killing these people would somehow strengthen the genetic heritage of the body of the German people, the great mythic *Volk*—like removing a cancerous tumor from an individual body, perhaps. And, of course, there were the economic reasons—"useless eaters" were taking resources better used in the German war effort.

Such arguments served to give a rational cover to what went on at Hadamar. But from what I could tell, what went on at Hadamar was not rational. None of the arguments held up. Many of the German citizens who were killed were not in great pain, were not dying; some were not even sick. Some were but temporarily disabled; others were gainfully employed. The disabling condition of many of them did not appear to be related to any readily discernible sort of inheritable genetic weakness. What *was* it the medical personnel at Hadamar were doing? What was it they thought they were doing?

And the patients—the thousands upon thousands of patients: what was going on with them? All but a few of them must have known they were on the way to death. After all, they talked with one another and with their friends among the nursing home and asylum staffs. The institutionalized patients were aware and concerned about the fate of their colleagues, who were shipped away on the gray patient-transport buses, only to be followed a week or so later by a flurry of simultaneous death notices. It was no secret. There are enough extant letters of appeal or farewell written by institution inmates, desperate letters written to the authorities by families of patients, to make it evident that patients were aware of what was happening. The dreadful and sickening smell of burning bodies that permeated the neighborhood of Hadamar served as a keen reminder, should anyone forget.

These people were not prisoners; they were patients. These people, these patients, had retained their physicians to act as their agents in the search for healing. Certainly they had not, under any contract known to medicine, given their physicians the authority to kill them at will. When it became evident that the doctors had become the enemy and that their lives were in danger from the doctors, why did the disabled not revolt, flee, protest?

It is true that many of the insane were in hospitals because they had been committed by a court proceeding, and they were being held there by the power of the state. And, of course, there were the SS guards and the barbed wire which had been placed around the hospital. Symbolically, as well as actually, the presence of the guards served to enforce the authority of the doctors and to discourage in an obvious way thought of escape or revolt.

Furthermore, Germany is a society that respects authority and places a high value upon strict observance of the rules and regulations imposed by that authority. At no time in the history of the German people was the power of authority greater than during the terror years of the Third Reich. It was physically dangerous—life-threatening—to question or resist the ruling powers.

And as anyone who has ever been a patient is aware, a hospital is an institution that rewards dependence and discourages personal autonomy. The *good* patient is the one who does what he is told: he takes his medicine, has his bowel movement, is passive and undemanding. The *bad* patient causes trouble: he complains, questions his medicines, acts up. As a result the bad patient is ostracized in the institutional setting, while the good patient gets the attention: his bell is answered sooner; he gets the extra dessert; he is better taken care of. No wonder the long-term patient in a medical institution all too often regresses into a helpless, childlike dependency. Such people are not good at revolution.

No doubt, I thought, these factors combine to explain why many went quietly to their death—many, but not all. I remembered stories of patients who had refused to get on the buses and who had been beaten into submission before their horrified fellow patients. I remembered accounts of daring escapes and of the occasional doctor who had assisted the patients to hide from their killers.

And, indeed, it was this scattered protest by the patients and their families and friends which had aroused the local villagers, the churches, and ultimately a large part of society in a manner unique in the history of Nazi Germany. In spite of the danger of protest, protests against the euthanasia program came from all over the country. There were public meetings, sermons, editorials, demonstrations, even small riots. There is reason to believe that Hitler and his advisers were startled by this domestic unrest, perhaps even fearful, coming as it did during the middle of the Nazis' disastrous Russian campaign. Not wanting a divided home front at this critical point, Hitler canceled the official euthanasia program.

When you consider the facts—and of this I am quite sure—the disabled have no reason to be ashamed of how they regarded the enemy—their physicians. The disabled struggled and resisted being killed. Their resistance served to alert their family, friends, and neighbors. Society rallied in support. The disabled confronted their enemy, rallied support from their allies, and, at least officially, won their battle.

Driving down the hill from the Hadamar Institute I mused: the disabled came out of it all right, but the medical personnel certainly did not.

In the trial held after the war concerning the deaths of some four hundred Polish and Russian nationals at Hadamar, Alfons Klein, the hospital administrator, told the court that everyone employed at the institution was aware of what was being done. He said that a Dr. Schwellenbach, who was medical director at the beginning of the killing program at Hadamar, had in fact given an indoctrination lecture to the staff to explain in detail what was going on. [13]

The Hadamar personnel worked together as a team. It appears that every effort was made to keep up this team spirit: there were parties and rallies. In my research, I was able to piece together an account of one such event:

One day in midsummer 1941, the administrator came into the staff dining room at lunchtime to make an announcement. Today was the day they would cremate the ten-thousandth body to go into the Hadamar furnace. There would be a small ceremony and a staff party to commemorate the event. [14]

Accordingly, doctors, nurses, orderlies, even grounds attendants gathered in the lobby of the right wing in the evening. Beer and wine were served, and then all present filed downstairs to the crematorium in the basement. [15]

The room had been decorated, and the oven itself was bedecked with fresh flowers. On a gurney in front of the oven was the naked body of a dead man—the actual ten-thousandth victim. The body was adorned with flowers and small flags with the swastika emblem. [16]

Standing with his back to the oven door, Dr. Brenner gave a short, inspirational talk about the importance of the work that was being done at Hadamar and his pride at being part of such a dedicated and hard-working team. With a nod from Brenner, the body was placed in a trough-like structure and shoved into the oven.

And then it was time for the fun. Mr. Merkle, the hospital bookkeeper, came out. He turned his collar about, put his coat on backward, and intoned a burlesque eulogy of the deceased insane person. The audience howled with laughter, although some of those present said later that they thought it in questionable taste to make fun of the clergy.

Music was provided by a local polka band; much more beer was served. There was dancing and laughter; and later, a drunken march around the sanitorium grounds with lots of singing and shouting. [17] Some of the staff members complained afterwards that the drinking had gotten out of hand.

Four years later, the U.S. Army newspaper *Stars and Stripes*, in its report of this affair, stated that the partygoers had sipped their wine from the skulls of their victims. This was vehemently denied by Hadamar staff members, who were shocked at the very idea. Simply not true, they said. [18] And, of course, the fact was, there were *no* skulls available: they had all been cremated along with the bodies, strictly according to regulation.

The staff knew what was going on all right. But, according to the testimony of both Klein and Nurse Huber, although everybody knew, nobody *liked* it. Nobody liked the killing. [19] Huber, for example, was, in her own words, "of plain country stock," a devout, churchgoing Christian. She cared for her patients, and she took risks on their behalf. Upon occasion, she would secretly bring a priest into the institution to hear the confessions of the patients before their deaths. In wartime Germany food was short and sweets were precious. Nurse Huber went about the town collecting cookies and candies for the children in her wards. American prosecutor Leon

Jaworski, later of Watergate fame, recalled, "I have no doubt whatever that at one time Irmgard Huber was a good woman."[20] If Nurse Huber was so good, and if she disliked the killings so very much, why didn't she leave, quit, go?

Administrator Klein had told the court, "Everyone who worked in this institution knew [of the killings] but nobody was forced to work in the institution." He went on, "Nobody was threatened with the concentration camp . . . and everyone worked there voluntarily, and was able to resign. If anyone says that he was forced to work there, and was not able to quit, it is a lie."[21]

And, in fact, while defendants did testify they were forced to participate against their will, the evidence presented tended to contradict their testimony. People *did* leave their jobs at Hadamar, although in the ordinary way. Nurses got married and moved away. Staff was transferred to other facilities. Some got better jobs; others joined the service. There was no indication, in all the material presented to the court, of anyone having left out of principle or protest. Of course, participants in the euthanasia operation received a generous bonus to their paycheck, a liberal leave policy, and the promise of rapid promotion. Of such routine personnel policies was the killing program built—the "banality" which Hannah Arendt observed in the Third Reich's evil.

Employees were warned that the killing program was extremely secret, and they were told that if they revealed what was happening at Hadamar they risked being sent to concentration camps; indeed, they had heard stories of one or two personnel from other hospitals who were sent there over the years.

It was all simple. There were inducements to kill, and the threat of punishment for those who told. The doctors and nurses did not like it, but they stayed. And men and women pledged to healing took to killing.

At the trial, Chief Nurse Huber broke down on the stand toward the end of her cross-examination. She had testified of the killing, "I knew it was very terrible and I suffered very much."[22] She testified she had been afraid to leave for fear of being sent to a concentration camp. "I was always afraid of it," she said, even though she had made no mention of such a fear in the written statement she had made to the U.S. Army of Occupation authorities before she was charged with murder. Now, in the cross-examination, she admitted she had never been threatened with being sent to a camp. She felt, however, that she could not have taken any steps against the killing. She said she had no way out. "Where should I go? I could not go away. We were working under pressure."

And then she began a wailing litany of helplessness, sad and human. "The death[s] . . . it was terrible, I know that. I never agreed to that, and I myself could not be satisfied with it. The lives . . . are just as valuable as my life, but I could not change anything there. I didn't have any say. I couldn't report anything. I avoided the matter."[23]

On the way up to the institution we had noticed that the town of Hadamar was having some sort of fall festival. Here and there throughout the town, people had put up poles with a small pine tree tied to the top. The poles had various streamers and, halfway up, there would be a teddy bear held tight by a wire wrapped round. On the way up, this had seemed only a part of local custom. Now, on the way back down the hill, everything had changed. The warm autumn sun had faded; dark clouds were filling the sky, and there was a cold wind rising. The teddy bear tied to the pole looked as if it was being crucified.

2

The Handicapped in Other Times and Places

Attitudes and behavior toward disability are not willy-
nilly affairs.

H. von Hentig, "Physical Disability,
Mental Conflict, and Social Crisis"

G erman people, of course, have special qualities. They have
made a unique contribution to Western culture. There can be
no doubt that German music, art, literature, philosophy, scholarship, archaeology, medicine, and technology have greatly added to
the quality of man's life and the pleasure of his existence. Germany
is unique; nevertheless, in essential ways it is very much an integral
part of Western civilization. Christianity, the Renaissance, the
Reformation, the Age of Reason, the Romantic movement, nationalism, and social reform—all of these had varying impacts upon
Germany, just as they did over the rest of Western Europe.

The Germans are not "different" from Americans in any critical
sense—they are very much members of the human family. How they
treated their insane, handicapped, and retarded during the Third
Reich was certainly extreme behavior—tragic and appalling—but
it was not inconsistent with patterns of social behavior that can be
traced throughout the history of the disabled over the centuries. The
German physicians actually acted on the basis of feelings which are
common, to a greater or lesser degree, to most men and women in
most societies.

And, in fact, there is no reason to believe that the attitudes of the Germans in the 1930s toward the disabled and the chronically ill were different in any essential way from the prevailing attitudes elsewhere. Indeed, in all nations the role assigned to the disabled has been difficult and troubled. And in all history, certain images and behaviors have persisted.

—

The German people who were killed by their doctors were perceived as "disabled." What does this mean? What does it mean to be disabled, and why does the society of man react in the ways it does to disabled persons?

It is not easy to define or explain what it is that distinguishes a disabled person from a person who is not disabled. For years, the American Congress and the courts have wrestled with legal definitions of disability. These will vary from law to law and from state to state. In general the definitions seek to include inability as the result of a physically (or mentally) limiting condition *and* an imposed inability as the result of social attitudes. A person with AIDS denied a job because of fear and someone in a wheelchair who cannot get to his workplace because of steps are both disabled, not just by their physical conditions, but by the action of society as well.

Of course, the biological or physical fact of being disabled often is evaluated differently in different times and societies. A condition such as poor eyesight is largely a trivial matter in a society where eyeglasses are readily available. In an aboriginal hunting society, poor eyesight is a calamity. In traditional Inuit society the insight of a schizoid personality is valued; in modern America it is often feared. Franklin D. Roosevelt, who was accustomed to a life of valets and chauffeurs, found his paraplegia a less disabling condition than would a poor man who was similarly paralyzed. There can be no doubt that the way a society perceives and deals with a handicap is a major factor in determining just how disabling—in a real sense—the handicap will be.

Ann Shearer, in her book *Disability: Whose Handicap?*, explains the process by which the disabled come to be devalued, even ostracized.

Each and every one of us has felt frustration at physical and mental limitations. . . . Not many of us have survived adolescence without sometimes being overwhelmed at our own apparent abnormality.

As life goes on, these moments probably get fewer. The inabilities no longer overwhelm us, for we find that the world will accept that we have abilities as well. We learn to avoid the places and situations that show up the first and find our way into those where we can use the second. At some point, somehow, some people are no longer seen as able in some situations and unable in others. Instead, a blanket description is thrown over them. They are "disabled."

Why the cutoff? The difference between the people called "disabled" and the majority is simply that [disabled people] have less room to maneuver as they make their way about their society. Most people can conceal their inabilities most of the time, or avoid situations where these will become apparent. People who have severe disabilities cannot, because their inabilities are in areas that are considered indispensable to coping with "normal" life and because the world is organized around an assumption that everyone has a range of fundamental abilities. It is a short step from that assumption to the perception of people with disabilities as being fundamentally different.

Commissioner Evan Kemp of the federal Equal Employment Opportunity Commission, who is himself a wheelchair user, adapts the Shearer argument:

1. Mankind naturally comes in different shapes, sizes, colors, and physical and mental abilities.
2. Nevertheless, society assumes that all people have the same range of abilities, that all are identical, interchangeable parts in a social machine.
3. People who are good at some things and not at others come to be viewed as not good at anything. They are, in other words, dis-abled.[1]

This is surely part of what social reaction to disability is about, but there is more to it than this. There are profound and subtle aspects to man's reaction to disability. These, if examined, provide a framework within which the behavior of the German doctors may be placed.

Disability in the Animal Kingdom

There seems to be no general pattern of behavior by animals toward members of their species which have been disabled as the result of birth deformity, illness, or accident. Certainly, the life of such creatures is often "nasty, brutish, and short," in the words of Hobbes. In the Darwinian sense, presumably such animals are less able to forage or hunt for their food, are less able to withstand the rigors of the wild, and less successful at courtship. The fit survive in the wilderness; the unfit do not.

A host of curious examples of animal behavior has been collected by E. Maisel in an unpublished manuscript quoted by Beatrice Wright. Goldfish that have suffered the amputation of a fin seem to be accepted fully by fellow goldfish. On the other hand, sharks will close in on another shark that has been injured, and will eat it. Not surprisingly, baboons are terrible toward an injured or physically weaker baboon. Chimpanzees can be most caring and supportive. Elephants are concerned when a fellow elephant is hurt, and porpoises have been observed helping an injured porpoise to safety. According to Maisel, an albino penguin—improperly dressed by penguin standards—is loved by his family, even though he is treated with hostility by penguin society as a whole.

From these examples, as Wright (among others) has pointed out persuasively,[2] there is no reason to assume that a disabled animal will be persecuted or ostracized by his peers. This both does—and does not—happen. The psychobiologist Robert Yerkes is quoted as saying, after more than fifty years' study in animal psychology, "I am quite unable to make with confidence any general statements" about the treatment of a disabled member by its peers in the animal world.[3]

Disability in the Aboriginal World

It is similarly difficult to generalize about the position of disabled persons in aboriginal societies. In some cases life itself was grim, and the very survival of the tribe was problematical. In such cases

27

the disabled did not fare well. Take, for example, the Inuits of north Alaska before their contact with Western civilization. Life was dangerous and short. The specter of hunger was ever-present. The people were nomadic, hunting the whale, following the caribou, eking a balanced diet from whatever meat, fish, birds, and wild plants were available. Nothing was wasted; everything was used. The people lived and moved in small family groups, as the vegetation upon the land was so sparse it could not support any larger population.

The Inuit loved their children and showered them with affection and attention. Nevertheless, they killed their deformed infants. The Inuit respected their old people and deferred to their wisdom and experience. Yet they abandoned them on ice floes when they could no longer travel with the band.

This was cruel, but cruel, too, was their way of life. A person who could not keep up, who could not handle his share of the work, endangered the life of the entire band. And the band was everything. No individual could long survive alone in the Arctic. The survival of each member of the band was dependent upon the survival of the band itself. And this is why the individual was sacrificed—when necessary—to insure the survival of the band.

The practices of man toward his handicapped brothers are as varied and changing as is man himself. Maisel went through some of the anthropological material available in the Human Relations Files at Yale University. He drew up a list of some of the behaviors of more than fifty tribes and societies.[4]

- Among the Siriono Indians, sickness not infrequently leads to abandonment and death.
- In the Azande tribe, infanticide is not practiced. "Abnormal children are never killed nor do they seem to lack the love of their parents. A supplementary fifth finger or first toe is surprisingly common amongst these [Azande] savages who are usually proud of the addition."
- Among the Navajo Indians, the ideals proscribe sadistic humor against those with physical deviations but in practice, "A great deal of enjoyment is derived from commenting verbally or through pantomime on the personal afflictions, infirmities, and peculiarities" of others. Uncomplimentary nicknames are not uncommon.

- Among the Masai, "misshapen and especially weakly children" are killed immediately after birth.
- Among the Dieri, a tribe of Australian aborigines, "infanticide is frequent, applying to the children of unmarried girls, and to deformed children."
- Among the Chagga, an East African tribe, cripples were felt to satisfy evil spirits, thereby making possible normality in others. Hence, they did not dare to kill cripples, who included children with more or less than five fingers as well as those with serious deformities.
- Among the Creek Indians, where "old age is revered to excess," the aged infirm were killed only out of humanitarian reasons, such as when they might otherwise fall into enemy hands.
- Among the Truk peoples of the East Central Carolines, only the healthy and strong are esteemed. The deaf and dumb are called *umes* (crazy people). Old people and the disabled are considered to be superfluous.
- Among the Wogeo, a New Guinea tribe, children with obvious deformities are buried alive at birth, but children crippled in later life are looked after with loving care.
- Among the Dahomeans of Western Africa, it is a singular fact that the state constables are selected from persons with deformities. Children born with anomalous physical characteristics are held to be under the guardianship of special supernatural agents. Some of these children are destined to bring good luck, and the fate of others must be determined by signs from the supernatural. They may even be "ordered" to be abandoned at the riverbank.
- Among the Ponape of the Eastern Carolines, "crippled and insane children" were treated like the normal children.
- Among the Witoto Indians of the North West Amazon, the new-born infant is submerged in the nearest stream, for "if the child was not strong enough to survive it had better die." If the child becomes deformed later, the medicine man declares that it was caused by some evil spirit and may work ill to the tribe, making it necessary to dispose of the person.
- Among the Jukun, a Sudanese kingdom, children with deformities are not allowed to live, but are left to perish in the bush or in a cave, for it is believed that such children are begotten by an evil spirit.
- Among the Semang of the Malay Peninsula, the person looked upon as a sort of chief to settle disputes and admonish if

necessary was a severely crippled man who could only move with the help of a long stick.

- Among the Balinese, sexual relations with "albinos, idiots, lepers, and in general the sick and the deformed," are taboo.
- Among the Maori of New Zealand, people with deformities meet with little sympathy and often receive a castigating nick-name.

There are two tentative generalizations which may be made about such a list. First, all peoples seem to recognize the "otherness" of the chronically disabled as significant—whether in a positive or a negative sense. Second, negative behavior patterns seem to be more prevalent than positive ones.

Disability in Western Society

The social scientist H. von Hentig has said that most people view disability as some sort of a moral judgment. These people—at some level of their consciousness—think of disability as a punishment.[5] Hentig tries to explain this by saying, in effect, that man cannot bear to live in a world in which punishment is meted out with an even hand to the innocent and the guilty alike. Man wants to believe that pain and illness—certainly terrible punishments—must be the consequence of evildoing. In such a simplistic world construct—life according to Disney—the good are rewarded and the bad are crip-pled and no good life is lived in vain.

This desire to blame the chronically ill and disabled for their condition, to hold them somehow guilty and punished for some undefined sin, perhaps, is caused by the degree of subconscious fear that the crippled arouse in the minds of most people. This has been suggested by the German Freudian H. Meng, writing in 1938.[6] He posits that the nondisabled have a subconscious fear that the crip-pled person has perpetrated some evil act—*or is about to* perpetrate something evil—that has brought on punishment.

An example of this fear of the potential of evil in disabled people is found in the behavior of various communities in the Middle Ages at the time of the plague. Surely, there must be, the townsfolk reasoned, something—or someone—causing this devastating epidemic. By such reasoning, it was probable that the person guilty of such a terrible deed belonged to an outside group—he was, as the Nazis would say, an asocial. Accordingly, the town would expel all its Jews and kill all its cripples.

It is not surprising, then, that in many languages the terms used to describe a disabling condition are often moral value words, heavy with implied meaning—something is *wrong* with his leg; he has a *bum* leg; his leg is not *right;* this is his *bad* leg; is it *good* to walk on?

Certainly, in the Old Testament chronic illness and disability are directly linked, cause and effect, to sin against God and his commandments. The disabled is a sinner, and—as spelled out in Leviticus 21:18—he is unclean, and thus may not be a priest, or even approach the altar. Twelve specific conditions are proscribed including "a blind man, or a lame, or he that hath a flat nose, or anything superfluous, or a man that is brokenfooted, or broken handed or crookbackt, or a dwarf, or that hath a blemish in his eye, or be scurvy, or scabbed, or hath his bones broken. . . ." Even the poor soul with a ruptured testicle is unacceptable to the harsh God of the Hebrews.

Just how harsh a God is seen in the utterly flat, chilling pronouncement of 2 Samuel 5:8—"The blind and the lame shall not come into the home."

Over the centuries, additional body flaws were added to the twelve of Leviticus, so that the later Talmudic scholars list some 142 varieties of disqualifying disabilities. The Romans barred the disabled from the priesthood of their pagan temples, a practice picked up by the Roman Catholic Church, which continued until recently to bar the disabled from its priesthood.

The medical historian Henry Sigerist discerned four differing social approaches toward the disabled: The ancient Hebrews believed disability to be caused by sin. The ancient Greeks considered it to be a matter of status and economics—the handicapped as social inferiors. The Christians looked upon the disabled as cursed or possessed, objects of pity and prayer. The world of science sees the disability in the clinical sense as a symptom of disease; and purports to see the disabled and the diseased as value-free victims.[7]

However, running as a constant from first to last is man's ever-present tendency to blame the victim for his condition. Even the wise and gentle Jesus said to the blind man, "I have healed you, go and sin no more," implying, thereby, that sinning had brought on his blindness. This theme continues up to the present time—as seen, for instance, in the view that people with AIDS have brought the disease upon themselves by their behavior as homosexuals. Even modern medicine, with its psychosomatic theory of illness, carries within it the implication that the sick are responsible for their sickness.

Interestingly enough, ancient Egypt seems to have been an exception to this kind of thinking. In Egypt, where the gods often took monster-like form, the physically deformed were not seen as "other" or excluded from society. They were simply accepted as being a part of the overall interrelatedness of all species. This contrasts with Greece and Rome, where disability was often taken as an omen of the anger of the gods, presaging bad luck or worse. Infants born with even relatively minor disabilities, a club foot or extra fingers, were regularly exposed—that is, taken to some secret place and left to die. [8] Thus in Egypt the figure of a deformed person could be the subject of worship, while in Greece such a deformed person would be sacrificed.

This hostility to the newborn disabled has been a recurrent attitude throughout the development of Western culture. It was, for example, Martin Luther's belief that such babes were surely change-lings, substituted by a diabolical mother of a deformed child. Luther advised that such disabled children should be severely beaten in the hope that the evil mother would be forced to return with the healthy child. Luther held that the killing of deformed infants was pleasing in God's eye. [9]

In general, however, Christianity has been sympathetic to disabled people. In Christian terms, the disabled were seen to be afflicted through no fault of their own. They might be freed from their affliction through prayer and divine intervention. Jesus cured the lame and made the blind see again. He met with the disabled in the Temple. The disabled, as all men, are made in God's image and are worthy of love and care. From Christian teachings sprang the Western tradition of charity as a social responsibility. Over the centuries this takes the form of almsgiving by the citizenry, the maintenance of almshouses and hospices by the Church, and finally, hospitals and institutions operated by the governmental authority.

At least as far back as Exodus, the social concept has been widely accepted that reparation must be paid to someone who has been disabled through the fault of someone else. This is, of course, the principle upon which today's workmen's compensation is based. Perhaps equally as old is the principle that men wounded and disabled in battle in defense of the nation or city-state should receive a pension from their government: a surviving speech by Lysias informs us that Athens, in the fourth century B.C., provided such benefits to its disabled veterans.[10]

In the fourth century A.D. the Code of Justinian provided assistance for the disabled but specified that the disabled must be genuinely needy. The Code defined this recipient as "the typical poor man who, afflicted with both poverty and sickness, finds himself incapable of supplying his own needs." The Code also prohibited healthy, nondisabled men from begging in the streets.

The Code offered a very early example of the close relationship which has existed historically between disability and poverty. So far as the state is concerned, the disabled person must be poor in order to receive help. If a man with a crippled condition is still able to work, then he is ineligible for aid. It is not his condition, per se, that determines his eligibility, but whether or not his condition is sufficiently severe to render him unable to earn a living. The criteria established in the time of Justinian are in use today. They are used by the American Social Security disability insurance program in its determination of eligibility for disability payments and Medicare.

The fear addressed in the Code that someone might receive assistance without being qualified for it has bedeviled society for centuries. The concept of the false beggar, tricking innocent people into giving him alms, has been the source of much derision and fear. Many laws have been passed designed to punish such miscreants. For example, a royal decree of 1750 in France specified that infirm beggars be confined to hospitals and nondisabled beggars sentenced to five years at sea in the galleys. This fear or derision of the false beggar—or the "welfare queen"—has often been raised as an excuse by those anxious to avoid charity altogether. Such excuses are as common today as they were in 1750.

Throughout Western literature disability has been used as a metaphor. In the *Iliad*, Therisites is described by Homer as being ugly in every way, deformed in mind and body. Like Homer, authors use the physical fitness of their characters as a symbol of their moral flaws. Richard III's hateful personality finds expression in his hateful hunchback. Captain Hook is evil, and he shows it with the hook on the end of his arm. The villain Long John Silver in *Treasure Island* has a peg leg. Likewise, of course, disability can be used as a sign of extraordinary worth or wisdom—as with the tubercular heroines of nineteenth-century romantic novels, or the blind minstrel Demodocus in Homer, who was able to create beautiful songs of the Trojan War, or even blind Homer himself. The crippled condition of Tiny Tim, or Laura in *The Glass Menagerie*, is used by the author as a signal to the reader to define character.

From the above representative examples of behavior and attitudes concerning disabled persons in Western society, it can only be concluded that a profound ambiguity exists. As the French social psychologist Dominique Le Desert has said, "Within a given society, the status of the infirm is nearly always ambiguous, contradictory. Each conception of the infirm seems to contain within it its opposite: the infirm is impure, but perhaps also powerful and sacred. People take pity on the infirm, but at the same time fear him. These contradictions characterize our own society."[11]

Psychological Studies of Disability

Psychological studies of the place of the disabled in society are not terribly advanced. Any study of societal attitudes must contend with so many variables that it is impossible to do much more than to generalize on the basis of what research work is available. Even so, a search of the available studies yields useful material, relevant to an understanding of the position of the disabled in German society and the behavior of the medical profession in the late 1930s.

American society has both positive and negative feelings about the disabled. It appears safe to presume that this is also true of German society. In 1944 a standard study of American attitudes[12] concluded that the disabled are widely believed to be more conscientious, to have more self-reliance, to work harder, to be more persistent, more alert, more religious, and so forth. From this, it would appear that the handicapped person is perceived as a thoroughly worthy individual. Wright points out, however, that these are views openly expressed in public; these are overt expressions of opinion. Covert views tend to be something else.

When asked, in confidence, whether they *liked* various categories of the disabled,[13] a group of professionals and business people had, thirteen years earlier, revealed feelings quite different from those expressed in the 1944 study:

RESPONSES TO PHYSICAL CHARACTERISTICS OF PEOPLE

	Liking	Disliking	Indifferent
Sick people	22%	28%	50%
Very old people	45	11	44
Cripples	29	19	52
Sideshow freaks	4	77	19
Blind people	25	16	59
Deaf people	16	25	59
People with hooked noses	4	38	58

The 1931 study compared these responses to those for more general characteristics:

RESPONSES TO GENERAL CHARACTERISTICS OF PEOPLE

	Liking	Disliking	Indifferent
People who borrow	3%	77%	20%
Blacks	13	32	55
Socialists	8	41	52
Athletic men	74	1	25

These polls were taken in the United States long ago. They do not necessarily correlate with attitudes held by German people of the same period. Nor, perhaps, do they correlate with the attitudes of Americans in the 1980s. What they *do* indicate, emphatically, is that disability has some sort of a major impact upon the way a person is perceived by others: Given no information other than what they see, people will feel good about a well-built athlete; they will respond a good deal less positively to someone with a physical deformity. Strong negative feelings are aroused by the sight of a crippling condition.

This verity is taken one step further in a 1969 study by L. M. Shears and C. J. Jensema.[14] These researchers found that the more intimate the relationship, the stronger the prejudice will be against disabled people:

PERCENTAGE OF SUBJECTS WHO WOULD ACCEPT CERTAIN ANOMALOUS
PERSONS IN TWO TYPES OF RELATIONSHIPS

Person	Work Partner	Marriage Partner
Physically handicapped (wheelchair)	93%	7%
Amputee (arm or leg)	91	18
Blind person	89	16
Person with a hare lip	80	8
Severe stutterer	74	7
Deaf-mute	67	10
Cerebral palsy (spastic)	51	1
Mentally ill person	37	2
Mentally retarded person	30	0

Here it is well to remember that the participants in the study were asked hypothetical questions; it is therefore not surprising that their answers revealed stereotypical thinking at its most bald-faced. In the old days down South, everyone knew the answer to the question "Would you want your daughter to marry a black?" "Would you marry a person in a wheelchair?" is such a question, and the answer it provokes reflects the same sort of stereotype. It is interesting that there is so little resistance to working beside a person in a wheelchair, and it is sad that there is such strong aversion to associating with the mentally ill and retarded persons.

There are two additional comments that may be made about these attitudes:

Observational studies[15] of children and adults interacting with disabled children in the familiar surroundings of home, neighborhood, and integrated schoolrooms indicate that these negative perceptions can be changed. Once the disabled person became known as a person, the importance of the disability, the burden of the stigma, faded into the background. "Under these circumstances, the focus of an associate's attention shifts from the superficial characteristics of physical appearance to deeper, more important traits of personality and behavior. . . . They [the participants] were not responding to a 'crippled child,' but rather to Nick or Patrick or Libby, as persons, who, almost incidentally, had a physical disability."

Thus it *may* be true that through "mainstreaming" and integration these age-old stereotypes, these prejudices, can be diminished if not actually eliminated.

It should not be thought, however, that these attitudes are trivial or easily dispatched. They are deeply rooted. As Hentig has observed, "Attitudes and behavior toward disability are not willy-nilly affairs . . . their underpinnings are solidly fastened to perceived cause-effect relations."[16] Hentig illustrates this with the example of mentally ill persons in times past who were thought to be—or to be possessed by—witches and demons. Such persons were regularly beaten or burned. This behavior was neither unjust nor irrational in the sense that it was an appropriate reaction to what was the perceived cause of the madness.

Just how tenacious and deep-seated such attitudes are can be seen in a report by John Gliedman and William Roth. Writing in 1980, they found "that expressed attitudes toward most groups of disabled people have remained unchanged over the past fifty years—remaining mildly negative to mildly positive—during a period in which expressed attitudes toward members of such stigmatized groups as Jews and blacks have registered dramatic shifts away from prejudice and toward tolerance."[17]

Why this should continue to be so—why prejudice against the disabled should be so widespread and so tenacious—has no answer. Certainly, the answer goes to the heart of the human experience. All men will die—"In the midst of life we are in death," says the Book of Common Prayer—all will become old, in one manner or another disabled along the way. Perhaps the visibly disabled are living reminders of the frailty of life and the vulnerability of man. And as messengers of the inevitable they are unwelcome.

They were certainly unwelcome in Germany. During the Nazi era, the Germans were out to build a new society, a Super Race. They saw themselves as the strong in triumph over the weak. How annoying the presence in their midst of seemingly helpless disabled and elderly persons must have been.

Spread, Devaluation, and Passing

In discussing disability attitudes, there are three terms that are helpful: *spread, devaluation,* and *passing.*

> *"Spread"* describes the phenomenon which occurs when some or all attributes of a person's character are thought to be the function of a handicap. Examples: George has cerebral palsy; his hands move in a jerky manner; therefore, he must be a jerky thinker, too. When a paraplegic happens to be a good student, this will often be explained in terms of his handicap. He is a good student because he cannot run and play like the other students. All he can do is sit and study. Beatrice Wright has labeled this view of things "physique as prime mover."[18] The German physicians were indulging in spread when they assumed that because a person's legs do not move, his life is worthless—or that a person whose brain function is not "normal" is subhuman.
>
> *"Devaluation"* is the depreciation of the worth of a person on the basis of his handicap. Devaluation comes in many guises, some of them sly and deadly. For example, the Jerry Lewis Telethon used to devalue its clients in what was almost a subliminal fashion. Children with muscular dystrophy were paraded before the television camera, while Jerry Lewis or Ed McMahon talked up their tragic, pathetic condition. The theory was: the more pathetic the victim, the more money would be contributed. In the process the child was devalued into a "victim" object. The German use of such terms as "worthless lives" or "lives not worth living" to describe institutionalized patients is an example of devaluation. The Nazi practice of referring to the physically handicapped and the chronically mentally ill as *Untermenschen* (subhuman) is devaluation taken to its limit.

"Passing" is used in the same manner as it once was used to describe fair-skinned black people who passed as white in the Caucasian world. In the same way, disabled people who make it in the world of the fit are no longer thought of by their able-bodied peers as being handicapped. Such people are said to be "passing"; they are accepted as though they were able-bodied. The existence of their deformity or whatever is denied, ignored, certainly never mentioned. The great example of this, of course, was the paraplegic President, Franklin D. Roosevelt, who had polio. A curious example was Josef Goebbels, Hitler's minister of propaganda, who was disabled by a congenital hip condition. As successful members of their society, neither they nor their associates thought of them as handicapped. They passed.

The Troubled Doctor-Patient Relationship

It must be emphasized that the disabled are a part of the society they live in; and, as such, they tend to share the prevailing social attitudes of that society. The disabled population is a minority in the civil rights sense, but it is a curious one. It is a minority that does not naturally think of itself as a minority: the disabled have no community, no history, no culture. They live scattered throughout the nonhandicapped population. Not surprisingly, the values and attitudes held by the disabled concerning their disability tend to be those of their family, their neighbors, their church, and their society.

As prevailing social attitudes tend to devalue the worth of disabled people, this, in turn, serves to encourage the disabled to hold themselves in low esteem. Various issues exacerbate this problem. One such matter involves the relationship that disabled persons have with their physicians.

A person with a chronic disabling condition in a twentieth-century Western nation will spend a lot of time with his doctors. This is particularly true of a child whose growth and development are complicated by his condition. The majority of doctors practicing in the Western tradition operate according to the "organ system." This views disease as organ-sited and treats the disease by treating the organ. As a result, the doctor concentrates upon the disease,

39

sometimes ignoring the person afflicted by the disease. He treats the organ—not the person as a whole. He perceives the person with the organ as an object.

This goes far to explain why the disabled so often feel that their physicians do not listen to them. By treating the disease, rather than the patient, the doctor is able to distance himself from the feelings his patient may experience. As a result, the disabled report that their legitimate complaints are too often dismissed by their doctors as "emotional maladjustments." These patients complain that they have experienced very little dialogue with their doctors. They say that too often they are treated as "patient material" rather than as human beings.[19] Often, in fact, the medical community—in Germany in the thirties, as well as in America today—has tended to concentrate so much attention upon the disease that the patient's view of himself has become sadly and inaccurately skewed. As an example, consider Jane, a small girl with cerebral palsy. Ask her, "And who are you?" and she will reply, "I am a C.P." The person comes to confuse the self with the condition.

If a man is told repeatedly by his doctors, his family, and his society that his disabled condition is detestable, and if tremendous medical efforts are made to mask or eliminate this condition, it is no wonder the person is apt to become confused; it is no wonder his self-esteem suffers. His doctors have caused him to see himself as defined by his handicap, and his handicap, he is told, is detestable. Therefore, he is detestable. Thus, the handicapped person himself becomes the victim of his own spread and devaluation reasoning.

And if the society in which he lives believes crippled people to be inferior, believes they are *Untermenschen* or that they lead "lives not worth living," then in most cases the crippled person will come to believe these things as well.

Disability: A Learned Inferiority

Gliedman and Roth have pointed out that the disabled have a history of learned inferiority.[20] They do not, *ipso facto*, consider themselves to be inferior to or less fortunate than their nondisability neighbors. They have to be taught. In the Germany of the 1930s, such lessons were taught as a matter of state policy. And these lessons were taught by the medical community.

That a feeling of inferiority can be taught is borne out by a 1965 study by Wright and Muth. [21] They report that mental health patients and welfare recipients believe that *as distinct groups*, the mentally ill and the poor are less fortunate than are other groups. Their beliefs in this regard are not different from those of control groups of housewives and college students. What is interesting is that when each participant in each group is asked how fortunate her own individual life has been, the answers are, again, indistinguishable among the groups. Almost without exception the mentally ill and the welfare recipients—just like the other groups in the study—consider themselves as individuals to be at least average in good fortune.

There are reasons to believe—according to the reports of disabled people based upon their own experience—that the disabled do not find it anywhere near as dreadful to be crippled as physicians and the general public believe it to be. This is a question which badly needs to be studied. Would a careful poll find that while the disabled believe the quality of their life is, on average, as good as anyone else's, the general public believes it to be markedly inferior? Would such a study indicate that physicians as a group believe the quality of life of a disabled person to be totally unacceptable? Empirical evidence seems to indicate this to be true.

It is not clear why physicians should believe that the life of the disabled is so very much worse than do the persons who actually have the disability. Experts in the field[22] have suggested that one reason may be that physicians have had no instruction on the situation of the disabled in modern society and have had little or no contact with independent handicapped people; nor have they associated with professional peers who are disabled. Usually the only disabled people that physicians come across are those with a continuing or severe illness.

There is an important distinction here that often becomes clouded: *most* disabled people are not, per se, sick people. Disability is a condition, not an illness. Disabled people get sick, just as other people get sick; but it is a mistake to think that disabled people are sick all the time.

As it happens, the handicapped people that the physicians do see in their practices *are* the sick ones; and it is perhaps natural that the physicians should extrapolate from this evidence that all handicapped people are sick, suffering, and in agony.

More on the Troubled Relationship

The above study of physicians' attitudes toward disability is, in a sense, corroborated by an analogous study of physicians' attitudes toward death.[23] Doctors were asked to rate their fear of death. Their answers were compared with the answers of seriously and terminally ill patients and with the answers of healthy individuals. It was found that physicians are significantly more afraid of death than are ill or healthy persons. The study went on to compare the attitudes of medical students with those of experienced doctors. Here, again, the doctors had a greater fear of death than did the students. Jay Katz suggests[24] that contact with death increases doctors' fears. He points out that physicians see the death of a patient—as they see a disabled patient—to be a failure in their doctoring skills. Physicians, like other people, fear and dislike failure.

Physicians are only human. They like cures; they like success. They do not like to be made to look ineffectual. And this is, of course, exactly the effect produced by patients who are disabled or chronically insane. Little wonder such patients have the feeling that their doctors are distancing them—not physically, but psychologically. Such patients feel a sense of isolation. Any handicapped person who has ever spent time in a hospital will have experienced the result: the physicians treat him with a gentle disdain, bordering on antipathy. Often the disabled patient is not listened to; he is ignored, occasionally actually abused. According to one observer, "Only the victims of problems for which remedies are known or anticipated have been treated sympathetically."[25]

This recurrent complaint by handicapped people that they are not listened to or heard by their doctors is a reflection of what Katz[26] has referred to as the feeling of psychological abandonment experienced by chronic patients in their dealings with their doctors. Illness and disability cause the patient to feel a loss of control. He feels a sense of self-estrangement and of abandonment. This is increased as the physician addresses the patient, not as a peer, nor, often, even as an adult, but rather as some sort of needy child for whom decisions will be taken without consultation—sometimes without explanation. And when the treatments decided upon fail or continue on and on, without effect, let alone cure, the patient's sense of abandonment grows larger.

This practice of telling patients only what the doctor thinks patients should hear dates back at least to Hippocrates. There is, indeed, a deep strain of authoritarianism in the Western tradition of medicine by which doctors know best, and a "good" patient does what the doctor orders. Physicians will argue they act this way only to spare the feelings of their patients, when, often enough, they do so to spare their own feelings. They are projecting their own fears upon their patients. The doctors fear death and crippling; they see these things as failures, and they do not want to talk about them.

Money and Status Make a Difference

It should be emphasized that in Western industrialized society, socioeconomic factors play a large role in disability. The richer and more educated a person is, the less debilitating will be a given handicap. There are two reasons for this. The first is that money can buy help. The second reason is more complex.

It is expensive to be crippled. In addition to the high costs of medical care itself must be added such things as the expenses of specially adapted transportation and housing and the costs of attendant care. These things tend to ameliorate the impact of a disability. With the proper equipment, with accessible facilities and dependable attendants, the handicapped person is often able to live a normal sort of life, independent and productive. Independent living, however, is not cheap, nor is decent institutionalized care.

So the effect of money is clear. Not so clear is what happens to social attitudes when a handicapped person has money and education. Psychologists report that people find a handicap less offensive or restrictive if the handicapped person is at a high social and cultural level. A rich man "passes" more easily than does a poor man.

Two interesting studies illustrate aspects of how these economic and social factors operate. The first considered children who were deformed because their mothers took the drug thalidomide during pregnancy.[27] According to the study, "The initial reactions of mothers of thalidomide children, their perception of their child's handicap (which, moreover, continued to evolve over time) and their emotional relationship with their child were always a function of the social norms of the surrounding social milieu. In every case the seriousness of the malformation only played a secondary role."

The second study was of the reactions of doctors to their paralyzed polio patients. The results are fascinating.[28] The study found that the higher the patient's family was on the socioeconomic scale—the richer it was—the less severe did the physician rate the degree of the patient's paralysis, and the more optimistic was the doctor's assessment of the extent of the patient's ultimate recovery of his motor functions. The conclusion is inescapable: that although money has no impact whatever upon the paralysis left by polio, it certainly seems to have influence on the medical judgment of the doctor.

In sum, society carries a mixed bag of emotions when it comes to disability: fear and hostility in full measure, but love and concern also. Disabled people are seen as sinners, cheats, miscreants; they are also thought to be childlike, uncommonly wise, inspiring.

When Hitler gave the German doctors license to deal with handicapped people, free from the restraints of law or ethics, when he allowed the doctors to proceed in secret away from the cleansing force of public awareness, the members of the medical establishment were free to act upon their most base and primitive feelings concerning the handicapped.

When Hitler signed the order making all this possible, what happened illuminates—as never before in history—the troubled nature of the position held by disabled people in human society.

All of these sociological and psychological observations serve to illuminate the events of the Third Reich. For in the Nazi years, the official institutions, the physicians, the citizenry of Germany acted out—in high relief—many of the fears and hostilities which have so dogged disabled people over the centuries.

3

Aktion T-4 Begins

If the physician presumes to take into consideration in
his work whether a life has value or not, the consequences are boundless and the physician becomes the
most dangerous man in the state.

Dr. Christopher Huffeland (1762–1836)[1]

In the fall of 1939 at the successful conclusion of the Polish
campaign, Adolf Hitler signed an order. Although Hitler actually signed this document later in the month, it carried the date
September 1, 1939. This was the day Germany invaded Poland, the
first day of World War II. The date was chosen to signify the order
as a wartime measure. The authorized program was to operate
throughout the duration of the war under the authority of this
informal Hitler directive. It was understood that after the war a
formal law would be promulgated.

By this stage of his rule, a directive from the Führer carried the
force of law. Even so, for the directive to take effect, form and
procedure had to be followed to the full: the directive written on
formal state stationery, signed officially by Hitler acting in his
capacity as Führer of the Third Reich, certified, and circulated to
the affected departments of government according to set administrative procedures. Such procedures were not followed in the case
of this order. It was feared that the new order would be controversial.
Public knowledge of the new policy might cause discussion; certainly the Church would object.[2] Such controversy would surely
alarm—unduly, felt the program's sponsors—the patients for whom
the program was intended and their families. Therefore, the order
was written on Hitler's personal stationery, plain except for the Nazi

insignia—eagle and swastika—embossed in gold at the top of the page. The Führer simply signed "A. Hitler" in his twig-like, scratchy handwriting, and the entire order was stamped "Top Secret."

Throughout the war, right through the Nuremberg trials, there was much discussion about whether this order of Hitler's carried the weight of law, as it had not moved through ordinary bureaucratic channels. This, of course, was a decidedly fine point, given the state of affairs in wartime Germany. As one of the trial defendants observed from the dock, "I should like to have seen anyone raise any objection at that time to any paper signed by Adolf Hitler, whatever its outward form might have been."[3]

Hitler's order read, in toto, "Reichsleiter [Reich Leader] Philip Bouhler and Karl Brandt, M.D., are charged with the responsibility of enlarging the authority of certain physicians to be designated by name in such a manner that persons who, according to human judgment, are incurable can, upon a most careful diagnosis of their condition of sickness, be accorded a mercy death."[4]

Hitler and Brandt together worked most carefully on the wording of the order. Brandt felt that it was impossible for a doctor to say with absolute certainty that a patient was incurable, and that, therefore, a certain leeway was required. Hitler, however, did not wish to give the doctors too much leeway; and, therefore, he insisted upon adding "upon a most careful diagnosis of their condition of sickness." Brandt gave this account in his testimony at Nuremberg. He emphasized repeatedly that the order was not an order to kill; it was instead an authorization to specifically designated physicians to do so if, in their judgment after "the most careful diagnosis," the patient was "incurably sick." The physicians were given a license to kill; they were not directed to do so.[5]

Hitler had often discussed the question of "mercy killings" with his medical advisers. According to Karl Brandt, Hitler had told Dr. Gerhardt Wagner in 1935 that "in the event of war he would 'take up and deal with this question of euthanasia.' " According to Brandt, the Führer was of the opinion that, in wartime, measures for the solution of "such a problem could be put through most easily and with least friction, since the open opposition which must be expected from the Church could not then in all the circumstances of war exert so much influence."[6] And that is why, having conquered

Poland, the Führer assured Brandt "that he now intended to bring about a definite solution to the problem of euthanasia."[7]

In particular, Hitler's attention had been focused upon the issue of mercy killing in the early part of 1939. He had received a petition from a Nazi Party member, a father asking that his handicapped daughter be killed. Hitler personally directed his escort physician (as Brandt was then) to investigate. Physician Brandt went to the child's home in Leipzig to assess the situation. He found, in his own words, "a child who was born blind, an idiot—at least it seemed to be an idiot—and it lacked one leg and part of one arm."[8] Having, as he saw it, confirmed the facts (the child *seemed* to be an idiot), Brandt was directed by Hitler to inform the family physician to proceed with euthanasia. Hitler did not want the parents to feel guilt about this. In the testimony of Brandt, "The parents should not feel themselves incriminated at some later date as a result of this euthanasia—that the parents should not have the impression that they themselves were responsible for the death of this child."[9] Lastly, Hitler directed that the minister of justice be informed that, should legal proceedings be brought against any of the participants in this murder, they would be quashed by the Führer himself.

Thus, with the very first official case of "euthanasia," the pattern was set. None of the participants knew whether the child was, *in fact*, retarded. With a young blind child it is difficult to tell—impossible, really, if one must rely only upon a cursory observation. No one asked what the child's wishes might be, nor what her life-style and productivity might reasonably be expected to be, given adequate education and prosthetic assistance. The fact that she, too, was a German citizen with as much access to legal protection as any other citizen was not seen as relevant. Also, note that the issue of whether her condition was genetically caused or transmissible was not even considered. She was killed "as an act of mercy." Care was given only for the convenience of the parents and the legal protection of the doctors.

As the story of the little Leipzig girl became known in medical circles, other families sent similar appeals to the Führer. It is surely some kind of comment on the state of German society at the time that people were petitioning their leader, asking that members of their family be killed.

Each of these appeals was carefully appraised by Drs. Brandt and

Bouhler. Reichsleiter Bouhler was in charge of the Führer's Chancellery, the office which provided immediate staff support for the Führer, rather as the Executive Office serves the needs of the American President. Administrative action was handled by Bouhler's deputy, Viktor Brack, who was in charge of the so-called Central Office. By the time Hitler signed the general authorization, he was regularizing a procedure which was already in place; and it is not surprising that he should have chosen Brandt and Bouhler to direct it. They were already doing so.

Bouhler was an owlish, obsequious little man. He wore spectacles, loved details, and bowed a lot. He had been with Hitler as a party functionary since the early twenties, and he could be trusted to carry out the Führer's directives with an unquestioning efficiency. Karl Brandt was something quite different. A good-looking young doctor, Brandt at the age of twenty-nine became a member of Hitler's inner circle by accident, literally. Hitler's niece and an adjutant were injured in a car accident, and Brandt happened to be the closest doctor available. He was well-liked by the Führer and his household. Hitler came to trust Brandt, and over the years elevated him to the position of Reich Commissioner. He thus became the supreme medical authority in the Third Reich, subordinate only to Hitler himself. Brandt was said to be an idealist of a philosophic bent. He was acquainted with Dr. Albert Schweitzer, later winner of the Nobel Peace Prize, and in medical school Brandt planned to join the great theologian-musician-missionary doctor in his practice at Lambaréné in the French Congo.[10] Young Brandt was kept from doing so because, as an Alsatian by birth, he would have been drafted into the French army had he moved to this French colony.

Brandt firmly believed that euthanasia could be justified ethically, and upon occasion during the war he discussed the matter carefully and in depth with Pastor Friedrich von Bodelschwingh of Bethel. Bodelschwingh, a well-known Protestant minister and the head of a famous institution in Bethel for epileptic people, was strongly opposed to euthanasia. He said so openly and often, and Brandt saw to it that the hospital was largely exempted from the killing program.

In a unique way, Hitler's life and thought reflected the life and thought of the Germany of his era. Hitler's personal failures before

World War I, his trauma from poison gas during that war, his frustration with the way the war had ended, his fury with the Weimar Republic—these mirrored the feelings and experiences of those who were his followers. To understand what was going on in Germany in the 1930s, it is therefore necessary to investigate what was going on in Hitler's mind.

The fact that it was possible to mount such a program, in contravention of established law and practice, is an indication of the absolute sway which Hitler held in the thirties over the citizens of Germany. Even a dictator as absolute as Hitler was had to have the support of his people. Without this, one way or another, his policies would fail, whether through inadequate enthusiasm, passive resistance, or acts of sabotage. At least at first, Hitler's killing policy did not fail.

The Germany of the Nazi revolution was a remarkable state. At its apex, at its center, was the Führer himself, Adolf Hitler. He dominated and personified the revolution. He was seen not only as the chief of state, but the chief architect, the chief attorney, the chief doctor. He was immensely popular. In a public election, honestly staged and without force, Hitler received some 98 percent of the votes cast. Many adored him, worshiped him as a living god. Such attitudes, of course, were encouraged by the sophisticated propaganda techniques of Goebbels and his department.

These attitudes were, nevertheless, quite genuine and widespread across Germany. Schoolchildren were indoctrinated from infancy. The children of Cologne, for example, recited before their lunch:

Führer, my Führer, bequeathed to me by the Lord.
Protect and preserve me as long as I live!
Thou hast rescued Germany from deepest distress,
I thank thee today for my daily bread.
Abide thou long with me, forsake me not,
Führer, my Führer, my faith and my light!
Heil, my Führer!

This mass adulation was not based upon propaganda alone. During the 1930s Hitler's dictatorship had been remarkably successful. Its achievements impressed the entire world. Hitler had taken a national economy, deep in depression, and transformed it into prosperity. Rearmament and a massive public works program all but eliminated unemployment as production surged. Germany became the first nation to build a system of superhighways—the autobahns. And it was planned that every worker's family would soon have a car of its own—the Volkswagen—to drive upon these beautiful new roads. Antipollution programs were put into place to cleanse the air and to keep the waters of Germany's rivers clean. City planning was stressed. Hitler made much of the common need for culture and beauty. Every city should have its parks, broad boulevards, and handsome buildings. Wages were increased, as were workers' benefits. Like FDR across the ocean, Hitler regularized and strengthened social security and old-age benefits. Health care was improved. Tuberculosis and contagious diseases declined, and infant-mortality levels fell below those of the United Kingdom. Police methods were brutal, but they were effective: crime rates were down.

The famous "Strength through Joy" campaign really did improve the quality of workers' lives. Thought was given to improving the esthetics of the workplace with flowers, fresh air, and planting. There were concerts in the factories, educational programs, and day trips for workers. Even vacations were of interest to the state. Cheap package tours and cruises were made available for all.

Two particular aspects of Hitler's revolution should be noted. First, there was a genuine attempt made to produce a social democracy. German officers really did eat in the same mess halls at the same tables as their men. In the factories German bosses ate in workers' dining rooms, played side by side on soccer teams with their workers. Germany, a nation with a deeply entrenched, complex social caste system, took a step toward egalitarianism in the Nazi years.

Also noteworthy is the improvement in the general well-being of the youth of Germany during the peace years of the Third Reich. A regime of good food, exercise, sports, and widespread educational opportunities significantly raised the confidence and morale as well as the health and strength of these young people. The sense of dolor and defeat brought on by the depression of the last days of the

Weimar Republic had been particularly hard on the young, coming of age after World War I. Hitler's programs reversed this trend.

These were not small achievements. Such is, of course, the plus side of the scale. The man who brought these things about also plunged the world into war, brought about the destruction of his own country, and annihilated the Jews. Hitler was a complex man. He was an intuitive leader who, like Lincoln, Roosevelt, and even Ronald Reagan, made his decisions largely on the basis of his own instinct. His genius, he said once, consisted "in not hesitating when an inner conviction demands that you act."[11] He seemed to understand the subconscious source of his behavior, and he had an absolute belief in the rightness, the correctness, of what it told him: "I go the way that providence dictates with the assurance of a sleepwalker."[12] Like Louis XIV and, perhaps, most dictators, he saw himself and the state he governed as inextricably linked. "The fate of the Reich depends only on me," he said at the beginning of the war, and later, "I shall never survive the defeat of my people."[13] Surely, it is not surprising that, at least through the peace years, the German people unquestionably shared Hitler's belief in the fusion of his fate with Germany and the infallibility of his intuition.

If euthanasia was the Führer's program, there were many who, when they learned of it, accepted it because it was his. Many of those who were appalled when they learned of the program believed it had been carried forward without his knowledge. "If only the Führer knew," they said, consoling themselves.

But there could be no mistake. The Führer knew and approved: he had spoken of such policies many times.

Hitler saw man's natural state as "characterized by an eternal struggle . . . between beasts and men themselves. The earth continues to go round, whether it is the man who kills the tiger or the tiger which eats the man. The strongest asserts its will; it is the law of nature."[14]

The Führer was worried about preserving the biological prowess of Germany. He wanted to strengthen the German race—as he believed it to be—and to protect it from "mongrelization." The race was threatened, in his vastly paranoid vision, by enemies from without and contamination from within. This contamination sprang not only from Jews and Gypsies and such, but from inferior, flawed

Germans—"the syphilitics, consumptives, hereditary degenerates, cripples, and cretins," as he listed them in *Mein Kampf*.[15] Such people as these were the products of weak genes. As they bred with healthy Germans, they threatened to weaken the general gene pool of the German nation; even their very presence marred and weakened the strength of the German *Volk*. Hitler admired ancient Sparta for dealing so directly with such problems: the Greek city-state simply disposed of its inferior children. Said Hitler, "The exposure of the sick, weak, deformed children, in short their destruction, was more decent and in truth a thousand times more humane than the wretched insanity of our day which seeks to preserve the most pathological subjects."

Hitler had nothing but scorn for the disabled. Writing in the early twenties, Hitler had said that his Reich would sterilize "those who are visibly sick and hereditarily tainted." Said Hitler, his Reich "must take care that only the healthy beget children; that there shall be but one thing shameful: to be sick and ailing, and nevertheless to bring children into the world."[16] Hitler repeated this theme many times in *Mein Kampf* and elsewhere: "He who is not sound and worthy in body and mind must not perpetuate his suffering in the body of his child . . . [the state] must declare and actually render incapable of procreation all those who are visibly sick and hereditarily tainted and thus infectious in turn." Clearly, the new Reich would be no fun for the disabled; however, their sacrifice would eventually serve to benefit all society. "If the capacity and the opportunity for procreation were denied to physical degenerates and mental cases for but six hundred years, it would . . . free humanity of an immeasurable misfortune."[17]

Hitler said this in his writings; he said the same in his speeches. He made no effort to hide his forceful views on human breeding practices. Speaking to the annual party convention in 1929 at Nuremberg, he said, "If Germany every year would have one million children and eliminate 700,000–800,000 of the weakest, the end result would probably be an increase in [national] strength."[18] He meant it.

Hitler's position was but a garbled and inexact version of the widely accepted eugenic doctrine of the day. Selective sterilization of those with hereditary genetic defects was much discussed in medical journals in the United States and Europe, and it is neither surprising nor exceptional that five months after taking power the Nazis promulgated a law for the prevention of hereditarily diseased offspring. This provided that "any person suffering from a hereditary disease may be rendered incapable of begetting children by means of a surgical operation [sterilization], provided it is established by a scientific medical experience as very highly probable that any children he might beget would inherit some serious physical or mental defect."[19]

Although other jurisdictions have had similar laws, none surely enforced them with the enthusiasm of the Nazis. Between July 14, 1933, and the beginning of World War II on September 1, 1939, the Nazis reported the sterilization of 375,000 persons. This figure breaks down into the following categories:

Congenital feeblemindedness	203,250
Schizophrenia	73,125
Epilepsy	57,750
Acute alcoholism	28,500
Manic-depressive insanity	6,000
Hereditary deafness	2,625
Severe hereditary physical deformity	1,875
Hereditary blindness	1,125
St. Vitus' dance	750
TOTAL	375,000

—From Deuel, *People Under Hitler*, 221

From the table, it is clear the Nazis were uncertain of what constituted a hereditary disease. A Hamburg study of the problem defined a severe hereditary deformity as "being [any condition] of a sufficient degree to interfere with normal life and the capacity to earn a livelihood." This definition gave enormous range to the authorities. In some jurisdictions, alcoholics, "perverts," and even accident victims were subject to sterilization.

There was, not surprisingly, substantial resistance to the operation popularly known as the "Hitler Cut," a play on the word *Hitlerschnitt* as a parallel to *Kaiserschnitt*, the German word for a Caesarean operation. Those who rebelled or ran away were referred to in an official document as "persons lacking in understanding." It was reported that the feebleminded were cheating on their written examinations, sneaking the correct answers provided by their more intelligent friends into the test room. The alcoholics, according to the Hamburg report, were the "group with the least understanding of their disease." The alcoholics found it hard to admit they had a disease. They denied that it was hereditary. As for sterilization, the report quotes the drunks as saying, "The law is a fine thing and they applaud it in principle. But, of course, there is no question of its applying to them."[20]

Few of the "persons lacking in understanding" managed to escape the Hitler Cut. Of the operations performed, 37.3 percent of the patients gave their approval, 24.1 percent had approval given for them by their legal guardians, and the remaining 38.6 percent were forced to submit to the operation.

The government was sensitive to the feelings of the victims, however, and it was anxious that those who had been sterilized not be made the butt of ridicule. Anyone caught making jokes about the sterilization program was sent to prison. Anyone actually involved in the operation of the program was sworn to secrecy; names of victims were not released. Violation of the secrecy restrictions was punishable with jail terms of up to twelve months.

Running concurrently with the sterilization program was one that castrated the "totally unfit"—presumably sexual criminals. The operation of this program was not officially described. Figures were released only for the years 1934 and 1935, in which 996 people were emasculated. Although no accurate total is available, a party committee called the Race Policy Office estimated that between fifteen hundred and two thousand persons were castrated between the years January 1, 1934, and the outbreak of war in 1939. There were rumors in prewar Germany that both the sterilization and the castration programs were being used to punish dissidents and political troublemakers, and to settle scores. This is unclear, but certainly extraordinary anomalies did occur. A workman in Saxony who lost his leg in an accident was said to have a diminished earning capacity. He was, therefore, sterilized against his will, and he later committed suicide. The German public, which joked about the program in spite of the "no-joke" directives, was amused by the report from Hamburg that retarded females with "a low threshold of sexual inhibition" actually asked to be sterilized. Such women were said to be the most popular whores in the city.

There was nothing bizarre or outré about Hitler's thoughts concerning the threat posed by the disabled. As shown in Chapter 4, his thoughts on sterilization and euthanasia derive quite naturally from the scientific and social theory of his day. The physicians of Germany (and the United States, too) had been discussing such policies for years.

Hitler was familiar with such discussions. He was, therefore, perfectly willing to entertain proposals made by German physicians to put a stop to this "insanity" and to authorize the institution of a program to destroy inferior German citizens—the deformed and insane.

The manner in which the Führer authorized the killing program is significant. He appointed Brandt and Bouhler to run it. These two men were not major powers in the Nazi galaxy, but they were close and trusted deputies. Hitler followed this strategy—using reliable juniors, going outside ordinary administrative channels, retaining immediate supervision—to carry out his most secret and controversial policies. The Holocaust, the movement of large populations, and the euthanasia program were handled in this manner. This served to keep both bureaucratic resistance and public attention to a minimum.

Bouhler was described by Brandt as "an honest man" who had become interested in "euthanasia." It was Brandt's testimony at Nuremberg that Bouhler—although reluctant to do so—took on the assignment "because he feared that in these circumstances, with the war on, certain district leaders might, now and then, take a hand in the matter and initiate measures in their districts without due guidance."[21] In other words, local leaders might take to the killing of the sick and aged in an overly zealous manner. Bouhler apparently felt he could keep some control over these impulses with a tight administrative management. Furthermore, as one of his clerks added in testimony, he wanted to keep the program out of the hands of Dr. Leonardo Conti, head of the Nazi doctors' association, and through him Martin Bormann, director of the SS, who was a very powerful man indeed. Bouhler feared, according to this testimony, that "Bormann would misuse his authority."[22] In fact, Bormann *had* been heard to remark of the euthanasia program, "It would be by no means restricted to the incurably insane."[23] This unvarnished enthusiasm alarmed even the Nazis. By keeping the management of the program away from Bormann, Bouhler was able to enlist the support of Göring, Himmler, and Frick, the minister of the interior—no mean lineup.

—

Legal or no, Hitler, the head of state of the National Socialist government of Germany, had authorized physicians to kill the incurably ill; and thus began the first such officially condoned program ever adopted by a Western industrialized nation.

From the very start, it was clear that the program would not be small, nor would it be limited to "mercy deaths" for the terminally ill. The organization to administer this program was set up in an orderly and businesslike fashion. Agencies were created in accordance with management principles. Regulations were prepared to govern the operation of the program. Standards were set and criteria fixed for the selection of those to receive "final treatment."

The people who set up the euthanasia program were not madmen; nor were they, at least at the start, killers. They were doctors and bureaucrats, efficient men, attempting by centralized structure, strict policy, and procedure, to alleviate what they perceived to be the burdens imposed upon society by chronic illness and disability. They sought to regularize and rationalize the disorderly state of nature: the life process is so often untidy and inefficient. In life, disease and disability burden the quality and usefulness of the afflicted, and place painful duties and expensive responsibilities upon family and society. Hitler's bureaucrats sought to impose a state-ordained tidy resolution of these hard matters.

These people envisaged a Germany in which everyone was healthy, fit, and productive. What they got, soon enough, was reflected in the famous boast of Karl Koch, commandant of Buchenwald: "In my camp there were no sick people, only healthy and dead people." It is instructive to see how this came about.

—

Brandt, Bouhler, and Bouhler's chief clerk, SS Colonel Viktor Brack, went to work. Brandt and Bouhler had other major duties in

Hitler's Chancellery, and so responsibility for the day-to-day administration of the program fell upon Brack. Brack was a thirty-six-year-old economist who had been a party member since he turned twenty-one. He was a methodical, ordinary sort of person, good with details and routine procedures. His rise in the party had been due rather more to accident than to ability: his father had been Mrs. Himmler's gynecologist; and Himmler, taking an interest in the young Viktor, hired him as a chauffeur. [24]

In addition to Brack, three other men were placed in charge of the organization. All three were physicians: Dr. Herbert Linden, who held the sub–cabinet level position of chancellor in charge of all sanitoriums and nursing homes within the Ministry of the Interior; Professor Dr. Werner Heyde and his deputy, Professor Dr. Paul Nitsche, who served as the chief medical experts of the euthanasia program. Heyde had held the position of professor of psychiatry at the University of Würzburg and was head of the University Clinic for Nervous Diseases. [25]

Although the operation was a part of the Führer's Chancellery, for housekeeping purposes the program was placed within the Ministry of the Interior with Dr. Linden acting as liaison. This allowed the new organization in its operation of the euthanasia program to make use of the already existing channels of communication and to work through the existing authorities.

The new operation was housed in an imposing villa, just down the road from the Chancellery itself, in a section of Berlin called Charlottenburg. The address was Tiergartenstrasse 4, and for this reason the program came to be known as T-4.

Three semi-independent corporations were set up to handle the actual operation of the program. These were given purposely vague and misleading names:

- Allgemeine Stiftung für Anstaltwesen, the Foundation for the Care of Institutions in the Public Interest, which handled the budgetary and financial aspects of the program—the costs of which were not small.
- Reichsarbeitsgemeinschaft Heil- und Pflegeanstalten, the Reich Association of Sanitoriums and Nursing Homes, charged with the actual administration of the program. The National Group developed the selection criteria, prepared the questionnaires, provided administrative support for the review commit-

57

tees, and actually operated the terminal "observation institutions."

- Gemeinnützige Krankentransportgesellschaft, the General Patient Transport Company, which organized and operated a unique, complex system for moving tens of thousands of the sick and helpless about the countryside. Soon enough the vans and buses of the company, clearly labeled, became a common sight on the streets of German cities.

Concurrently established, although separately administered, was the Reich Committee for Research on Hereditary and Constitutional Severe Diseases. This committee was charged with "assisting the dissolution" of mentally afflicted, severely handicapped, or "idiotic" children. The authority under which this last committee functioned was a decree issued by the Ministry of the Interior on August 1938, which in fact predated Hitler's euthanasia order.

It was later claimed that the children's operation was separate and unconnected with the euthanasia program. True enough, its procedures were different, but it, too, was headquartered at T-4.

Several hundred workers were recruited in a short period of time. People were needed to generate and process the paperwork, to structure and operate the widespread transportation system, to handle and care for the disabled people being shipped to the euthanasia-centers, and to provide the medical care, nursing, and support required to operate these killing facilities. Such disparate duties as the scheduling of the buses and seeing to their fueling and upkeep in time of war; arranging for the preparation of meals for euthanasia-center staff and patients; the placing of ashes into urns and then wrapping them for shipment to survivors; the recording and filing of death certificates—these and many others had to be fitted into job descriptions and the positions had to be filled.

Because of the secrecy of the program, employees had to be screened carefully for loyalty to the party and the Führer. Many of the staff were civil servants, seconded by their old agencies to T-4. Others were recruited. The war had just begun, and there were many people who had come to Berlin to make their contribution to the war effort.

T-4 was a glamorous place to work. It was a hush-hush operation attached to the Führer's Chancellery. A T-4 job meant extra pay, as well as the status of working directly for the Führer. To get a job at

T-4 took contacts, "pull." A former employee remembered after the war, "I was working in a fashion boutique and I was desperate to do something more useful for my country. A friend told me she thought she might be able to help me get into the Führer's Chancellery where she was working as a secretary. 'Secret work,' she said. Well, that sounded very exciting, so I went. And I got in. I had no idea what it was until I was in there."[26]

There is a term used by psychiatrists which is relevant here—detoxification. This describes the process by which the unacceptable, the taboo practice, is rendered somehow acceptable by clothing it in a new name. The euphemism is used to "detoxify" the "poison." Thus, the physicians of Germany in their committee meetings referred to "negative population policies" instead of mass extermination. They spoke of "specialist children's wards," when they meant the places where the children were killed. And, of course, they said "euthanasia,"* and they meant murder.

Both before and after Hitler's order of September 1939, secret meetings were held with selected physicians across Germany. At these meetings much detoxification was practiced. Many euphemisms were used to describe the program. There was never a doubt, however, as to what was being discussed. The leading psychiatrists, physicians, and medical professors were carefully briefed on the new euthanasia program.

These men were told that the Führer-authorized euthanasia program was a part of the "breakthrough campaign" necessary to obtain the new medicine of the Third Reich. The sorting out of "unprocessed inferiors" then resident in the hospitals and sanitoriums of the Third Reich was to be done as part of a long-term, scientifically oriented program to upgrade and radicalize the therapeutic activities of German medicine. This was described in terms of ongoing "supportive research," the introduction of new therapeutic facilities, and the basic reorganization of "the Reich Association of Medical and Care Institutions."

---

* Euthanasia (Greek: *eu*-well and *thanatos*-death): act or practice of painlessly putting to death persons suffering from incurable and distressing disease (*Webster's New Collegiate Dictionary*). In common usage today, euthanasia is used to describe the process of "pulling the plug" on persons who are terminally ill, in great pain, or comatose, and dependent for their survival upon the machines of medical technology. This was not the usage, nor the purpose, of the German physicians.

In terms of the "racial hygiene" practiced by the German medical community during the Nazi years, the physically deformed, the handicapped, and the mentally ill constituted a threat to the body of the *Volk*. These flawed people were thought to have infected the collective body of the German people, and they were to be dealt with the way a physician would deal with a pathogenic infection of an individual body—by isolation and disinfection. Dr. F. Klein, who was at Auschwitz, made the analogy clear when he said, "Out of respect for human life, I would remove the purulent appendix from a diseased body."[27]

In both the minutes of the "Reich Committee for Scientific Research of Serious Illness of Hereditary and Protonic Origin"—a high-level physicians' committee which met regularly with the Reich Chancellery—and in the reports of the briefing meetings with rank-and-file physicians, it was fiercely argued that the radical modernization of therapeutic activity could not be achieved without—and, in fact, had to go hand-in-hand with—the elimination of these "refractory therapy cases."[28]

Postwar testimony received in a trial at Koblenz gave details of one such meeting held in July 1939—*before* Hitler's order—at the Chancellery in Berlin. Psychiatrists, professors, and other experts were officially informed of a secret program to be initiated by direction of the Führer. At this meeting they were told by Viktor Brack that *all* the insane persons in Germany were to be liquidated under plans which would be carried out by "euthanasia." The audience was invited to participate in the program. It is reported that all present agreed to participate, with the exception of a Professor Ewald of Göttingen, who explicitly declined his services.[29]

Testimony was received at Nuremberg from Dr. Fritz Mennecke about another such meeting held in Berlin in February 1940. Some ten or twelve doctors attended. They were sworn to secrecy and then were briefed on the program. They were asked if they would be willing to participate in the patient-selection process. The doctors were assured that participants in the program would in no way be punished. According to Dr. Mennecke, "The other doctors present were all elderly people, including, as I afterwards learned, some of high reputation. As they all unhesitatingly agreed to participate I followed their example and offered to act as an assessor."[30]

Another physician present at the same conference, Dr. Walter Schmidt, testified that when questions were raised from the audience concerning the legality of the euthanasia program they were being asked to participate in, the questioners were told that it was all quite legal; that Hitler had issued a secret decree for which the jurists had determined he had full authorization. They were told the scheme had been planned since 1932, and that any sabotage of it would be considered a criminal offense.

The program was, of course, to be secret because, in Dr. Schmidt's words, "The patients were not to have knowledge of such a measure beforehand because otherwise they would become excited." This solicitude for the feelings of the patients was continually stressed throughout the life of the program. Even the infamous SS captain Christian Wirth—who at the beginning of the program at Brandenburg was shooting patients through the back of the head at close range with a pistol—said, "The people must not be allowed to realize that they are going to die. They have to feel at ease. Nothing must be done to frighten them."[31]

Not all the meetings were as acquiescent. At one held two months later in April, there was much discussion. According to reports, "vigorous protests were raised by some of those present." Nevertheless, the physicians, as one of them stated after the war to a Düsseldorf court, agreed to participate on the grounds that even though they were "in a position from which there was otherwise no escape," they might nevertheless "find an opportunity to restrict in some way, or at least an indication of how such restriction might be achieved, the execution of the program, and so to rescue as many patients as possible."[32]

A pattern was set at these meetings that persisted throughout the life of the euthanasia program. Most physicians went along with the authorities. Most of those who did not agree with the program or its operation kept their peace. Only a few raised open objection.

Open disagreement with a policy of the Führer was, of course, dangerous business in Third Reich Germany. On the other hand, physicians who chose not to participate in the program were not forced to do so; nor were they reprimanded or otherwise harassed in their practice of medicine. In several cases objecting physicians were even enabled to protect their patients from the selection process for euthanasia.

Such cases, however, were very few. Most physicians just went along.

Nothing of the grim process, from the concept of mercy killing to the Holocaust, was ordained, not at any step of the way. It was throughout a human undertaking, and as such revocable, alterable. Each step followed from the preceding one for innumerable reasons, from innumerable causes. The number of principals, participants, and precipitant events grew and grew. The physicians of Germany may have had it in their power to stop organized mercy killing. Their mass refusal to participate—even the public refusal of a significant number of them—could well have halted that program in its tracks. Said Dr. Andrew Ivy, who worked with the prosecution at Nuremberg, "Had the profession taken a strong stand against the mass killing of sick Germans before the war, it is conceivable that the entire idea and technique of death factories for genocide would not have materialized."[33]

The "ifs" of history are pointless. What "if" Caesar had stayed home that March morning; what "if" Columbus had turned back? It did not happen, and what *did* happen is all there is. Nevertheless, *had* the doctors acted differently, had they said no, things would have been different. An early link in the chain of events leading to the Holocaust would have been broken.

It must be said that, by and large, the physicians of Germany participated without objection in the program. Of course, only a small percentage of these doctors were involved in the actual proceedings—that is, in the selection of the candidates or in their execution. Nevertheless, *all* of the physicians of Germany were participants in the sense that they were aware of the program's existence. They had to be—for all physicians were required to fill out lengthy documents on the condition of each of their chronic patients. Selection was made on the basis of these documents, and patients selected would be transferred to the killing institutions. No doctor could have been unaware of the depletion of the hospital wards or the disappearance of his patients. The doctors stood silent as their chronic patients received medical referrals to other doctors who would kill them. They did not protest—neither alone nor through the respected medical societies of Germany. It may have been the case that once the program was well under way, in realistic appraisal, the physicians could not have saved their patients; in fact, they did not try.

As recently as 1983, some forty years after initiation of the euthanasia program, the German medical journal *Deutsches Ärzteblatt* was still rationalizing the behavior of these physicians with an argument unworthy of the honored traditions of German medicine: "Would it have changed anything if the physicians' organizations had resisted the pressure of the administration, and if they had not submitted voluntarily?"[34] This is a question which cannot be answered because the German medical establishment did not resist.

There can be no doubt that the existence and operation of the euthanasia program was general knowledge within the medical community of the wartime Reich. It was even the cause of some professional anxiety among psychiatrists. As the chief physician of the army, Professor Woth, reported to a professor of psychiatry named Bumke, "I warned him [Dr. de Crinis] of the danger of psychologists and psychotherapists taking over psychopathy and 'neurosis.' And with mental patients being taken care of by euthanasia, who will wish to study psychiatry when it becomes so small a field?"[35] This cry was taken up by the eminent psychiatrist Karl Schneider, who warned at a congress of psychiatrists in 1941 that sterilization and euthanasia might even put psychiatry out of business. He warned his colleagues, "Should not eugenics, racial improvement, and other measures taken by the state be able so to free the *Volk* from the social, moral, and economic burden of the insane that psychiatry will no longer be needed at all?" He urged psychiatrists, if they wished to keep their jobs, to broaden the field of their psychological interests—particularly "into the religious, philosophic, and mythic ideas of the whole *Volk*."[36] Whatever this may say about the ethical priorities of German psychiatrists, it shows Schneider understood where his economic interests lay, and he had no small sense of humor.

Bouhler and his deputy Brack moved quickly to institutionalize the authority Hitler had given them. They appointed between ten and fifteen doctors chosen for their "political reliability" to act as assessors. Above them were appointed review committees of chief overseers made up of university professors of psychiatry and medicine.

An organizing conference was called in which the professors of psychiatry and the chairmen of the departments of psychiatry at the medical schools of the universities of Berlin, Heidelberg, Bonn, and Würzburg were participants. Continuing meetings of this oversight group were conducted on a quarterly basis under the direction of the professor of psychiatry at Heidelberg.[37]

The "Reich Committee" oversaw the preparation of a registration form designed to elicit the information it regarded useful in determining which persons were "worthy of help" and which were "useless lives," candidates for "final medical assistance." An instruction leaflet was also drawn up, giving detailed directions on how the form was to be answered. Many thousands of copies were printed by the Reich minister of the interior. These were distributed to the long-term hospitals, sanitoriums, and asylums, along with a covering letter from Dr. Leonardo Conti, chancellor of sanitoriums and nursing homes, saying that a form had to be completed in full for each patient, filled out by the attending physician; the information provided had to be typewritten, with three carbons. The forms were to be completed at once, explained Conti's letter, owing to "the necessity for a systematized economic plan for hospitals and nursing institutions."

The Reich Minister of the Interior,
    Berlin NW 40, Koenigsplatz 6, 16 November 1939
    IV g 4178   39–5100
        Telephone:
        Dept. Z, I, II, V, VIII 11 00 27
        Dept. II, IV, VI
        (Unter den Linden 72); 12 00 34
        Tel. Address: Reichsinnenminister.

To the Head of the Hospital for Mental Cases,
Kaufbeuren,
or his deputy in Kaufbeuren.

With regard to the necessity for a systemized economic plan for hospitals and nursing institutions, I request that you complete the attached registration forms immediately in accordance with the attached instruction leaflet and return them to me. If you yourself are not a doctor, the registration forms for the individual patients are to be completed by the supervising doctor. The completion of the questionnaires is, if possible, to be done on a typewriter. In the column "Diagnosis" I request a statement, as exact as possible, as well as a short description of the condition, if feasible.

In order to expedite the work, the registration forms for the individual patients can be dispatched here in several parts. The last consignment, however, must arrive in any case at this ministry at the latest by 1 January 1940. I reserve for myself the right, should occasion arise, to institute further official inquiries on the spot, through my representative.

per proxi: DR. CONTI

Instruction Leaflet.

To be noted in completing questionnaire.

All patients are to be reported who—

1. Suffer from the following diseases and can only be employed on work of a mechanical character, such as sweeping, etc., at the institution:

Schizophrenia,

Epilepsy (if not organic, state war service injury or other cause),

Senile maladies,

Paralysis and other syphilitic disabilities refractory to therapy,

Imbecility however caused,

Encephalitis,

Huntington's chorea and other chronic diseases of the nervous system; or

2. Have been continously confined in institutions for at least five years; or

3. Are in custody as criminally insane; or

4. Are not German citizens or not of German or related stock according to their records of race and nationality.

The separate questionnaires to be completed for each patient must be given consecutive numbers.

Answers should be typewritten if possible.

Latest date for return _____

INSTRUCTIONS

Diagnosis should be as precise as possible. In the case of traumatically induced conditions the nature of the trauma in question, e.g., war wounds or accidents at work, must be indicated.

Under the heading "exact description of employment" the work actually done by the patient in the institution is to be stated. If a patient's work is described as "good" or "very good" reasons must be given why his release has not been considered. If patients on the higher categories of diet, etc., do no work, though they are physically capable of employment, the fact must be specially noted.

The names of patients brought to the institution from evacuation areas are to be followed by the letter (V).

If the number of Forms I sent herewith does not suffice, the additional number required should be demanded.

Forms are also to be completed for patients arriving at the institution after the latest date for return, in which case all such forms are to be sent in together exactly one month after the date in question, in every year.

[DOC 825.]

Registration Form 1   To be typewritten
Current No.
    Name of the institution_____
    At_____
Surname and Christian name of the patient_____
At Birth_____
Date of Birth_____ Place_____ District_____
Last place of residence_____ District_____
Unmarried, married, widow, widower, divorced_____
Religion_____ Race_____
Previous profession_____ Nationality_____
Army service when? 1914–18 or from 1/9/39_____
War injury (even if no connection with mental disorder) Yes/No
_____

How does war injury show itself and of what does it consist?
_____
Address of next of kin_____
Regular visits and by whom (address)_____
Guardian or nurse (name, address)_____
Responsible for payment_____
Since when in institution_____
Whence and when handed over_____
Since when ill_____
If has been in other institutions, where and how long_____
_____
Twin? Yes/No_____ Blood relations of unsound mind_____
Diagnosis_____
Clinical description (previous history, course, condition: in any case
    ample data regarding mental conditions)_____
_____
Very restless? Yes/No_____ Bedridden? Yes/No_____
Incurable physical illness? Yes/No (which)_____
Schizophrenia: Fresh attack_____ Final condition_____
    Good recovery_____
Mental debility: Weak_____ Imbecile_____ Idiot_____
Epilepsy: Psychological alteration_____
    Average frequency of the attacks_____
Therapeutics (insulin, cardiazol, malaria, permanent result
    _____ Salvarsan, etc., when?)_____ Yes/No_____

Admitted by reason of par. 51, par. 42b German Penal Code, etc.,
    through_____
Crime_____ Former punishable offences_____
Manner of employment (detailed description of work)_____

_____

Permanent/temporary employment, independent worker?
    Yes/No_____
Value of work (if possible compared with average performance of
    healthy person)_____
This space to be left blank
            _____ Place   Date_____

                  Signature of the head doctor or his
                  representative (doctors who are not
                  psychiatrists or neurologists, please
                  state same)[38]

Naturally, there was a good deal of confusion concerning who was to be selected for killing. When Dr. Schmidt, who had attended one of Brack's early briefings, was asked which "people were concerned," he replied, "The incurably sick. However, it was not quite clear to me where the line was to be drawn."[39]

At the beginning of the euthanasia program, it certainly was not clear to the unbriefed rank-and-file physicians filling out the forms. They did not know why the information was required or what purpose was to be made of it. Indeed, one rumor had it that the state was looking for additional common laborers. On the basis of the information received from the forms—according to this rumor—the state intended to remove the less seriously afflicted patients from the hospital and put them to work in the fields. This rumor was said to have caused some physicians to exaggerate the condition of their patients so that they might avoid recruitment; thus, unintentionally, these doctors sealed the fate of their patients.

At the briefings, Dr. Schmidt had expressed confusion over who was to be covered by the program. His confusion was certainly not relieved by Conti's letter, the registration form, or the instruction leaflet. This material does, indeed, provide a puzzling and imprecise picture of what facts were sought or for what purpose.

The registration form included three questions on the patient's work, ability, and experience—more than on any other topic. There were only two questions related to genetic theory: Did the patient have a twin? Did he have blood relatives of unsound mind? The twin question was easy enough to answer, but the term "unsound mind" was so general as to be meaningless. No conclusions about the genetic origins of the patients' conditions could be drawn from such sketchy information.

The form asked for information on the patient's race, religion, and military service. Without going into the Nazi theories of race superiority, it is probably safe to assume that here—as well as everywhere else—the purpose of the race question was to separate the Jews, Gypsies, and lesser races from the German Aryans. But why was this particular question included on this particular form? Brack insisted at Nuremberg that only German citizens of pure stock had been eligible for the euthanasia program: "The government did not want to grant this philanthropic act to the Jews."[40] This sounds reasonable when one recalls that one of the professed original intentions of the program had been to strengthen the German race by culling its weaker members. Not wanting to strengthen the Jewish or Gypsy stock, they were—at least at the start—exempted from the program.

But this left the program directors with a curious dilemma. If they killed *only* German asylum inmates and not the others, the asylums of Germany soon would be left with no patients *except* for disabled Jews and Gypsies—"useless eaters" and expensive to care for. And this was certainly not their intent.

How they resolved their dilemma is revealed in the fact that at the end of the war there were virtually no chronically ill Jews left in Germany. This was so because, despite the protestations to the contrary by the defendants at Nuremberg, Jews were included very early in the euthanasia program. The supposed "genetic" principles of the program directors fell before the sweeping efficiencies of large-scale killing.

This killing of the Jewish insane can be traced through official documents. A decree of August 30, 1940, ordered the segregation of Jewish patients. On September 4 of the same year, the Bavarian State Ministry of the Interior ordered that all Jewish insane be sent to Eglfing-Haar, outside Munich. They began arriving at the hospital on September 14; they were taken to the euthanasia unit on the twentieth, and soon they were all dead.[41]

The indefatigable Dr. Hermann Pfannmüller, director of Eglfing-Haar, was able to report to the Bavarian State Ministry on September 20, 1940, that "from now on my institution harbors only mentally diseased Aryans. In the future I shall decline admission of mentally diseased full Jews. In my institution there remains only one mentally diseased full Jew, whose home is in the Protectorate of Bohemia and Moravia, and whose transfer to an institution of the Protectorate should be initiated as soon as possible."[42]

It was the very strong and consistent testimony of Karl Brandt and others at Nuremberg that military veterans were to be exempted. This is why military-service information was requested on the questionnaire. The exemption of veterans was for public relations reasons: German boys were giving their lives, their limbs, their sanity, fighting at the fronts, East and West. It would surely shake their morale, and that of their families at home, if the state were to begin killing the invalid survivors of battle.

This reasoning shows again the confusion of thought of those who shaped this program. The directors believed it was essential that the program be kept secret. Therefore, all personnel were sworn to the highest secrecy, and death was the price for leaking information to the press or public. Yet the directors must have known it could not remain secret. You cannot wipe out hundreds of thousands of citizens without people noticing. The fact that they exempted veterans *in deference to public opinion* indicates they expected the program to become public knowledge, as, in fact, it did.

The exemption for veterans makes so much sense it is hard to believe that Brandt and the others would order that veterans be taken along with the others—but taken they were. It is likely this was done without the knowledge of the program directors. Once the killing process got started, it developed a momentum of its own; and many of the original controls and restraints fell by the wayside.

In due course, the veterans' exemption was altered so that only veterans who had been wounded or decorated were to be spared. Decisions as to which vets were to be taken and which excused were under the direction of a Mr. Jennewein at T-4 headquarters.[43] As a result, many veterans of World War I and even shell-shocked veterans of the Russian campaign of World War II went to their deaths. When news of the killing became known on the Russian front, troop morale was disturbed to the point that Field Marshal Wilhelm Keitel complained to Hitler about the killings.[44] When news that veterans were being killed by the government became generally known, it created a major furor—just as Brandt had feared it would.

Also exempted from the killing program were the wives, children, and close relatives of the T-4 employees. This last exemption is surely an important one. If a man is expected to put his heart into killing people, he must be assured that he will not be asked to kill one of his own loved ones. And also, for their part, the authorities must insure that a state-authorized killing program not be used by a corrupt employee as a tidy method of dispatching his mother-in-law.

There is ample testimony by the Nuremberg defendants that the program was conceived as a privilege of citizenship and not a punishment of the state. However, this claim is belied by the request in the registration form for the patient's criminal record, if any. Information obtained from these completed forms made it possible for the authorities to locate the criminally insane of Germany. This they did with efficient alacrity; and as a result the criminally insane, as a block, were eliminated. Like the Jewish insane, by the end of the war they were no more.

The accompanying instruction leaflet listed the categories of patients for whom forms should be completed. These were so general, so vague, as to include virtually *all* residents of the long-term asylums and institutions. The first category consists of the mentally ill, including but not limited to schizophrenics, the senile, epileptics, paralytics, and "the feebleminded"—the last a meaningless term. The second category consists of those who have been institutionalized for more than five years. The criminally insane are in category three, and the fourth category is made up of those who are not of German stock or nationality.

Brandt insisted that to qualify for euthanasia a person must have been mentally ill *and* resident for five years or more in an asylum *and neither* criminally insane nor a foreign national. Here again the wording of the paperwork shakes the credibility of his testimony. In the listing of the categories to be covered, the instructions read, "All patients are to be reported who are 1 . . . ; *or* 2 . . . ; *or* 3." The presence of the "ors" indicates that being a member of any one of the categories was sufficient grounds for being written up as a potential participant in the euthanasia program.

Speaking in medical terms, the form was a trivial business. The information requested was not sufficient to make any real diagnosis or to draw any valid conclusions concerning the prognosis or state of well-being of most of the patients. The forms had "No disposition about tests. No place to build up the diagnosis. No place to judge the person."[45] As a witness testified at Nuremberg, "On the basis of the questionnaires it was impossible for experts or top experts to form an exact medical opinion on the physical state of the patients."[46]

Dr. Brandt agreed that the form was superficial, but insisted it was always intended that the patient's medical history records as well as direct observation were to be used in addition to the form in determining who was to be eliminated. In fact, as the program operated, neither records nor observation was used for the vast majority of the victims.

None of this makes much difference. If a society decides to eliminate its disabled—without much regard for whether or not they are productive, tax-paying citizens—it is easy enough to identify the paralytic, the dwarfs, the blind, and those with afflictions such as Huntington's chorea. This was done straightaway.

It is not so easy, however, to sort out the mentally ill. The difference between the mentally healthy and the insane is a matter of degree rather than kind. There is no given point at which a person stops being sane and becomes, instead, insane. Most people are sometimes a little crazy; most insane are sometimes fairly "normal." Schizophrenics and depressives can be among society's most creative and productive citizens. Persons incapacitated by mental illness today may come out of it tomorrow and resume normal lives with full productivity. Diagnosis is a subjective matter. As a rule of thumb, perhaps as many as half of the insane can be considered curable; many simply become "cured" on their own. When the German doctors decided to kill their insane patients, they destroyed the lives of many productive, valuable citizens.

The physicians who watched their mental patients disappear from the hospital were fully aware that many were only temporarily ill. Others were aware, too: in a strong, brave letter of protest to the authorities from the bishop of Paderborn, who objected to the euthanasia program, "in the name of the Fifth Commandment of God . . . in the name of humanity," he pointed out that "among those unhappy human beings who are destined to be killed or who have already been killed, there are many who aside from partial disturbances are mentally completely clear and who know what is going to happen to them."[47]

In analyzing the questions asked, it is apparent that a patient's medical situation was to be only one of the factors weighed by the physician assessor in determining who was to live and who to die. Also to be considered was how much work he could do, how much his care was costing the state, how much it had already cost, and whether or not he was a criminal. With this information, the doctor assessors were to sit as judge and jury in a kangaroo court, without benefit of law or precedent, and decide, based upon their own appraisal of medical, economic, and moral factors, which of their fellow citizens should live and which should die. In making this decision eugenics did not appear to play an important role, nor was the "mercy" aspect of the killing given particular emphasis.

4

Aktion T-4 Origins

We have no business to permit the perpetuation
of citizens of the wrong type.

President Theodore Roosevelt

G erman physicians, Nazi Party members, and Adolf Hitler
were—inescapably—the product of their culture and their
times. Similarly, the program to provide "final medical assistance"
to the chronically disabled was not a spontaneous idea, the sudden
irrational impulse of a diseased mind. It was, rather, the practical
application of principles and proposals which had been widely
discussed and debated in scientific and medical circles for more
than half a century. This debate had been carried on, not only in
Germany, but throughout the Western world, in the United States
as well as in Europe. These discussions were held within the context
of the newly developing science of eugenics, the social movement
called Social Darwinism, and the social philosophy called monism.
Final medical assistance was the bastard offspring, the unforeseen
product, of the extraordinary flowering of inquiry and activity in
biological sciences following publication of Charles Darwin's *Origin
of Species*.

—

The nineteenth century was a time of great advances in the quality
of life and well-being of the disabled. The rise of democracy, the
Industrial Revolution, the widespread improvement in the standard
of living, the great scientific discoveries, the optimistic belief in
progress, and the enthronement of science as key to the universe—

all these developments promised and delivered significant improvements in the status and care of the disabled in society:

- Basic improvements in medicine—antisepsis, anesthetics, germ theory—served to keep many more disabled people alive and to lessen their pain and suffering.
- Public health practices and improved living standards—safe water, indoor plumbing, central heating, etc.—greatly improved the quality of all lives, including those of the disabled.
- The rise of medical specialties, especially orthopedics, at the end of the century increased the mobility of the physically disabled, thus enabling them to participate more actively in society.
- The development of a concern for social welfare and the resultant growth of charitable organizations channeled food, money, and resources to the needy disabled.
- Hospitals, asylums, and schools were built to house and treat the disabled. Although hardly "enlightened," these were, in most cases, superior to the common prison cells in which, hitherto, the destitute, physically disabled, and the insane had been incarcerated.

In the middle of the nineteenth century, there came an event of absolute watershed importance. In 1859, Charles Darwin published his *Origin of Species*, which changed, thereby and forever, the lens through which man examines the world about him. Unfortunately, in the process Darwin and his followers altered significantly and severely the attitude of society toward the disabled.

Darwin's argument concerning the evolution of the species is more subtle than it appears. Darwin's theory was (and is) a profound insight, so simple that it is easily and widely misconstrued. Darwin held that the members of a species will have various and sundry variations, and that these variations will, in one way or another, influence the ability of the individual member to survive. Thus, in general, the individuals more fit for the struggle will survive, while lesser ones fall by the wayside. This, said Darwin, was the principle of "natural selection," expressed by his follower Herbert Spencer as the "survival of the fittest."

Darwinian theory came like a revelation to the life scientists.

Natural selection, plus the Mendelian laws of heredity and genetics, seemed to provide a wholly convincing explanation for the operation of the biological world. All at once, it seemed that, armed with these tools, scientists could with careful examination come to understand any and all of the phenomena of nature. There was an explosion of interest in the study of botany and biology, natural history, zoology, paleontology, and even anthropology. Close observation produced remarkable and varied discoveries in these fields. For example, it was found that wolves were part of the natural ecosystem of the caribou, following after the herd, culling its weaker members, insuring the health and survival of the herd as a whole. It was seen that the butterfly with a pattern upon its wings, which seemed to give it the fierce eyes of an owl, was more apt to escape its predators' attack than was his less gaudily decorated neighbor. And it was thought that the evolutionary development of the bird, of the horse—yes, even of man!—could, at least in part, be traced through fossils, the record-keeping system of the ages.

In such excitement and ferment it is not surprising that thoughtful persons soon sought to apply the principles of natural selection and survival of the fittest to the organization of human society and the making of social policy. This was to have a lasting and ominous impact upon the rights of the disabled.

Darwin himself did not flinch from what he saw as the lesson evolution offered man. In *The Descent of Man* (1871), he said, "We civilized men, on the other hand, do our utmost to check the process of elimination; we build asylums for the imbecile, the maimed, and the sick; we institute poor-laws; and our medical men exert their utmost skill to save the life of everyone to the last moment. . . . Thus the weak members of civilized societies propagate their kind. No one who has attended to the breeding of domestic animals will doubt that this must be highly injurious to the race of man." He expressed the wish that "both sexes ought to refrain from marriage if they are in any marked degree inferior in body or mind." But he added, "Such hopes are utopian and will never be even partially realized until the laws of inheritance are thoroughly known."[1]

It should be pointed out at once that there was a general confusion as to what constitutes a weak member of civilized society or what constitutes survival in society. It is by no means clear that the stereotypical scrofulous Gypsy stealing horses, the street urchin picking pockets, or the welfare mother is any less adept at survival in the real sense of the term than is the upper-middle-class university-trained biologist. As Homer repeatedly emphasized in the *Odyssey*, it was not Odysseus' physical prowess, but rather his wiliness that allowed him to escape every pitfall, to survive every danger. Just what constitutes survival strength or weakness in the human race is a complex issue with many ramifications. The relationship between prosperity in an industrialized society and survival and selection in the natural chain of evolution is not as clear as the first evolution enthusiasts believed it to be. This, however, in no way slowed the Social Darwinists, as they were called, in their rush to apply the scientific principles of natural biology to the organization of human society.

The knowledge and insights provided by evolutionary theory and Mendelian law were brought together in the new eugenics in the early twentieth century. This was concerned with the study, evaluation, and ultimately the manipulation of human breeding practices. It was the avowed purpose of the eugenicists to make use of their scientific findings in the betterment and strengthening of the human race. Charles Davenport, a leader in the eugenic movement, explained it as "the science of the improvement of the human race by a better breeding."[2]

The turn of the century was a period of vast confidence, even smugness, among members of the educated classes of the Western industrialized world. Their empires covered the face of the globe. Their railroads spanned continents. They built great cities, made great discoveries, harnessed the forces of steam and then electricity. Anything seemed possible to these people. This was also a period of sweeping social reform. These people were determined to remake society—to insure health, safety, and justice for all citizens. This could be done "scientifically," using the vast resources of the industrialized state, using the newfound tools of science and engineering—and eugenics.

These were not bad people, but they were exceedingly arrogant.

In the United States these people tended to teach in the better colleges and universities and gather under the flag of the progressive movement. They were out to make a better world; they were united in their desire; and they were *ethnocentric*. They had no doubt what shape and color this better world would take. It would be a world in which all people of whatever race or nationality would live just the way the American progressives did. They meant well, but they sought to impose their values and behavior patterns upon all classes, all people everywhere.

Eugenicists were an integral part of the progressive movement in the United States. Their policies were jumbled in with such other progressive issues of the day as electoral reform, government regulation of commerce, international disarmament, women's rights and suffrage, prohibition, and birth control. Policies based on eugenics were endorsed with an honest and, at times, innocent intensity and the arguments used to support these policies were often inconsistent. Birth control offers an example: it was argued that readily available birth control would improve the status of women and raise the quality of life for many—as, indeed, it has. Some eugenicists saw birth control as something more—a tool which could be used to alter the birth rate for their own eugenic purposes. Overpopulation could be controlled; poor breeding stock—the "lower" races, the poor and the degenerate—would be able to improve their wealth and status by producing fewer children. The basic flaw in this thinking was seen at once by others in the eugenics movement: the people who needed birth control most were the ones who would use it least. The "right" stock would use it to have *even* fewer children, while the lower types would not use it at all. This meant, these eugenicists feared, that the least fit would survive in even greater numbers while the most fit—the chaps like the eugenicists—would dwindle away.

Eugenicists worried that the educated, well-to-do classes, the good old American stock descended from the Puritans of Massachusetts and the cavaliers of Virginia, the Anglo-Saxon aristocracy which had built America and kept it great—the WASPs—were not reproducing themselves. America's native stock appeared in danger of being overwhelmed by the great tidal wave of immigration bringing millions upon millions of people of lesser races to American shores. America's native stock was in danger of disappearing altogether, and the eugenicists called for government action before it was too late.

Teddy Roosevelt was impressed by the eugenicists' fears. His call to arms (as it were) to his fellow Americans of the right sort was clear and unambiguous: "A race is worthless and contemptible if its men cease to be willing and able to work hard and, at need, to fight hard, and if its women cease to breed freely." As he said in a private letter to eugenicist Davenport, "Someday we will realize that the prime duty, the inescapable duty, of the *good* citizen of the right type is to leave his or her blood behind him in the world; and that we have no business to permit the perpetuation of citizens of the wrong type."[3] Roosevelt felt that poor genetic types, including criminals, should be sterilized.

Although T.R., as a personality, was quite unlike the careful, thoughtful, and conscientious scholars of eugenics, his statement illustrates nicely the underlying bias and conceit of the science as it was practiced. The eugenicists used value-judgment words freely; they spoke of persons and peoples of superior or inferior blood. In their scientific articles, in many textbooks, and in the general press the races of the world were rated. Africans and Hottentots were apelike; Northern Europeans were superior to Mediterranean types; and clearly, the American model derived from Colonial times of English, Scotch-Irish, Dutch, and German blood was the finest of all. As the president of something called the National Institute of Immigration announced, "It is not vain glory when we say that we have bred more than sixty millions of the finest people the world has ever seen. Today there is to surpass us, none. Therefore any race that we admit to our body social is certain to be more or less inferior."[4]

The English philosopher Bertrand Russell made an observation once that is relevant to such thinking. He said that the whole great progress of evolution proceeds from the poor single-cell protozoan up, through the struggle of survival, over eons of time, to the ultimate culmination of nature's evolutionary force: the philosopher. "Of course," mused Russell, "it is the philosopher who makes this judgment, and not the protozoan."[5]

Progressive eugenicists strove to change things, to perfect man and his society. America's Social Darwinists were different. These men, such as William Graham Sumner, were conservatives, who used their philosophy to justify the status quo. They enjoyed a comfortable cultural elitism. They were virtually without exception white Anglo-Saxons of Northern European extraction. They believed their race was superior to all others. They believed the well-to-do and the powerful received their rewards from society because they deserved them. The successful were genetically superior to the failed. The rich deserved to be rich; the poor deserved to be poor. They regretted it, but they were forced to conclude that traditional American democratic values were nothing more than unscientific sentimentality. They found it unlikely that the poor and hereditarily disadvantaged, even with education and opportunity, could rise in society. Lastly, and this caused them a good deal of moral pain—for they were not bad people—they came to the conclusion that welfare programs were not only harmful to the recipients, but actually dangerous to the health of the race. As Charles Loring Brace warned in 1874, charity "degrades all that is manly and self-respecting in a human being, and destroys all habits of industry and self-support." If such charity programs were continued, "A community of paupers transmitting pauperism to children of like character would soon become one of the most degraded and miserable on the face of the earth."[6]

It is not possible here to summarize in detail the work of American eugenicists over the decades that surround the turn of the century. Their efforts were extensive. There were numerous studies of a scientific nature, numerous textbooks, numerous accounts in books and periodicals for the general reader of the findings of the eugenic investigation into race and heredity.

Perhaps the saga of the Jukeses and the Kallikaks is the most famous and, in some sense, characteristic of these studies. In 1874 Richard Dugdale painstakingly put together the family tree of the Jukeses of upstate New York. He traced the family back through six generations to Max Jukes and his two sons in Colonial times. Working from poorhouse and prison records and the memories of old residents, failing to take into account those progeny who had escaped the family environment, Dugdale came up with a staggering portrait of family degradation. According to his count, over the five generations there were 709 Jukeses or persons married to Jukeses. Of these, seventy-six had been convicted of crimes; more than two hundred were on relief; 128 were prostitutes; and eighteen owned houses of prostitution.

In 1897 a social worker named Elizabeth S. Kite assembled the records of another family, that of Martin Kallikak. During the Revolutionary War, this Kallikak had an illegitimate son by a feebleminded girl. This son, later known as "Old Horror," spawned a family fully as dreadful as the Jukeses. Over the generations, Old Horror had 480 descendants. One hundred and forty-three were feebleminded; eighty-two died in infancy. There were three criminals, three epileptics, twenty-four alcoholics, thirty-three prostitutes and other immoral persons, twenty-six illegitimate children, and only forty-six "normals." According to Kite, Old Horror's father, Martin Kallikak, later married a Quaker girl of good family. From *that* union there descended a line of doctors, lawyers—intelligent, decent people all.[7]

The Jukeses and the Kallikaks obtained nationwide notoriety. They became a symbol of the supposed threat posed by the unlimited reproduction of the lower classes, who were assumed by nature to be the morally weaker, intellectually impoverished segment of the population. This segment was also assumed to include the psychologically and physically disabled.

The eugenicists and Darwinists, for all their scientific pretensions, made no distinctions within the unfitness category. Crooks and prostitutes, the blind, the paralyzed, the retarded, all were degenerate, all were unfit. These were people with weak genes. The degeneracy of their character, as well as the flawed nature of their bodies, was seen to be inherited. There was no point in attempting to train them. And as has been shown, charity would be misplaced. It would only serve to support them in their evil ways and encourage their reproductive habits. Families with weak genes were prone to crime, prostitution, paralysis, and insanity: these were but some of their flaws. In W. Duncan McKim's book *Heredity in Human Progress* (1900), heredity is blamed for, among other things, "insanity, idiocy, imbecility, eccentricity, hysteria, epilepsy, the alcohol habit, the morphine habit, neuralgias, 'nervousness,' Saint Vitus' dance, infantile convulsions, stammering, squint, gout, articular rheumatism, diabetes, tuberculosis, cancer, deafness, blindness, deaf-mutism, color blindness." It is, McKim said, "the fundamental cause of human wretchedness."[8]

This kind of thinking, of course, caused handicapped people and their families to be ashamed and embarrassed by their condition.

Disability was a sign of genetic inferiority. The retarded child, the paralyzed person in middle-class families were hidden away, kept inside the house with blinds drawn. There was something shameful about the disabled person—perhaps, if the scientists were right, something shameful about his family, too.

The ever-present tendency to link evil with physical deformity found clear expression in a curious turn-of-the-century development called criminal anthropology. In a variety of books and pamphlets published in the United States and in Europe, it was claimed that criminals could be shown to have definite anatomical peculiarities. For example, the Italian Cesare Lambroso believed it possible to identify a criminal by his face and his physique. He acknowledged that there were exceptions, but he believed in general that criminals had a primitive brain, a hairy body, large teeth, a flat nose, long arms, monkey-like feet. Murderers, in particular, he believed had cold eyes, big jaws, long ears, and dog-like teeth. There was such a thing as "murderer's thumb." The assumption underlying criminal anthropology was that the capacity for committing crimes, as well as imbecility and all the rest, was an inherited characteristic. A bad boy was born bad, and you could no more reform him than you could change the color of his eyes. The linkage here between physical defects and criminality was, of course, an example—this one dressed up in scientific terminology—of the old belief that a disabled person either had done or was about to do something unspeakably evil.

The social programs devised in America to counteract the threat posed to a decent society by the rapidly reproducing Jukeses and Kallikaks and their expanding band of criminals, lunatics, and paralytics were simple. These undesirables must be kept from breeding by sterilization or, ideally, internment.

Debate over the efficacy of sterilization as a tool of social policy waxed and waned in the United States over the first half of the twentieth century. In 1907 Indiana became the first state to authorize the sterilization of the feebleminded and the hereditarily unfit. Over the next ten years fourteen other states passed variations of the law. Progressive Hiram Johnson, when governor of California, sponsored such legislation, as did Woodrow Wilson when he was governor of New Jersey. In all, thirty states approved sterilization measures. The particulars of these laws varied from state to state. In general they authorized a board or commission to order the sterilization of persons found to be unfit and thought likely to pass their unfitness on to their progeny. There was a good deal of variation, state to state, as well as a good deal of confusion generally about what constituted such unfitness and whether or not it was an inherited trait and, hence, subject to sterilization. Virtually all of the laws provided for the sterilization of the retarded, the chronically insane, and epileptics. Also covered were such disparate groups as drunks, homosexuals, drug addicts, and recidivist criminals. Haller quotes a Missouri proposal that would have authorized the sterilization of those "convicted of murder (not in the heat of passion), rape, highway robbery, chicken stealing, bombing, or theft of automobiles."[9]

There was, throughout the period, much controversy over the morality of sterilization, particularly of criminals. In support of such a policy it was argued that the offspring of criminals would be fully as depraved as their parents, "helpless, unfortunate children of the degenerate and criminally depraved who are brought into the world handicapped at their birth, cursed before they see the light of day, stunted mentally, morally, and physically."[10] Of course, here again physical disability is linked with and becomes a visible metaphor for moral corruption.

The argument over whether the supposed therapeutic use of sterilization was constitutional reached all the way to the U.S. Supreme Court. The case before the Court turned on whether a state had the right to sterilize a retarded woman, whose mother and first child were said also to be retarded. In a famous decision Oliver Wendell Holmes wrote, "Society can prevent those who are manifestly unfit from continuing their kind. The principle that sustains compulsory vaccination is broad enough to cover cutting the Fallopian tubes. . . . Three generations of imbeciles are enough."[11]

Constitutional questions were raised concerning other aspects of sterilization. The Constitution prohibits "cruel and unusual" forms of punishment, and there can be no doubt that sterilization *as* a punishment is both cruel and unusual. By the 1920s, most of the states had so structured their sterilization laws as to avoid all appearance of the use of sterilization as a punitive measure. Care was taken to see that the law was equally applied, to those both within and without institutions, so as to insure equal protection of the laws and to avoid class legislation. Finally, most states provided some form of due process so that the rights of the victims to be sterilized could be heard and appealed through the courts.

Twenty years before the German Third Reich approved a sterilization law, the United States led the way among Western nations in the sterilization of the chronically disabled. Although the heyday of American sterilization came in the 1920s, sterilization procedures continued in some states throughout World War II and on into the 1950s. By 1958, over 60,000 American citizens had been sterilized.

The German law was passed in 1933. By that time thirty American states had sterilization measures on their books. In 1928 the Canadian province of Alberta had followed suit. Over the next two years, Denmark, Finland, Sweden, and Iceland also adopted sterilization policies. The issue was closely debated in Great Britain, but no authorization law was ever approved by Parliament.

American eugenicists sought not only to sterilize the disabled but to intern them for their own safety and that of society. Many articles were written about the dangers inherent in allowing the so-called feebleminded to wander the streets. It was felt that, invariably, such people would turn to a life of crime and debauchery. No doubt, unsterilized women would become pregnant, thereby thrusting yet another generation of the crippled upon burdened society. With the support of the eugenicists, the superintendents and medical directors of state institutions for the retarded and the severely handicapped pushed for enlarged facilities. They envisaged a system of enclosed dormitories, work farms, and colonies. The sexes were to be segregated—separate dormitories, separate workplaces—so that there would be no chance of procreation. They sought enforced commitment laws which would authorize the internment of the disabled with or without their consent on a lifelong basis. This was called permanent custodial care. The campaign to provide such facilities in each of the several states attracted much favorable attention. It received the support of the major philanthropists of the day, including General Coleman Du Pont, Henry Clay Frick, and Mrs. E. H. Harriman.

The campaign was full of good intentions, and its tone was as patronizing as a Jerry Lewis telethon: "It is the thing to do for the feebleminded—get them out of the big world where they have such a hard time because they are not like other folks."[12]

The turn of the century was a period of great growth for these custodial-care institutions. By the year 1923, forty-three states operated institutions with an overall resident population of 43,000. Testing standards and techniques varied from institution to institution. The internees were American citizens. Many of them were capable of living an active life on the outside. Others could have lived quietly with their families. Many of the internees were held against their wishes and without due process of law.

It should be emphasized that the leaders of this campaign for enlarged programs of mandatory custodial care were the officials who would benefit most from it. Human nature being what it is, perhaps it is not surprising that the director of an institution would seek to enlarge his domain, extend its authority, and increase his paycheck. The argument used was that lifetime internment would increase the well-being of the unfortunates in their care. But, in fact, in most cases institutional life was a punitive existence—a form of lifetime imprisonment without pleasure, reward, or parole.

Over these same years some forty states passed laws governing who was eligible to enter into a contract of marriage. Epileptics, the feebleminded, and the chronically insane were uniformly forbidden to marry. In some states alcoholics were added to the list. Though the laws were on the books, in most cases they were awkward to enforce and had little effect.

After an extensive campaign of many years' duration, Congress in the 1920s clamped down on the free immigration of "the lesser" races into the United States. Virtually all Oriental peoples were denied citizenship. The flow of immigration from Southern and Eastern Europe was cut by four-fifths, and only immigration from the Anglo-Saxon Nordic European states was allowed to continue at its previous rate.

In the first decades of the twentieth century, the American program to clean up and strengthen the gene pool thus consisted of internment, sterilization, marriage control, and finally, tight immigration restrictions. Prewar America was a nation anxious to conserve its racial heritage and strengthen its genetic pool through selective breeding practices.

—

Germany was just as anxious to preserve its racial heritage. The impact of Darwinian theory upon German thought was not less than it had been in Britain and America. If anything, it was wider and deeper. Darwin cast a long shadow over the development of National Socialism and the Third Reich.

The causes of racism lie deep in history and the subconscious. Racism is complex and not easily explained. However, the intellectual framework, the rationale of twentieth-century German prejudice—particularly anti-Semitism—was taken largely from the Social Darwinist arguments of the biologist and philosopher. National Socialism, in fact, was understood by its supporters to be the application of the biological principles of natural selection—again, as they understood them—to the political process: political biology.

In the half century before the rise of Hitler, Germany was a newly united country, operating under a frail federalism. Wilhelmine Germany was a nation alive with great intellectual, creative, cultural ferment. Rich in art, music, literature, science, and medicine—it was an amazing era. The trauma of World War I and its appalling aftermath added a cynical, nihilist twist to this creativity, but did not end it.

Over this era, biological and Social Darwinists were generally found under the banner of monism, a small, yet influential, philosophic movement dedicated to the oneness, the wholeness of the universe; mind and body, man and nature, all were one. For these people, science revealed to man nothing less than the immutable laws of nature to which man and all other creatures are bound. Hitler, perhaps not a monist but heavily influenced by the movement, explained, "Nothing that is made of flesh and blood can escape the laws which determine its coming into being." For the thinkers associated with monism, the ideas and theories of Social Darwinism took on many of the attributes of an evolutionary religion. This was, for many, a genuinely German response to the soft and selfish appeals of the Western European Romantic movement. Germans, they believed, should be made of sterner stuff. It is not surprising that many in monist literary circles drifted off through German mythology and pre-Christian paganism into the further reaches of vegetarianism, sun worship, and nudism.

The monist belief that the laws of nature should be and, in fact, are the laws of society had a far-reaching effect. In particular, the belief that the principles of biological selection mandated the institution of so-called racial hygiene policies was to have a catastrophic impact—and not just upon the German disabled.

The ideas of the German monists and their followers concerning social policy toward the disabled were not different from those of American eugenicists and social reformers, although they may have been more emphatic. Typical were the views of famed biologist and social scientist Ernst Haeckel. His book *The Riddle of the Universe*, published in 1899, became one of the most widely read science books of the age. It sold more than 100,000 copies its first year. It went through ten editions before 1919 and sold over half a million copies by 1933, and ultimately was translated into twenty-five different languages.[13] Haeckel was a scientist of immense prestige whose thinking had significant influence upon the German intelligentsia through the first half of the twentieth century. It was his conviction that "such ravaging evils as consumption, scrofula, syphilis, and also many forms of mental disorders are transmitted by inheritance to a great extent and transferred by sickly parents to some of their children, or even to all of their descendants." He was outraged that "hundreds and thousands of incurables—lunatics, lepers, people with cancer, etc.—are artificially kept alive . . . without the slightest profit to themselves or the general body." He warned that "the progress of modern medical science, although still little able to cure diseases, yet possesses and practices more than it used to do the art of prolonging life during lingering, chronic diseases for many years." This was not only a drain on the economy of society but presented a growing danger to the very health of the race. "Now, the longer the diseased parents, with medical assistance, can drag on their sickly existence, the more numerous are the descendants who will inherit incurable evils, and the greater will be the number of individuals again, and over the succeeding generations, thanks to that artificial 'medical selection,' who will be infected by their parents' lingering, hereditary disease." Haeckel stated clearly and without equivocation what must be done. "We are not bound under all circumstances to maintain and prolong life even when it becomes utterly useless." He proposed that a commission be set up in Germany to determine which of the deformed, chronically insane, and diseased should be allowed to live and which should be condemned to death—which he referred to as a "redemption from evil." He suggested that such death be brought about by means of a quick and rapid poison.[14] Haeckel was not alone in his proposal. Other books and pamphlets of the era discussed such matters. Here, for example, is an excerpt from a widely read book of 1910: "Our humanitarianism one-sidedly considers the well-being and complaints of unfortunate individuals who are alive at present and is extremely indifferent or blind to the suffering which they inflict by their complacency on the next or later generations." Said this author, "Instead of always increasing healing and nursing asylums for the spiritually and mentally ill, homes for cripples, etc., it would be a more farsighted expression of humanitarianism to provide for better human selection by favorable measures so that such unfortunates should not be born so frequently."[15]

Like their fellow American and British Darwinists, these people assumed mistakenly that such conditions as schizophrenia, depression, paralysis, and epilepsy were in every case inherited and not acquired characteristics; and they used this belief as justification for their desires to intern, punish, and kill those more vulnerable than themselves. Like so many primitive peoples before them, these scientists saw the disabled as the bearer of evil, and they sought redemption therefrom.

And, like the American and British eugenicists, the German monists and their followers tended to lump the disabled together as one degenerate group. People who were deformed of body were, no doubt, deformed of mind and morally degenerate. Professor Heinrich Ziegler, one of Haeckel's followers, was confident that "most murderers were feebleminded or epileptic." So, too, Ziegler believed that most alcoholics and criminals were also disabled. Crime, he said, is an inherited trait like blue eyes and blond hair. In fact, he said, the disabled—and like the eugenicists, he was particularly concerned about the mentally retarded—were the "worry children of the state." They were the poorest, they suffered the most, they were the most unemployed, they were untrustworthy, dishonest, and drunken. They stole, they murdered, they cheated and gambled, and they were vagrants. Ziegler, who considered himself a scientist, stated as a scientific fact that poor neighborhoods were "hotbeds of moral decay." Not only were they "constant centers of various infectious diseases, especially infectious sexual sicknesses," but they were also centers of social unrest. In these poor neighborhoods, it was alcohol which triggered the crippled and feebleminded to revolt. Drawing upon his research, Ziegler asserted that in 76 percent of such cases of unrest in these poor neighborhoods, drunkenness had been found to be the direct cause of the disturbance.

As in the United States, proposals were discussed to provide for the sterilization, even in some cases the castration, of the unfit—and, again, this was to include not only the retarded, but the chronically insane, the congenitally disabled, syphilitics, sex offenders, homosexuals, and alcoholics. The monists and their brethren were convinced that such people were profligate breeders. What was worse, they were convinced, was that the better types of Germans, the healthy Aryans of the upper class, were failing to breed in adequate numbers. In fact, Europeans as a whole were not breeding vigorously enough, and over the course of time stood to be overwhelmed by the "yellow peril," the rising tide of the Oriental population explosion. Inside Germany itself, they believed it to be a truism that the lower races bred in quantity, while the upper races bred in quality.[16] It was vital that the superior races and classes reproduce, more and faster. Along this line, the monist Dr. Wilhelm Schallmayer proposed a law that would require unmarried persons to marry and childless couples to divorce and remarry. "For every healthy man and every healthy woman not to marry is a shame and a violation of their obligation to the state."[17]

Monists came to believe strongly—at times even hysterically—that the physically and mentally degenerate must not be allowed to breed, must not be allowed to participate in society, and ideally, should be put to death. Professor Haeckel, who never flinched from a logical conclusion and who always had a way with a phrase, supported the idea of killing the disabled, the alcoholic, the very poor, and, of course, criminals. With a great passion Haeckel defended capital punishment. "Capital punishment for incorrigible and degraded criminals is not only just, but also of benefit to the better portions of mankind; the same benefit is done by destroying luxuriant weeds, for the prosperity of a well-cultivated garden." His passion for killing, he assured those who might be similarly inclined, had a sound Darwinian basis. "By the indiscriminate destruction of all incorrigible criminals, not only would the struggle for life among the better portions of mankind be made easier, but also an advantageous artificial process of selection would be set in practice, since the possibility of transmitting their injurious qualities would be taken from those degenerate outcasts."[18] Thus, in a perversion of Darwinian principle, Haeckel sought to hurry along the process of natural selection.

Dr. Ziegler went Haeckel one curious step further. Ziegler believed that since crime was a hereditary characteristic, it was both pointless and foolish to attempt to rehabilitate, reform, or retrain the degenerate wrongdoer. It was, however, said Ziegler, sensible to punish them. "One has the right to punish feebleminded and abnormal personalities," said Ziegler, "and they should not have the right to plead innocent by reason of insanity or mental incompetence. Everyone must be held accountable for his actions—whether or not he, in fact, is able to exercise control over these actions. It is the same as dealing with your house pet. When someone maintains that punishment should only be carried out when one believes in free will, then I may inquire of him if he ever had a dog; if this is the case, I can show him that he surely often punished the dog without asking if the dog had free will." Clearly Dr. Ziegler had come up with a justification for punishing those one was not allowed to kill.

Dr. Ziegler argued that if society persists in unreasonably restricting the use of capital and corporal punishment upon congenital miscreants, then, at the least, such persons should be interned away from decent people. He proposed that all such people should be put away, permanently. He sought the establishment of large work colonies in which the alcoholics, the vagrants, the poor, the retarded, and the crippled could be interned. "If one wishes, for example, to prevent a drunkard from committing a crime, one must place him in an asylum for drunkards or forcibly prevent him from drinking in some other way . . . the vagrant must be placed in an institution where he can be put to doing appropriate work. . . . In regard to feebleminded offenders, especially young murderers and arsonists, human society has the greatest interest in being lastingly protected from such people." Writing in his prize-winning book of 1918, Ziegler proposed the establishment of securely isolated compounds to house the deviates and disabled of society on a permanent basis. These undesirables would be housed in large camps. "Such institutions could be built according to the plan of modern insane asylums and must be provided with farms and workshops, with schools and churches." There would be no escape from these camps. There would be no alcohol available to its inhabitants. They would work at menial labor from dawn to dusk. Men and women would sleep in separate dormitories. All would be supervised closely at all times, so that there could be no question of crime, sex, or reproduction.[19]

Ziegler, Haeckel, and others were esteemed scholars who received all the prestige and respect German society bestows upon its wise men. Thoughts such as theirs were not limited to scholarly or scientific circles. They were widespread. For example, the great Krupp works sponsored a national contest for the best book of the year to apply scientific Social Darwinist principles to state politics. The Ziegler book, in fact, was a Krupp prize-winner. In 1920 a popular book dealing with the economic chaos following the Great War expressed concern that the disabled, particularly the large number of crippled war veterans, were consuming the resources of the healthy. In *Moral der Kraft*, author Ernst Mann called upon these veterans to perform one "last heroic deed"—that is, to kill themselves—thus sparing the state the burden of their pensions. Said Mann, "It's just not right to spend the millions of marks on the cripples, the diseased, and the incurable, when hundreds of thousands of the healthy blow their brains out because of the economic crisis." This volume was a best-seller when it was first published, and it sold well when it was reissued a decade later in 1933.

Perhaps most influential was the 1920 book *The Permission to Destroy Life Unworthy of Life*, written by psychiatrist Alfred Hoche and lawyer Karl Binding. These men were professors of reputation and importance. They argued that the medical profession should participate not only in health giving but, under certain circum-

91

stances, in death making as well. With a carefully reasoned argument, defining their terms precisely, their analysis concluded that certain people should be exterminated for racially "hygienic" purposes. They argued that the retarded, the deformed, the terminally ill, and those who were mentally sound but severely damaged by disease or accident should be put to death. They believed that the death should be painless and expertly administered—that is, by a physician. According to their reasoning, the right to "grant death" was a natural extension of the responsibilities of the attending physician. Binding and Hoche were widely read and vigorously discussed. One of their readers was the young Adolf Hitler, who had read a good deal on eugenics and monism prior to his writing of *Mein Kampf*. Later Hitler even allowed his name to be used in advertisements for Hoche's books.[20]

By the end of the twenties, the belief was widespread in German society that to be handicapped mentally or physically was shameful. Such a life was, indeed, widely believed to be not worth living. This was reflected not just in the works of scientists but in the popular media as well. Scholar James M. Gardner has reviewed twenty-five films dealing with mental illness and retardation made in Germany before Hitler's rise. He concluded that these films presented the mentally retarded as being exclusively from the lower classes. The mentally ill, on the other hand, came from the upper classes. Both the insane and the retarded were seen to be dangerous, indulging in murder and mayhem. They never recovered, and all but three of the characters came to a violent end. The three survivors were all upper class—a lawyer, a professor, and a count.[21]

An exceedingly popular movie of the mid-thirties dealt entirely with the issue of euthanasia for the disabled. *I Accuse* was the story of a young woman suffering from multiple sclerosis. Her husband, a doctor, after lengthy soul-searching, kills his wife as a fellow physician in the next room plays softly and funereally on the piano. Another film of the Nazi years illustrated the unbearable life of the insane with particularly grisly shots of defectives. This was made for the use of medical societies. The film was often screened at gatherings of physicians and was shown to the Nazi Party meeting of 1935 by Dr. Gerhardt Wagner, leader of the medical delegation.

Even Nazi schoolroom textbooks encouraged the devaluation of disabled lives. A mathematics text, *Mathematics in the Service of National Political Education*, set the following problem: "If the building of a lunatic asylum costs six million marks and it costs fifteen thousand marks to build each dwelling on a housing estate, how many of the latter could be built for the price of one asylum?" Another asked how many marriage-allowance loans could be given to young couples for the amount of money it cost the state to care for "the crippled, criminal, and insane."[22]

The long-discussed sterilization program became law in 1933, only after the Nazis had assumed full authority and thus were able to break the legislative block which had so bedeviled the Reichstag under the Weimar Republic. The proposed program had been debated in the Reichstag before, but without majority support. The new law met with worldwide interest and approval in the medical community. As a prewar report of the American Neurological Association, funded by the Carnegie Foundation, assured its members, "It is fair to state that the Sterilization Act is not a product of Hitler's regime in that its main tenets were proposed and considered several years earlier before the Nazi regime took possession of Germany. There was no doubt," it concluded, "that the Act conforms closely with the present knowledge of medical eugenics."[23]

In the fall of 1933 the Ministry of Justice, as part of the Nazi reform of the German penal code, proposed that a law be passed to authorize euthanasia. This proposal, too, was widely reported, not just in Germany but in the United States. A front-page story in *The New York Times* gave details of the proposal.[24] It quoted the ministry as proposing, "It shall be made possible for physicians to end the tortures of incurable patients, upon request, in the interests of true humanity." The law as proposed by the ministry outlined the procedure to be followed. Incurability must be determined not only by the attending physician but also by a review committee of two official doctors appointed by the state. These doctors were to review carefully the history of the patient and examine him personally. The ministry believed that the participation of the expert committee would insure, the *Times* reported, "that no life still valuable to the state will be wantonly destroyed."

This was, of course, the basic structure of the killing program to be instituted by the Nazi regime some six years later. There was no secret about it in 1933, and there was a significant outcry from the major religions of Germany. An editorial in *Germania*, a Catholic newspaper, condemned the proposal without qualification. "The Catholic faith binds the conscience of its followers not to accept this method of shortening the sufferings of incurables who are tormented by pain."[25] Lutheran authorities were also upset. As a result of the outcry this section of the penal code reforms was quietly dropped from the legislation.

Throughout the 1930s and on into the war years, occasional articles appeared explaining and discussing the issues raised by the German social experiments in sterilization and euthanasia. The *Journal of the American Medical Association* had a correspondent in Berlin who filed regular reports on medical events in Germany. In an editorial comment *JAMA* advised that judgment on the sterilization program be postponed until full evidence became available. By and large the reports in the eugenic journals were highly enthusiastic. One Paul Popenoe fairly bubbled in the *Journal of Heredity* for 1934. The Nazis were moving, he said, "toward a policy that will accord with the best thought of eugenicists in all civilized countries."[26] The July 1942 issue of the *American Journal of Psychiatry*, the official publication of the American Psychiatric Association, contained two articles, one in favor, one opposed to the killing of severely retarded children. The author in favor of the idea, Dr. Foster Kennedy, proposed that the defective child—the "hopelessly unfit" child, "nature's mistake"—should be relieved "of the agony of living." However, said Dr. Kennedy, the child should not be so relieved until he or she had reached the age of five and had been found by a competent medical board to be unfit. The board should review its findings two times at four-month intervals before it proceeded to "grant death" (using the phrase of Binding and Hoche). It is clear from the text that Kennedy was aware in 1942 of the German killing program. Speaking of the higher grades of so-called imbeciles, he said, "They are greatly needed for the simpler forms of work. They are necessary for the work of the world. *It would be improper, I am sure, for their disposal to lay down any such arbitrary law as has come into existence in Germany by dictatorial method* [italics added]."[27] With masterful ambivalence, the editors of the journal in an editorial seemed to feel that in due course euthanasia, like sterilization, would become a widely adopted practice in the United States. Because the editors felt the general public might find it difficult to accept such a program, the editorial suggests that a public education campaign might be helpful to overcome resistance. It also suggested psychiatric intervention to overcome the "resistance" of family members to such a proposal. "It is in the evaluation and melioration of this parental attitude that the interest of the psychiatrists in the whole question must center."[28]

It is not surprising that Dr. Kennedy was aware of the Nazi killing program for the disabled. It had been described fairly accurately by William L. Shirer in his best-selling book *Berlin Diary*, published in 1941. Shirer had spent the 1930s in Berlin as a well-known radio correspondent for CBS and returned to America in the winter of 1940. An article describing the killing program was extracted from this volume and published in the June 1941 *Reader's Digest*—the magazine with the largest circulation in America. Shirer was not aware of the size or scope of the program. It was, after all, a high state secret. Shirer had to piece his story together on the basis of rumor and gossip. He got some of the details wrong, but in general his was an accurate report. The story was available for any who wished to read it.

—

There can be no doubt that the concepts of sterilizing, interning, and killing the disabled were widely discussed throughout intellectual Germany—and not just in Germany—for many years before the rise of the Nazi state. There was nothing creative or innovative about Nazi social policy in this regard. The Nazis were consistent and effective in the implementation, but responsibility for the origins of their policies rested with others—the medical profession, the scientific community, and the intelligentsia generally.

95

5

Aktion T-4 in Action

This is murder by assembly line.
Reich Minister of Justice Franz Gürtner

The Aktion T-4 program was soon in full-scale operation.
Little more than a month after Hitler's authorization the
completed questionnaires began to flow in. Each form received was
copied in triplicate and sent off to the physician members of the
assessment committees.

The paperwork generated was enormous. Thousands upon thousands of completed questionnaires flooded into T-4. Each receipt
was noted and a file established for each. Files and forms and copies
were stacked in the corridors, everywhere. Forms and files were sent
out to the assessors in bulk. These men already had full-time
duties—as medical directors, psychiatric professors, and the like.
Appraising the questionnaires was an additional task piled on
top of their heavy wartime responsibilities. Take, for example,
Hermann Pfannmüller, the manager of a large psychiatric institution. He agreed to serve as an assessor. During the fifteen months
from January 1940 through April 1941, Pfannmüller received 159
separate shipments, each containing between two hundred and
three hundred questionnaires for him to evaluate.[1] Dr. Pfannmüller
actually passed medical judgment on 2,058 patients over an
eighteen-day period during which he continued his daily management duties.

There was, of course, a financial incentive for the doctors doing
the appraisals. They were paid ten pfennigs per questionnaire when
they processed up to five hundred per month; this payment dropped

to five pfennigs per questionnaire up to 3,500 a month. There are one hundred pfennigs in a mark, and the mark was then worth forty cents in 1940 U.S. dollars. This works out to between twenty and seventy dollars per month.[2]

The physicians of the appraisal committee would review the information contained in each of the questionnaires, and determine which of the patients should live and which should die. Originally, a death warrant required the approval of all members of the appraisal committee. However, as the program came into operation, a majority of two out of three or three out of four members was usually sufficient.

The decisions of the appraising physicians were gathered and forwarded to a senior expert—usually a professor and head of a medical department at one of the major universities. Final decisions would be made by this senior expert. Names of the patients to be killed were then routed to Dr. Herbert Linden, who served as representative of the Ministry of the Interior. Linden worked in conjunction with the General Patient Transport Company to arrange for the transfer of the selected patients from the nationwide array of mental institutions, nursing homes, and long-term facilities to the "observation institutions." The principal ones were Eglfing-Haar, Kempten, Jena, Buch, and Arnsberg.

At the observation institutes, according to *theory*, the patients were to be observed for one to three months by the physicians in charge before a final decision on their disposition. At the Nuremberg trial there was testimony that some 4 to 6 percent of the patients observed were rejected for euthanasia and returned to the facility from which they had come. This was sharply rebutted by witnesses, and it seems clear that the observation institutions were principally used as gathering stations from which the patients were taken in large groups to the euthanasia institutions.

There were six major euthanasia institutions. T-4 referred to them by letter. They were:

A. Grafeneck, in the Black Forest, southwest of Ulm
B. the "old jail" at Brandenburg, near the hospital at Görden, southwest of Berlin
C. Hartheim, northwest of Linz in Austria

97

    D. Bernberg, in central Germany

    E. Hadamar, in Hesse, north of Frankfurt

    F. Sonnenstein—often called Die Sonne—near Dresden in Saxony

Characteristically, these were located in large houses or castles on the edges of small towns in out-of-the-way places. Schloss Hartheim, for example, had been built as a private house. It had served as an orphanage and later a hospital. It was complete with gardens, great trees, archways, turret, and courtyard. Hadamar had been an asylum for many years. Bernberg was a church-operated institution. Grafeneck looked like an old resort hotel, deep in the Black Forest. Sonnenstein was an abbey-like structure, high on a hill over Pirna, near Dresden.

The first euthanasia station to open its doors was at Brandenburg, located only a few miles southwest of Berlin. It was set up in an abandoned prison and guarded by a unit of the Anstaltpolizei under the direction of the infamous SS captain Christian Wirth.

Wirth was a genius, an enthusiastic genius, at killing. At first he dispatched his charges by shooting them, one by one, in the back of the neck.[3] He later claimed to have invented the use of shower stalls as gas chambers; and after the formal end of the euthanasia program he was transferred to the conquered Eastern territories, where he pioneered the extraordinarily efficient assembly-line type procedures for killing large numbers of persons which made the Holocaust possible.

The Wirth style of killing did not last long in the euthanasia program. It should be remembered that the program was conceived as a medical matter; death was to be a therapy, "final medical assistance," as it was called. It would not do for it to be administered by a psychotic hoodlum, no matter how efficient he might be. The shootings were soon halted and replaced by physicians with hypodermic needles. From then on, throughout the life of the program—whether death came by pill, starvation, or carbon monoxide shower—it came at the hand of a physician. It was Brack's firm and oft-stated belief that "the syringe belongs in the hand of a physician."[4]

Bouhler was insistent that a way of death be found that would not only be painless but also imperceptible to the patient. He did not want to frighten the patients or make them uncomfortable. These things must be "done according to his orders, and in a dignified and not a brutal fashion."[5] It was the conviction of a chemist, Dr. Kallmeyer, that carbon monoxide provided the most humane and economic means of killing large numbers of people. He briefed the leaders of the Aktion T-4 program, who were much intrigued. Accordingly, one cold day in December 1939 or January 1940, when the snow was on the ground, Dr. Brandt, together with Dr. Leonardo Conti, the Reichgesundheitsführer (German health minister), Bouhler, and Brack, drove down from Berlin to the Brandenburg killing center to witness an experiment. Other doctors were present for the show, but their names have now been lost.

The experiment consisted of leading four men, supposedly "mentally incurable" according to Brack,[6] into a small room, shutting the door, and turning on a canister of carbon monoxide supplied by the famous German chemical firm I. G. Farben. "After the gas was let in, the patients became sleepy and tired and died after a few minutes," testified Brack. Others reported that death came sooner, in a matter of seconds. The doctors took turns watching what happened through a peephole in the door. After the patients were dead, the bodies were immediately cremated—again at the insistence of Bouhler.[7]

These doctors and officials were witness to—and participants in—the first mass murder by carbon monoxide in the history of the world. This was the very small beginning of what was to become the largest crime of the twentieth century. There is a plaque on the wall under the grandstand at Stagg Field on the University of Chicago campus which commemorates the spot where mankind first triggered a nuclear chain reaction. There should be such a plaque on the wall of Brandenburg prison. In its way, what man started at Brandenburg is no less important than what happened at Stagg Field.

Hitler was said to have been delighted with the report he received from Brandt and Bouhler. "On the basis of this experiment Hitler decided that only carbon monoxide was to be used for killing the patients," said Brack.[8]

It was the concern for the peace of mind of the patients that made the shower-stall concept so attractive. As explained by defendant

Brack at Nuremberg, ". . . the photographing of the patients, which was only done for scientific reasons, took place before they entered the chamber, and the patients were completely diverted thereby. Then they were led into the gas chamber which they were told was a shower room." And this ploy worked—sometimes. One of the patients was heard to remark, "We will have a real bath now and get other clothes."[9]

The patients never knew what was happening to them. This was the theory. And, at least at the beginning, this was the fact. As the program went into operation all over Germany, the existence of the gas chambers and ovens became common knowledge. People talk, patients and medical personnel talk, and there can have been but few of the later victims who were not aware of their fate—and the purpose of their "shower."

It is not clear who came up with the bathroom ruse. Brack gave Bouhler credit for it.[10] Of course, the "Savage Christian," blood-thirsty Captain Wirth, claimed that he had invented it.[11] And throughout the T-4 operation, the gas chamber/shower room was known—in that particularly German form of gallows humor—as the "Brack remedy."[12] Whoever was initially responsible, one senses that they were *all* rather proud of their invention.

Transfer arrangements were not simple. The patients were allowed to bring their personal possessions, their money, and such articles of value as they might have. These items were to be recorded on separate special lists which were kept in duplicate. Hospital reports and medical histories on each patient were required and had to be presented to the director of transport at the point of transfer. Items of clothing were labeled with a strip of adhesive tape on which the patient's name had been written. Such a label was also required to be affixed to the back of the patient himself between the shoulder blades. There were various other forms and fees to be noted and provided for. In cases where the trip was to be a lengthy one, food was to be provided for the well-being of the patients.

The administrators of the program could be extraordinarily persnickety, insisting that their directives be carried out to their last detail. Take, for example, the following scolding letter, surely an essay in surrealism: the patients are to be killed shortly after transfer; neither their clothing nor their personal belongings will be returned. Nevertheless, their effects must be separately packed and labeled; effects must be listed in quadruplicate; pocket knives must be placed here, driver's licenses placed there, and so forth. This surely is madness.

From
State Sanitorium Herbron   May 26, 1941
Phone : 341
File # D

To
the Director
or Assistant Director   State Sanitorium
State Sanitorium at   Merxhausen
Merxhausen   received: May 27, 1941
Kassel—area

Re: Transfer of a female patient from
    Merxhausen to Herbron

During transfers from other sanitoriums to this institution the following administrative difficulties/shortcomings have been observed and are brought to your attention:

The patient's name is written on a strip of adhesive tape which is then attached to the patient. Often the tape has detached itself so that we have great difficulties in establishing the true identity of the patient. In these cases we have found ourselves totally dependent on the statements of other patients accompanying this person in transfer. We therefore suggest to write each patient's name between his/her shoulder blades, preferably with an ink pen.

For patients with very common names, such as Müller, Schmidt, Meyer, etc., it is recommended that you also add their dates of birth in the same space.

It has happened occasionally that patients were wearing clothes which had name tags of other patients attached to them. Please be certain to have your patients wear only their personal clothes.

All belongings accompanying the patient must be listed.

The list is to be divided into two parts. One for his personal belongings and the other for the hospital's (sanitorium's) property which he is allowed to take along.

Should there be any personal belongings then a further selection will have to be made: one part listing new or unused items and the other for used or old items.

Our superiors demand that all possessions must be listed.

It has happened that a patient was in possession of a pocketknife which had not been listed.

It would be best if all those unnecessary items could be confiscated and put into a package with his/her personal belongings. (For example: handkerchief.)

Furthermore we ask that a patient's belongings be packed in his own package/container, and not in a package/container together with everybody else's.

Each container/package has to have the patient's name, date of birth, and first name printed on it legibly. This has to be done in a way safe enough to prevent smudging or erasing. Please supply the head of the transport detail with an accurate typewritten list of all patients to be transferred. Include first name, family name (maiden name for married women), date of birth, place of birth, and place of residence.

We would appreciate this list in triplicate or better yet four copies. This should not pose more work for you and your staff. It would make this endeavor easier for us, since we are quite overworked with all these transports.

Please do not insert the patient's file card for clothes into his/her personal files. Rather send them separately, together with his/her personal papers such as passports, driver's licenses, and other important documents and valuables.

The Director[13]

At the commencement of the killing program, when the patients were little aware of what was happening to them, the transportation procedures worked smoothly. The killing institutions were operated as regular medical facilities. At Hartheim, for example, the medical staff consisted of two physicians, Dr. Renno and Dr. Lohnauer. Lohnauer was austere and said to have been coldly professional, but Renno was a warm and popular doctor. Renno would greet the new patients upon their arrival and visit them in their wards to see that they were comfortable. (After the war, Lohnauer committed suicide; Renno was excused from trial for reasons of ill health.) There were fourteen nurses, seven men and seven women. They were pleasant and solicitous.

Over the course of the program, a variety of killing methods were used. Poison gas, of course, was the preferred "humane" method. With young children and the very weak elderly, food was withheld until death occurred, although all other ordinary nursing care would be continued. In some cases, death would be administered by injection of lethal doses of such drugs as morphine or scopolamine. All six of the killing institutions had gas chambers by the end of the programs, but no more than four were operable at any given time.

It was Dr. Brandt's thesis at the Nuremberg trials that the variety of killing methods utilized was evidence that the program was not centrally directed. He insisted that the participating doctors, using whatever procedures seemed to them to be most efficacious, made their own killing decisions. While it was Brandt's position that no guilt should be attached to the intent or early operation of the euthanasia program, he insisted that whatever guilt there might be rested more properly with the individual doctors freely participating in the program rather than with the program's originators.

The original regulations envisioned a "conservative" program with careful review procedures. In operation the program became a matter of killing in wholesale lots. The psychological reasons why physicians were willing to participate in these killings are no doubt complex. There is, however, an aspect of the program's structure which made it easier: there was no single point of responsibility—no place in the procedure at which it was possible to say, *Here* is where the patient receives his death warrant; no point where it could be said, *This* physician is responsible for this patient's death.

The local practicing physician simply filled out the question-naires as he was required to do. The members of the assessing committee simply gave their individual opinion on each case. Nothing more would happen unless the members were in substan-tial agreement. The senior review physician simply went along with the committee or else expressed an objection. He was expressing a medical opinion, nothing more. Neither the assessors nor the review physicians ever saw the patient. The transportation staff was involved in transporting patients—but it was no business of theirs where or why the patients were being moved. The staff which ran the centers were simply doing their jobs. Even the physician whose job it was to operate the gas chamber was not responsible for the death of the patients—after all, he played no part in their selection; he knew nothing of their cases. He was only following the procedures laid down by his superiors, carrying out the policy of his government as advised by the most eminent members of the medical profession.

Responsibility was diluted. Any one of the participants could say, "I am not responsible for the killing. The others are responsible."

Even so, there were guilt feelings. In a 1941 letter from the County Court of Frankfurt to the Ministry of Justice which complained that the killing program had lost its secrecy, it was said that "at night [the killing] experts picked up the Berlin Gestapo . . . drink themselves to oblivion in the little Hadamar Gasthof, where the regular customers take care to avoid them." Franz Stangl, an Austrian who served as one of the security guards at Hartheim, reported that at first he felt "that I didn't think I could stand it. . . . I had heard that the police official who had the job before me had been relieved upon his request because he had stomach trouble. I, too, couldn't eat—you know, one just couldn't." Over time, of course, he learned how and went on to serve later in the concentration camps. Nevertheless, in recounting his story to a reporter after the war, the Austrian said, "I hate . . . I hate the Germans for what they pulled me into. I should have killed myself in 1938."[14]

Disposal of the bodies of the dead patients presented a fairly sizable logistic program. The German nation was in an all-out war posture, and it was simply not practical to clutter up the transportation system by shipping corpses all over the landscape. It was for this reason, as much as public health concerns, that Bouhler insisted upon immediate cremation at the major centers. Permanent furnaces were constructed at some of the sites, but other hospitals relied upon an ingenious device, a furnace on wheels. After the official end of the program, these furnaces were hauled to Poland and used in the Holocaust. The director of the Institution for the Mentally Sick in Kaufbeuren built his hospital its own crematorium, modeled on the ones used by the official killing centers.[15] All these ovens were fueled either with coke or oil.

Some of the centers were so mechanized as to have a conveyor-belt system installed to carry the corpses from the gas chamber to the oven. This made it easy: After the gases had been evacuated from the chamber, the ports were opened. Forty-five minutes were allowed to insure that all the poison gas had left the room; after this staff members would enter. The physician in charge would certify that all the disabled patients were dead, and the bodies would then be placed on the belt and moved to the oven. If there was no conveyor, the bodies would be lifted onto a stretcher-cot device and carried out, one by one, to the oven. As the Frankfurt County Court letter explained, "The corpses enter the furnaces on a conveyor belt, and the smoke from the crematorium chimney is visible for miles."

The ash remains of the deceased were gathered from the oven, placed in ceremonial urns, and delivered to their families. Each urn was numbered by means of a small imprint on the bottom of the vessel. No effort was made to distinguish the ashes of one victim from another. The family receiving an urn assumed they were receiving the remains of their own loved one—the letters surely indicated as much—but they were not.

It was not just mass-killing techniques that were pioneered at the medical killing centers. As part of the reception procedure for new patients, they were given a dental inspection. This involved looking in the patient's mouth to determine if he had any gold teeth or inlays. A code number was then stamped on the patient's chest with a rubber stamp and ink pad. After the patients had been gassed, a man specially trained for the job—at Hadamar his name was Loeding—would break off the gold teeth and send them to Berlin where they were melted down into gold ingots for the Reichsbank. This aspect of the euthanasia program was under the direction of the T-4 Central Accounting Office. [16]

In the Germany of the 1930s, just as in America today, medical treatment was an expensive business. Someone had to pay for a patient's care—either the insurance company, the family, or the welfare system. "Euthanasia," or "final medical treatment," was not cheap. The special equipment, treatment, and expert attention cost money. Whenever possible, these expenses were charged to the families of the victims. Dr. Leo Alexander, a major in the U.S. Medical Corps, made a study of the killing program in August 1945. According to his report, "special fees were charged for the

105

killing as indicated by a letter from the Gemeinnützige Kranken-transport G.m.b.H. to the Cure and Care Institution in Eglfing-Haar, dated February 25, 1941, to the effect that the institution should communicate to the transport company the names and ad-dresses of the paying relatives of all those Jewish patients who had been transferred to the general government area of Poland (pre-sumably Lublin), as well as the daily rates which those relatives had been paying, so that these relatives could be sent a bill according to those rates."[17]

The euthanasia program was not conceived by its creators as an opportunity for laboratory medical research. Once it was under way, however, physicians saw at once that the simultaneous deaths of large numbers of mentally ill and disabled made available a unique resource of "patient material."

Scientists made requests of the authorities seeking specimens for their research from the cadavers of the patient victims. And the authorities were happy enough to cooperate with their fellow phy-sicians in the name of science. The bodies were headed for the crematorium anyway.

Munich, 24 November 1942

To: Head Physician Dr. M. Leinisch, Gunzburg
Re: Letter of 13/11/42

Dear Doctor:

In your letter of 13/11/42 you requested me to send suitable epileptics for the carrying out of your research work. I had an opportunity of discussing this with the Obermedizinal-raten Doctor Falthauser and Doctor Pfannmüller. Both will willingly deliver to you suitable patients. For various rea-sons patients from the Institution at Kaufbeuren are primar-ily to be chosen. If this institution has no suitable material I agree to the transfer of patients from Eglfing-Haar to Gunzburg for your research work. I request you to get in touch with Dr. Falthauser.

Heil Hitler
Gaum[18]

106

Robert Jay Lifton, in his book *The Nazi Doctors*, tells of his interview with a "Doctor F." who as a junior physician worked in an institution where disabled and impaired children were put to death. This man now refers to the deceptions of the program as "diabolical" and emphasizes, "The physician . . . has been educated to help the sick, to heal the sick and not to kill the sick." Even so, Dr. F. does not condemn the killing program out of hand. He has done extensive work—both during the Nazi regime and after—with the brain specimens he obtained from the killings. As he explained to Lifton, "One is interested in finding out what was wrong with the person: What is going on there, why is he sick? . . . Why is this child an imbecile? Why is it paralyzed? There was a high scientific interest present—I must point that out."[19] The reader must wonder why Dr. F. refers to a person with paralysis as "it."

Another physician, a neuropathologist by the name of Professor Julius Hallervorden, at the world-renowned Kaiser Wilhelm Institute for Brain Research—now the Max Planck Institute—received over six hundred brains of adult and children victims for use in his laboratory. Hallervorden is well-known for his work in brain disease and a hereditary disease is named in his honor—Hallervorden-Spatz disease. The professor gave the killing institutions very specific directions as to how the brains should be selected, removed from the skull, preserved, and shipped to him for his microscopic studies. The brain-tissue specimens were delivered to him in lots of 150 to 200 at a time by the General Patient Transport Company.[20]

After the war Hallervorden explained his behavior as follows: "I heard what they would be doing so I went over to them and said, 'Look here, people, when you kill all of these people, then please at least take the brains out, so that I will be able to use the "material." ' They asked me, 'How many can you study?' And so I said some limitless number—'the more the better.' I gave them a rate, vessels, and instructions for the handling and preparation of the brains and they brought them in a delivery wagon from a furniture store."

After the war there was some discussion as to whether this work by Dr. Hallervorden served to implicate him, to make him a party after the fact to the euthanasia. This suggestion was dismissed by a professor of psychiatry at an American medical school who wrote that the physician's behavior presented no ethical problem. Hallervorden, he said, "merely took advantage of an opportunity."[21]

This issue—whether the use of tissue material is "tainted" by its origin—is of more than scholarly interest to the medical community. Current advances in medical technology, as well as current social policy, present physicians with the very sort of "opportunity" that Dr. Hallervorden exploited. It is now possible to detect all manner of genetic abnormalities in utero; these abnormal fetuses, once detected, are most commonly aborted. Concurrently, medicine is finding a wide range of uses for so-called fetal material. For example, fetal tissue has been found to play a key—and, perhaps, unique—part in the regeneration of nerve cells. Research in this area is of enormous importance for persons with central nervous cord trauma, including paraplegics, and for those suffering from Parkinson's disease.

Today the practice of abortion makes fetal material available to the scientist—just as in the 1930s the killing of deformed children made brain tissue available to Dr. Hallervorden. There are now reports that the issue has been taken one step further. There are reportedly women who have become pregnant for the sole purpose of aborting the fetus in order to sell the fetal material. Would Hallervorden be buying?

The euthanasia program generated a great deal of correspondence. Family and friends were understandably anxious to locate their loved ones. Of course, T-4 insisted that the whereabouts of these patients be kept secret. Many thousands of desperate letters of inquiry were written to the authorities.

Here, for example, is a letter from an American, written before the United States and Germany were at war, addressed to the therapeutic establishment of Warneck in Würzburg:

November 1, 1940

Gentlemen:

I learned that my mother Frau Gertrud Sonder is supposed to be no longer in Warneck.

As her only child and as an American citizen who has contributed to the costs of my mother's upkeep I request you kindly to give me an indication as to the present whereabouts of my mother.

I should be very thankful if you would give me such indication by return airmail. Please charge any eventual expenses to my privileged frozen account.

Respectfully,

Hans Sonder
c/o Topsy's
112-01 Queens Boulevard
Forest Hills, New York, U.S.A.[22]

And here is another letter, typical in its concern:

Mainz, 1 December 1940

To the Management of the Therapeutic and Nursing Establishment

Eglfing-Haar:

I beg to inquire herewith whether my cousin Herr Oswald Feis is in your establishment. He reported to me some time ago from the Therapeutic and Nursing Establishment in Ansbach that he was being transferred to Eglfing. I wrote him directly three times enclosing a stamped envelope for answer without receiving any news from him. A parcel sent to him was also returned to me.

I request you kindly let me have some news <u>as soon as possible</u> as to the state of his health and whether he is still staying in your establishment. I would like to prepare a Christmas treat for him.

Most respectfully,[23]

Whether the letters of inquiry were addressed to the local hospitals or to the state agencies, they were answered with essentially the same form letter. No information of any sort was given out, nor was there any follow-up. Even if the inquiry came from another government agency, no information was given out. Take, for example, the correspondence of one hospital, Eglfing-Haar: according to the American Dr. Alexander, who reviewed the files of the infamous director Dr. Pfannmüller, "evasive replies were sent to the district court of Furth, the district attorney, and the mayor of Landau, I. D. Pfalz, the government insurance company in Berlin, the county welfare association in Würzburg, the Lord Mayor of Nuremberg, and to the district court of Munich and to the Ministry of the Interior in Munich itself, in a case submitted through the guardianship court of Stuttgart."[24]

This is the form such replies would take:

To: Mrs. Johanna Sara Moritz
Subj: Rubell Marin, your letter of 1 December 1940

We have forwarded your letter to the competent agency because the name of the receiving center is unknown to us.
J.[25]

The sought-after loved one had disappeared into an unknown "receiving center," and the correspondence was referred to a nameless agency; and the letter was initialed, rather than signed, by a nameless bureaucrat. Mrs. Moritz, and thousands like her, were left in limbo.

There were occasional exceptions. These officials did not have hearts of stone. They could be moved by a sad letter from a loving mother:

Dachau, 14 December 1940

Greatly Honored Herr Direktor:
Please forgive me if I approach you personally with a heavy mother's heart in these days which also for you must be full of suffering.

On 2 December I received an announcement from the institution that my daughter Anny Wild, House 8, had been transferred because the house had to be cleared and that the receiving institution would notify me, but to date I have not heard anything.

I beg you urgently to tell me as soon as possible where my daughter is now.

At the same time I want to express to you, Venerated Herr Direktor, and to the other doctors who helped to care for my daughter in her many days of severe suffering, my deeply felt gratitude. If you realize that she has been bedridden for almost a whole year but now at this season had to go on a journey, you will understand my great solicitude; and also if you consider that the holidays are near, when we would have liked so much to visit her.

I beg you urgently for an immediate reply.

With German greeting.

Elise Strohmaier,
Dachau
Hermannstrasse 10

I can be reached by telephone at Burgmeier T-364.

To this moving plea, Dr. Pfannmüller replied at once, and for once he did not use the standard form:

16 December 1940:

Greatly Honored Mrs. Strohmaier:
In reply to your letter of 14 December 1940, I regret not being able to tell you to which reception institution your daughter has been admitted, since I personally was not informed about the matter. However, I have been assured that you will be informed about the condition of your daughter, Anny Wild, in a short time by the receiving institution. The transfer of the patient occurred within the frame of a planned evacuation of the institution for the purpose of making room for evacuees upon the direction of the Commissioner for Defense of the Realm. The direction of this institution has no influence upon the transfer of patients.[26]

Unfortunately, these courtesies changed nothing, and Mrs. Strohmaier's daughter Anny Wild died along with her fellow patients at Eglfing-Haar.

This Kafka-like state of affairs was often of short duration. For soon enough after the transfer of a person from his institution to the so-called receiving center his family would receive another sort of letter. This would be typed on the stationery of the hospital and signed by the doctor handling the case. The letter would announce

111

with sadness the death of the patient. It would explain the cause of death, offer condolences, and remind the family that now the patient's suffering was ended. The matter of the suitable disposition of the remains was discussed, and the wording in all the letters was always very similar.

Personalized form letters, signed by the physician, were sent to the patient's relatives. A typical example is the following, which was sent by the director of Grafeneck:

6 August 1940

To: Frau B . . . Sch . . .

My dear Frau Sch . . .
We are sincerely sorry to tell you that your daughter F . . . Sch . . . , who had to be transferred to this institution in accordance with measures taken by the National Defense Commissioner, died suddenly and unexpectedly here of a tumor of the brain, on the 5th August 1940. The life of the deceased had been a torment to her on account of her severe mental trouble. You should, therefore, feel that her death was a happy release. As this institution is threatened by an epidemic at the present time, the police have ordered immediate cremation of the body. We would ask you to let us know to what cemetery we may arrange for the police to send the urn containing the mortal remains of the deceased. . . . Any inquiries should be addressed to this institution in writing, visits being for the present forbidden as part of the police's precautions against infection. . . .

Dr. Koller[27]

Different, but overall quite similar, is the following letter from Brandenburg:

Brandenburg on the Havel

20 February 1940

My dear Doctor _____ :
We regret to inform you that your son, who had to be transferred to our institution, has died here unexpectedly as

a result of abscessed tonsils on 17 February. We are sorry to say that all our medical efforts were in vain. He died quietly and without any pain. With his serious and incurable disease death means relief for him.

Due to the present danger of epidemic here, the body of the deceased had to be cremated immediately according to police request. We are asking you to inform us at your earliest convenience whether you want the urn with the earthly remains interred at any special cemetery. In that case we ask you to name the cemetery and give its correct address so that we can have the urn transferred to the administration of that cemetery. If you have no special wishes as to the burying or if you fail to inform us within a month, we will have the urn buried here free of charge. The belongings of the deceased had to be burned due to the danger of spreading of disease.

We enclose two copies of the death certificate which you will carefully keep in order to submit eventually to the authorities.

Heil Hitler
by order

Dr. Meyer[28]

Brack was anxious that these letters be personalized, so as to comfort the family and deflect their suspicions. In a message to "My dear party comrade Dr. Schlegelberger" stamped "Strictly Confidential" with "Top Secret" written beneath in Brack's own hand, the program chief sets out his view on "the death notifications to the relatives of the patient. These are to be kept somehow different according to the district and kind of relatives; they must be altered frequently to avoid stereotype texts and therefore a form letter would only irritate."[29]

The physicians took pains to find a cause of death that was suitable to the patient. The patient's medical chart would be assessed: if he had weak lungs, death from pneumonia might be chosen; if he had a history of appendicitis, death by peritonitis resulting from a ruptured appendix would be selected. Cause of death was considered an important matter, because it had to be listed on the death certificate, an official document which was filed with both the local and national authorities.

One of the doctors at Nuremberg testified that it would not have looked "right" for a physician to put down carbon monoxide asphyxiation as the cause of death for all the patients in his care. It would have been "unprofessional" to have assessed the true cause of death upon the certificates. Hence, the physicians maintained their sense of propriety by lying, by fabricating credible causes of death for the patients they had murdered.

At the trial after the war, the chief physician at Hadamar insisted that the killing program was fully legal. In that case, he was asked, why the false death certificates? He replied, "I did not want to scare the population by not filling in a diagnosis. I could not put down on the death certificate, 'We killed them.' "

A guide was prepared, probably by one of the T-4 physicians' committees, for the use of the doctors as they were preparing the fake certificates. This helped to insure that the cause of death assigned and the medical history of the patient were internally consistent and medically sound. For example, in discussing septicemia as a cause of death in the mentally ill, it was explained that these patients frequently had boils which they scratched and "It is most expedient to figure four days for the basic illness and five days for the resultant sepsis." Doctors were warned that this diagnosis "should not be used with patients who are meticulously clean"; instead, it is "preferable for young, strong patients who smear readily." However, the guide warned, if septicemia was used as a cause of death for the young, it should be noted that "seven to eight days have to be allowed for the illness to take effect, since their circulation is relatively more resistant."[30]

—

Of course, there was not just correspondence with the families of the deceased. This was a government-operated program, and there was naturally much bureaucratic paperwork. Throughout the killing process a flood of letters, directives, reports, and receipts were all carboned and filed with copies sent to T-4 in Berlin, according to the appropriate administrative procedures. It was somehow important to the credibility of the program, in the eyes of the medical personnel carrying it forward, that everything be done in a proper and fully correct manner.

The following letter was sent from Berlin dated May 12, 1941, to the director of the hospital of the District Association of Swabia, Kaufbeuren/Bavaria:

Dear Director:

By order of the Reich Defense Commissioner I must remove mental cases from your institution from the branch of Irrsee to another institution. A total of 140 persons are to be transported, seventy on 4th June and seventy on 6th June. I forward to you herewith transport lists number 8, 9, 10, and 11 in triplicate. The additional spaces on the lists are intended for possible deficits (discharged meanwhile, died, etc.).

The marking of the patients is most suitably done by means of a striped adhesive tape, on which the name is written in ink pencil, to be pasted between the shoulder blades. At the same time the name is to be put on any articles of clothing.

The hospital reports and personal histories are to be prepared for transportation and handed to our director of transport Herr Kopper in the same way as the personal possessions of the patients, as well as money and articles of value.

I enclose property information cards and information cards as to the defrayer of the expenses, which, accurately filled out, must be handed in at the time of transportation. Money and articles of value besides being noted on the property information cards must also be noted on separate special lists (in duplicate).

Our director of transport Herr Kopper will visit you the day before in order to discuss further details with you.

I further request you to provide the patients with food (2–3 slices of bread and butter each and some cans of coffee).

Heil Hitler!

[*signature illegible*]
Public Utility Ambulance
Transportation G.m.b.H.[31]

115

Confirmation, 30 August 1940, of the Transfer of Mental Patients with List of Transferred Patients Attached

CONFIRMATION

In accordance with the decision of the State Ministry of the Interior (Public Health Division), dated 8 January 1940, on orders from the Reich Association of Sanitoriums and Nursing Homes [Reichsarbeitsgemeinschaft der Heil- und Pflegeanstalten] and as chief responsible for the General Patient Transport Company [Gemeinnützige Krankentransportgesellschaft], I have taken charge of the transfer to a Reich institution of the patients enumerated in the list below.

[*signature illegible*]
Eglfing, 30 August 1940
Commissioner of General Patient Transport Company[32]

Transfer Memorandum for Niedernhart

Handed over were:

1. 149 patients with their own clothing, underwear, money, and belongings.
2. 149 files with personal records (case histories).
3. A list of the amount of money of each patient. A receipt was made out for this purpose.
4. A list of the names.

Eglfing-Haar, 30–8–40

Head Nurse Lotte Zell[33]

Provincial Association for Social Welfare
Swabia

Address: Augsburg 1, P.O. Box Regierungspraesident

Tel. No. 582
Cashier's Office:
Principal Govt.
Cashier's Office Augsburg
Post Office check account:
Munich No. 1624

Director Dr. Falthauser, of the Hospital,
Kaufbeuren

Your reference: 2080 Your letter of 13 November 1940.
Our reference: (must always be referred to). II–B–7–2

Augsburg, 6 May 1941

Concerning the transfer of patients.

I have the honor to inform you that the female patients
transferred from your institution on 8 November 1940 to the
institutions in Grafeneck, Bernburg, Sonnenstein, and
Hartheim all died in November of last year.

[*signature illegible*]

Enclosures[34]

The official, centralized euthanasia program lasted from the fall
of 1939 through the summer of 1941. By that time the program's
existence was widely known. The churches had raised strong and
vocal objections. There had been public demonstrations in opposition to the killings. The German army was deep in the Russian
campaign, and Hitler had no wish for public unrest at home.
Accordingly, the Führer, without ceremony or discussion, ordered
a halt to the euthanasia program in a conversation with Dr. Brandt.
This did not, however, bring an end to the killing of the disabled

and the insane. Physicians across Germany continued to administer "final medical treatment" to patients they considered as having "lives not worth living." The killings continued, but the decision-making and the criteria used in these decisions became those of the immediate doctor rather than the assessor committees and the review professors. The "children's campaign," by which retarded and deformed infants were put to death, continued unabated—not just until the end of the war, but for some time thereafter, according to the records of the U.S. Army occupational forces. As the bombing of German cities increased, Brandt undertook to evacuate institutionalized patients to the countryside. Many of those evacuated were also killed by their physicians. On the eastern ramparts of Germany—in Danzig, Pomerania, and West Prussia—as well as in Poland, mentally ill patients were simply shot by the local SS and police forces.[35] Operation 14 f 13 practiced wanton killing of the sick and disabled in the camps and elsewhere, and what the Germans at the time referred to as "wild euthanasia" led to additional, widespread, unorganized, and indiscriminate killing. As Dörner has said, "Unplanned groups and individuals were murdered: welfare wards, asocials, wayward children, healthy Jewish children or those of mixed blood, homosexuals, political offenders, elderly wards of nursing homes, sick and healthy Eastern workers."[36]

It is not possible to tell with any accuracy how many disabled German citizens were put to death during the Nazi years. No reliable figures exist for the spontaneous killings. Figures survive for the official centralized T-4 killings:

	Anstalt	*1940*	*1941*	*Sa*
A	(Graf.)	9,839	–	9,839
B	(Brand.)	9,772	–	9,772
Be	(Bernb.)	–	8,601	8,601
C	(Hartheim)	9,670	8,599	18,269
D	(Sonnes.)	5,943	7,777	13,720
E	(Hadamar)	–	10,072	10,072
		35,224	35,049	70,273

—Ernst Klee, *"Euthanasie" im NS-Staat, Die "Vernichtung lebensunwerten Lebens,"* 1983.

In some of the trial documents, the figure 120,000 is given as the overall number of inmates killed in public institutions. According to Aly and Roth, this number is on the low side and does not include those who died in such programs as the children's operation, random euthanasia, and the "Brandt campaign" in which 20,000 lost their lives.[37] Dr. Leo Alexander, who served with the Office of the Chief of Counsel for War Crimes at Nuremberg and who performed the major study of the euthanasia program for the court, has estimated that 275,000 persons were killed.[38] The psychiatrist Fredric Wertham has looked into hospital records. He found, for example, that the province of Brandenburg in 1938 had 16,295 mental patients from Berlin. By 1945 there remained but 2,379 patients. In an institution called Berlin-Buch, out of 2,500 patients five hundred survived. Kaufbeuren in Bavaria had 2,000 patients at the beginning of the war, and two hundred remaining at war's end. Many mental institutions simply closed their doors because of lack of patients. In 1939, for all of Germany there were some 300,000 mental patients. In 1946 there were 40,000. This is not to say that all these persons were destroyed by the German state in the course of its euthanasia operation. The German war losses were colossal. In all, it has been estimated that no more than 15 percent of the mental patients of Germany survived the killing programs of the Third Reich.[39]

More than 4.5 million Germans lost their lives—a million of them civilians. No doubt the lives of many of these patients were lost in the general conflagration. Nevertheless, it cannot be doubted that the euthanasia program swept out entire wards, cleaned out entire hospitals. It decimated the entire German population of the severely disabled and the chronically insane.

6

The Children's Program

The object was to obtain possession of these abortions
[the newborn disabled] and destroy them as soon as
possible after they had been brought into the world.

Karl Brandt[1]

A ktion T-4 did not extend to children and infants. This does not
mean they escaped the baleful eye of the eugenic scientists
and the racial hygienists, who dominated German medicine during
the Third Reich. Children born with birth defects or who were
thought to be retarded came under the purview of the children's
program.

—

Western society has a profound ambivalence toward its children. Children are the heart of the family; they provide their parents
with a sense of continuity and bring meaning and importance to life.
All people agree that children are to be nurtured and protected.
They are the hope of the future. *Everyone* likes children; everyone is *supposed* to like children. Billions of dollars of advertising
are based upon the good feelings generated by the depiction of
cute, happy kids eating breakfast cereal, Campbell's soups, and so
forth.

All this is true; and yet there is a dark side to how society deals
with its children. Consider that in America child abuse is endemic.
Child neglect is common—and not just among the poorer classes.
Sex-abuse cases involving children are not usually punished as
severely as cases involving the rape of adults. The convicted mur-

derer of a baby is seldom given life imprisonment or capital punishment. Infant mortality rates in America are twice as high as in Japan or Sweden. American society does not give its infants the care and attention they need.

Medical practices over the years graphically illustrate the ambivalent manner in which children are treated. It is true that medicine has saved and improved the quality of the lives of millions of children. Even so, it must be said that physicians have carelessly, and even wantonly, harmed their patients. In times past, they regularly prescribed such substances as gin, morphine, and laudanum to quiet a fretful or colicky baby. Chronic use of these drugs can in no way have been good for the infant patient. Over the last century or so, deformed children have been strapped into the most bizarre and painful assortment of orthopedic devices which cause much pain, heartache, and, oftentimes, little improvement. Psychiatrists, discarding the evidence of their own eyes and ears, have for years denied that young children can be vulnerable to depression. This denial served to keep depressed children from treatment. In a similar manner surgeons have routinely performed surgery—as minor as circumcision, as major as heart repair—on the very young without benefit of proper anesthetics, even though they were available. These surgeons told one another that the nervous system of their patients was not sufficiently developed to feel pain, even though all the indicators—shallow respiration, rapid heartbeat, kicking and screaming—said otherwise.[2]

It is difficult to draw conclusions from such practices. Cruelty to children—in one guise or another—exists everywhere, and the blame for this cruelty is not exclusive to one profession or nation. It is universal. It is a fact that an infant is perceived as less than the adult, helpless and weak and more easily transgressed. The adult can demand his dignity and rights; he can cause harm, wage war—he can be dangerous. The child can do none of these things. He is a victim, ready-made.

Knowledge of this, knowledge of how easy it is to victimize a child—and how widespread the practice is—provides a perspective with which to appraise the German children's program. The German experience is instructive: it is easy to cloak torture as science, killing as medicine. But it is still torture, still killing.

In Germany people drive very fast. On the autobahn routine traffic can move over one hundred miles an hour. Main arterial roads run through the centers of small towns, past the old houses built right on the street; and the cars and trucks barely slow down as they pass. To a stranger, everyday traffic in a German village is like the Grand Prix at Monte Carlo.

At least through the 1960s the carnage from traffic accidents was terrible. A 1965 study found that for every 10,000 cars on the road, fourteen people a year were killed. In the United States, in comparison, for every 10,000 cars there were 5.2 deaths a year.[3] German children in the small towns play on their stoops, sometimes even on the roads themselves; and as a result a disproportionately large number of those killed each year were children. For a long time no one paid much attention.

The respected German sociologist Ralf Dahrendorf has observed that in German society, rather more than in other Western societies, the "normal role"—the concept of the citizen for whom and around whom social behavior and practice is organized—belongs exclusively to the healthy male adult. This immediately excludes four-fifths of society. What is "normal" is not female, not old, not young, not sick, not disabled, and certainly not foreign. This leads, among other things, to a certain hardness, a macho quality that is seen on the nation's highways and everywhere else, too.[4]

According to Ralf Dahrendorf, there is a brutal quality that runs as a constant over time through German society. This fosters a respect for the strong, a disdain for the weak, which reveals itself in many ways, large and small. For example, it is well-known that German dentists, at least until recently, have insisted it is quite impossible to use painkillers while drilling because it is necessary to gauge the exposure of the nerve on the basis of the pain experienced by the patient. And in marvelous understatement, Dahrendorf observes that in Germany one is not treated politely "when one is in error or has stepped on someone else's feet by mistake."[5]

This brutal quality is reflected in the way children have been treated. Heddy Neumeister, writing about the place of children in German society, observed a child waiting to be served in a busy bakery. The women customers smiled warmly at the child, gave him motherly pats—as they shoved ahead of him, repeatedly denying the child his turn at the counter.[6] She wrote of similar situations on streetcars or buses where children are all but crushed in the rush to get on or off. And, most grimly, she writes, "The little scene that occurred in the baker's shop may be observed every day in hundreds of shops. . . . One can watch it in the frightening indifference with which the public takes notice of the murders of children—and old people—who are run over."[7]

There is an old saying that the Germans treat their cupboards like children and their children like cupboards—giving their cupboards the loving attention they deny their children. Perhaps, in the twentieth century, this should be changed. The Germans treat their *cars* the way others treat their children.[8]

—

Cruelty to children is universal. Infanticide—the killing of unwanted children—has been practiced, one way or another, at one time or another, everywhere and in every society. Germany has no monopoly.

In the United States in recent years there have been several well-publicized cases in which young disabled babies were starved to death by order of their physicians, and a good many more such cases which were not publicized.

The most famous case was that of Baby Doe, an infant born with Down's syndrome, a disorder of the chromosomes leading to mental retardation, and a malformed esophagus. It was not possible to determine in infancy whether the baby would grow up to be slightly or seriously retarded. It was certain, though, that the baby would not grow up at all unless he had immediate surgery on his esophagus so that he could eat. This operation was not major and had a 85–90 percent success rate. Baby Doe was unlucky. His physician and his parents decided not to operate. In spite of valid offers of adoption, the courts ruled for the parents, and Baby Doe was starved to death. His physician had testified to the court, "Some of these children . . . are mere blobs. . . . These children are quite incapable of telling us what they feel, and what they sense, and so on."[9]

A lesser-known case involved Drs. Raymond Duff and A. G. M. Campbell of Yale–New Haven Hospital. These doctors in the 1970s wrote widely in the professional journals–the *New En-*

gland Journal of Medicine, Pediatrics, the *Journal of Medical Ethics*—about their work with disabled children, both the severely impaired and borderline cases such as those with spina bifida, Down's syndrome, and physical deformities. It was their work which spoke openly of "death as a management option." They practiced something they called "selective nontreatment," and the criteria they used involved estimates of the child's ability to love and be loved, the concern of the parents for their child, and its chances of institutionalization. These two doctors over a thirty-month period oversaw the deaths of forty-seven of their patients from "selective nontreatment." They concluded, "If working out these dilemmas in ways such as we suggest is in violation of the law, we believe the law should be changed."[10]

From 1977 through 1982, doctors at the University of Oklahoma Health Services Center at Tulsa carried out what they thought was a novel experiment. It was not, of course, so novel. Drs. Richard Gross, Alan Cox, and Michael Pollay published the results of their experiment "Early Management and Decision Making for the Treatment of Myelomeningocele" in the October 1983 issue of *Pediatrics,* the journal of the American Academy of Pediatrics. They explained that the subjects of their experiment were newborn infants with spina bifida. Persons born with this condition require corrective surgery to the spine and the installation of a shunt to drain spinal fluid from the brain. The surgical techniques are not major, but without them the persons will die. Persons with spina bifida are apt to experience further health problems. In later life, some must use braces when walking and some will suffer decreased intellectual development. This cannot be determined with certainty in infancy.

The Tulsa doctors, making use of a mathematical formula devised by a pediatric surgeon named Anthony Shaw, undertook to decide which of the spina bifida babies under their care should have the life-giving surgery and which should not. Dr. Shaw is director of the Department of Pediatric Surgery at the City of Hope National Medical Center in Duarte, California, and clinical professor of surgery at the UCLA Medical School. He is the chairman of the Ethics Committee of the American Pediatric Surgical Association.

The formula was $QL = NE \times (H + S)$.

QL—quality of living the child is apt to have if it lives

NE—natural endowment of the child, intellectual and physical

H—the contribution the child is likely to have from home and family, based on emotional stability of the parents' marriage, the educational levels of the parents, and their wealth

S—the quality of social services that will be available to the child from his community

A team consisting of physicians, nurses, physical and occupational therapists, a social worker, and a psychologist reviewed the records of each of the babies and their families and assigned numerical values to each for NE, H, and S. The babies with the highest resultant QL's were recommended for "active vigorous treatment." The others were not.

Parents were not told about the formula, nor about the evaluative procedure. They were simply told by their child's physician that surgery was advised—or was not. They were assured this advice was a medical judgment. They were told nothing of quality-of-life estimates.

From the viewpoint of the authors of the report, the experiment was a great success. All thirty-six of the patients who had received "active vigorous treatment" were alive and doing well. All twenty-four who, with their parents' uninformed consent, had been denied treatment died. As the article put it, "The 'untreated survivor' has not been a significant problem in our experience." They died as scheduled. In commenting on the Tulsa case, civil rights attorney Martin Gerry, formerly with the Department of Health, Education and Welfare, said, "What you have here is a conspiracy to commit murder."[11]

This judgment is, no doubt, a harsh one: the medical professionals at Tulsa were, no doubt, well motivated. Nevertheless, the results of what they were doing were the same as the results obtained by the German doctors who participated in the children's program.

The children's program authorized the pediatricians of Germany to kill their deformed and retarded infant patients. Unconnected with Aktion T-4, the children's program had a similar and parallel development with T-4. Like T-4, it began small and unofficially. It became a major operation, with the selection of victims handled by a central committee of physicians in Berlin, and these broke down into widespread killing by local pediatricians, acting entirely on their own volition and without supervision, reporting their behavior to no one.

Dr. Brandt testified at Nuremberg that the German program for disabled children was a natural outgrowth of the 1933 sterilization law, "for the prevention of the birth of children suffering from hereditary diseases." He pointed out—accurately enough—that similar versions of this law were in effect in numerous nations, including the United States.[12] While this law did not authorize the killing of defective babies, it certainly conferred a stigma upon them and upon their parents. And Brandt was right: with passage of such a law the state had, indeed, launched a campaign against defective children.

In their influential 1920 study, *The Permission to Destroy Life Unworthy of Life,* Binding and Hoche had insisted that in cases of "human ballast" such as people with brain damage or retardation, killing is not like other killing but is, instead, "an *allowable, useful* act."[13] Although there was much discussion on this issue, pro and con, in general it is believed that the idea of killing deformed newborns had general acceptance in pre-Nazi Germany. This belief is supported by the poll taken in 1920 that concluded, "Seventy-three percent of the parents and guardians of mentally deficient children favored extermination of the latter."[14]

As Amir has said, killing was in the air in Nazi Germany. Unofficially, and without sanction, physicians since 1933 had begun to act on their own, dispatching those babies they thought not fit to live. This "spontaneous killing," as Aly and Roth have called it, was generally not punished. What criminal proceedings there were in the 1930s were dismissed on such grounds as "insignificance" or "lack of evidence."[15]

It is not known how widespread the killing was before the start of the official centralized program. The evidence is anecdotal. It is known, for example, that Dr. Pfannmüller at Eglfing-Haar hospital outside Munich was systematically killing his little patients by means of starvation. This is revealed in one of the depositions filed with the Nuremberg court, by a psychologist named Ludwig Lehner. [16] He was one of a group of psychologists and social workers taken for a tour of the hospital in September 1939. He stated in his deposition,

> I remember the gist of the following remarks by Pfannmüller: "These creatures (he meant the children) naturally represent for me as a National Socialist only the burden for the healthy body of our *Volk*. We do not kill (he could have used a euphemistic expression for this word kill) with poison, injections, etc.; then the foreign press and certain gentlemen in Switzerland [the International Red Cross] would only have new inflammatory material. No, our method is much simpler and more natural, as you see." With these words, he pulled, with the help of a . . . nurse, a child from its little bed. While he then exhibited the child like a dead rabbit, he asserted with a knowing expression and a cynical grin, "For this one it will take two to three more days." The picture of this fat, grinning man, in his fleshy hand the whimpering skeleton, surrounded by other starving children, is still vivid in my mind. The murderer explained further, then, that sudden withdrawal of food was not employed, rather gradual decrease of the rations. A lady who was also part of the tour asked—her outrage suppressed with difficulty— whether a quicker death with injections, etc., would not at least be more merciful. Pfannmüller then praised his methods again as more practical in view of the foreign press. The openness with which Pfannmüller announced the above-mentioned method of treatment is explicable to me only as a result of cynicism or clumsiness. Pfannmüller also did not hide the fact that among the children to be murdered . . . were also children who were not mentally ill, namely children of Jewish parents.

Thus it was that the stage was set—more than set—for the Knauer child case [17] and the favorable publicity it attained. The father of the deformed Knauer child had sought permission from Hitler to have his daughter killed. Hitler's instructions to Dr. Brandt were limited

127

and precise. (Or at least they were precise in Brandt's careful accounting at Nuremberg.) Brandt was asked at the trial, "What did Hitler order you to do?"

Brandt replied, "He ordered me to talk to the physicians who were looking after the child to find out whether the statements of the father were true. If they were correct, then I was to inform the physicians, in his name, that they *could* carry out euthanasia [emphasis added].

"The important thing was that the parents should not feel themselves incriminated at some later date as a result of this euthanasia—that the parents should not have the impression that they themselves were responsible for the death of this child."

And then came perhaps the key sentence: "I was further ordered to state that if these physicians should become involved in some legal proceedings because of this measure, these proceedings would be quashed by order of Hitler."[18] As the child-killing program developed over the ensuing years after the Knauer child episode, this immunity from prosecution freed the doctors from the usual social constraints—with quite horrid results.

Even before the Knauer affair, a committee had been set up in Berlin to consider the addition of mercy killing to the already existent sterilization program so as to improve racial hygiene. This was called the Reich Committee for Scientific Research of Serious Illness of Hereditary and Protonic Origin. Members of the committee were Karl Brandt, psychiatrist Hans Heinze, pediatrician Werner Catel, Ernst Wentzler, and Helmet Unger. Unger was an ophthalmologist who had written a popular novel which romanticized euthanasia. Operating in a businesslike fashion out of the Ministry of the Interior, the committee met several times with the Führer's Chancellery; and on August 18, 1939, issued, under the minister's signature, a decree requiring that all defective newborns and infants under the age of three be reported.[19] Doctors, midwives, and hospitals were required to report when "serious hereditary diseases" were suspected, including such conditions as deformed limbs, head, and spinal column; paralysis and palsy; dwarfism; blindness and deafness; and idiocy, Down's syndrome, and various brain abnormalities.[20] Midwives were paid two Reich marks per report. Failure to report could bring a fine of 150 marks or four weeks in jail.[21]

The purpose of this reporting was explained in the order: "It is

128

contemplated in these cases to carry out treatment of these children with all means of medical science in order to prevent them from lapsing into permanent infirmity. For this purpose, the Reich Committee . . . will erect special institutions or special departments in existing institutions."[22]

The explanation sounded straightforward and legitimate. What could be more reasonable and worthy than to use the advances of modern medical science to cure the infirmities of the newborn? This was not—as it turned out—what the committee had in mind.

Brandt, testifying at Nuremberg, explained the committee's intention quite explicitly: ". . . in the case of the children it [euthanasia] was desired, if only on account of the trouble they would cause their families and for similar reasons, to prevent their growing up. The object was to obtain possession of these abortions and destroy them as soon as possible after they had been brought into the world."[23]

The confidential order was refined several times over the next five years; additional information was requested. A questionnaire was prepared by the committee which was required to be used by those reporting. This sought a careful and detailed medical history on each baby, its condition, and the race, religion, and status of the parents, particularly hereditary conditions and such matters as alcohol and tobacco abuse. The quality-of-life expectations of the baby were to be appraised.

Although the information gathered was similar to that used in the Tulsa experiment, the decision-making procedure used by the German physicians in the Third Reich was a good deal more sophisticated, providing the infant patient with greater protection against the possibility of what might be called a "mistaken" diagnosis.

Each completed questionnaire was submitted to the committee of physicians: Drs. Wentzler, Catel, and Heinze. Each member of the committee would review each case. Upon each file the member would place a mark: a " + " signifying "treatment," a " − " signifying no treatment. The files were passed from member to member, so that each was able to see the judgment of his colleagues. If—and *only* if—all three physicians concurred, a certificate would be issued authorizing the killing of the deformed infant patient.

This process went on throughout the war. It was not stopped when the official euthanasia program was brought to a halt; in fact, it ended only with the fall of Hitler's Germany.

The committee was quite serious about its work, very scientific. Dr. Pfannmüller, director of Eglfing-Haar mental hospital, one of the participating hospitals, was called to a special meeting of "physicians active on behalf of the Reich Committee" on November 26, 1940. Dr. Pfannmüller took notes at the meeting. Pfannmüller had arranged for these and other papers to be burned as he fled the occupation forces of the U.S. Army. Fortunately a good many of his papers survived, and from them it is possible to reconstruct how the children's program operated.

At the Berlin meeting, physicians were informed of the following:

1. In every case the hereditary situation has to be fully investigated.

2. Indication for the treatment is determined by the likelihood of permanent unfitness for productive life.

3. Every case said to be considered on its own merits. For instance, bilateral blindness or bilateral deafness alone are insufficient indications for the treatment. In myelomeningocele it should be investigated whether palsies are present. Among deformities, only the most severe cases with extensive deformities are to be treated; in mongolism, only severest cases which are combined with mental deficiency of a high degree.

4. In every case one should ask for history of attempted interruptions of pregnancy, and also for severe psychic trauma of the mother during pregnancy.

5. All cases are to be cleared up diagnostically to the last detail. In addition to a complete history, including history of heredity, special examinations such as encephalography, arteriography, X-ray studies, and others are to be performed. In mongolism, mere mongoloid habitus should be differentiated from mongoloid idiocy.

6. Investigations performed hitherto in children with idiocy have shown that idiocy in almost a hundred percent of cases was caused by damage during infancy, not caused by heredity. Idiocy in most cases develops prenatally or intranatally, in some cases even postnatally.

7. Also the question of heredodegenerative development disturbances and diseases are to be cleared up in every case.[24]

130

It can be argued that the official German medical program was no less humane—although certainly more efficient—than the Tulsa and the Yale–New Haven experiments. At Tulsa the baby patients were killed slowly by denying them access to antibiotics, corrective surgery, or even sedatives to ease their pain during the death agony. Baby Doe was simply starved to death.

This passive approach to killing is argued by some to be somehow morally superior to active killing. It keeps the attending physician's hands clean. The distinction is not a happy one—standing by and doing *nothing* is certainly a form of doing *something*. It is a distinction of words and not of fact.

Of course, killing techniques varied from hospital to hospital. For example, the infamous Dr. Pfannmüller employed an ingenious stratagem for killing in a vain attempt to keep the program secret from his staff. He called the medical team of the children's ward together for a meeting. He told them that a new drug was to be used that was designed to cure their patients. The drug was experimental and dangerous, he explained, and it might be expected that some of the patients would die from its effects. Pfannmüller then began a series of toxic injections of his young patients. He diluted the level of poison, injected it regularly, gradually raising the toxic level in the system of each patient until death occurred. This was a slow and painful death. Pfannmüller's little stratagem did not work. It was not long before the staff noticed that not just some but *all* of their patients were dying.

Once the Reich Committee physicians had made their decisions, the babies selected would be transported to the killing centers. There were twenty-eight official centers, usually a wing of an existing, often distinguished, hospital (such as Idstein, Brandenburg-Görden, Eglfing-Haar) and commonly referred to as the Children's Department. Here the babies and infants would be killed.

The German physicians generally killed their baby patients with a massive shot of such drugs as morphine-hydrochloral or luminal and a poison compound specially prepared in Vienna called "modiscop." This was active killing, but it was quick and the suffering was minimal.

Over the course of the German program, it is said some five thousand babies were authorized to be killed, and *were* killed. This was, however, only the beginning.

131

Thanks to the invaluable files of Dr. Pfannmüller, rescued from destruction by the American army doctor Leo Alexander, it is possible to learn something of what it was like to operate a Children's Department killing center.

Dr. Pfannmüller's successor at Eglfing-Haar told Lifton that the doctor was a "soft, depressive type," who in normal times would not "hurt a fly."[25] He was a short, roly-poly man with perfectly round, black-rimmed glasses. The doctor was a deeply committed Nazi who saw the elimination of "unworthy lives" as a cleansing of the body politic, a part of the purification of the *Volk*. Pfannmüller was also a clever bureaucrat and something of a scrounge.

Pfannmüller first learned officially of the children's program at a meeting of asylum directors of Bavaria, held in Munich the summer of 1940. There the directors were briefed by Dr. Wentzler of the Reich Committee in Berlin.

In a letter to Wentzler, Pfannmüller announced that the Eglfing-Haar hospital would participate in the program—provided he be allowed an expense-paid junket to Vienna. "Before I shall definitely decide to place a building of my institution at disposal for this activity, I regard it as essential to obtain a firsthand impression about the organization involved by a visit to the first institution of this kind of which you spoke, namely the one which has been erected at the Steinhof [the state institution of the insane] in Vienna."

He said that after his trip to Vienna, and after a survey of the estimated patient load had been completed, he would meet again with Wentzler.

> The purpose of our future discussion in Munich should be an agreement concerning the economic arrangements with my institution, the number of beds. . . . the number of personnel. . . . the food to be supplied and other economic questions. Not until then shall I be in position to make a rough calculation as to the mode of economic settlement with your organization.
>
> Heil Hitler

A month later Wentzler in Berlin replied that Eglfing-Haar would probably be chosen as the program's third special institution, after Steinhof and Brandenburg-Görden.

More than six weeks later, on September 21, 1940, Pfannmüller informed Berlin that he had appointed Dr. Herbert Jung to head the new department. He said that Jung was a good Nazi Party member and politically reliable, and concluded, "I am glad that positive work in this children's matter can finally begin at last."

Wentzler's successor, Dr. von Hegener, was also pleased that the program was under way at Eglfing-Haar. He said so in an October 11, 1940, letter enclosing ration tickets for a precious thirty liters of gasoline, because "in view of the appointment of a new physician you will have to make an increased number of trips to Munich."

Von Hegener took an interest in the institution's admissions policy in a letter of November 2; and in a follow-up letter, November 13, 1940, sent Pfannmüller another thirty liters of gasoline coupons, "to be used for trips on behalf of the Reich Committee."

By November 30, Pfannmüller was able to submit his first report to von Hegener: eleven children had been admitted in November and already five had "died."

After a December trip to Berlin, where Pfannmüller took the notes cited above, he sent a personal letter to von Hegener, full of praise, assuring the Berlin doctor of the great pleasure of working with him, and emphasizing what a great help to the program it was to have extra gasoline coupons. Von Hegener, in response to Pfannmüller's obvious flattery, sent him coupons for an extra 100 liters of gasoline. [26]

Dr. von Hegener was no fool, however. Pfannmüller was an enthusiastic and efficient participant in the child-killing program, a valuable man, as the surviving records illustrate. Of 275 children who were admitted to the program at Eglfing-Haar during the years 1940–42, 213 received "Authorization" and were killed. [27] Pfannmüller earned his gasoline coupons.

Parents were not generally a problem. Pfannmüller often found encouragement and reassurance in his work from a memorandum, which he kept on his desk, of a conversation he had with the mother of a child named Lothar Hubsch. In the memorandum the mother said, "I do not know why an injection is not given to such human beings to make them fall asleep. It makes really no sense to spoon-feed them while the healthy ones are being killed at the fronts. If I knew where I could go to make such arrangements I would do it. If the child were dead I could peacefully die myself, but as it is, I would worry who would take care of him. [28]

At Eglfing-Haar, Lothar's mother had found the place she was looking for.

Defendants at Nuremberg insisted that approval was obtained from the parents before the infant patients were killed. Undoubtedly, in some isolated cases this was true. In general, however, the parents were told only that their child had been selected for advanced therapy and that the prognosis was uncertain. Few objected. If they did object, however, in many cases their baby would be spared. The hospital had no authority to hold the baby contrary to the wishes of the parent. Pfannmüller tells of one case in which the parents took their baby home, in spite of all the medical advice. The case upset him greatly. "It [the baby] was handed to the parents upon their insightless urging. There were no legal means to retain it in the institution by force."[29]

With that curious selective sensitivity that often occurred, Pfannmüller always tried to arrange a farewell visit for the parents of the victim so that they might see their baby for the last time. After Pfannmüller received authorization to kill a child, he would invite the parents to visit their "sick" child. He did not, of course, tell them that he intended to kill the baby immediately after their visit. Such information was a top-secret matter and could not be divulged.[30]

In general, the correspondence concerning the operation of the authorized killing program is similar to that of the euthanasia program. Parents would write asking the whereabouts of their child and receive in reply the usual bureaucratic runaround. They were notified of their child's death from a variety of causes: pneumonia, postsurgery developments, communicable diseases. Because of the possibility of spreading disease, by law the infant body had to be cremated.

In one fairly typical case of administrative confusion and moral cynicism, the parents of a child who was in an Austrian nursing home at Gallneukirchen received a letter. This came from officials of the hospital at Sonnenstein, informing them that their daughter had been transferred to the facility because of wartime precautions. They would be allowed to see their child, but only with previous written permission. The father immediately sent a telegram, "Can I visit my daughter tomorrow?" By return, he received a telegram saying, "No. Await details by letter." A few days later the parents received the usual letter informing them their daughter had died of an epileptic seizure. Her body had been cremated, according to section twenty-two of the health code for communicable diseases. In fact, relates Klee, the little girl had been dead for some time.[31]

Parents were required to pay for the food, lodging, and health care of their child in the killing institution, right up to the date of death. In the case of Jewish families there is evidence that parents sometimes were billed for the care of their children long after the date of their dying. There are cases in which Jewish parents were not told of their child's death for as long as six months after the actual date of death: they were sent monthly bills and in all innocence they paid them.[32]

In one particular case, an eight-year-old Down's syndrome child named Erwin was brought to the clinic by his parents, a young Jewish couple who were to be transported east at four o'clock the next morning, by order of the Gestapo. They entrusted Erwin to the institution for safekeeping. The mother, in tears, told the nurse, "I'll leave my son in your personal care, because I know he will be in good hands with you.[33]

Erwin was killed and so were many others. Although at first only the very young were to be included, soon enough the age limit was lifted from three to five—ultimately even teenagers were included. In some places the selection process was turned over to nurses and orderlies. Qualifying asocial characteristics came to include such things as bed-wetting, pimples, a swarthy complexion, or even annoying the nurses.

This was how the authorized children were killed at Eglfing-Haar and elsewhere. In addition to the authorized children, many others were killed: there is no way of knowing how many. In November 1942 the Bavarian authorities ruled that institutionalized children *not included* in the program should nevertheless be denied all forms of medical therapy and their food rations cut to the starvation level. Thus, by order of the government, institutionalized children across Bavaria went to their deaths for lack of food and care.[34]

And, in fact, children all over Germany—as a matter of policy— were systematically starved to death by their attending doctors and nurses. Sometimes they were denied heat in winter and died of exposure. In some hospitals the children were kept clean and tidy as they died. In others they were simply left to die. Eyewitness accounts tell of small children in hospital nurseries being fed nothing but greens, dying of diarrhea in their cribs, lying in pools of their own excrement.

In the little village of Velpke in Hanover, there was a nursery for the babies of Polish women forced to work at the Volkswagen factory in Brunswick. These were not, of course, German citizens; but neither were they deformed, retarded, or, when they came to the nursery, sick. They were just babies. From May until December 1944, ninety-six infants died at the Velpke baby home. Fourteen survived and one was spirited away by his mother.

The nursery windows looked out on a well-traveled path. The villagers could see what was happening inside—but they did nothing. A village dog was found playing with a bloody, hairy baby's skull. Nothing was done. A local doctor visited the nursery twice a week, but only to sign death certificates. The mayor and other local officials inspected the place on a regular basis—but they, too, did nothing.

In the trial which took place after the war, the counsel for the prosecution, Major G. I. D. Draper of the Legal Staff, H. Q., British Army of the Rhine, said in his opening speech, "It is the case for the prosecution that these children were never meant to live, but by a system of willful neglect consisting of improper feeding, premature separation, dirty conditions, insufferable heat with shut windows and a stove in a corrugated iron shed in summer, lack of attention in the changing of bedding and clothing and treatment, bedsores, lack of medical attention, except to sign death certificates, lack of trained nurses, no running water, insufficient hygienic precautions with bottles, sour milk and too full a diet and failure to nourish either by passing it through the body by vomiting or diarrhea; by all these things it was intended that they should die, and die they did.[35]

By the last year of the war Germany had become a living hell, a charnel house of a nation.

Hitler saw life as an "eternal struggle." He had said, "The strongest imposes its will, it's the law of nature," the law of the jungle. In ten years the Führer had turned Germany into a jungle state.

Scientists studying behavior of primates in the wild have described terrible scenes, when under certain circumstances of "increased aggression levels," apes will turn upon their young, killing and eating their babies.[36] Just so, Hitler's people, caught up in their paroxysm of destruction, turned upon and killed their own children.

136

7

Aktion T-4 at Absberg

. . . the wildest scenes imaginable.

U.S. Nuremberg War Crimes Trial,
1946–1947

A bsberg is a small town on a low hill in south central Germany. From Langlau on the valley floor, the road passes by a small lake used for boating and sailing and winds up the hill, with pleasant views on all sides of the gentle rolling countryside. The road through Absberg itself is lined with old houses in the Bavarian style: peaked roofs, small balconies, boxes of flowers at every window, and flowerpots on many stoops. Absberg is an exceedingly comfortable town.

Absberg has been a modest farming center for centuries. The market square, in the middle of town, is edged with fine old trees; and, to the side, there is a stone watering trough for horses and dogs, dedicated to St. George. The parish church sits on one side of the square; the Ottilienheim Abbey on the other. For the last century the abbey has been run by nuns as a home for retarded and disabled people. Most of the abbey's residents are from the neighborhood, members of the Catholic families of the local farmers and tradesmen.

The church is a typical Bavarian onion-domed Roman Catholic chapel. There is a clock in the bell tower, with a weathered rooster weather vane atop the dome. There is a little flower garden at the dooryard, with a small marble obelisk at its center, a tribute to the village dead from three wars: the Franco-Prussian, World War I, World War II. The keystone over the church door carries the date 1500.

The church interior is simple—stone slab floors, clear windows, a dark, smoky, wood-beamed ceiling, almost primitive woodwork

137

and trim. The pews, on either side of a center aisle, are old and worn. The altar, too, is simple and the reredos is lovely, managing to be both Baroque and modest at the same time. The bouquets on either side of the altar are of local flowers: geraniums, marigolds, chrysanthemums. They are carefully arranged and clearly lovingly attended. This is a church both loved and used. On the stone wall by the door are two plaques listing the names of the village men killed in the two world wars. It is a long list for such a small village.

Across the road, the abbey has a walled flower and vegetable garden which can be seen through open gates. The abbey itself is an old barn of a place, all cupolas and gables, built in the seventeenth century. The building is stuccoed, painted a gentle gray with a surprising, yet pleasing, peach-colored trim. Red geraniums are in boxes at many of the windows, on the balconies, and in pots on the doorsteps. All in all, it is a sunny, cheerful place.

There is a cobbled carriageway leading from the town square into the abbey. A large yet delicate crucifix at the entrance, with the elongated Christ in gilt, is set off against the blackened wooden cross. The great wooden doors of the carriage passageway are open.

In the courtyard there is a simple stone statue of the Virgin and Child on a short pedestal. At its base fountain waters splash into a shallow basin. The air is cool, fresh, pure, and the sounds of the splashing water mix with the occasional shouts and laughter that can be heard from the residents—disabled persons and nuns—within the building.

—

Absberg's troubles started in the fall of 1940. One day a big gray bus rolled down the narrow streets of the town, through the market square, past the horse trough, and under the abbey entryway into the courtyard. The abbey gates were shut behind the bus.

The bus caused lots of attention. Absberg is off the beaten path; and, even though World War II was raging, the little town seldom saw traffic much larger than a farm tractor.

Villagers were watching, then, when half an hour later the bus pulled out of the abbey and drove out of town. On the bus that day, according to the report of a local official, were twenty-five of the disabled residents of the abbey. The local constable, in his report, had it that only eight were taken. Both, however, agreed on what happened next. Quoting from the later report of the local constable, all but one of those taken "were said to have died very shortly afterwards of influenza and low blood pressure which set in. Only one person returned to Ottilienheim in Absberg."

These deaths caused a good deal of unrest in Absberg. It is not known how many of the victims had families in town, but that didn't matter. The townsfolk knew the disabled persons on a personal basis. The abbey was a part of the town and so were its residents. Those who could moved freely about the community, just like everyone else. Some worked in the fields or tended the gardens. Others helped with the housework in the village homes. In the afternoon, laughing, sometimes singing, they would go down to the town store for a sweet or stop at the bakery for a pastry. The nuns and the disabled were always a part of town festivities and were present in church for Christmas and Easter.

The deaths of the Ottilienheim residents were felt by the whole community. "The country must be in pretty bad shape if it has to kill poor people to free up money for the war effort," grumbled one resident.

The town is rural and religious, and the Nazis were never very popular here. It is not surprising that there was a lot of agitation over what had happened. The constable, however, took pains to explain to his superiors that "the population of Absberg, of both religions, are good Christians and although individuals may have found fault among themselves . . . they obey all official orders and do not allow themselves to be carried away to excesses."

Things went along like this for several months. And then, one day in mid-February 1941, a delegation of strangers arrived in town. "The strangers thoroughly inspected Ottilienheim and made notes as to the size of the rooms, etc.," according to the local Nazi leader Kirchof. This, of course, caused much talk and a flood of rumors. As Kirchof reported, "The population of Absberg now fears that their Ottilienheim may possibly be evacuated and made available for other purposes."

With all of this in mind, it is not hard to understand what happened next—on Friday, February 21.

The mother superior Gugenberg had known for some time that seventy-five more of the abbey residents were to be transported. She had been so informed by the authorities. They said the bus would arrive on the twenty-first of February, and it would make two trips on that day to pick up all seventy-five. They told her this was a state secret, and she was ordered not to tell the secret to any of the families or friends of those who were to go. She did not. Nor did she tell the village priest or the other sisters.

The mother superior became sick, perhaps because of the terrible secret she was carrying. She could not bring herself to tell her charges what was coming; yet she felt it important that they be told. Finally, the night before they were to leave, she told the local priest, Father Joseph Zottmann. She asked him to tell them the next morning.

It is unlikely that either Gugenberg or Zottmann slept well that last night.

Early the next morning, before dawn, while the town lay dark and still in the February cold, the nuns awakened their disabled residents. All were dressed and bundled into their coats and mufflers.

As the day was breaking, the residents and the nuns moved across the market square to the church for a special service. Father Zottmann was waiting for them at the church door. The church was lit by candles on the altar. A Mass was said, and each member of the home was offered confession, communion, and absolution. Those who could make it to the altar on their own legs did so. Those who could not, who needed help, were half carried to the altar rail by the nuns.

This act, the least and, sadly, the most that the priest and nuns could do for their charges, took much courage and faith on the part of all concerned.

In his later report to party officers, local Nazi leader Kirchof describes the scenes in almost incredulous terms: *"It is even said* [his emphasis] that these poor victims—as they are regarded by the clergy and the religious inhabitants of Absberg—were taken to the Catholic church for confession and communion shortly before their departure. It seems absolutely ridiculous to attempt to absolve, by a moral confession, the possible sins of people, some of whom completely lack all mental powers."

After Mass, the mother superior called all the residents to a meeting in the abbey hall. There, Father Zottmann rose and told of the plans of the officials to transport seventy-five of the residents to another facility. They knew what that meant.

At ten o'clock sharp the big bus lumbered up the hill into town. It passed through the carriageway of the abbey into the courtyard, and the great doors were shut behind it. Everyone in town knew it was there.

An hour later the gates were opened and the bus emerged, fully loaded, and headed out of town toward Geiselsberg. There was no one in the market square as it passed by.

The bus returned at three in the afternoon. Reports conflict, but apparently this time it stopped in the market square, just outside the gates of the abbey. There were people in the square, and as the village school had just let out, the children, following the bus, joined them there.

The small crowd stood in silence as the bus crew emerged and went into the abbey. There were four in the crew: a medical professor from Erlangen and three "nurses," according to the constable. As events began to unfold, more and more of the villagers moved into the square, until—according to original reports—virtually the entire village was present.

The abbey residents who were to be transported were by then, according to Kirchof, "thoroughly stirred up." Perhaps, had they been able-bodied citizens, the Nazi would have acknowledged them as persons fighting for their lives. But as they were only "imbeciles and feebleminded and were said to have other epileptic diseases as well," they were seen as "stirred up," like animals.

The residents refused to leave the abbey and get on the bus. They had to be taken forcibly, one by one, fighting and shouting the whole way. "The people were taken away in the most conspicuous manner imaginable," commented Kirchof disapprovingly.

There are no eyewitness accounts of this struggle by the disabled people of Absberg for their lives. There are, however, reports from other such institutions where other such scenes took place. These reports give a sense of what went on in Absberg that afternoon:

A sister at the Ursberg home said, "Some of the patients hung on to the nuns for dear life. It was terrible. They felt what was happening. It was especially terrible with the girls. They knew instinctively that there was something bad going on. They cried and screamed. Even the helpers and the doctors cried. It was heartbreaking."[1]

According to information from the Evangelical Home at Stetten:

> . . . As K.W., an eighteen-year-old insane girl, realized that she was to be taken to the buses, she tried to run away. Two of the transport personnel removed her by force. She tried to hang on to anything she could grab, but to no avail. Her crying and screaming reverberated through the halls and was heard in the courtyard.
>
> ". . . Miss Sophie, stay here. I want to stay here. . . . " Even after two of the henchmen had bundled her into the bus, you could hear her. . . . "Miss Sophie, Miss Sophie, get me back."
>
> L.M. was screaming when she was taken by two helpers and two "sisters" into the bus. In her fear she resisted with such a force and strength that the four persons had difficulty in subduing the almost fifty-year-old woman.
>
> Others were petrified and could only show their terror with screams. Wide-eyed, white as a sheet, they stood trembling with fear. E.S. raised her arms over her head and screamed, "I don't want to die."[2]

As the "nurses" were coming to drag her to the bus, one woman at Emmendingen screamed, "Here come the murderers!"[3]

At Reichenau, as a woman patient was dragged off, one of the orderlies said, *"Auf wiedersehen"* (see you again). She responded, "There will be no seeing you again. I know what they are going to do to me according to this law of Hitler's."[4]

At Weinsberg one of them cried, ". . . you will pay for this with your blood." Elsewhere, another cursed, "We are dying, yes, but the devil will get Hitler!"[5]

The impact of such scenes as this upon the decent townsfolk of Absberg was immediate and great. There were murmurs, talk, and then shouts. There was pushing and shoving and attempts were made to help the residents in their struggle to keep off the bus. There were, in the shocked words of the local Nazi Party leader, "the wildest scenes imaginable." The Nazis were cursed. Threats were made. Dangerous and treasonous words were shouted to the roof-tops. Lamentations were heard and many began to cry.

It was all to no avail, of course. Force was used to load the bus, as the patients were strong-armed aboard by the crew, the women of whom were just as tough as the men.

The doors shut on the loaded bus and it pulled out—the crowd of agonized townsfolk giving way as it passed through the square and down the street. On the square, on the stoops, and at the windows of the houses of the street, the people of the town stood and waved and wept, as their friends from the abbey were transported to their death.

Reports of this dismaying scene reached Berlin soon enough. The demonstration had taken place on the twenty-first of February. By the twenty-fourth, local Nazi official Gerstner had written a report to his superiors. Fellow Nazi Kirchof also filed a report. On that same day local constable Pfister, based at Langau, down in the valley, was called by his district prefect and asked to prepare an immediate report in writing of the incident. He did so. On the first of March, making use of this information but placing most of his reliance on the reports of the party members, local chief of staff Sellmer reported to the Security Service (the SD) of the SS in Nuremberg. He also sent copies of the reports to Dr. Hans Hefelmann, the chief physician at the T-4 euthanasia program headquarters in the Führer's Chancellery in Berlin. Hefelmann had already learned of the unrest at Absberg and had been on the phone with Sellmer previously.

The reports received from the three locals—Kirchof, Gerstner, and Pfister—were not in agreement on key points. This is not surprising. Pfister was a Roman Catholic and clearly anxious to downplay the events and to exonerate the villagers, if possible. As Kirchof, the village Nazi cell-group leader, reported to the party, he and other local officials feared "that Pfister—who is judged and regarded as strongly Catholic by us—may not take effective steps against his own fellow believers in this matter." Kirchof, for his own part, was not considered to be entirely believable by his fellow party member Gerstner. Gerstner, in forwarding Kirchof's report to higher-ups, warned, "The report of party member Kirchof is in fact of no importance, as it does not include any real facts but merely relates the events as told by third persons."

Gerstner insisted that, contrary to Kirchof's report, the bus did not stop in the square but passed directly into the courtyard. He said it was a mistake in psychology for the bus to have scheduled two trips in one day: the abbey personnel knew the bus would be coming back and so, in time, did the villagers. As a result a crowd assembled in the square, awaiting the bus's return. Gerstner maintained that it was not possible to find *any* party members who participated in the uproar. He called a party meeting in Absberg on March 1, a week after the disturbance. "Here also I could not ascertain that any party member had wept or misbehaved in any other way during the removal of the asylum inmates. In any case, it has been proven much noise has been made about nothing here." This sounds like Pfister was not the only one trying to protect the locals. It is not hard to imagine what would have happened to a Nazi Party member found to have participated in, or indeed merely been present at, an antigovernment demonstration. The local party was not about to incriminate one of its own.

Not all the correspondence survives, and it is not known whether the top officials of the Nazi government were informed of the goings-on at little Absberg. Nor is it known whether any retaliatory or punitive measures were taken against the town or the abbey residents. The ruling circle was remarkably alert and sensitive to signs of unrest amongst the citizenry, so it would not be surprising if the report was circulated in Berlin. In a somewhat similar case of unrest and protest—this time in the neighborhood of one of the killing institutions—the matter went all the way up to Himmler's desk. His response was interesting, extremely cagey in its sensitivity to public relations:

Top Secret

19 December 1940

SS Standartenführer Viktor Brack Staff Leader at Reichsleiter Bouhler's Office Berlin W 8

Dear Brack,

I hear there is great excitement on the Alb because of the Grafeneck Institution.

The population recognize the gray automobile of the SS and think they know what is going on at the constantly smoking crematory. What happens there is a secret and yet is no longer one. Thus the worst feeling has arisen there, and in my opinion there remains only one thing, to discontinue the use of the institution in this place and in any event disseminate information in a clever and sensible manner by showing motion pictures on the subject of inherited and mental diseases in just that locality.

May I ask for a report as to how the difficult problem is solved?

Heil Hitler!

H[einrich] H[immler][6]

8

Aktion T-4 in Trouble

What happens there is a secret and yet is no longer one.

U.S. Nuremberg War Crimes Trial, M887,
Tape 17, Doc. No. 018

What happened at Absberg was only a part of the troubles experienced by Aktion T-4. These problems brought on by red tape, confusion, and protest reflected fairly accurately the general state of affairs in Hitler's National Socialist state.

Even the most efficient, well-engineered machine breaks down. The Nazis had dreamed of creating a bureaucracy which would be as efficient and as well-designed in operation as one of their Mercedes-Benz cars. They had aimed for perfection, but they missed. The fact is, they did not come close.

Hohne, writing about the SS in *Order of the Death's Head*, says, "The Third Reich was not a totalitarian state; it was a caricature of one."[1] To master the existing bureaucracy Hitler destroyed it and replaced it with a "confusion of private empires, private armies, private intelligence services."[2] There was, claims Hohne, a virtual "anarchy of authority." He quotes Hannah Arendt as saying that this confusion led to a state among the Nazi administrators of "permanent frustration." Speaking of the hated Gestapo, Hohne sums up, "In fact, the SS world was a bizarre, nonsensical affair, devoid of all logic."[3]

This might well describe what happened to the medical delivery system of Germany. The Aktion T-4 bureaucracy had been superimposed upon the existing management structure—national, state, local, religious, and private. Aktion T-4 transferred thousands of patients of extended-care institutions back and forth across Germany without informing attending physicians, without coordinating with

146

the local hospital administrators, operating by and large outside, and in addition to, the regular management channels of the Division of Nursing Homes of the Interior Ministry. Some patients were killed without knowledge of their doctors. Doctors killed their patients without the knowledge of their families. All of this was contrary to formal law and precedent, and often it was carried forward without the knowledge, let alone approval, of the local government or judiciary. All of this caused the most terrible confusion of jealous jurisdictions, squabbling bureaucracies, and tangled records.

There was an unmistakable aura of Spike Jones—a determined cacophony—as the T-4 physicians went about their work.

The trouble started at once. There were the usual administrative foul-ups. This report gives an example:

> The following cases should naturally not have occurred:
>
> 1. Through an oversight one family received two urns.
> 2. One notification of death indicated appendicitis as the cause of death. The appendix, however, had already been removed ten years previously.
> 3. Another cause of death quoted was a disease of the spinal cord. Relatives of the family had visited the patient, then in perfect physical health, only eight days before.
> 4. One family received notification of death, although the woman still lives in an institution today and enjoys perfect physical health.[4]

The authorities were upset by such mistakes, but on the whole understanding. As a Nazi Party official explained in a confidential note to a colleague dated December 6, 1940:

> For some time, the inmates of mental institutions have been visited by a commission . . . the patients are examined . . . and then the decision is made whether they should be released from their sufferings.
>
> The body is cremated and the ashes are placed at the disposal of the relatives. Small mistakes in notifying are naturally always liable to occur, and in the future it will not be possible to avoid them. The commission itself is anxious to avoid all mistakes. . . .
>
> I believe that we National Socialists can welcome this

action which is *extraordinarily serious for the affected individual* [emphasis added]. I beg you, therefore, to oppose all rumors and grumblings. . . .

> Heil Hitler!
> Sellmer
> Gaustabsamtsleiter[5]

The letters of notification of death sent out to the families caused some of the rumors and grumblings referred to in Sellmer's letter. It might happen that the parents of a retarded child who had been transferred from a local institution would receive a letter from the authorities telling them that the child had died of such a cause on such a day in such a place. By comparing letters with the parents of other retarded children in the same village, they would find that they were identical: *all* their children had died in the same place, often on the same day. They were puzzled at first, and then angry as they concluded that their children had been killed.

Brack, of course, had been anxious to see that such mistakes not happen: "the death notifications to the relatives of the patient . . . are to be kept somehow different according to the district and kind of relative; they must be altered frequently to avoid stereotype texts and therefore a form letter would only irritate."[6]

How right he was—irritate they did. When the letters went out, the complaints began. The Nazi state was a tyranny, and it was dangerous for a citizen to complain. Nevertheless, people were outraged, and they did not shrink from expressing their anger. There were complaints to the authorities, letters to the editor, and lawsuits filed in court.

Party leaders began to be concerned. There was nothing democratic about Nazi rule, but even the most totalitarian of states must pay attention to public opinion. A government without the support—active or passive—of a majority of its citizens is not stable and, in the long run, cannot survive. And the Nazis wanted to survive. Theirs was a stable government, ruling with the general consent of its citizens. The party leaders kept track of what the public was thinking. They used modern polling techniques and public opinion analysis to do so. They were aware of public opinion: they responded to it, and they attempted to manipulate it with a sophistication ahead of its time.

Hitler had known euthanasia would be a controversial matter. He had said it could be done only under cover of general war and an all-out war effort. He had feared the reaction of the churches. Now his top officials watched public reaction to the euthanasia program with close attention.

Here, for example, is a note from Hitler's right-hand man, Martin Bormann, to a Nazi official in Franconia, concerning the complaints being stirred by the duplicate letters. Bormann was anxious that Nazi Party members do all that they could to counter criticism and provide support for the authorities running the killing program.

> The text of the notifications of relatives varies in its composition, as I was once more assured yesterday; it can, however, naturally happen sometimes that two families living close to each other receive similarly worded letters.
>
> It is natural that the representatives of Christian theology speak against the Commission's measures; it must be equally natural that all party officials should, as much as necessary, support the work of the Commission.[7]

It is evident the party did not see the program as shameful or indefensible. To Nazi officials the secrecy with which it was shrouded was simply a tactic necessitated by the recalcitrance of the unenlightened, rather than any moral concern over what was being done.

When party members complained about what was going on—and when there was no question about the loyalty of the member—they were brought into party headquarters and given a full briefing on the program. The following is a letter received at the killing institution of Sonnenstein:

12. Maria Kehr
     To the Provincial Mental Institution
     Sonnenstein/near Pirna/Elbe.

     Nuremberg 27.11.40
     Schweppemannstr. 44

                    [Stamped:] Kreisleiter advised
                    _____

                    Received 29. Nov. 1940
                    506
                    _____

I have received your letter of 22 Nov. 1940 and acknowledge the death of my sister Christine Ortmann.

My brother-in-law, Herr Hans Lindemann, whose wife, Ottilie Lindemann, née Ortmann, has died there, too, and who was also a sister of mine, will get in touch with you about the dispatch of the urn with the mortal remains.

I request that the personal affairs of the deceased be placed at the disposal of the NSV [National Socialist Welfare Organization].

The unexpected deaths of both my sisters within a period of two days appear most improbable to me. Their illnesses were fundamentally different, the difference in their ages amounted to nine years.

You must realize that one is bound to draw a certain conclusion if one receives news of the death of two sisters in the very same day, and nobody in the world can convince me that this is just a coincidence.

I could regain my peace of mind only if I knew for certain that *a law* of the Reich authorizes mercy killings of people with incurable diseases. This is obviously a blessing both for the sick persons themselves and for their relatives, and a great relief for our Reich and people.

I should be very grateful to you for the transmission of this order which gives the authority for mercy killings of these sick people.

I myself and my family stand solidly behind the Third Reich and would certainly not oppose this decree, as I have had to watch the misery for a great many years myself, and on innumerable occasions my sole wish was that both my sisters might soon be relieved of their great suffering. I cannot believe, however, that this secret wish of mine should have been realized in a period of two days.[8]

The authorities were particularly touched by this letter. A Dr. Schumann referred it to Professor Heyde, the chief doctor at Aktion T-4, seeking permission to call the woman in to explain the program to her:

Dear Professor Heyde,
Enclosed I submit to you a letter of a relative whose two sisters have died at our place.

I ask for information, whether in this case the writer is to be asked here for a discussion, or whether as usual the necessary precaution is to be used especially in explaining that the death of two sisters has occurred in a natural way.

I have sent a copy of this letter to Dr. Hofelmann because he is interested in such letters [handwritten continuation] and since he considered particularly to give reasonable hints in the letters to the relatives.

Heil Hitler

Provincial Mental Institution

Sonnenstein-Saxony Dr. Schumann

5 December 19[*illegible*]
B 042003[9]

Permission was given to the local party to inform the woman. She and her brother-in-law were called in to Nazi headquarters in Nuremberg on January 9, 1941, and given a full briefing on the program which had brought about the death of her two sisters. According to the party file note on the meeting:

In absence of the Gaustabsamtsleiter, Party member Seila and acting on his orders, I received today Frau Kehr and her brother-in-law, and informed them in a very discreet manner with regard to the question put forward by Frau Kehr in her letter.

Frau Kehr and her brother-in-law were at once satisfied with the explanation and emphasized that they understood the measures which had been taken and that they were almost grateful for it. They only wanted to hear from a competent office that they were not confronted with a case lacking all legal foundation.

Nuremberg, 9 January 1941
Kalminsky[?] 297/20[10]

In order to avoid the situation which befell Frau Kehr, a strict rule was issued which prohibited the taking of brothers and sisters together in the same shipment to the killing hospitals. Their killing was supposed to be spaced out over a period of time—kill one and then, after a month or two had passed, kill the other. [11]

The Kehr family was not the only one that did not object to the killing of the chronically handicapped. Many family members were pleased to learn that a deformed or demented relative "had been given a happy release from their suffering"—according to Brandt's testimony—and was thus no longer a burden to the conscience of the family. "During the euthanasia scheme we put through in the years 1940 and 1941," Karl Brandt told the court at Nuremberg, "we received a great number of letters expressing perfect understanding and agreement with our work."[12]

That this was, in fact, so, receives some corroboration from a poll taken in 1920, which had surveyed two hundred parents or guardians of severely disabled children. Of the 162 who responded, 47 had opposed and 119 approved the proposal that physicians be allowed to end the lives of the disabled. [13]

These responses seemed to indicate that Hitler had known what he was doing when he insisted the program be run in such a manner as to absolve the families of the victims from all responsibility for their deaths. When freed of this responsibility, there were many, apparently, quite willing to go along with this program "which every sensible person should only welcome," in the words of Nazi Party member Gerstner. [14]

Of course, not everyone who supported the Nazi program felt this way. As knowledge of the existence of the program grew more widespread, people of good conscience become concerned, even though they were not directly involved in the program or personally affected by it. Such people—whether or not they were Nazis, and certainly most Germans were Nazi sympathizers—loved their country and feared their God. Such people could not believe that innocent German citizens were being killed, simply because they were disabled. These people took risks and wrote letters in opposition to the killing.

The anguish felt by such people is beautifully captured in the following letter by a Frau von Löwis. An aristocrat and a supporter of the Führer, she wrote from her castle to Frau Buch, the wife of the chief justice of the Nazi high court, a high-ranking, longtime

Nazi close to Hitler's inner circle. Frau von Löwis clearly intended that her letter be brought to the attention of the Nazi Party leaders and that its subject matter, the terrible impact of Aktion T-4, be brought before the Führer himself. The matter-of-fact courage displayed by Frau van Löwis in stating her views to the authorities is impressive. She could well have been sent to a concentration camp.

The letter states emphatically that the wanton killing of the disabled is contrary "to all right and justice." Von Löwis is in despair that such a policy has become state policy, and she warns that the confidence of the people in their government and in their Führer is at risk.

There is, throughout the letter, a fine sense of the dreadful fix in which the decent people of Germany found themselves as Hitler's Third Reich moved along its evil and ineluctable path. These people had made it possible for him to seize power, and now they found there was no escape.

Mauren, 25 November 1940

Dear Frau Buch!

The simplest way is probably for me to direct this letter to you with the request to forward it to your husband or to hand it to him when he returns home if you think it better. Doris wrote us some time ago that he is in Poland?

The problem which brings me to you today is not a personal matter but it concerns all of us and would seem to me to be the hardest of all those which we have had to tackle so far. Until now nothing could shake my confidence in the successful overcoming of all difficulties and dangers which the "Greater Germany" is meeting on its way, and with my faith in the Führer I have unswervingly fought my way through thick and thin; but that which looms up before us now simply takes the ground from under our feet, as a young 100 percent party member, a coworker in the office for racial policy, said to me yesterday.

Undoubtedly you know about the measure now used by us to dispose of incurable insane persons; still, perhaps you do not fully realize the manner and the scope of this, nor the horror it creates in people's minds! Here, in Württemberg, the tragedy takes place in Grafeneck, on the Alb, as a result of which the name of that place has taken on a most ominous meaning. In the beginning one instinctively refused to believe the tale, or in any case considered the rumors extremely exaggerated. On the occasion of our last business meeting at the Gau School, in Stuttgart, about the middle of October, I was still told by a "well-informed" person that this involved only idiots, strictly speaking, and that application of "euthanasia" applied only to cases which have been thoroughly tested. It is entirely impossible now to make anybody believe that version, and individual cases established with absolute certainty spring up like mushrooms. One might deduct perhaps 20 percent but even if one tried to deduct 50 percent this would not help. The terrible and dangerous part is not so much the fact in itself; if a law had been created on the order of the sterilization law which subjects certain categories of sick people to the most thorough examination by experts, patients in whom there is no longer left even a spark of recollection or of human feeling, then I am convinced feelings would calm down after the initial indignation and people might have become reconciled with it, perhaps quicker than with the sterilization law. Perhaps, after a few years, one might even have asked why this merciful law had not been introduced long before? But considering how matters are now being handled the effects are truly unfathomable from every point of view. Opinions may vary on how far men can arrogate to themselves the right to decide on the life or death of their fellow men, but one thing should be sure, anyhow: This right must be strictly established by law and it must be administered with utmost conscientiousness or else doors will be opened wide to the most dangerous passions and to crime. It once was a well-established practice, for instance, to get rid of embarrassing relatives by declaring them insane and lodging them in insane asylums.

I am of the opinion that the people have the right to know about the law, just as they knew of the sterilization law. The most awful thing in the present case is "the public secret" which creates a feeling of terrible uneasiness. We can not possibly be expected to guard the secret indefinitely even though he who gives it away becomes liable to capital punishment, as is said to be the case in this instance. It was equally unheard of to expect people to <u>believe in the mysterious "epidemics"</u> to which the relative was said to have succumbed; a mistake which never can be made good again! Those who are responsible for those measures, have they no concept of <u>the measure</u> of confidence they have thereby destroyed? Everybody must at once ask: What then can still be believed? Where is this path taking us and where should the boundary line be established? It is not that only hopeless idiots and mentally deranged persons were affected but, as it seems, <u>all</u> mentally incurables will gradually be included—also epileptics whose minds are not at all affected. Frequently there are among them persons who still take some part in life, who accomplish their modest measure of work, who are in contact with their relatives by mail, persons who, when the gray motor car of the SS rolls up, know where they are to be taken. And the farmers on the Alb when they see these cars pass know also where they are going and day and night they see the smoke from the crematory. We also know that among the mentally incurables there are many persons of highest intellect; those who are deranged in part only, and those who are deranged periodically only and who for periods in between have a perfectly clear mind, with enhanced mental energies. Was it not enough to sterilize them and is it not horrible to think of those whom this is hanging over?

While I am writing down all this, I am again so overwhelmed by the ghastliness of these things that I feel I am having a bad dream from which I must wake up! And to think that just now women are to come forward for a huge campaign! And what is the canvas material for the Catholic Church!

How the people still cling to the hope that the Führer does not know about these things, that he <u>could</u> not know, otherwise he would have to take action against it; that in no case does he know about the manner and extent of these things which take place. I feel, however, it must not go on that way much longer or this confidence will be shattered also. It still is so moving to come across this confidence, just among the simple people: "Of course the Führer does not know of it," and this weapon we must keep shining as nothing else! We cannot do this, however, by trying to throw dust in people's eyes, keeping them quiet as long as possible with subterfuges and hushing-up when they ask us, with excuses which we do not believe ourselves. I am also convinced that we will pay bitterly for this attempt to stultify the people's sound feeling of resistance against these happenings and to silence it; it is the feeling of right and justice without which a people invariably goes astray. Again, one must not permit the wave of indignation to become so strong that it breaks an open path for itself by force or that it—which could be worse still—begins to consume us from the inside out. The matter must be brought to the Führer's ears before it is too late and there must be a way by which the voice of the German people can reach the ear of its Führer!

Much could still be added on this subject but I believe I have said what is essential, and I do not want to abandon the hope that the unified strength of those who recognize the danger clearly and who muster the necessary courage will help us to find the way out of this labyrinth. I do hope that you and your family are well and that, particularly, you are receiving good news from your sons on the front and that despite all you are all looking forward to a merry Christmas in wartime. I still have my daughter with her two children here; probably she will be here throughout the war, that is, as long as we still can live in the castle; much to our regret we had to decide to rent it to the Women's Labor Service last spring; otherwise we would not have been able to hold the farm financially. We hope soon to build a small house in the garden where we can get along with one maid; the question only is where we are going to be until that little house is finished. At the end of the week my daughter-in-law, an Englishwoman by birth, will also come with her little child because they cannot find an apartment in Chemnitz; thus, before vacating the castle it at least will once more be fully utilized.

With kindest regards to your husband also and

> Heil Hitler!
> your
> Else von Löwis

A quiet moment in the garden for the T-4 medical consultants: (left to right) Erich Bauer (chauffeur), Dr. Rudolf Lonauer, Dr. Victor Ratka, Dr. Friedrich Mennecke, Dr. Paul Nitsche, and Dr. Gerhard Wischer. *Ernst Klee*

Hadamar Institution, 1941: "The corpses are said to be transferred on a conveyer belt to an incineration chamber. . . . The thick smoke of the incinerator is supposed to be visible every day over Hadamar." (From a report to the Minister of Justice.) *Ernst Klee*

Hadamar in 1987: "The sweeping lawns were bright green in the sharp fall sun. And everywhere there were flowers." *Steven H. Sanders*

The loading dock at Hadamar: "Care was taken to see that the patients were unloaded . . . in a place where their screams could not be heard. Here at Hadamar, a special wooden garage . . . was constructed in the courtyard behind the main building." *Steven H. Sanders*

"Absberg's troubles started on a fall day in 1940. . . . A big gray bus rolled down the narrow streets of town . . . and passed under the abbey entryway into the courtyard. The abbey gates were shut behind the bus." (Roland Marcotte with the author at the abbey gates, Absberg.) *Steven H. Sanders*

Altar, village church at Absberg: "The residents and the nuns moved across the market square to the church for a special service. . . . Each member of the home was offered confession, absolution, and communion. Those who could make it to the altar on their own legs did so. Those who could not—who needed help—were half carried to the altar rail by the nuns." *Steven H. Sanders*

"The bishop sent word to the Gestapo that they could arrest him if they wished. They would find him standing at the door of his cathedral, arrayed in his full bishop's regalia, the miter upon his head: in his hand, the great crosier or crook." *The Library of Congress*

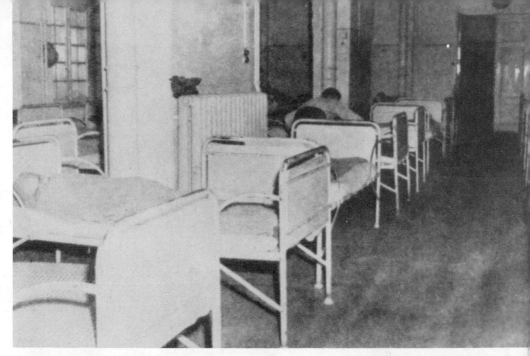

Ward I-B, Hadamar Institution, 1945. Patients unknown. "Most of the rooms were small and bleak. There was little furniture other than beds and these, without exception, were old and uncomfortable." *The Library of Congress*

Hadamar in 1945: "The building itself resembled a morgue, cold and forbidding." *The Library of Congress*

Hartheim near Linz, 1988: "Schloss Hartheim had been built as a private house. It had served as an orphanage and later a hospital. It was complete with gardens, great trees, archways, turrets, and courtyard." A total of 18,269 patients were killed at Hartheim in the years 1940 and 1941. *Paul Waggaman*

The Hadamar staff in court. Front row: Dr. Adolf Wahlmann, senior attending physician; Mr. Heinrich Ruoff, chief male nurse; Mr. Philipp Blum, doorman, telephone operator, and grave digger. Back row: Mr. Karl Willig; Mr. Adolf Merkle, bookkeeper; Miss Irmgard Huber, chief nurse; and Mr. Alfons Klein, administrator.

"The body . . . was shoved into the oven. And then it was time for the fun. Mr. Merkle . . . turned his collar about, put his coat on backward, and intoned a burlesque eulogy of the deceased insane person. The audience roared with laughter." *The Library of Congress*

Nurse Irmgard Huber on the stand: "The lives . . . are just as valuable as my life, but I could not change anything there. I didn't have any say. I couldn't report anything. I avoided the matter." *The Library of Congress*

Dr. Karl F. Brandt, personal physician to the Führer, Reich Commissioner for Health and Sanitation, and director of the T-4 euthanasia program, stands on the scaffold next to the hangman moments before his death on June 2, 1948. (The face of the hangman has been scratched out on the negative by U.S. military authorities to protect his anonymity.) *U.S. National Archives*

The wife of Chief Justice Buch did exactly as was intended by the writer. She gave the letter to her husband, the chief of the Nazi Party court. He, having been with Hitler since the 1920s, had seen a lot—including leading an investigation into the appalling anti-Semitic outrages of Kristallnacht. Nevertheless, he was both surprised and distressed by its contents. Justice Buch passed the letter on to Heinrich Himmler, head of the Gestapo. In his covering letter, Buch asks for an explanation of the outrages set forth in Frau von Löwis's letter.

The Chief of Counsel
of the NSDAP

Munich 7 December 1940
Telephone 50812–50815, 50825

To the Reichsführer SS and Chief of the German
Police Herr Reichleiter Heinrich HIMMLER

B e r l i n SW 11

Prinz Albrecht-Strasse 8

Personal

Confidential

Registered

Dear Party Colleague HIMMLER,

Enclosed I send you a letter from one of my oldest acquaintances, Frau Else von Löwis of Menar, expressing a moral distress that—if I may say so—cries to high heaven. My dear HIMMLER, there have been three women in my life whom I felt bound to set apart from all others. For me, these three were Nordic goddesses descended from heaven rather than women and whom I had the privilege to approach on the same level. One of them was Karin GÖRING, the other two the sisters Grete and Else von DUOCH (now Frau von Löwis). Their father was a Baden minister of justice, a friend

165

of my own father. When the family, parents, sisters, and brothers came together, all of them from 1ᵐ 80 to 1ᵐ 90 tall, everything else sank into insignificance. I have never in my life seen such marvelous, Nordic figures. The brother Alex was, until his recent death, the right hand man of Robert WAGNER at the Regency at Karlsruhe.

Had I not an unlimited trust in my Reichsführer SS and therefore the assurance that nothing will happen to the woman as a consequence of her letter, I would never have sent it on. But I know that this woman, who is only slightly older than I, is an ardent follower of the movement and, from her family residence at Mauren Castle, District of Böblingen in Württemberg, has already accomplished a great deal as leader of the women's organization. If she has written to us, it is only because she is bewildered in her distress and witnesses things that are beyond her. She understands them as little as I do. I have never heard of such things. I can imagine what is wrong but I am of the opinion that there must be something false about the report if it stirs such a disturbance. There are certainly things which a man can stand but access to which should not be allowed to a woman.

Therefore if we must today undertake certain things because we want to fight for the eternal life of our people, things before which a woman would shudder, they must be handled in such a way as to keep them really concealed.

My request is that things should be carried on without further unpleasantness for this woman for whom I absolutely vouch. There must be something false about it all and injurious to the movement, else the good soul would not have been so distracted.

Heil Hitler!

Yours faithfully

Walter BUCH

Enclosure

Himmler's reply, informal and personal, acknowledges Hitler's authorization of Aktion T-4, but places responsibility for its operation on the shoulders of the physicians. He avoids all mention of the concerns Frau von Löwis has expressed—that the program will corrupt the people and wreck confidence in the Führer. The privileged position of the aristocracy, even under the Third Reich, is brought out by Himmler's pledge that "Frau von Löwis will not be implicated in this affair."

SECRET NATIONAL MATTER

Mei/C   Va/23 19 December 1940
To: The Chief of Counsel of the NSDAP
      Party Member Walter BUCH,

M u n i c h 33

Dear Party Colleague BUCH,
Hearty thanks for your letter of 7 December 1940. The proceedings in the place in question, I may inform you confidentially, are carried on by a commission of physicians by virtue of an authorization of the Führer. The selection is carried out as conscientiously and justly as is humanly possible, not by an isolated individual but by a commission, of which every member first gives his decision independently.

The SS only helps with vehicles, motorcars etc. It is the doctors, experts conscious of their responsibility, who give the orders.

I agree with you on one point. If the matter has become so public as you say, the process must be faulty. On the other hand, it is clear that it is always a difficult process. I shall immediately contact the competent headquarters and bring the defects to their notice and advise them to drop Grafeneck.

Of course Frau von Löwis will not be implicated in this affair.

When we meet again, I shall give you some more detailed information verbally so that you can inform Frau von Löwis more accurately should you have the opportunity.

#867   Cordial greetings

Heil Hitler!

Himmler[15]

167

The twentieth century has seen so many mass killing programs that they have lost their power to shock. It is only when the killing is personalized—when the victim has a name, when the specifics of a particular case are known—that it is possible to grasp the injustice and to sense the anger it caused.

Here are some individual cases, selected at random:

There was young Koch, an eighteen-year-old who, with his aged mother, worked the family farm. Koch was known as an affable fellow, very popular in his little village. He was an epileptic. He was sent to the hospital to be sterilized under the terms of the "Law for the Prevention of Genetically Impaired Progeny." His mother wrote him in the hospital telling him to hurry his recovery, as she needed him on the farm. She sent him sweets with her love. Unfortunately, Koch was caught up in the euthanasia sweep—he was both sterilized and killed. His mother was in despair, the villagers both angry and puzzled.[16]

In another case, Pastor Paul Gerhard Braune, one of the most public, outspoken critics of the killing, tells, in a report he wrote in protest to the Reich Minister of Justice, about the deaths of six young women: "In one case with which I am particularly familiar, six girls were included in a transfer to the killing institution, despite their impending discharge from the institution in order to become domestics in people's houses."[17]

There were cases in which patients were taken by sheer accident or saved by mere chance. A Dr. Joseph Jordans told about one such case:

> I myself was transferred . . . at the end of March 1942 because it became known that I was opposed to the killings. After I left, one of my patients, an adult man, a Gypsy, was killed by injections. He was on the list of persons to be shipped out for killing at another asylum, but I had saved him four times. Immediately after I left, he was killed, according to my wife who was at that time still at Wieslech. This man was in no way feebleminded. In fact the institute made money out of him because he was an expert basket-maker. His killing was part of the program to kill psychopaths.[18]

A man named Otto was more lucky than the Gypsy—although he had a close call:

> Otto M. was a schizophrenic and worked for Georgenthal Goods. He was on the list and was to be picked up from Georgenthal on the day that the transport was to leave. . . . He looked good and nearly normal, just like other people. Therefore I went to Director Muller and asked if he wouldn't take another look at this Otto M. to see if he might be held back. He replied, "Oh, so what, I don't do that anymore. I can't bother with such things, no, no!" This did not leave me in much peace of mind. I pondered, over and over, what more I could do. Soon enough the transport bus arrived with Transport Director Seip—and the telephone rang.
>
> It was a woman on the line, inquiring about Otto: had he already been shipped to Hadamar? She begged me to please hold him back. She would look after him and bear all the costs of his upkeep. She had heard that he was to be shipped out immediately. And then she said that he was a veteran of the 1914 War. I immediately thought that World War I veterans were supposed to be exempt from shipment to Hadamar. Transport Director Seip was just leaving, I pleaded with him that the patient will be claimed by his relatives, he is reported to be a veteran of combat. Seip replied: "If he is a veteran, I shall not take him, he will have to stay here." Quickly, I telephoned through to Dr. Mennecke—who happened to remember Otto's case. . . . Director Mennecke replied that he would accept the responsibility; Otto was an orderly person who could be held back and saved. Now by this time, Director Muller was with Seip at the old folks' home and the transport bus was almost ready to go. I quickly shouted out and someone told me the patients were already in the bus. I continued shouting; shouting and running toward the bus. I got him back. They pulled Otto out of line just as he was boarding the bus. He is still living to this day.[19]

Otto was lucky; a hapless soul named Keller was not so lucky. Keller was a patient at the Wieslech Clinic. He is described in medical records as a mildly schizoid person. According to hospital personnel he was a talented painter, gentle and harmless. Keller's bad luck was that there was another patient at Wieslech, also named Keller, who was not so gentle. This Keller was sorely troubled and his name was on the list to receive "final medical treatment." When the transport bus arrived, the troubled Keller was taken off to his last reward, all right; but along with him, through a mix-up, went the medical records of the mild Keller. As a result, the family of mild Keller received formal notice of his death, and in due course, "his" ashes in an urn. When the officials realized their frightful error, they did what any good bureaucrat would do. They killed mild Keller. Since they had already classified him as dead, they went ahead and killed him.[20]

A patient named E.B. almost made it, but not quite. According to the medical records, E.B. was a quiet, mentally retarded woman, dependable and hard-working. She worked as a cleaner at the hospital, and she never missed a day's work. Nevertheless, her name was on the list. When the bus arrived she followed her orders seemingly without hesitation or qualm. Calmly, she walked alone, out the doors of the hospital to the waiting bus. When she got to the bus, E.B. just kept on going, behind and not into the bus. Unnoticed, she circled the building and reentered the hospital through the back door. After the transport had gone, the orderlies discovered her back at work, in the process of washing the transportation number off the back of her hand. E.B.'s freedom was short-lived. Fifteen minutes later, the bus returned and picked up its missing patient.[21]

Another such tale was told by a Dr. Reuter, at a trial after the war. A young peasant arrived at a killing center as one of a group of patients scheduled for final treatment. As it happened, the patient was an old friend of one of the male nurses. The peasant was undressing for the "shower" when his friend and Dr. Reuter tried, in front of the other patients, to persuade him that he did not really need a shower; he was not that dirty, the shower could wait. No, replied the young man, at his daily job there was no shower, and this would be a rare treat. With that he went to his death.[22]

Maria Mader's mother intervened on behalf of her twenty-four-year-old daughter. It was in April 1941, and the word was out that patients were being killed at the state institutions. In a strange twist

Mrs. Mader did not object so much to the idea that her daughter might be killed as she did to the idea that her body would be cremated. The following is a note to the files made at the time concerning Maria's case:

> The mother of the patient Maria Mader, born 16.9.1917, Mrs. Anna Mader, born Rein, Munich, Analienstr. 95/I, appeared today before the director of the Institution and declared:
>
> "I request immediate release of my child Maria Mader to my care. In spite of all difficulties I want to take her home. My reason is that I have learned that people who are transferred from institutions die soon and that their bodies are then cremated. Only the ashes are sent to the relatives. Since I find it unbearable to have my child cremated, which is against my principles, I want to take my daughter home with me. At any rate I would like to take possession of the corpse of my daughter if anything should happen, so that the child could be buried in a decent ritual manner in a cemetery. According to your advice I shall submit a petition so that I can take my daughter away with me."
>
> Since the patient had already been scheduled for the transport of 25 April 1941, the director declined to return the patient immediately to her mother. I put it at the discretion of the director of the Cure and Care Institution in Niedernhart, as transition institution, to possibly return the patient to the mother upon request. The mother threatened immediate suicide if she were to learn that her child, Maria, was cremated.
>
> Eglfing 23 April 1941
>
> Direktion der Heil- und Pflegeanstalt des Bezirks-verblands Oberbayern Eglfing-Haar[23]

Mrs. Mader's appeal had a short-term effect. Her daughter had been scheduled for the April 20 transport to the killing hospital, but she was held back for a while. However, her name was added in pencil to the bottom of the list for the April 29 transport, and Maria went to her death—and cremation. Whether the mother made good on her suicide threat is not known.

The German historian Goetz Aly, who is doing important research on Aktion T-4, believes that the program was generally popular with the rank and file of the German citizenry.[24] Mention has already been made of the 1920 poll of the parents of the chronically disabled, which showed a wide acceptance of the concept of "mercy" killing. Twenty years later, with T-4 under way, letters from these parents were received by the hospitals and killing centers actually asking that their children be killed. There is no way of ascertaining how many such letters were received, but there were enough to make an impression upon the directors of the hospitals.

Certainly, the existence of the program and its intent to do away with the dependent chronically ill were acceptable to a sizable segment of the population. But to another sizable segment, it was most certainly not acceptable.

The protest at Absberg was but one of the demonstrations—again, it is impossible to say how many—which took place here and there across Germany. They did occur, and they did worry the authorities. There was, for example, trouble in Württemberg in February 1940.

Thirteen epileptic patients had been taken away from the Pfingstweide-bei-Tettnang, the oldest institution for the treatment of epilepsy in Germany, in a big gray bus. They were transferred to Schloss Grafeneck. Shortly thereafter, their relatives received notices of their deaths. These hitherto healthy people had died, simultaneously it seemed, of flu, inflammation of the lungs, or apoplexy.

People were angered and, bravely, they expressed their anger in a protest at the offices of the Ministry of the Interior. Apparently, the victims had been chosen from an alphabetical list of the institution inmates, and the names selected for "final medical therapy" happened to start with the letters "A" and "H." It is said the protesters made much of the coincidence that these letters were also Adolf Hitler's initials.[25] Thus was the demonstration both antieuthanasia and anti-Hitler.

Within the month that trouble broke out at Absberg, there was a similar disturbance not far away in the little town of Bruckberg. Again, the local party leader reported to his superiors, "The news of the removal of some of the inmates of the Bruckberg Institution has caused the greatest unrest among the members of the population of Bruckberg, unrest which was further increased by the fact that some of the inmates to be removed, namely those who, in the opinion of the villagers, are still 'in their right mind,' visited almost every house in town to say good-bye."[26] The party official found it hard to believe that these visits—which had served to alert the town to what was happening—could have been the idea of the disabled people themselves: "One could almost be led to believe that it is a question here of a 'farewell carried out on orders,' but I am informed from reliable sources that the inmates acted on their own, feeling it was their duty to say good-bye and that probably it was a case of one imitating the others."

But it *was* the idea of the disabled people, and it worked. The visits served both to alert and to alarm the townsfolk. The Nazi official, unaware of what was in store for the institution inmates, sought permission to still the villagers' unrest. He said he intended, at the next meeting of party members, to set forth the facts of the matter, "and above all quash the rumors that have arisen to the effect that the inmates would very soon be put out of the way, done away with or poisoned."

Another official, Wolf, to whom this request was addressed, passed it up the line to one Sellmer, the same man who was so involved in the troubles at Absberg. Wolf said to Sellmer, "I, however, am of the opinion that it is better now as before not to talk about this matter at all and I ask you to notify me accordingly if you hold different views. . . . As I evaluate the situation, a certain amount of unrest will naturally continue to arise. . . ."

In a handwritten note across the bottom of this report, Sellmer wrote, "Party member Wolf was informed by telephone on 3.3. Nothing is to be announced officially. The Org.P.T. [local official] is to be informed." Case closed.[27]

The villagers of Absberg and Bruckberg, the protesters of Württemberg, were upset over the loss of their friends. Also upset were those medical personnel of the extended-care institutions for whom the inmates were not only patients but friends as well.

Typical of such a response was the account of nurse Amalie Widmann, as told to the American doctor Leo Alexander on August 5, 1945, shortly after the war. This nurse almost lost her life because of her concern for her patients. The following is taken from Dr.

Alexander's notes recorded immediately after his interview with Nurse Widmann:

> Miss Widmann stated that the first transport of patients to a killing center left Wieslech on 19 February 1940. Among the patients were a good many who had become endeared and attached to Miss Widmann. After they had been taken to the killing center, Miss Widmann became unable to take her mind off the sad fate of these patients, and she became unable to rest day or night. She had to think about them all the time. She finally felt that it might give her ease of mind if she could actually see what happened, and she decided to visit the killing center in Grafeneck herself. So she asked for a furlough, not telling anybody what she planned to do, and she went to Grafeneck on 22 July 1940. When she got off the train at Marbach a.d. Lauter bei Munzingen, which is the railhead for Grafeneck, the people whom she asked for directions to Grafeneck looked at her in a peculiar way as if there was something strange or funny about her. When she finally arrived in front of the institution in Grafeneck, she found a sign reading: "Entry strictly prohibited because of danger of infection." There were heavily armed men in green uniform, obviously police about the area. Suddenly Miss Widmann felt gripped by an overwhelming feeling of anxiety and she ran away over an open field crying bitterly. She sat down and cried for a while. She then saw that she was on the premises of a stud farm. The farmer came and asked her whether he could do anything for her, and she told him that she wanted to go and see the institution in Grafeneck. The farmer then told her: "Do not go there. One must not say anything." Shortly afterwards, an SS man appeared, accompanied by other SS men, with hounds. They took her into the building, where she was brought before an official who asked her what she wanted. She said that she wanted to see some of her old patients and find out how they were. The official then stated that the patients liked it so much there that they would never want to leave again. He then interrogated her sharply about her antecedents and her connections with any group, if any. He then called up Dr. Mockel. Miss Widmann added that she felt she owed her life to Dr. Mockel because if he had not talked for her they would have

killed her. The reason why she went there was because of her deep feeling of close relationship with her patients.[28]

Only the families of Aktion T-4 medical personnel were exempt from the program. The families of other medical people were fully eligible. There were physicians whose loved ones went to their deaths, who received the "final medical therapy" at the hands of their fellow physicians.

In one such case, a physician in Stuttgart had a daughter, Helene, with severe epilepsy who was a patient at the Liebenau institution. In the summer of 1940, Helene smuggled a letter past the censors to her father. She told him that patients were being transported from Liebenau to Grafeneck, where they were killed. She believed her name was on a list of those to be taken, and she feared for her life. She begged her father and brother to save her.

The family was terribly concerned. Because the father had heart disease, it was the brother who went to the health department officials in Stuttgart. He was referred to a public health doctor with whom he met. He told the doctor of his sister's fears and, expecting reassurance, he asked if it could possibly be true that her life was in danger. He could not get the medical official to give him a straight answer.

This worried the family even more. The father, heart condition or no, went directly to the authorities at Liebenau. He had several meetings and, at each, he was encouraged to believe that Helene was safe. They assured him there would be no change in his daughter's situation—she would not be transported—without his receiving prior notification. In addition, he wrote to Aktion T-4 authorities in Berlin, seeking an official letter guaranteeing her safety, and this was promised.

In the middle of these efforts, the family received another letter from Helene. It was a letter of farewell.

> Dearly beloved Father:
> Unfortunately nothing has changed. I must report to you today my departing words to this earthly life into eternal Heaven. Reflect, that I must be permitted to die as a martyr, not without the will of my godly redeemer appearing, in

accordance with my year-long yearning. Father, good Father, I do not want to part from this life without asking you and my dear brothers and sisters again for forgiveness, for what I have always felt through you my whole life. Please, dear God, accept my sickness and these victims as atonement. Dear Father, please, don't hold it against your child, who has so profoundly loved you, and always think and think again, that it is going on to Heaven, where we will all find each other with God and our deceased ones. Dear Father, I am going with determined courage and trust in God and never doubt in his good deeds, which he exercises upon us, even though we might not understand (or be enlightened about them) at the time. We shall soon be rewarded. God commanded. Please, tell my sisters and brothers of my life.

I don't want to suffer anymore, but on the contrary I want to be happy once again: I give you this little picture to remember me by, so goes your child onward to the savior. It (He) embraces you in true love and with the certain promise, which I gave to you at our last departure, that I will staunchly stand by to wait.

Your child, Helene

. . . Please, pray for my calmness. Until we see each other again, good Father, in Heaven.[29]

Shortly thereafter, the family received an official letter from the institution at Brandenburg to which Helene had been transferred: Helene had died unexpectedly as the result of an unfortunate accident. Because of an epidemic her body would be cremated, and the ashes, etc., etc.

———

As the program switched into high gear, as more and more people became aware of what was going on, the level of protests began to build. There was never an organized outcry; it was always inconsistent and spotty, depending upon the specific impact of Aktion T-4 upon the particular region of the country. Some areas were only lightly affected; in others, whole wards were emptied, entire nursing homes closed down, and many families lost their loved ones.

It is traditional in Germany to place a notice in the newspaper to announce a death in the family, giving the date the person died. Thus, in some local newspapers, an entire column might be filled with the death notices of persons from a particular asylum or nursing home, all of whom had died on the same day. The notices themselves provided damning evidence of what was going on, and they were looked upon by the authorities as a form of protest. This problem was met by ordering an end to death notices.

Other protests were not so easy to end. The struggle of the disabled to remain alive, and the efforts of their families and friends to save them, have been described. It is important to understand the motives of the physicians in resisting as well as assisting the killing. It is important to understand what efforts the attorneys and the judges made to protect the rights of disabled German citizens—and what they did not do. Most important of all in bringing the centralized killing program to an end was the impact which the churches of Germany were able to bring to bear—in particular, the impact of the public pronouncements of certain brave members of the Roman Catholic hierarchy upon Nazi leaders. These leaders had power, and they used it in the face of Aktion T-4.

9

Aktion T-4 and the Doctors

Let us say it openly and without exaggeration: the doctors
were happy and joyful in Nazi times when they could
dispose of human lives, the lives of others.

Eugene Ionesco, *Le Monde*, 1974

I n order to gain some sort of understanding of what motivated the
behavior of German physicians during the period of the Third
Reich, it is important to examine the extent of their resistance—or
the lack thereof—to the Nazi killing policies. It is necessary to look
at the economic incentives which were so strong during the Nazi
years, and it is necessary, also, to appreciate the strength of the
appeal to the physicians of policies based upon the supposed
imperatives of modern biological science. These things provide a
circumstantial framework for developing an explanation for the
behavior of the doctors; there were, also, psychological factors at
work, and these, too, must be examined.

Resistance

The resistance of the medical community to the euthanasia program
is difficult to assess. There were brave physicians who simply
refused to participate. There were physicians who protested, both
within and outside official channels. There was even some attempt
to put together an organized resistance. By and large, however, it
must be said that such objections as were raised were notably few
and far apart.

As has been shown, a physician in practice in Nazi Germany in the 1940s could not help but know that chronically ill patients were being put to death in large numbers across the country. Whole wards in major hospitals were emptied; nursing homes and insane asylums were emptied and shut down. Indeed, the killing became, as Himmler had said, "a secret that is no longer one."

There were about 15,000 physicians in Germany. Close to half were members of the Nazi Party, the largest percentage of members of any of the professions.[1] Probably no more than 350 doctors in Germany were ever actively engaged in the official killing program itself,[2] although Dr. Alexander Mitscherlich told Robert Jay Lifton that this estimate represents only the tip of the iceberg. An Aktion T-4 executive, Dietrich Allers, said after the war that at least 20,000 people had direct knowledge of the program's operation.[3] Large numbers of doctors supported the racist policies of the Nazi regime, and the profession went well beyond official government-set quotas in purging their ranks of communists, social democrats, and Jews.[4] They espoused the prevalent eugenic beliefs of the day, but it is doubtful that more than a small portion of the German physicians were genuinely committed, as a matter of philosophy or public policy, to the slaughter of the "useless eaters." The fact, however, that distinguished professors of medicine and psychiatry and quite well-known physicians agreed to participate, and that detailed briefings were given not just to medical leaders but to sizable numbers of practicing doctors, leads to an inescapable conclusion: the medical establishment of Germany, leadership and rank and file, raised no very significant objection to the program, placed no hindrance to its pursuit. Muller-Hill reports that—with the admirable exception of one Professor Gottfried Ewald—of all the many letters and petitions received by the authorities protesting the killing of mentally ill patients, not one is known to have been written by a psychiatrist.[5]

Life in Nazi Germany, particularly during wartime, was a time of terrible stress for most people. The nation was trapped. Escape was impossible. Protest led to the concentration camps; informers were everywhere; terror was public policy; and death was in the air. There was an overwhelming sense of helplessness. It has been noted that in the face of such a situation, many chose—voluntarily or unconsciously—a form of "internal exile" or "inner immigration."

In such a state the person withdraws into himself, numbs his senses, does his job, keeps his head down, his mouth shut, hunkers down and simply endures. This gray depressed state is found in prisoners, concentration-camp internees, and starving Ethiopians. And this was the way many German physicians went through the war.

If patients were disappearing out from under their care, so be it. If after 1942, in violation of the Hippocratic Oath, physicians were ordered to break the rules of confidentiality and report to the state various aspects of their patients' private lives and health, so be it. If fellow physicians, taking advantage of a general license, insti- tuted their own policies of killing troublesome or refractory patients, so be it.

An example of this sort of inner exile can be found in the interview immediately after the war with Dr. Wilhelm Mockel, director of the Badische Heil- und Pflegeanstalt, a state hospital near Heidelberg. According to Mockel, he had strongly disapproved of the killings of his patients, but he had done nothing about them. "I never wanted to hear about what they did at Grafeneck [one of the killing centers]. It always nauseated me." So what *did* he do? "Later I could not stand it any longer. Whenever a transport [of patients bound for Grafeneck] was to leave at night, I usually left the institution at noon and did not come back until the next day."[6]

Nothing noble about it: it was a survival technique and it worked. The rank-and-file physicians of Germany tended their patients as best they could with what they had. They obeyed the laws, followed the regulations, caused no trouble.

Brandt, in his powerful defense argument at Nuremberg, insisted that no doctor was forced into the killing and that each participated according to his own free will. "In no circumstances is it to be understood that any doctor serving under this scheme was ever obligated to perform euthanasia in a case where he himself had not decided that it was necessary."[7]

This, no doubt, overstated the case. The killing was official policy, and for anyone to object to official policy in the Nazi Third Reich was, often enough, a capital offense. Nevertheless, there were examples of doctors who surreptitiously worked in opposition to the killing program, and there were even a few who quite openly declined to participate and lived to tell the tale.

These people were heroes:

Professors Pohlisch and Panse called a secret meeting of physicians in Bonn to work out a strategy to sabotage the killing program. Health official Professor Creutz worked with them, and the Landesrats (government members) of Hanover and of Münster were aware of their activities; and it was even said the Landeshauptmanns (provincial or state leaders) of Hanover and of the Rhineland Province cooperated, at least in part, with their efforts. Physicians privy to the plan were instructed in how to fill out the euthanasia questionnaires: Most patients were labeled as fit to work and important to the war effort—hence exempt. Seriously insane persons were mislabeled as suffering from various senile ailments—and the senile were not yet being called. The really hopeless cases were identified as "instruction material" for the medical schools—and they, too, were exempted. These ruses saved lives. [8]

After the war, a court in Düsseldorf found that the efforts of Pohlisch and Panse had been effective: their "proved countermeasures had met with considerable success." As for Professor Walter Creutz, the court held that he had managed to save "at least 3,000" of some 4,000 patients who had been scheduled to be sent to their deaths. Creutz's "unmistakably proved opposition and consequent action led to equally unmistakable success." [9]

Some doctors simply said no. A doctor identified only as Dr. Schn. actually took his patients off the transport buses. Another, a Dr. Schi., flatly refused to allow his patients to be taken, as did an unnamed director of an institution who said "the way to his patients was over his dead body." [10] Klee records the case of a psychiatrist named H. Jasperson who strongly opposed the killing program and tried openly, but in vain, to get the directors of the psychiatric departments of the medical schools to join him in a group protest. [11]

There were other acts of courage by unknown doctors and nurses. Relatives were called and told to come fetch their family members from the institutions. In other institutions, patients were simply released. Others were sent to hide in the woods on the days the transport buses were scheduled.

After the war one patient recalled what it had been like. The nurses had told them to flee. "We went through the forest, ran around, because we did not know where to go. . . . When the nurses came to fetch us, many started to run again. . . . We hid in barns a few times. . . . One was safe nowhere. . . . As soon as a car came, the head nurse called, 'Get up, march, hide yourself. If someone comes, don't stand still.' "[12]

A remarkable example of courage was set by Professor Gottfried Ewald, director of the University Clinic for Nervous Diseases at Göttingen. He was summoned to one of the T-4 briefings in Berlin for doctors and psychiatrists arranged by Dr. Heyde. At the meeting he spoke forcefully in opposition to the killing program. Asked to leave by Heyde, Ewald was reminded of the high secrecy surrounding the program.

Back in Göttingen, Ewald prepared a long and powerful memorandum, arguing the case against the killing of the mentally disabled. The argument was cast in Nazi terms, for Ewald was a Nazi supporter, but it was a strong argument nevertheless. He did not believe a doctor should attempt to "interfere with fate." He insisted that a mother's love for her child *"demands respect"* (Ewald's italics). And in further emphasis, *"Do we really know that all the patients who fall under the law are incurable?"* Ewald concluded, "I cannot choose a profession whose daily business is to eliminate a sick person because of his sickness after he or his relatives have come to me, trusting and looking for help."[13]

Ewald sent copies of his memorandum to Heyde, to Conti, to the dean of faculty at his university, to the administrative leader of his state of Hanover and, most audaciously, to Matthias Göring, a psychotherapist in Berlin and nephew of Hermann Göring. Ewald asked Matthias to pass the memorandum directly to his uncle, the Reischsmarschall who was Hitler's second-in-command. Not surprisingly, Ewald warned his wife that he might well end up in a concentration camp.[14]

Professor Ewald was an enthusiastic supporter of the National Socialists. He had tried in the 1930s to join the Nazi Party, but had been turned down because, as a soldier in World War I, he had lost a forearm. He was a disabled person and thus not acceptable as a party member—just as he was ineligible to join the army, the foreign service, to become a priest or minister, or even to apply for a Rhodes Scholarship.

It is of interest that another of the few physicians to oppose the killing was also a disabled person. A Dr. Kuhn had lost a leg by amputation.[15] As professionals, both of these men held privileged positions in German society. Nevertheless, as disabled persons, each had experienced the discriminatory practices commonly meted out to the disabled. And, as such, they had reason to understand more clearly the cruelty and injustice of what was being proposed for their fellow cripples.

Nothing ever came of Professor Ewald's memorandum. It changed nothing. But significantly, the memorandum had no adverse impact upon the career of the professor. He continued his practice in Göttingen. He was not forced to participate in the euthanasia program against his will; he was not removed from his post; neither was he reprimanded, nor was he sent to a concentration camp. This was, in fact, standard. In the very few cases where protest was made within a medical context and not through public channels, there was no punishment or retribution.

The following letter confirms the point that it was possible simply to walk away. Dr. F. Holzel had been offered a job on the killing staff of the children's staff at Eglfing-Haar. After much thought he decided he was just too soft for the job. He apologized for the weakness, but as he loved working with children he thought he would find it hard killing them. The director of the hospital simply initialed the letter as having been received and filed it. The job was given to someone else.

28 August 1940

Schwarasee bei Kitzbühel

Dear Herr Direktor:

The heavy rains during the first half of my vacation had the advantage of giving me sufficient leisure for reflection, and I am very grateful to you for your great kindness and consideration in giving me this time to make up my mind. The new measures are so convincing that I thought I could let personal considerations go by the board. But it is one thing to approve of measures of the state with full conviction, and something else to carry them out *oneself* in their full consequence. I am reminded of the difference which exists

183

between judge and executioner. Therefore, in spite of all intellectual insight and the goodwill on my part, I cannot escape the realization that according to my personal nature I am not suitable for this job. As vivid as my desire is in many cases to improve upon the natural course of events, it is repugnant to me to carry this out as a systematic job after cold-blooded deliberation and according to scientific objective principles, and not urged by medical feeling toward the patient. What has endeared the work in the children's house to me was not the scientific interest but the physician's urge, amid our often fruitless labor, to help and at least to improve many of our cases here. The psychological evaluation and the curative and pedagogic influence were always much closer to my heart than anatomical curiosities, no matter how interesting they were. And so it comes about that, although I am sure that I can preserve my full objectivity in giving expert opinions, I yet feel myself somehow tied emotionally to the children as their medical guardian, and I think that this emotional contact is not necessarily a weakness from the point of view of a National Socialist physician. However, it hinders me from combining this new duty with the ones I have hitherto carried out.

If this should force you to place the work in the children's house in other hands, it would certainly be a painful loss to me. However, I consider it more right to see clearly that I am too soft for this job, instead of disappointing you later.

I know that your offer to me is a sign of special confidence, and I cannot honor your confidence in any better way than by absolute honesty and openness.

Heil Hitler,

Your very devoted,

F. Holzel

After the war there were numerous assertions that the program had been opposed by one and all. As Muller-Hill has commented, everyone "discovered" that the acts of persecution in which they participated "had in fact been cleverly designed subterfuges to help the persecuted."[16] Ernst Ganzer, a male nurse at Ansbach since 1929, insisted, " . . . all of our doctors and the entire hospital personnel were firmly opposed to and condemned this action. . . ."[17] While this statement is untrue on its face, it must be said that many of the personnel seemed to have been troubled by what was going on. There were various reports of heavy drinking, fighting, and even violence among the professional members of the killing teams. One report to the Ministry of Justice read, "The staff employed on the work of liquidation at these institutions is obtained from other parts of the country and the local inhabitants will have nothing to do with them. These employees spend their evenings in the taverns, drinking heavily."[18]

In "The Emperor's New Clothes" the whole world goes along with a delusion until it is punctured by a small boy blurting out the truth. This shows how dangerous one person speaking truth can be. Something of the sort *may* have taken place at the Grafeneck euthanasia institution on June 4, 1940. What is clear is that the head nurse was shot dead in the hospital by the chief physician, Baumhardt.

There are several versions as to how this came about, but in any case it cannot be denied that the death took place in an extraordinary climate of violence in which doctors carried guns in the line of duty and routinely shot patients point-blank in order to "avoid the contamination" of their sickness. It is an extraordinary story.

In the summer of 1940, the newspapers of Berlin carried the following announcement, released by T-4:

On Tuesday June 4, 1940, while performing her duties
our very gifted and loyal coworker

Party member Anne H.—Head Nurse at the state
sanitorium of Grafeneck—died accidentally.

As an active National Socialist, charged
with a difficult assignment in a responsible
position, her achievements were unusual.

The Sanitorium Foundation

Funeral services will be held on Friday, June 14, 1940, at 2 P.M.,
New Cemetery, Minden/Westphalia.

Nurse Anne had been in Berlin for a few days' vacation at the end of May 1940. She had visited with her family and with former coworkers at the Berlin-Buch hospital. Her nurse friends wanted to know about her new job at Grafeneck. Their patients were being transported to Grafeneck, and they never came back. What was happening? The persistent questions visibly upset Nurse Anne. Agitated, she would only reply, "I can't bear it anymore, it is inhuman. I am under an oath of secrecy, I cannot talk about it. But I won't be able to deal with this psychologically."

Within the week she was shot dead by the head doctor at Grafeneck. Had she voiced her objections? Had she broken psychologically? No one knows.

No one seems to have been present at the scene of the crime. There were no eyewitnesses.

Typical was the testimony of a fellow nurse at Grafeneck: "I only saw her afterwards. She was already mortally wounded. She remained alive for maybe twenty to thirty minutes. My knowledge of the incident stems from conversations with others."

Otto Mauthe, an official of Württemberg who looked into the incident after the war, concluded, "Later on, as was printed in the *Völkische Beobachter*, a nurse died accidentally while performing her duties. When I questioned head doctor Dr. Baumhardt as to the facts of the incident he was very evasive in his response. Baumhardt told me, not very convincingly, that the nurse had gotten herself killed when she stepped into the line of fire of an SS guard who was attempting to shoot an escaping patient. I have to assume that this nurse was shot because she didn't want to participate anymore. Resistance would have been senseless, even stupid."

A different story was told by a woman employed at the institution to write the letters of condolence. This woman was engaged to be married to the physician who supposedly did the shooting.

It was the summer of 1940, July 4, to be exact. I was lying in bed with a concussion when a transport of patients arrived. Among the people was a patient with leprosy whose face had been partially eaten away, according to the nurses. Dr. Baumhardt killed him immediately with a handgun to avoid contamination of the nurses. Baumhardt had ordered everybody to stand still. But Nurse H. moved to the side anyway and was struck by the bullet. Dr. Baumhardt told this to me himself. He was very disturbed about the incident. He wanted to commit suicide.

The incident must have had a memorable impact upon the other arriving patients. It is a sign of the remarkable times in which she lived that this witness should consider the shooting of a patient with leprosy to be a reasonable explanation for the "accident." Her statement mentioning murder, accidental killing, and suicide in a single paragraph illustrates, as Amnon Amir has said, that death was indeed "in the air."

As it happens, the local justice of the peace was in the hospital at the time of the shooting. His postwar account stated:

In May or June of 1940 the head nurse, Anna H., was shot and killed by Dr. Baumhardt due to his negligence. I was in the office at the time and, after being alerted to the incident by a nurse, had to write down the testimonies of the witnesses. According to the statements of the witnesses and the interrogations of Dr. Baumhardt the following had transpired: An insane patient had gotten loose and was terrorizing the nurses and staff. Dr. Baumhardt drew his pistol and fired at the patient. The bullet passed through the patient and hit nurse H. in the chest. She had gotten herself into the line of fire while trying to escape from the patient. Dr. Baumhardt was subsequently charged with the murder of Nurse H. due to negligence on his part. The paperwork was sent to the prosecutor's office at Ulm.[19]

Nurse H. was buried, and the case against Baumhardt was dropped.

Incentives and Imperatives

Germany has always been famous for the quality of its medicine. Between 1901 and 1939, German scientists were awarded the Nobel Prize in Medicine eight times, far more than the scientists of any other nation. Many of the important advances in modern medical treatment and many of the major discoveries in drug therapy were made by German physicians working in German laboratories and hospitals.

The medical schools of modern Germany had a universally acknowledged reputation for excellence: "Their scientific achievement and intellectual probity were the envy of the world. Berlin, Heidelberg, Marburg, and Frankfurt were the Meccas of postgraduate studies for physicians and surgeons from all over the world."[20]

Physicians hold an important station in German society; they have always been treated with deference and respect. In the years preceding the rise of Hitler, these physicians displayed the expected values of their time and station: the majority were nationalist and conservative. As the daughter of the famous professor Dr. E. Fischer has said of her father, "He was a nationalist and a conservative, but they all were at that time: that's not a matter of politics."[21] Historian Michael Kater has said of the German physicians of the era that they had "a strong proclivity toward authoritarianism, promilitary leanings, a pronounced antifeminism, and, most importantly, anti-Semitism."[22]

The intensity of this militant patriotism can be felt in the so-called Manifesto of the Ninety-three. This was issued at the beginning of World War I, shortly after the Imperial German Army had overrun neutral Belgium. The world was appalled by the brutality of the German forces. In Louvain, for example, local officials had been shot, the city shelled, the ancient cathedral severely damaged, and the university library burned to the ground.

In their manifesto, the leading physicians and scientists of Imperial Germany declared, "We strictly refuse to pay the price of a German defeat just to preserve artistic or cultural objects. Without German militarism, German culture would have been wiped out. The German army and the German people are one and the same. This we guarantee with our names and our word of honor." The signers included such world-renowned men as Planck, Roentgen, and von Wassermann.[23]

It was not easy to become a doctor. Medical school admission standards were extremely high and completely objective. The education was arduous. It took ten years of training and supervision before a student could begin a practice on his own. The certifying boards were operated under the supervision of the ministries of health and education in an impartial and scrupulous manner. Admission to the medical profession in Germany was on the basis of ability—without discrimination. As an illustration of this, it may be noted that 13 percent of the 50,000 physicians in Germany in 1933 were Jewish; fully 60 percent of the physicians of Berlin and 67 percent of the physicians of Vienna were Jewish. (These are Nazi figures and hence perhaps suspect. They are, nevertheless, indicative—despite widespread anti-Semitism—of the openness of the medical profession before the Nazi takeover.[24]

The German Medical Association, founded in 1871, served as a national organization and clearinghouse for the numerous local medical societies. Also, there were separate associations for the various medical specialties as well as an organization known as the Hartmann Bund, which supervised various administrative and financial aspects of the profession. Since 1881, in Bismarck's era, Germany has had compulsory health insurance for all employees, and the Bund handled collective bargaining on behalf of the physicians in their negotiations with the health insurance companies.

A significant portion of physicians' income was in the form of payments from the health insurance companies. The level of payment for various medical services was determined by negotiations. However, the standards for the operation of this government-mandated health program were determined, of course, by the government and the Reichstag. Professors at the medical schools and scientists at work in the laboratories of these schools were civil servants and, as such, paid by the government. As the result of this century-old arrangement—which gives the government an extraordinary say over the income of the medical profession—the physicians of Germany have more closely participated in the making of policy and have lobbied for their interests with government authorities longer and more extensively than have the physicians of most other countries.

The eminent position of the physicians in the social system of Germany and the extreme gravity with which they presented their views on policy served to make the physicians influential and effective lobbyists. By 1933, at the accession of Hitler, the physicians of Germany were a politically sophisticated interest group.

The Nazi revolution was not only fought in the streets. Battles for control were waged across the whole spectrum of German society— in the schools, the churches, and the professions. In medicine the supremacy of the German Medical Association was challenged by the militant National Socialist German Physicians' League. This group of bully-boy doctors warred with the Socialist League of Doctors, shouted down speakers, broke up meetings, and generally denounced established medical traditions.

They certainly did not behave anything like traditional physicians. To the astonishment of the medical community in other countries, they behaved more like members of some Hell's Angels gang, without the motorcycles. For example, on what was called "Boycott Day" in Berlin on April 1, 1933, members of the German Physicians' League in the early hours of the morning broke into the apartments and homes of Jewish and socialist doctors. They were dragged from their beds, beaten, and then hauled off to an area near the Berlin Lehrter. There, stripped of their clothes, they were forced to run laps about the track as they were subjected to hazing, pistol shots, and beatings with sticks. Many of them were then taken to the cellars of the Hedemannstrasse jail, where they were tortured further before being released.

The Nazi doctors called for a new medicine: "The ill-conceived 'love thy neighbor' has to disappear, especially in relation to inferior or asocial creatures. It is the supreme duty of a national state to grant life and livelihood only to the healthy and hereditarily sound portion of the people in order to secure the maintenance of the hereditarily sound and racially pure folk for all eternity. The life of an individual has meaning only in the light of that ultimate aim, that is, in the light of his meaning to his family and to his national state."[25]

These sentiments were often cloaked with references to the great history of German medical science, to such eminent figures as Hufeland, Correns, even Paracelsus. Lip service was paid to the Hippocratic tradition, but a reasonably intelligent child would have perceived the difference between the medicine of Hippocrates and the medicine of Hitler.

If the German medical establishment was so conservative and well-placed, how could it be that they would embrace a program so alien to the traditions of German medicine? How could they, why should they, stomach such tactics, such trash?

They were desperate. The years of the Weimar Republic had been hard ones for the physicians—as, indeed, they had for all Germans. These years had been times of literal starvation, staggering inflation, social turmoil, and then economic collapse. From 1929 through 1932, the German economy was brutalized by the worldwide Great Depression; the nation's gross national product had fallen 40 percent. For years the medical schools had been producing far more doctors than there were positions available to be filled. As a result, doctors' incomes fell sharply—from an average 13,200 RM in 1927 down to 9,600 RM in 1932. Many doctors found it hard to get work, and some were even said to face starvation.[26]

With the rise of Hitler and the National Socialist state, all this changed.

In the Third Reich, the authority and prestige of the doctors—already great—became greater. In fact, the Nazi administration was as close as the world has come to being a medical state: a government run in accordance with "doctor's orders." To the extend that Nazism can be said to have had a political philosophy or principle, it was based upon the application of Social Darwinist concepts as propounded by the doctors and biologists of Germany. For as Hitler, the great doctor of the people, had proclaimed, his government was to be "the final step in the overcoming of historicism and the recognition of purely biological values." National Socialism, said one party official in 1934, was to be "applied biology." Nazism would be "applied racial science," said Rudolf Hess.[27]

The Nazis saw it as their purpose to strengthen public health—to improve the strength, vitality, and health of the German *Volk*, and to purify it of "corrupting" racial elements. For the Nazis, "racial hygiene," the application of their ideas of racial superiority, was a part of public health care. And by making race a matter of public health, as Proctor has pointed out, they, in effect, "medicalized" the prevalent social prejudices of the day: anti-Semitism, bigotry directed against Gypsies and "asocials," hostility toward the disabled.[28]

The Nazis set up new schools of public health. Institutes for racial hygiene and public health clinics were established and the number of persons employed in public health–related activities was greatly increased. Organized nationwide propaganda campaigns were designed to educate the public on the benefits of nutritious food, exercise, fresh air, and adequate rest. The merits of fresh vegetables, whole grain, and unadulterated foods were advertised, and there were campaigns against tobacco and alcohol use. The government imposed stiff fines for driving while intoxicated, and the first large-scale testing of blood for alcohol levels was undertaken. Germany instituted mass X-ray testing for the early detection of tuberculosis, dental care programs in the schools, and nationwide physical exams for schoolchildren at ages six, ten, fourteen, and eighteen. The Third Reich campaigned for the "return" of the family doctor and the reinstitution of house calls. The Nazis also, of course, mandated the sterilization program which caused the hospitalization of 300,000–400,000 citizens for this not inconsiderable surgical operation.

The sterilization law—the "Law for the Prevention of Genetically Impaired Progeny"—was remarkable, not only in its operation but in its organization. As originally planned, there were to be 1,700 Tribunals of Hereditary Health and appeals courts, operating at an estimated annual cost of 12 million RM.[29] Although this scale of operation was never obtained, the sterilization program was of major size.

Probably for the first time anywhere, physicians were impaneled as *judges* in what amounted to a nationwide medical court system. Each tribunal consisted of a lawyer and two physicians—one local and the other a genetic specialist. Proceedings were secret. The person being considered for sterilization often was not informed until the tribunal was actually in session. He had no right to inspect the evidence presented, and a request for legal representation could be denied by the tribunal without explanation.[30] Decisions of the tribunal could be appealed, but the overwhelming number of decisions appealed were affirmed by the appellate court. The tribunal case records were—and remain—confidential.

The "health in marriage" law of 1935 specified that before a couple could receive a marriage license they had to present a certificate from a physician stating that they had passed a genetic health exam and were fit to marry.

These two laws gave the doctors of Germany extraordinary power over the lives of their healthy, law-abiding fellow citizens. This was a power quite beyond the traditional definition of a physician as a man practiced in the art of healing. It is not healing to sterilize a person against his will—it is, in fact, harmful. This is a violation of the Hippocratic Oath.

Whatever benefits all these programs may have brought to the German people, they certainly served to benefit the medical profession. Physicals, X-rays, operations—these are medical services which are performed by doctors, for which doctors must be paid. All this new activity meant a rapid rise of income for the average physician during the Nazi years: in 1933, his average taxable income was 9,280 RM; by 1938 it had risen to 14,940 RM.[31]

The Nazi government severely restricted the number of places in the medical schools; and as a result, by 1935 the number of new physicians entering the marketplace each year had been reduced by half.[32] In addition, the government proceeded with its despicable policy of driving Jewish physicians out of practice. By the end of the decade, a government official was able proudly to proclaim, "Today, no man of German blood is treated by a Jewish doctor."[33] This relieved, in a dramatic fashion, the glut of doctors which had so depressed income and opportunity in the days of the Weimar Republic.

Thus, under the Nazi regime, the non-Jewish physicians of Germany found a greatly increased demand for their services, an end to the overcrowding in their field with a greatly improved opportunity for advancement, and, of course, a significant increase in their income.

So far as the physicians were concerned, it was the dawn of a new day. The policies which they had endorsed were now the policies of the nation. The whole country was health-conscious. Major figures in the administration were themselves doctors, and doctors received major university appointments from the administration. Leading medical scientists and professors were appointed to various boards and commissions; their views were sought, and in numerous situations their recommendations were accepted and acted upon. And, of course, physicians were newly rich and getting richer.

While it may be reprehensible, it is surely not surprising that no profession in Germany was more enthusiastic in its support of Hitler and the Nazis than were the doctors.

Motivation

Physicians had an economic interest in the Nazi movement. Many endorsed the Nazi racial theories. This does not, however, explain how the doctors of Germany came to participate in a program designed to kill their patients.

As has been shown, this program was designed by physicians. In all but a very few cases, the killing was done by physicians. They were not ordered to participate; they did so on a voluntary basis.

Karl Brandt, Hitler's personal physician, the man entrusted by the Führer with the responsibility for instituting the deadly procedures, insisted upon the point repeatedly.

> Each doctor took personal responsibility for what he had to do within the framework of these measures, which culminated finally in euthanasia. The individual doctor took full responsibility for his judgments as assessor, as the surveyor did in his. Doctors at both the observation and the euthanasia centers also assumed full responsibility for their actions. In no circumstances is it to be understood that any doctor serving under this scheme was ever obliged to perform euthanasia in a case where he himself had not decided it was necessary. On the contrary, it was his duty, if he did not agree with any such decision, to decline altogether to perform the operation. [34]

This was asserted many times in other persons' testimonies. In 1964 at the aborted war crimes trial of euthanasia bureaucrat Hans Hefelmann, he confirmed, "No doctor was ever ordered to participate in the euthanasia program; they came of their own volition." [35]

This program was not imposed by the Nazis, although their authorities assisted in its implementation. Himmler, Reichsführer of the SS and the Gestapo and director of the concentration camps, had made the distinction quite clear in his letter to Judge Buch. "What happens in the place in question [a psychiatric hospital] is carried out by a commission of physicians. . . . The SS furnish only help in vehicles, cars, etc. The medical specialist, expert and responsible, is the one who gives the orders."[36]

Of course, the government knew what was happening and did all it could to lift the restraints and the punishments which hitherto had hindered such happenings; but, nevertheless, within the hospitals patients were going to their deaths because their doctors prescribed death therapy in precisely the same manner they prescribed any other therapy. They were functioning in their professional capacity as physicians; and they became for the Nazi state, in the words of Leo Alexander, "the unofficial executioners, for the sake of convenience, in formality and relative secrecy."[37]

The killing of ordinary patients, as performed by ordinary physicians, was done—where else?—in hospitals and sanitoriums. As the pace of the program accelerated and many thousands were put to death each month, special killing centers were established. These centers, however, were in medical surroundings, often a wing of an already-established hospital. The Eglfing-Haar institution had a pediatric unit—the Kinderhaus—for chronic and long-term patients. The killing—four or five children a week—was done there in a small room especially set aside for the purpose. The nurse, whose duty it was to keep the equipment and drugs on hand and who assisted the attending physician during the "therapy" itself, kept a potted geranium in the window of the sunny room so that it might be bright and cheerful.

How can such behavior be explained? Really, it cannot be. Certain aspects of an explanation can be advanced, however. These aspects are certainly part of the whole—but only part of the reason the physicians of Germany turned to killing their patients.

No doubt there were pathological killers at work in the program. As in the Holocaust there were persons who took perverse, sadistic joy in murdering their innocent brothers and sisters; alas, such mad dogs, of whatever race or nation, are let loose in war unfettered by the ordinary restraints of peacetime society: this is a pestilence of war. Such persons are horrid, but they are not surprising.

Nor are they the ones for whom explanations must be sought. The patient-killing program was the work of the medical profession of Germany: doctors, psychiatrists, professors, scientists, nurses, and technicians. These were not psychotic killers, nor were they all

195

members of the Nazi Party. They were distinguished practitioners, many of them with worldwide reputations in their fields.

Here, selected at random, is a list of some of these participants:

Professor Dr. Paul Nitsche—director of various state hospitals, author of books and articles on prison psychoses, ranking medical man at Aktion T-4 headquarters. Tried for murder, convicted, and executed in Dresden, 1947.

Professor Dr. Hermann Voss—before the war, professor of anatomy at the University of Leipzig; in 1941 became professor of anatomy and director of anatomical research at the University of Posen. After the war, served at the University of Jena. During the war, with his assistant Dr. R. Herrlinger, conducted research at Posen Gestapo headquarters on spleens removed at the guillotine. Research results were published in 1947, 1948, 1949, and 1950. The two men published a major anatomy textbook in 1946. It is still in use. In 1956, Professor Voss was given the honorary title of "Excellent Scientist of the Nation" for furthering the development of science in the service of peace.

Professor Doctor Werner Catel—pediatrician, head of the children's clinic at the University of Leipzig, 1938–39. Was principal medical expert for the Nazi Children's Program. After the war became professor of pediatrics at the University of Kiel, 1954–60. Author of books and articles, including a textbook for pediatric nurses and *Borderline Situations of Life*, published in 1962, advocating infant euthanasia.

Dr. Klaus Endruweit—under the pseudonym Dr. Bader, was physician at Sonnenstein where 13,270 disabled people were killed over a fourteen-month period in 1940–41. Since 1946 has practiced medicine at Bettrum. Member of the Medical Board of Registration, Hildesheim district, 1955–57 and 1962–65. Member board of the Medical Insurance Union, district Hildesheim, 1956–64.

Professor Julius Hallervorden—department head, Brain Research, Kaiser Wilhelm Institute, 1938; department head, Max Planck Institute of Brain Research, after 1948. Hallervorden-Spatz disease is named in honor of Dr. Hallervorden. He used more than six hundred brains of euthanasia victims in his research.

Dr. Max de Crinis—professor of psychiatry, University of Berlin, and director, Psychiatric Department, Charity Hospital;

author of books and articles, including a respected study of somatic origins of emotions. Killed himself in 1945.

Professor Dr. Werner Villinger—during the war was professor of psychiatry, University of Breslau; member, Aktion T-4 team of experts; formerly at Tübingen and Bethel; professor at University of Marburg, 1946–56; participant in the 1950 White House Conference on Children and Youth. Committed suicide to avoid trial.

Professor Karl Schneider—professor of psychiatry at Heidelberg; chief of Race Policy Bureau, Heidelberg; active member of Aktion T-4 expert team; director of physicians at Bethel; author of respected books and articles on mental illness, particularly schizophrenia. His text *The Psychology of Schizophrenia* is still referred to. Committed suicide to avoid trial.

Dr. Werner Heyde—professor of psychiatry and director of clinic at University of Würzburg; major participant in Aktion T-4 killing program. After the war he practiced for twelve years as a "Dr. Sawade." Served as expert witness in numerous trials. His identity was widely known and protected by the medical community. After his apprehension, his trial was repeatedly postponed for four years. He committed suicide in his cell. [38]

There were many more such men. They had held their posts for years before the Nazis came to power, and a good number of them held their positions for years after the fall of the Nazis. They were the writers of textbooks still used, the authors of articles and research still of importance. These doctors and nurses trained in one of the oldest, finest traditions of humane medicine. They had taken the Hippocratic Oath to respect only the rights of the patients and none other—not the state nor their own—as they administered their therapy, and to do no harm. These doctors and nurses for years before and after the Nazi nightmare tended their patients with compassion and concern. During the nightmare, they killed them.

These doctors and nurses were the same persons before, during, and after the Nazis; and yet their behavior toward their patients was radically altered. What caused this change of behavior?

Here are some suggestions:

Fear. Nazi Germany ran on fear, every level of fear. The doctor, confronted with a situation in which his patients were taken from him and sent away to be gassed, was too frightened to object. He was afraid if he did object he would lose his job. He was afraid he would lose face in his profession, perhaps even be expelled from his profession. He feared he might lose his liberty, be sent to a concentration camp as a "person lacking understanding," or lose his life. All these fears were rational and possible.

Ostracism. All the physicians participated in the program. Virtually none of them objected to it. If everyone agrees that black is white, who am I to say otherwise, even though I know it to be untrue? I doubt myself: Perhaps I am color-blind; perhaps my knowledge of what constitutes white is flawed; perhaps my definition of black is in error. Perhaps I should be quiet about this in order to avoid being laughed at, ignored, or worse. In a society of discipline and order such as Germany, the threat of ostracism by one's peers is a powerful weapon. In a profession as status-conscious as medicine, ostracism was, as it remains, a very powerful threat indeed.

Blood—"Blutkitt" (blood cement). This was a technique that Hitler was said to have consciously borrowed from Genghis Khan. It was most evident in the SS, but the principle applied throughout German society of the 1930s. Dr. Leo Alexander believed the principle could be used to explain the behavior of the physicians.[39] Under *Blutkitt*, loyalty is tested and proven by the commission of a crime that is contrary to one's own moral code or interest, but is said to be in the service of a greater cause. As these crimes were repeatedly performed, the person, perforce, came to believe he was performing extraordinary service to the cause. This bound him closely to the movement, for— should he break away—he had to face the fact that he had violated his own values and self-interest. With the party he was everything; without it he was less than nothing, for he had destroyed his self-esteem. This is a powerful technique, as effective in a medical setting as it was in the concentration camps with the infamous SS.

Chicken. There was, among the German physicians of the day, a kind of "chicken" game being practiced, based upon a fear of ostracism and the technique of *Blutkitt*. The physician wanted to appear as strong to his confreres as he was loyal to the state. Over and over he was told how difficult it is to build a new society. Painful things must be done, sacrifices made, suffering endured to obtain the New Order. This sadomasochistic view of man's state and human progress was central to the Nazi message. Are you strong enough, man enough? It takes a superman to build the super race. The physicians proved their manhood by murdering their patients. Those who refused to participate were considered weak, unreliable by their peers, and—given the climate of the times—often by themselves. When Dr. F. Holzel declined an offer to operate the children's division of Eglfing-Haar, he apologized that he was "too soft" for the job, that his "temperament was not suited to the task."[40]

The psychological relationship between a physician and his chronic patients is a difficult one. Part of the effectiveness of the physician is that he believes in his own abilities to cure disease, to alleviate suffering—as a sorcerer believes in his magic, a medicine man believes in his medicine. Medicine is a science, but it is also an art; and it is not mumbo jumbo to say that both doctor and patient must believe in the power of the doctor. The chronic patient challenges this belief. The doctor uses all his therapies, but the condition remains; the patient does not improve. The patient continues in need of relief, and the doctor is rendered helpless, impotent. This state of antagonistic symbiosis is present—if only in degree—in all physician–chronic patient encounters. Examples abound: At the end of the nineteenth century the fledgling specialty of orthopedic medicine was unable to do much to relieve its paralyzed and deformed patients. Nevertheless—or perhaps because of this frustration—it prescribed an array of bizarre braces, casts, and confining devices, hideous and torturous, with which to torment what it could not cure. In modern times psychiatrists, unable to assist their chronically agitated patients, sought to calm them with a surgical technique in which a common ice pick was stuck through and behind the eye socket into the front lobe of the brain where it was wiggled back and forth in a random effort to destroy the offending brain cells. The man who invented the technique received a Nobel Prize for his work. This widespread practice was without supporting medical evidence, and it was for a time routinely performed by psychiatrists without surgical training. Whatever else such examples may illustrate, they demonstrate the problem the chronic patient presents his physician.

What the Nazis did in Third Reich Germany was to remove the

restraints upon the physician which are normally present in the patient-doctor relationship. The physician swears in the Hippocratic Oath to think only of the benefit of the sick, commonly thought of as "do no harm." The laws of liability and the injunction against murder serve along with the Hippocratic tradition to protect the interests of the vulnerable patient in his transactions with his doctor. As has been shown, the Nazis did not direct their physicians to kill but instead lifted the sanctions against such behavior—and they did so in the name of science. The age-old taboos were gone. The physician in the service of science and the new order could act out his inner hostility, could eliminate his frustrations—his patient. This authorization of license in the service of science proved irresistible.

The physician involved in this equation is, of course, not just a professional. He is also a human being, frail and mortal. Whatever support he may receive from his belief in the *Volk* or from the more usual promises and rewards of the traditional religions, he remains—like all men—frightened of his own helplessness, decrepitude, and death. The physically disabled and the mentally deranged are living reminders of this fear, and this reminder often generates hostility. Illustrations of this hostility toward the disabled are legion throughout history. In different ways and different places, the impaired have been ostracized, imprisoned, starved, tortured, and jeered at.

Physicians, rather more than ordinary men, are particularly sensitive, vulnerable to feelings of fear and hostility in the face of disease and disability. They alone among the professions have pledged themselves to a lifelong struggle against such adversities. They are *at war* with all that makes man frail and mortal. This war is the centerpiece of their professional lives. Others may come to some sort of terms with disease and death; but to the person who has chosen to be a physician, they must always be the enemy. And the fact is that death and disease are personified by the chronically disabled: they are the very symbol, the metaphor of what the person who is a physician most fears as a person. And as the Greeks killed the messenger with bad news, it is not surprising to find what the physicians of Germany did when the restraints were lifted.

Two things here are of great importance:

First, the euthanasia program was carried out under the cover of secrecy. Various reasons were advanced for this: to skirt the objections of the churches, to avoid the complaints of the International Red Cross and the propaganda charges of Germany's enemies, so as not to trouble the families of the victims or to alarm the intended victims. All these reasons were no doubt valid in their fashion. The key reason for secrecy was more basic. In a letter discussing the pros and cons of extending the "special treatment" of the euthanasia program to the tubercular patients of Poland, a Dr. Karl Blome argued, "If absolute secrecy could be guaranteed, all scruples—regardless of their nature—could be overcome."[41] Man will do in secret what he will not do in public. He will break the taboos, overcome his scruples. The triggering mechanism of the debaucheries of the Hell Fire club of the eighteenth century, child prostitution in Victorian England, the Ku Klux Klan in the American South, hazing in the initiation rites of college fraternities—the sine qua non of such activities is, at the start, the promise of secrecy. A mother will tell her child not to play with excrement—nor will he, until he gets the chance. And so it was with the physicians of Germany.

Second, the euthanasia program was carried out in the name of science. The physicians and the medical professors constantly assured each other and themselves that what they were doing was in the cause of the advancement of science, a refinement of the great traditions of medicine, and in the interests of their patients. These men sought to "radicalize therapeutic activity." They were after new "active therapy" that would *do* something, produce results. In the thirties they were enthusiastic participants in "hereditary biological stock-taking." They found their pursuit of scientific efficiency continually thwarted by "refractory therapy cases" and it is not hard to understand their interest in what they spoke of as "negative population policy."[42] These psychiatrists spoke to one another of the killings as the "further development of psychiatry"[43] even as they worked out extraordinarily complex logistics for transporting the tens of thousands of helpless and infirm persons to the euthanasia centers.

They congratulated each other on breaking loose from the foolish and unscientific sentiments of the past which had served to weaken the family of man. Dr. Ernst Rüdin, professor of psychiatry at the universities of Munich and Basel, warned his colleagues to guard against the "excessive compassion and love of one's neighbor characteristic of past centuries."[44] The physicians sought new "active therapies," efficient and scientific, commensurate with the new Germany. They dismissed in the name of science the precepts of the past. As Dr. Brandt explained with conviction at Nuremberg, "I am convinced that if Hippocrates were alive today he would change the wording of his oath . . . this prohibition as formulated by Hippocrates [explained by Brandt as forbidding "a physician to administer poison to an invalid even upon demand"] can assuredly no longer be regarded as valid in view of modern advances in diagnosis and prognosis and our present recognition of the limitations of therapy."[45]

All was science and, of course, the *authority* of science. There could be no doubt of their behavior. They were *scientists*, and what they did *was* science. And what they did was endorsed by the most eminent scientists of Germany. Consider the director of the Hadamar center, who had presided over the cocktail party in commemoration of the killing of their ten-thousandth patient. He testified, after the war, "I was of course torn this way and that. It reassured me to learn what eminent scientists partook in the action: Professor Karl Schneider, Professor Heyde, Professor Nitsche."[46] Another begged off, "I was always told that the responsibility lies with the professors from Berlin." A third witness, Dr. Fritz Mennecke, who came to serve as director of an observation center where "those not worthy to live" were sorted out from those "worthy to be helped,"[47] told the Nuremberg court how he was brought to the program. He and ten or twelve other physicians attended a meeting in Berlin in February 1940. The program was explained and "we were asked if we would be willing to act as assessors. . . . The other doctors present were all elderly people, including, as I afterwards learnt, some of high reputation. As they all unhesitatingly agreed to participate, I followed their example and offered to act as an assessor."[48] Brandt comforted himself with the assurance, with the same assurance passed back and forth within the medical profession: "Were not the regular professors of the universities with the program? Who could be better qualified than they?"[49]

And so it went. This was a scientific program, this had to be a scientific program. For if it was not a scientific program, then just what sort of program was it?

These men were arrogant. They had the authority—and they believed their position gave them the right—to implement these theories upon their fellows, whether or not objection was raised.

These men had no respect for the diversity of humankind; rather, they sought conformity: conformity with their own concepts of a society modeled upon themselves. They saw themselves as the very culmination of the evolution of man, and they sought to "perfect" German society by eliminating those who did not conform to their concept of what was acceptable.

These were arrogant men, who sought perfection—a fool's game and a dangerous business.

Dr. Leo Alexander was one of the U.S. Army physicians who investigated the Aktion T-4 euthanasia program for authorities at the Nuremberg trials. In 1949 he wrote a thoughtful article in the *New England Journal of Medicine* concerning what he had learned in his investigation. "The lesson of the T-4 euthanasia program," wrote Dr. Alexander, "applies not just to Germany but to modern medicine." He discussed this lesson within the context of what he called "the situation in the United States." Dr. Alexander's warning was important when he wrote. Forty years later, it is even more important.

Physicians have come dangerously close to being mere technicians of rehabilitation. This . . . attitude has led them to make certain distinctions in the handling of acute and chronic diseases. The patient with the latter carries an obvious stigma as the one less likely to be able to be fully rehabilitated for social usefulness. In an increasingly utilitarian society these patients are being looked down upon with increasing definiteness as unwanted ballast. A certain amount of rather open contempt for the people who cannot be rehabilitated with present knowledge has developed. This is probably due to a good deal of unconscious hostility, because these people for whom there seem to be no effective remedies have become a threat to newly acquired delusions of omnipotence.

Hospitals like to limit themselves to the care of patients who can be fully rehabilitated, and the patient whose full rehabilitation is unlikely finds himself, at least in the best and most advanced centers of healing, as a second-class patient faced with a reluctance on the part of both the visiting and the house staff to suggest and apply therapeutic procedures that are not likely to bring about immediately striking results in terms of recovery. . . . From the attitude of easing patients with chronic diseases away from the doors of the best types of treatment facilities available to the actual dispatching of such patients to killing centers is a long but, nevertheless, logical step.[50]

10

Aktion T-4 and the Lawyers

I would rather commit an injustice than endure disorder.

Goethe

Old Germans today reminisce that, say what you will, in the Third Reich one could leave a bicycle unlocked without fear of having it stolen, and long-haired hippies did not wander the streets—they were locked up. [1] Such thoughts reflect something of the respect the German people have for social order, even now, after all that it has cost them in the past.

The cost of social order during the Nazi years was measured in terror—terror institutionalized as an instrument of public policy; and the German courts and jurisprudence system, along with everyone else, were induced to accept it as such. This terror at first was applied to what Peukert has called "community aliens," that is, those groups who were said to be the cause of social problems. These included alcoholics, the homeless, the disabled, thieves, Gypsies, and, most famously, the Jews. These persons—separated from the social norm, either by their nonstandard behavior or simply their nonstandard category—were systematically subjected to terror. They were blamed, and they were persecuted for the social problems they were thought to cause or represent. Of course, as the ills of society failed to disappear, official frustration mounted and the persecution and terrorism increased. [2]

This use of terror was not secret. It was known, talked about, and generally approved of. Nazi officials proclaimed its use, and church leaders did not object. Friedrich Dibelius, the general superintendent of the Protestant Church in Brandenburg, said in a 1933 sermon delivered in the presence of Hitler and Hindenburg:

205

A new beginning in the history of the state is always marked, in one way or another, by the use of force. For the state *is* power. . . . the power of the state must be employed effectively and with vigor whether internally or externally. . . .

If the state carries out its duties against those who undermine the foundations of state order—against those, in particular, whose coarse and corrosive words destroy marriage, expose faith to contempt, and slander those who lay down their lives for the fatherland—then let the state carry out its duties, in God's name![3]

It was *popular* to lock up Gypsies, homosexuals, and "professional" criminals.[4] After the turmoil of the Weimar years this is not surprising. In the 1960s in the United States, when the middle-class establishment felt threatened by change and various social pressures, there was a similar widespread support for arresting and locking up the long-haired, the foul-mouthed, and the "troublemakers"—the deviants from the social norm, the community aliens. Of course, by and large, over time, the Bill of Rights kept this from happening.

The German legal system is old and honored. Based upon the Mosaic, Judaic, and Roman legal codes, it has for generations guaranteed to the German people a fair and ordered society. German law did not contain the guarantees of personal liberties of thought, word, and behavior embodied in the American Bill of Rights, but it did provide for the sanctity of person and property. During the Second Reich, under the Kaisers, the very sovereign himself was subject to the law. Not only did he enforce, he obeyed the law. The Reich was called—and proudly so—by its citizens, a *Rechtsstaat*—a state of law.

The *Rechtsstaat* was conservative but trustworthy. Judges were men of high dignity who were treated with great respect. The legal system was largely independent of political pressure and highly esteemed by the populace. During the days of the Weimar Republic, judges were protected from arbitrary removal, and their independence was subject only to the law. The judiciary was extraordinarily conservative in political terms; and in the chaotic years preceding Hitler's accession, with German society sustaining violent attacks from both extreme right and left, the courts aligned themselves in the public eye with the right. In several celebrated cases the courts dealt harshly with violence of the left and appeared to condone the violence of the right.

It is perhaps not surprising that, once in power, the Nazi revolution debauched German jurisprudence as easily and as quickly as it destroyed the honor of German medicine. This is a tribute to the effectiveness of Hitler's masterful combination of "terror and seduction."[5] It is also a reflection of the fragile nature of the German legal system. When a doctor works he is dealing with something "real"—a cancer, a broken bone, a common cold. Whatever perversions of medicine took place in the Third Reich, most physicians, most of their working time, continued to treat patients for their ills according to the principles of their profession. Lawyers were different: lawyers do not deal directly with the "real" in the sense that doctors do. They operate at an abstract level, one step away from the real. Courts are man-created, and so are laws and legal procedures and precedents. When the Nazis poisoned the legal system, the poison polluted every judge and attorney participating in the system. Under the Nazis, the law (or the absence of law) was itself perverse, and all who sought to uphold the law were perverted.

Hitler came to power January 30, 1933, as the legal head of a coalition government. On February 27, 1933, the day after the dramatic and suspicious burning of the Reichstag, Hitler induced President Hindenburg to issue an emergency decree—as allowed by law—"for the protection of the people and the state." This decree effectively abolished individual freedom in Germany: "Restrictions on personal liberty, on the right of free expression of opinion, including freedom of the press; on rights of assembly and association . . . are also permissible beyond the legal limits."[6] The emergency decree continued in effect throughout the life of the Third Reich.

By March of the same year, the Reichstag had approved and Hindenburg signed into law the Ermächtigungsgesetz, the Enabling Act. This act gave Hitler and his cabinet the authority to legislate by proclamation, without the approval of the Reichstag, and the authority to "deviate from the constitution" at will.

Thus, within sixty days of taking power, Hitler had obtained, by legal means, full dictatorial and supraconstitutional authority—

"what Bismarck, Wilhelm II, and the Weimar Republic had never dared to attempt."[7]

The Enabling Act granted great power to the dictator, but it imposed various procedural steps upon his lawmaking—or breaking. For instance, laws had to be published in a journal available to the public before coming into effect. Secret law was supposed to be null and void. Even these restraints were swept aside by the act of April 26, 1942, in which the Reichstag voted unanimously to give Hitler absolute authority of life and death over every citizen of Germany.

This progress toward absolute power was important to the deliberations in the war crimes trials of medical personnel after World War II. In these trials prosecutors and defendants agreed that Hitler had authorized the murder of innocent patients in 1939; and he had done so in an order typed on his personal stationery. The order was secret and never published. Did the existence of this secret order mean the doctors were acting legally when they killed their patients? Did Hitler's ruling have the force of law? If not, then did the 1942 act with its absolute power make the force-of-law question irrelevant? If so, then the question "Did the doctors kill before or after April 26, 1942?" became a matter of importance. In the end this issue fell before the argument, which the judges of Nuremberg found to be persuasive above all others, that the killing of the chronically ill was murder; and murder, whether by definition or by recourse to a higher ethical or natural law, cannot *ever* be legal.

The Nazis institutionalized terror. Dissatisfied with the existing court system, they set up and operated a parallel system known as people's courts. These had the authority to try citizens for treason. They functioned in camera, using a sort of court-martial procedure. They had the authority to sentence the convicted to torture, death, or the concentration camps. The people's courts were hated and feared.

The Nazis' disdain for precedent and the traditional court system of law was clear and never hidden. Speaking to the Academy of German Law on October 11, 1936, Gestapo head Heinrich Himmler boasted, "It makes no difference to me whether the letter of the law says I can or cannot do something."[8] Hans Frank, speaking before the same body in November 1939, made the point: "We are proud of having formulated our legal principle [which consists of] the maxim—that which serves the Nation is right, and that which harms it is wrong."[9]

Here, again, as in so many other areas, the Nazis did things without any fine regard as to whether they had the authority to do them. They ruled on the basis of what in their own terms they considered to be good for the country; in many cases they simply ignored existing law, and they did what they wanted.

The Nazis left the routine enforcement of the routine laws to the established courts and worked their will on the side. This caused enormous legal confusion. German legal scholar Albrecht Wagner has called it "a confusing jumble." There was, he said, "a hardly discernible mass of legality, seeming legality and lawless injustice."[10] This was of immense frustration to the order-loving conservative members of the legal profession. The lawyers and jurists were but one more Third Reich group in that state of "permanent frustration" identified by Hannah Arendt.[11]

Whether or not Hitler's directive was seen as legal after the war, the directive to the physicians was carried out with enthusiasm; and it caused all sorts of chaos in the legal system. The courts were caught in a macabre situation.

Amazing things began to happen. Defendants in court cases would be sent to psychiatric hospitals for evaluation and simply disappear. Lawyers would have their clients vanish without a trace. The sad case of Karl Stieberitz is typical: He was committed to an institution in 1938, at the age of twenty-eight. A court ordered his release on appeal June 1, 1940, but by then he had been killed. Ernst Schmiedel, a laborer, was convicted of indecent assault at the age of forty in 1937. He was imprisoned for a year and four months, with a five-year loss of civil rights. Released from prison, Schmiedel was ordered castrated and committed to a sanitorium. According to court documents, Schmiedel was of "entirely sound mind"; nevertheless, he was killed in 1940 under the euthanasia program without the knowledge of the court which had committed him.[12]

An in-house memorandum of the Ministry of Justice details some of the problems: "The courts are unable to protect their wards, probate is confused; court proceedings, even trial, retrials, and appeals have proceeded, even though the subject has already died.

Relatives go to court and file murder charges against defendant doctors."[13]

A particularly graphic account of the effect the wanton killing of chronically ill citizens was having in the communities at large is found in an official communication from the Frankfurt am Main Provincial Court of Appeal addressed to the minister of justice:

> People living near sanitoriums and convalescent homes, as well as in adjoining regions, sometimes quite distant, for example throughout the Rhineland, are continually discussing the question of whether the lives of incurable invalids should be brought to an end. The vans which take patients from the institutions they occupy to transit stations and thence to liquidation establishments are well-known to the population. I am told that whenever they pass the children call out: "There they go again for gassing." I hear that from one to three big omnibuses with blinds down go through Limburg every day on their way from Weilmunster to Hadamar, taking inmates to the Hadamar liquidation center. The story goes that as soon as they arrive they are stripped naked, given a paper shirt and immediately taken to a gas chamber, where they are poisoned with prussic acid and an auxiliary narcotic. The corpses are said to be transferred on a conveyor belt to an incineration chamber, where six are put into one furnace and the ashes then packed into six urns and sent to relatives. The thick smoke of the incinerators is supposed to be visible every day over Hadamar. It is also common talk that in some cases the heads or other parts of the body are detached for anatomical investigation. The staff employed on the work of liquidation at these institutions is obtained from other parts of the country and the local inhabitants will have nothing to do with them. These employees spend their evenings in the taverns, drinking pretty heavily. Apart from the stories told by the people about these "foreigners," there is much anxiety over the question of whether certain elderly persons who have worked hard all their lives and may now in their old age be somewhat feebleminded are possibly being liquidated with the rest. It is being suggested that even old people's homes will soon be cleared. There is a general feeling here, apparently, that

proper legal measures should be taken to insure that above all persons of advanced age and enfeebled mentality are not included in these proceedings.[14]

The Secretary of State and Acting Reich Minister of Justice Dr. Franz Schlegelberger wailed in a letter to Dr. Lammers, chief of the Reich Chancellery, that the situation was "equivalent to the execution of a death sentence without a previous trial in court."[15] Later, in another lengthy letter to Lammers in March 1941, Schlegelberger set forth the legal confusion caused by Aktion T-4 and detailed some of the rumors and fears caused in the public mind by the legal confusion:

Difficulties have arisen for trustees in cases where judges have opposed the transfer of insane persons in the charge of guardians or trustees to other asylums. Often the courts were given no official information as to the whereabouts or the decease of insane wards, though the personal and financial affairs of any body of trustees, the communications between trustee and ward and the regular inquiries by relatives must enable the authorities to state the address and subsequent circumstances of any such ward. . . . Public prosecutors have also been embarrassed when relatives or third parties have lodged charges of the murder of persons who have disappeared. One prosecutor-general intends to cross-examine an official physician accused of having falsified the medical history of a patient who had "died." Details of problems which have arisen for criminal lawyers may be found in Enclosure 2. Serious doubts have affected the minds of authorities conducting trials under the legislation against malicious attacks on state and party when defendants have alleged the killing of persons in good physical health. As the liquidation measures are kept secret, the most various rumours have been spreading among the population, have been encouraged by subversive elements, and have reached immoderate dimensions. The secrecy involved and public ignorance of the extent of the measures are proving fertile soil for the spread of rumors that even perfectly sane inmates of penal establishments and actually persons suffering from war injuries, as well as elderly German citizens past work and the politically undesirable, are being included in the scheme. Trials in camera of persons accused of malicious gossip in the dissemination of such talk would also appear to involve special risks, as the investigation of individual features of the case would bring the whole problem of the extermination of lives not worth living into the open. In these circumstances, too, unscrupulous agitators would escape the punishment they deserve. Confidence in the medical profession, especially in the directors of sanitoriums and convalescent homes, is being severely shaken. People are saying that the deaths reported are due to doctors' blunders and that insane patients are being used for military experiments, such as the testing of poison gas and other weapons of war. Other rumors reveal anxiety over the food situation which it is felt must be precarious if remedies are already being sought in the liquidation of some hundreds of thousands of the mentally afflicted.[16]

It was all particularly embarrassing for the Justice Ministry because the euthanasia program had been organized and operated within the Ministry of Interior; and no one at Justice had been even so much as aware of its existence until the letters of complaint and outrage began to flood in.

The file cabinets at Justice were filled with the legal correspondence generated by this "confusing jumble." The district attorney of Naumburg an der Saale wrote concerning the suspicious demise, all on the same day, of insane asylum inmates in his district—which "permit the assumption of mass death resulting from catastrophic events, as for example fire." He could not conceive of the true cause of the deaths.[17]

Chief Public Prosecutor Holzhäuer had some idea of what was going on, and he warned in a letter to the Justice Ministry "that confidence in the state leadership will be terribly shaken in the widest circles of the population. It will be said that such a 'mass murder' never could have happened if it had not been ordered from above or at least tolerated."[18]

District attorneys were horrified as evidence of wanton killing in the hospitals became clear. These were "unlawful killings," cried the district attorney of Graz, killings worthy of Stalinist

Russia, and they had to be stopped or the people's faith in the justice system would be lost. The district attorney of Graz began a criminal investigation for murder against the doctors of one of the euthanasia hospitals.[19] These and others, what the minister of justice would later call "irresponsible instigators,"[20] caused the officials at the careful and correct Ministry of Justice a great deal of embarrassment.

In a rush of bureaucratic indignation the Reich minister of justice had written to Chancellery Chief Dr. Lammers, demanding that something be done. It was not only shocking, it was embarrassing. Forwarding several of the complaints that had been received, he wrote to Lammers, "From the enclosures you can see for yourself how embarrassing a situation has been created and no doubt the number of such inquiries will increase. It is extraordinarily difficult to reply officially to them, for no reference to either the existence or the content of the Führer's order can be made. And yet it is impossible for our authorities to pretend that the Reich Justice Administration knows nothing of the matter."[21]

This was an intolerable situation.

It is not unfair to say that throughout the legal community there developed a strong desire to have the killing *codified*. The concern expressed in letter after letter is not that the killing be stopped, but that proper legal procedures according to law be established so that the killing could proceed in a proper and organized manner. Here, for example, is a letter from a Pastor Schlaich, director of the sanitorium at Stetten:

On account of the complete secrecy and camouflage under which the measures are carried out, not only are the wildest rumors created among the people (for example, that all people unable to work on account of age or injuries received during the world war have been done away with or are to be done away with) but also the impression that a totally arbitrary manner prevailed at the selection of the persons concerned.

If the state really wants to carry out the extermination of these or at least some mental patients, shouldn't a law be promulgated, which can be justified before the people and would give everyone the assurance of *careful examination*

213

whether he is due to die or entitled to live and would also give the relatives a chance to be heard, in a similar manner as provided by the Law for the Prevention of Genetically Impaired Progeny.[22]

In fact, efforts were made in several quarters to come up with legal language to authorize and codify the program which was under way. This has been carefully documented in a brilliant article by Goetz Aly and Heinz Roth.[23] As early as 1937, a secret committee, the Reich Committee for Scientific Research of Serious Illness of Hereditary and Protonic Origin, located in the Führer's Chancellery, was at work on a number of health policy issues including sterilization, abortion, and marriage regulations concerning the handicapped. In time the committee began to formulate broad, sweeping population policy. The well-known killing of the disabled Knauer baby in Leipzig in 1937 serves as a symbol of a change in administration thinking; population control need no longer be limited to sterilization and confinement. Now "negative population policies," the actual elimination of deviant minorities, could be considered.

Starting certainly in 1938, perhaps before, something called Division Four of the commission of criminal law in the Ministry of Justice was analyzing the question of how to provide immunity from prosecution for those who kill for "medical" purposes. This question was taken up by the commission on August 11, 1939. Minutes of the commission meeting show that draft language for a new law in this regard was discussed:

> Paragraph 1. Any person suffering from an incurable illness seriously hindering himself or others, or leading to certain death, may, upon his own express wish and with the permission of a specially authorized physician, have access to mercy killing.
> Paragraph 2. The life of a person who, as a result of incurable mental illness, requires permanent care and who is incapable of keeping up with life may be terminated by medical means without any pain being felt by this person.

After Hitler's secretly approved killing program was under way, and as the complaints and confusion began to mount, there was a flurry of efforts to produce language for a law which, with Hitler's approval, would authorize the program. There were meetings and revisions and more meetings. Both Aktion T-4 director Brack and Chancellery head Lammers produced draft versions. The title of such a measure evolved from "Law on the Mercy Killing of Persons Incapable of Life" to "Law on Mercy Killing for People Incapable of Life and for Foreigners to the Community" to "Law on the Termination of Suffering for Persons Incurably Ill and Incapable of Life" to the final draft, "Law on Mercy Killing." No complete copy of this proposal is known to exist.

Hitler was kept informed of these activities along the way. His response to such briefings was consistently noncommittal and evasive. As the head of the Reich committee testified at Nuremberg, "the Führer did not approve of it [the draft] but . . . did not reject it altogether."[24] The promulgation of a law "which would first have to be considered by all the ministries" was ultimately rejected; it was "uncongenial to Hitler on political grounds," said Lammers[25]—probably because notice of lawmaking would have provoked opposition, as circulation to government departments generally does.

By July 1940 it was clear that the Führer was not going to approve *any* formal law. The simplest explanation for this is that by mid-1940 what was going on in the hospitals was a mass slaughter far removed from what was envisaged by the careful and arch language of the draft law. The doctors were as much in violation of the proposed draft law as they were of the old law against murder.

No new language, no new law, would make what the doctors were doing easier to stomach.

From the first, Hitler had said he could proceed with the killing of the disabled only under cover of war. He feared that the churches would be able to rally public opinion against such a program in peacetime. He had said that not until "after the war" would it be possible to try for a legal euthanasia program.

If he had a rationale for his present behavior—a *large* "if"— perhaps he felt it necessary first in a brutal and swift, illegal sweep to empty the hospital wards of the chronic patients; and only then after the war, after the "recalcitrant" therapy cases had been cleared away, to establish an official legal euthanasia program with careful selection procedures, proper safeguards, and so forth. Perhaps. This was Brandt's understanding: Hitler's order "applied to the methods by which euthanasia was to be operated during the war. After the war, so I understood, it . . . was to be formulated in different terms."[26] Hitler, who was so open with his thoughts and prejudices, was often opaque in explaining the timing or the reason for his actions. He was a man who acted according to his instincts and intuitions. Intuition can only be explained so far.

Amir has suggested[27] that Hitler knew he could commit mass murder and also knew he could not make a law of it. Law codifies behavior, and mass murder is behavior beyond codification. Mass murder is behavior beyond the bounds of law. Mass murder, in fact, is what codes of law and society are designed to prevent, not enforce.

It is perhaps not coincidental that Hitler's most grave and appalling programs were carried forward without benefit of *any* formal legal authority—the Nacht und Nebel (in which untold numbers of suspect citizens simply vanished into the night and fog), the Holocaust, and euthanasia. Such things are possible. They are done. But no law known to man can authorize or justify them.

The euthanasia program would have to proceed on the basis of Hitler's informal directive. By August the Ministry of Justice seemed to have resigned itself to the fact that, as Lammers testified, "in issuing his authorization the Führer had laid down the law." Reich Minister Gürtner "was apparently of the opinion that this was a valid order of the Führer"[28] and, as such, was to be accepted as legal by the judicial system of Germany.

Charges against the doctors, brought by relatives of the deceased and by prosecuting attorneys, were ordered quashed. Inquiries and protests were ignored. Cases against untimely dead defendants were dropped. The records of vanished wards of the court were simply filed away. At this wholesale prostitution of justice only one judge is known to have protested.

Dr. Kreyssig, judge in Brandenburg an der Havel, protested first by letter and then in person. In his letter to the minister he said, "Right is what is useful to the people. In the name of this frightening teaching which has not yet been contradicted by all the guardians of Justice in Germany, whole territories are excepted from the domain of Justice, as for instance the concentration camps, and now

216

the institutions for cure and nursing. What influence this will have in the future remains to be seen."[29]

Unsatisfied with the situation, Kreyssig protested in person to Undersecretary Freisler, threatening to file charges against the directors of the program. He then met with the president of his province, who urged him to be quiet and to go along with orders. Kreyssig refused and was finally called to Berlin where he met personally with the Justice minister.

Minister Gürtner showed Kreyssig a copy of Hitler's top-secret order authorizing the killing. This did not impress the judge. He responded, "Injustice cannot be turned into justice by formally correct positivistic legislation." Upon this, Gürtner closed the meeting, saying that a judge who "does not recognize the will of the Führer as the source of law . . . cannot be a judge anymore."[30]

Such courage was seldom seen. Kreyssig was allowed to retire from the bench. He survived the war and lived to see the rebirth of German justice.

As part of a program to forestall such behavior and to end the filing of proceedings against the participants in the euthanasia program, the ministry arranged for a briefing on the supposedly legal, supposedly secret, program for the "presidents" or chief judges of the courts of appeal of all the states of Germany and the district attorneys. Also present was Judge Erwin Bumke, the president of the Reich Court, the highest in the land. Bumke had been on the high court since his appointment in 1929, in the days of the Weimar Republic. This most unusual meeting took place on April 23, 1941.

Viktor Brack, Reich Leader Philip Bouhler, and Dr. Werner Heyde were present, along with Minister Schlegelberger and Undersecretary Freisler. Brack and Heyde addressed the meeting. Brack passed out copies of the Führer's order, explained its humanitarian intent, and said that the program was an experiment which would serve as a model for legislation on the subject in the future. He apologized for the inadvertent mistakes which had been made in getting the program under way.

Dr. Heyde was professor of psychiatry at the University of Würzburg and director of its medical clinic. The hospital clinic at Würzburg holds an important place in medical history—its tradition of caring humanely for the mentally disabled at Würzburg hospital

217

dates back to the sixteenth century. It was Heyde's task at the meeting to explain the medical rationale for the program. He assured the justices that the medical history of each patient was reviewed by a panel of doctors before a decision to apply final medical therapy was made. He, for his part, passed around some 150 photographs of persons "in extremis" as examples of those who would benefit from the program.

The program described to the judges was in no sense an accurate description of what was going on, at that very moment. They were not told about the wholesale emptying of the wards that was under way. Instead, as Amir points out, a program was described that conformed with the proposals made by Binding and Hoche in 1920, which had been widely discussed throughout Germany. The jurists were *not* told that, by the time of their meeting, the wave of euthanasia had spread to the concentration camps; or that it had been decided to kill *all* Jewish insane, without regard to condition or prognosis.

However limited the briefing, this surely was an extraordinary meeting. The representatives of a long, distinguished tradition of jurisprudence had met to be told that the state had awarded the physicians of Germany an absolute and secret authority to kill citizens. In doing so, the physicians would be accountable to no law or court; nor would there be a right of appeal from their decisions.

It was said that when a jurist from Hamburg raised questions concerning the policy he "was rebuked by Dr. Freisler with the remark that criticism of the Führer's measures was not permissible and would not be tolerated." [31] Other reports say that the judges listened in silence to the talks and attempted no discussion at all. According to a judge who was present, the feelings of the group were those of "gloom, abhorrence, and indignation." [32]

Such was the fix in which the good people of Germany found themselves. The disabled could expect no help from the courts. By then the courts were helpless, too.

11

Aktion T-4 and the Church

The anvil outlasts the hammer.

Bishop von Galen, 1941.

The churches of Germany attacked euthanasia as they attacked no other Nazi policy. Church leaders spoke from the pulpit in strong defiance; they rallied public support and—on *this* issue— forced Hitler and his henchmen to back down. One question may fairly be asked and must be carefully and respectfully examined: what would have happened had these leaders spoken in just such a united and forceful manner on other issues such as the extermination of the Jews, the savage cruelty to the peoples in the occupied territories, the bombing of civilian populations? This is not a simple question. Nor is the question of why the churches united in opposition to euthanasia, but not to the other issues.

In order to understand this behavior of organized religion and its impact during the Nazi regime, it is necessary to understand something of the historic position of the church in German society.

The population of United Germany under the Kaisers was approximately one-third Roman Catholic and two-thirds Protestant. The Protestant sects were largely of Lutheran and Calvinist origin. Generally speaking, the Catholics were located more to the south and to the west of the country; the Protestants tended to be concentrated in the north and the east.

There is some reason to believe that by the time of the rise of Hitler, religious practice for many Germans had become rather more a matter of ritual and symbolism than an ongoing confessing faith. In a 1939 census all but 5 percent of the population declared themselves to be members of a Christian faith: of the remainder, 3.5 percent said they believed in the existence of a God, and only 1.5 percent declared themselves atheist.[1] However, many of those professing a religious denomination were only nominal members— using a church ceremony to mark the major life passages of birth, marriage, and death, but not otherwise active. Church attendance, actual participation in church affairs, had been on a long decline. Even before World War I, it was found that only 8 percent of Protestants in Hamburg received communion. In Berlin this number rose to 15 percent, but only because of the social and official nature of religion in the Wilhelmine state—a French observer noted that in Berlin no one but "the official world, taking its cue from the Emperor, still went to church."[2] This process of secularization was greatest in the industrial cities, among males, and in the Protestant churches; it was less pronounced in the rural areas, with women, and in the Roman Catholic church.

The years of the Weimar Republic after the First World War were a time of skepticism, cynicism, chaos, and despair. The decline of the importance of the organized Christian church to German society continued in the face of intellectual and political attack and the ongoing collapse of traditional moral structure.

By the time of Hitler's accession, it can fairly be said that Germany was not a fervently religious country.

The principal Christian churches of Germany—the Protestant and the Roman Catholic—for centuries had been closely linked with issues of German nationalism and the authority of the state. To a degree quite alien to American experience, the churches had been major players in the political process.

Martin Luther and John Calvin, the founders of the two great branches of the German Protestant church, preached that resistance to the authority of state was sinful. They took as their text the words of Saint Paul: "Let everyone be subject to the higher authorities, for there exists no authority except from God, and those who exist have been appointed by God. Therefore he who resists the authority resists the ordinance of God; and they that resist bring on themselves condemnation."[3]

Luther, who was able to implement his reforms of the German church only through the cooperation of the ruling German princes, was insistent upon the duty of citizens to accord absolute obedience to their prince. He wrote, "The princes of this world are gods, the common people are Satan. . . . I would rather suffer a prince doing wrong than a people doing right."

Further, Luther said, "It is in no wise proper for anyone who would be a Christian to set himself up against his government, whether it act justly or unjustly." He also wrote, "There are no better works than to obey and serve all those who are over us as superiors. For this reason also disobedience is a greater sin than murder, unchastity, theft, and dishonesty, and all that these may include."[4]

Thus, the Lutheran Church, in many ways the dominant denomination in the making of a modern united Germany[5], preached as it had always preached: unquestioning obedience and respect for the governing authority.

As far back as the Peace of Augsburg (1555), the ruler of each of the dozens of the princely states which constituted the Holy Roman Empire of the German nation was free to decide which of the religions should become the established church of his state. Under this arrangement, the prince of each of the Protestant states was simultaneously the *summus episcopus*, or supreme bishop of the church. It is not surprising, therefore, to find that more often than not, positions in the church hierarchy were dispensed as a form of princely patronage. And over time, it became the principal task of these appointed church officials to see that the local pastors, in their sermons and in their teaching, laid heavy emphasis upon respect for and obedience to the prince, his government, and its policies.

Therefore, over time and in a general way, the Protestant churches of Germany—whether of Calvinist or Lutheran persuasion—came to be perceived as apologists for, as well as accomplices of, the power of the state.

The case of the German Roman Catholic Church was different. It had been the established church of the Empire until 1803. At this time its favored position was lost; church estates were sold off forcibly; and many of its monastic institutions were dissolved. In the 1870s Bismarck, the architect of modern Germany, fomented a struggle against the independence of the Catholic Church, a campaign which came to be called the Kulturkampf, "the conflict of civilizations." Among other charges, it was said that the German

Roman Catholic Church was guilty of ultramontanism—its hierarchy more closely pledged to the supremacy of the pope of Rome "over the mountains" than loyal to Germany. It served the Iron Chancellor's purposes, both domestic and foreign, to do battle with this internal "enemy."

The Church was badly bruised in the battle. Ecclesiastical supervision of local schools was ended; the Jesuit order was dissolved and its members ordered out of the country. Various bishops and priests were imprisoned or expelled on various charges. Catholics felt themselves to be victims of persecution by the state, and the focus of their resistance was found in the Catholic Center Party, whose sole purpose was the defense of the Church.[6] This party became large and powerful in the Reichstag: it was an important member of the various coalition governments which sought to govern Germany in the years before Hitler.

Thus, by the time of the rise of Hitler, while the Protestant churches were often seen as the tool or accomplice of the state, the Catholic Church still was perceived as being somehow *alien*, as having an uncertain loyalty to German nationalism. The Church felt pressure to prove itself genuinely German.

During the years of the Weimar Republic (1918–33), the hierarchies of both major churches found themselves on the defensive. Church leaders generally tended to be old and aristocratic, defenders of the ancien régime. They were monarchists and conservative. They felt severely threatened by the new republic and the godless communism, anarchism, atheism, individualism, and all the other "isms" that flourished during the rich ferment of the Weimar era.

The core of Nazi ideology was, of course, anathema to Christian doctrine. Catholics had been forbidden to join the party throughout its early life. The Protestant sects, like the Catholic Church, were appalled by the racial superiority claims of the Nazis. Nevertheless, there was much in the Nazis' early program that the religious leaders of Germany found attractive.

The churches of Germany were not particularly prodemocratic—they had no such tradition—and they made no notable protest as the democratic structures of the Republic fell before the Nazis. There had been a good deal of disturbing social unrest, and church leaders did not object as Hitler's government adopted stern measures designed to repress the unrest by interning the so-called asocials in the newly established concentration camps. Church leaders were as patriotic as any other Germans, and they responded as enthusiastically to Hitler's assertions that the First World War was lost because the nation had been betrayed—the "stab in the back"—by the false pledges of the Allies. Lastly, it must be said, there has been "a traditional Christian hostility to the Jews" in Germany, to quote a recent essay by theologian Ingrid Genkel.[7] Church leaders were notably silent as the persecution of the Jews began.

Potsdam Day, March 21, 1933, was, so it was said, a glorious day for Germany. The new chancellor Adolf Hitler; the old president of the Republic, Field Marshal von Hindenburg; and the entire government, together with Crown Prince Wilhelm and Field Marshal von Mackensen, went in great procession to the venerable Garrison Church at Potsdam. In this great shrine to Prussia's military victories are buried the bones of Frederick the Great. Here, the Hohenzollern kings of Germany worshiped. On the way to the church, Hitler, in an open car with the aged Hindenburg, the very personification of the spirit of old Germany, passed down great alleys of massed flags, flanked by row upon row of soldiers in dress uniform.

The ceremony in the church celebrated the installation of the new chancellor and the opening of the Reichstag. Presiding as pastor was Otto Dibelius, a general superintendent of the Prussian Evangelical Church. Newsreel cameras and radio microphones had been located in strategic places about the church, and the entire proceedings were broadcast live to all of Germany. Everything was most formal and traditional, as solemn as a coronation. Before all the world and to all appearances, Hitler was anointed to his new position by the Protestant church and the establishment of Germany.

On July 20, 1933, the papal secretary of state, Cardinal Pacelli, later Pope Pius XII, signed a treaty, the Concordat, with the Hitler government. This agreement guaranteed the right of German Catholics to practice their religion unimpeded by the state and their politics unimpeded by the Church. It guaranteed the sanctity of church property in Germany, and pledged that German Roman Catholic priests and hierarchy would take no part in the politics of the nation.

The Concordat, the first ever with the united nation of Germany, came as a surprise to the governments of the world. It was widely interpreted to constitute—at least to some degree—Vatican approval for the policies of the new Hitler government.

Cardinal Pacelli, before his post as Vatican foreign minister, had served for twelve years as papal nuncio to the German government in Berlin. In 1919 on the steps of a cathedral in Munich, a communist had held a pistol to the cardinal's head and threatened his life.[8] Now Pacelli explained his agreement with the Nazis using similar terms. "A pistol had been pointed at his head and he had no alternative. The Germans had offered him concessions . . . wider than any previous German government would have agreed to, and he had to choose between an agreement on their lines and the virtual elimination of the Church in the Reich."[9] Pacelli always seemed to be acting under the pressure of a pistol to his head.

To give Pacelli his due, he had no illusions concerning what he had signed. He understood, he told a British diplomat, that "if the German government violated the Concordat—and they were certain to do so—the Vatican would have a treaty on which to base a protest."[10] And indeed there would be many protests over the life of the Third Reich.

The Concordat was hailed generally by German Catholics. Four days after its signing, Cardinal Faulhaber sent a telegram to Hitler: "Your statesmanlike farsightedness has achieved in six months what the old parliaments and parties failed to achieve in sixty years."[11]

All of this was ready grist for Adolf Hitler's mill. By tradition, law, and popular support, the religions of Germany, indeed, held genuine power. It was a basic tenet of Nazism that there could be but one center of power in the state—the Führer. It was unacceptable that church leaders should have separate, even competing, claims upon public support.

The details are complex and at times inconsistent, but overall it was Hitler's policy to castrate the historic power of church authority by playing to its weakness. He was not willing to launch a frontal attack upon church power; indeed, he always professed a respect, even envy, for the authority and influence of the Roman Church. He did not relish a direct confrontation, saying that such would come only after the war: "The war will be over one day. I shall then consider that my life's final task will be to solve the religious question." [12]

In fact, no such direct attack was needed so long as the Protestants continued to weaken their authority with intradenominational fighting (dismissed scornfully as "parsonical squabbles" by Hitler, whose agents kept them stirred up). [13] And for its part, the Roman Catholic Church, always afraid of another Kulturkampf, was kept off balance by Nazi propaganda which caused the hierarchy to make endless efforts at proving their allegiance to Germany—the *Volk*, the *Vaterland* (the native land), and the *Heimat* (the country).

Many of the nursing homes and long-term care institutions in Germany are church-owned and operated. In the years between the two World Wars, the Christian officials with responsibilities for the care of the chronically disabled in these institutions were, not surprisingly, influenced by eugenic doctrine.

The concept of "differential treatment" received much attention. In a 1931 report on a eugenics conference issued by the Central Committee of the Inner Mission, a Protestant agency, it was argued that changes in population growth were producing a decline in the size of families of "socially strong and genetically sound" character. This decline required a new orientation to both public and private welfare. This report called for a differentiated approach to care to replace traditional equalitarian welfare. Considerable expenditures should only be made for those who were expected to be fully rehabilitated. As for the others—the long-term chronically ill—treatment should be limited to no more than humanitarian board and custodial care. [14]

Catholics, too, were influenced by eugenics. Professor Dr. Franz Keller, editor of the yearbook of the Caritas Institute of Science, wrote, "Even the Caritas [the central Catholic welfare agency] has to practice welfare as racial hygiene. . . . The Caritas has to adapt its activities of providing help to the society as a whole. Care of those incapable of living, sick people, must not be overemphasized to the detriment of the healthy and vigorous." [15] The Jesuit eugenicist Dr. Hermann Muckermann argued that the expenditures upon the chronically ill—"paid for by the healthy and moral people . . ."—had grown so great "that even the simplest problems of health maintenance can no longer be solved. A tragic vicious circle diminishes the number of the healthy and increases the number of the inferior."[16]

These were, of course, simply the same eugenic arguments which were being heard in medical and scientific circles, as well as the councils of the National Socialist party.

Already eugenically aware, the churches reacted to the 1933 Nazi law providing for the obligatory sterilization of the genetically unfit (and others) in a not entirely negative manner. Generally speaking, the Protestant churches raised no objection. Their institutions participated as required by law. There were numerous sterilizations performed in the institutions of the Inner Mission. And in the well-known and respected Bethel Mission, which cared for epileptic patients, 1,093 sterilizations were performed over the years 1934–45.[17]

Catholics opposed sterilization—with certain exceptions—and had done so publicly for years. The Catholic position had been spelled out with some force in the 1930 encyclical *Casti Conubii:* ". . . the eugenicists are going so far that they rob those [thought to be genetically flawed] of their natural faculties through medical techniques even against their will not as corporal punishment for crimes nor to prevent future crimes of the guilty but arrogating against all right and justice a power for the secular authorities which they never had nor could ever rightfully have."

These strong words did not stop the continuing discussion of the sterilization issue in Catholic circles. Hermann Muckermann, the Jesuit eugenics professor at the Kaiser Wilhelm Institute, published many articles warning of the threat posed by the high birth rates of genetically inferior people. With an act of high sophistry, he interpreted the encyclical so as to allow certain eugenic sterilizations: ". . . the papal encyclical rejected sterilization only for eugenic reasons but not when there were medical indications . . . that the welfare of society required such a measure or as punishment to prevent future crimes."[18]

Dr. Joseph Mayer was a theologian at the Caritas Institute of Science, and he, too, was a strong advocate of eugenic principles. In 1927, he published a volume, *Legal Sterilization of Mental Patients*, which had the imprimatur of the Catholic Church. In this he argued that sterilization carried out under the authority of law was not necessarily an evil, *if* the operation is done in order to achieve a moral good. He spoke of the inherited horrors of epilepsy and Huntington's chorea. So far as the mentally ill and the retarded were concerned, Mayer solved his problem with an adept use of devaluation: "Moral law applies only to the mentally normal, rational individuals. Mental patients do not belong in the moral order, neither as subjects nor in terms of implementation." [19]

By denying mentally ill persons the protections afforded by moral law, he relegated them to a subhuman class. Such thinking, so prevalent in the Germany of the thirties, of course, made the mentally ill terribly vulnerable—as the euthanasia program demonstrated. Mayer's position was certainly not that of the Catholic Church.

The sterilization law coming so very soon after the ratification of the Concordat presented Catholic authorities with a dilemma. Sterilization was against Church doctrine: there could be no compromise on that point. On the other hand, the Church was not anxious to get into a bitter struggle with the Nazis, a struggle which might threaten the Concordat and its limited guarantees of the integrity of Church property and the independence of Church operations.

During the discussions which preceded the ratification of the treaty, Nazi Interior Minister Frick had promised the German bishops that the government would review the whole sterilization issue. [20] Nothing came of this promise. The German Church hierarchy met with the government in an effort to head off the implementation of the sterilization law. Bishop Gröber suggested that the Church might be able to live with the law if sterilization were made voluntary on the part of both physicians and hospitals. [21] This, of course, was not acceptable to the Nazis; and, indeed, in 1935, the scope of the law was actually broadened by authorizing the sterilization courts to order abortion when the mother was adjudged to be genetically inferior.

Cardinal Faulhaber met with Hitler on November 4, 1936. One of the subjects discussed was sterilization policy and the Church's position. Faulhaber recommended to the Führer a program of permanent institutionalization, rather than sterilization. This apparently did not please Hitler. He asked, ominously, how long this Church fight against the racial laws of the Third Reich was to continue. Faulhaber, backpedaling rapidly, reminded the leader that "even under the monarchy there were laws (e.g., allowing divorce) which the secular authorities considered a necessity but which the Church rejected." As in the days of the Kaiser, Faulhaber hastened to assure the Führer, "A modus vivendi will be found."[22] And so it was. The Church continued its opposition and the government continued its program.

There is reason to believe that Hitler's Chancellery made an effort to find out how the churches would react to the euthanasia program before it was actually under way.

Albert Hartl, chief of Department IVB (religious opponents) at Gestapo headquarters, testified after the war that he had been told in 1939 by his boss, Reinhard Heydrich, that Hitler had grave reservations about euthanasia in the light of the protests he expected from the churches. Heydrich asked Hartl to inquire among his contacts in the Protestant and Catholic churches to determine what specifically their positions might be should the government undertake a policy of providing final treatment for the chronically ill. Hartl testified that because he was unable to provide an expert opinion himself, he had asked the Roman Catholic theologian Dr. Joseph Mayer, author of the book *Legal Sterilization of Mental Patients,* to prepare a study and Mayer had agreed to do so.[23]

There should have been little doubt of the churches' position. Both the Roman Catholic Church and Protestant denominations opposed euthanasia. As far back as 1934, the primate of the German Roman Catholic Church, Archbishop Bertram, had thought it necessary to warn the government publicly that the Church would always oppose euthanasia.

This did not faze Mayer. Again, according to Hartl, Mayer worked six months preparing his report. He talked to church officials and scholars and thoroughly researched the Church's attitude toward euthanasia. His conclusion was ambiguous: he could find no categorical condemnation of euthanasia. Mayer concluded there were reputable moral arguments which could be made on both sides of the question; and, therefore, euthanasia of the chronically mentally and physically ill was a *defensible* position to take.[24]

No copy of Mayer's study has ever been found. Catholic officials deny all knowledge of it. The Nazi Hartl, a fallen-away priest and organizer of a spy network against the Roman Catholic Church, is not the most reliable of witnesses. However, his testimony seemed to be quite certain and specific concerning the report. After the war, the aged Professor Mayer, testifying as a witness, at first denied authorship of the report; but later, under cross-examination, he did acknowledge preparing it. [25]

The euthanasia program began officially in the fall of 1939. The first *public* protests from religious authorities were not heard for well over a year. During this interval, there was a good deal of communication between the religious leaders and state officials. There were private protests, both in writing and in person. There may, in fact, actually have been negotiations. Historian Martin Hoellen believes that Bishop Heinrich Wienken, director of the Secretariat of the Fulda Bishops Conference, was negotiating with the government, trying to obtain an exemption for Catholic institutions in exchange for something like a pledge of silence on the issue. [26]

The protests, although made in private, were in many cases both brave and strong:

On March 19, 1949, Theophil Wurm, Lutheran bishop of Württemberg, wrote a passionate letter to Interior Minister Frick. Getting no response, Wurm wrote another blistering letter in September, deploring the "planned extermination of the insane, feeble, and infirm" as constituting a "great danger and scandal. . . . Must the German nation be the first civilized people which in its treatment of the weak returns to the customary practice of primitive people? Does the Führer know of this matter? Has he approved of it? Do not leave me without an answer on this extremely serious matter." Wurm finally received an answer by registered mail from Dr. Conti of the ministry. The answer was most unsatisfactory. The bishop was assured that everything was in order; the euthanasia program, although secret, was being carried out in a manner strictly according to law. [27]

On June 1, 1940, Roman Catholic archbishop Gröber of Freiburg sent a letter to the minister of justice of Baden protesting the reports of killing and asking for clarification. Gröber, the protector of Caritas, later protested to the head of Hitler's Chancellery and offered, on behalf of the Church, to assume the costs for the care of all those who had been selected to die, should they be spared.

In August and November, Cardinals Bertram and Faulhaber sent strong protests to both Lammers and Reich Minister Gürtner, who was himself a Catholic. Old Cardinal Bertram drew "attention to the indignation aroused by the killing of patients arbitrarily declared unworthy of life. Such destruction of the innocent not only violated the Christian moral law, but offended against the moral sense of the German people and threatened to jeopardize the reputation of Germany in the world."[28]

There were many other written protests from the religious hierarchy of Germany. The Bishop of Limburg wrote a moving letter. Bernhard Lichtenberg, provost of St. Hedwig's Cathedral in Berlin, filed a powerful complaint. The Roman Catholic bishops of Paderborn, Cologne, and Osnabrück sent a joint letter claiming to speak on behalf of ten million Catholics. Even parish priests sent letters of outrage. One such, from a priest named Baumann, said, "In the name of the Fifth Commandment . . . I object to this systematic mass murder."[29]

These were protests made in private in writing. The public had no way of knowing anything about them. Thus the protests did not, in the eyes of the government, interfere with the carrying forward of public policy. Furthermore, most of these letters were written by eminent and respected Church leaders. To take action against them—to put them in concentration camps or worse—would attract significant attention and arouse public concern. Therefore, for the most part, the Nazi officials took no action against these men; their letters were barely acknowledged, often ignored altogether.

Not all of the protesters escaped punishment. A pastor named Ernst Wilm gave a lecture on euthanasia in 1940. He was arrested and sent to Dachau, where he stayed until the end of the war. A pastor named Stellbrink was condemned to "death and the permanent loss of his honor" for listening to the overseas radio and distributing copies of a statement against euthanasia by the bishop of Württemberg.[30]

One of the most important critics of the euthanasia program was Pastor Paul Gerhard Braune, director of the Hoffnungstaler long-term care institutions and vice president of the Central Committee of the Inner Mission, the welfare agency of the Protestant churches. In the spring of 1940 he began receiving reports from Inner Mission institutions all over Germany that patients were dying under mysterious circumstances. Braune took these reports to the Reich Chancellery and the Ministry of Justice but received no satisfactory answer. Officials at the security headquarters of the Wehrmacht high command asked him to investigate the charges and prepare a report for them. Braune agreed to do so, and he worked up his report over May and June 1940.[31]

Braune's report was an authoritative document, fifteen pages long. In it he was able to piece together a remarkably accurate account of the euthanasia program's operation. Braune reported a rising concern across the country over the large number of patients being transported from hospitals and institutions. He cited reports from hospitals whose patients had been transferred for "economic reasons," sometimes transferred more than once. These transported patients would then be reported to have died, unexpectedly. Their remains would be cremated, and the families notified by form letter. He supplied copies of these letters.

His report concluded that there could be no doubt that these deaths were part of a large-scale operation to do away with thousands of so-called unworthy lives. It was general talk that national defense somehow made it necessary to do away with "useless eaters," and that the killing was part of a plan to upgrade the German race by culling out the mentally deficient and other hopeless cases. Braune quoted a magazine article which estimated that there were about a million such people in Germany.

Braune described in graphic detail the terrible conditions in the killing hospitals. He said the patients were very aware of what was going on. He explained about the starvation diets, and by analyzing the numbers inscribed on the base of the funeral urns he was able to estimate the number of persons already killed.

He pointed out that the general population was learning about the killings from the families and friends of the victims. He warned that this was causing great anxiety and undermining the people's trust in physicians and nurses.

Braune explained how difficult it was to define unworthy lives, giving the example of six girls who were in the process of being released from a hospital to take up jobs that were waiting for them. "These girls of clear mind were caught up in the operation, transferred, and killed. How can you tell," he asked, "who is abnormal, asocial, or hopelessly sick? What will happen to soldiers fighting for the fatherland who contract an incurable illness?"

He urged the authorities to stop the dreadful program and to review carefully its legal, medical, ethical, and political ramifications. [32]

Braune took his courageous report in person to Church Affairs Minister Kerrl. According to Braune, writing after the war, Kerrl had never heard of the program and was frightened to learn of it. Braune took the report to Minister of Justice Gürtner, who appeared to be most upset and who called the program nothing more than "murder on the assembly line." [33]

Braune, hoping that the Führer himself would see the report, gave it to Minister Lammers at the Reich Chancellery. Braune also sent a copy to Hermann Göring, through the good offices of Göring's nephew.

No official comment was ever received by Braune from any of the men who had seen the report. Unofficially he was told by a friend in the Chancellery that Lammers had, indeed, taken up the matter with Hitler, and that while the Führer had refused to end the killing, he had asked that it be done in a "decent" manner.

Braune received no official response; instead, on August 14, 1940, he was arrested by the Gestapo. He was held under the direct orders of Heydrich, head of the secret police. Braune was imprisoned for ten weeks. He was interrogated twice, his questioners emphasizing that he had not been arrested for writing the memorandum, since its subject was the euthanasia program which was an official secret and therefore, officially, did not exist. [34] Braune was released from this catch-22 nightmare only after he promised not "to take further actions against measures of the state or the party." [35]

Poor Braune even had trouble with his fellow officers of the Inner Mission. The president of the organization, a Pastor Constantin Frick, was not terribly concerned; he believed the killing program to be legal, and he had been assured that only mindless, vegetating patients would be taken. And as Braune summed up in 1967, "the official church remained silent, the official Inner Mission did not dare to do anything. After my release I was reproached by the treasurer of the central committee for having put myself in jeopardy over such a matter."[36]

One of the leading figures in Protestant Germany was Pastor Friedrich von Bodelschwingh. His father had founded the great Bethel Mission, a large long-term-care institution, famous for its treatment of persons with epilepsy. When his father died in 1910, Pastor Bodelschwingh took over direction of the center. He was highly respected by his peers and famous for the power and conviction of his sermons.

Bodelschwingh was a man of acknowledged integrity and leadership. In 1933, as the "German Christians"—Nazi-oriented Protestants—were trying to seize control of the churches through the application of the so-called Führer principle—the concentration of all power in an organization in the hands of a single leader—Pastor Bodelschwingh was elected Reich bishop by a large majority over the Nazi-backed candidate. Hitler was not pleased, expressing in his ominous way, "extreme regrets that the efforts for the reconstruction of the German Evangelical Church had taken a difficult and decidedly unlovable turn."[37] Bodelschwingh was at first successful in building resistance to Nazi encroachments on the operation of the churches, but within months he was forced into resignation by the government appointment of a National Socialist Commissar for the Evangelical Church of Prussia.

Bodelschwingh was no friend of the Nazis. His reputation and popularity allowed him to say things and take actions which the Nazis would not have tolerated from those less powerfully positioned. He was strongly opposed to euthanasia and, throughout the life of the program, refused to allow his patients to be taken in the transports.

When Braune was preparing his report on the killings, the killing program had not yet extended to Westphalia, where Bodelschwingh's Bethel Mission was located. He was unaware of what was happening until he was told by Braune. Deeply concerned, Bodelschwingh accompanied Braune to his meetings with the ministers of justice and religion and officials of the Reich Chancellery.

In June 1940 Bethel received three thousand copies of the T-4 questionnaire with instructions that they be filled out and returned by the first of August.[38] Bodelschwingh knew at once what was afoot, and he refused to allow his staff to fill them out. His staff was unanimous in support of this position. Bodelschwingh wrote at once to Minister of Health Conti, asking for a meeting. Although Conti refused to see him, he was able to meet with two ministry officials who admitted that, indeed, the completed questionnaires were to be used in the selection of persons to receive "final medical assistance."[39]

Bodelschwingh addressed a very strong letter of protest to the governor of his local district on September 28, 1940. In the letter he complained that in spite of his protests and those of others, the situation had not changed. He warned that the killing program was causing great anxiety among the general population, and said that families no longer dared to send their sick family members to the hospital.

He said he had been told, on a confidential basis, by Pastor Frick, president of the Central Committee of the Inner Mission, that the program, although secret, was fully legal. Bodelschwingh emphasized how difficult it was for the heads of institutions to participate in a euthanasia program which was not only directly contrary to their Christian convictions but was also, so far as most people were aware, illegal under the criminal code. If the legal authorization must be kept secret, he observed, what were they to tell the grieving parents and relatives of the victims?

Bodelschwingh asked that the whole program be reconsidered. If the program was not ended, he asked that the Bethel hospital be exempted from its operations. He promised to abide by all other government actions, provided only that Bethel was exempt from this one. He promised that the institution would pay all the costs of maintaining the rescued patients, and he volunteered to make space available in the buildings of Bethel for the use of the Department of Health, should it have the need of additional facilities.[40]

Bodelschwingh had meetings with other officials and wrote other letters of protest. In January 1941, he addressed a plea to Hermann Göring by way of Göring's nephew. In his letter, Bodelschwingh described the program and its scope; he urged that it be brought to an end. In reply he was informed that Hitler's personal physician would come to him and provide accurate information on the program. His own information, he was told, "was inaccurate and in great part false."[41]

Brandt did come to Bethel. The two men, the devoted young Nazi and the Lutheran minister, began a dialogue on the efficacy and morality of killing the chronically and severely disabled. The two continued the discussion by correspondence, and Brandt returned to Bethel for several more meetings. Something like a friendship grew up between them. According to Brandt at Nuremberg, "I had several talks with Dr. Bodelschwingh. . . . It was our mutual need for discussing these questions." Brandt had always felt with some conviction that euthanasia could be justified in moral terms. Bodelschwingh did not agree, although, again according to Brandt, he did acknowledge that exceptions might be made for certain extreme cases. Brandt claimed, "The longer we talked and the more we came into the open, the closer and the greater became our mutual understanding," and, perhaps, he was not entirely wrong.[42]

The Nazis were troubled by Bodelschwingh, but uncertain as to what to do about him. At one point Berlin ordered his arrest, but the local police officials refused to touch him, saying that he was so esteemed and loved that his arrest would cause great unrest in the neighborhood. Let the Gestapo do it, said the police. The Gestapo did not arrest the pastor; instead, a bomb was planted in the institution and duly exploded—as a warning.[43]

Because Bodelschwingh refused to comply with the euthanasia program, and because he protested forcefully and effectively, not one single patient at Bethel was taken directly from the institution to the killing centers. Bethel was left alone by the operators of Aktion T-4. This does not mean that all Bethel patients escaped the killing. It is not possible to say how many, but it appears that some patients were transferred to other long-term-care institutions and were transported from there. It is known, for instance, that of twelve Jewish patients at Bethel, the staff was able to hide five; but the remaining seven were sent to Poland where, soon enough, they were reported to have died. This was confirmed in a statement issued in 1985, on the fortieth anniversary of the fall of the Hitler state, by the Allied Boards of the Bodelschwingh Institutions of Bethel: ". . . we sadly state that inmates of Bethel were among the victims. . . . We have to assume that an unknown number of patients were killed when they were transferred to other institutions." [44]

Not all the extended-care institutions were so fortunate. Bethel had flatly resisted. Other religious institutions tried, as it were, to coexist with Aktion T-4. Officials of the Protestant facility at Alsterdorf believed that if they participated to the least extent possible, perhaps they would be able to save most, if not all, of their patients.

Pastor Friedrich Lensch, director of Alsterdorf, was afraid that if the institution failed to cooperate it might lose its designation as a charitable operation; and this would mean loss of its tax-exempt status. This, in turn, would force the facilities to close, leaving the patients without shelter in time of war.

Lensch actually began his hapless and ill-fated cooperation with the Nazis before the war. In 1937, in accordance with the "correct" thinking of the time, Pastor Lensch wrote to the Hamburg health authorities, asking that his Jewish inmates be transferred elsewhere. The authorities complied, and the "Aryanization" of Alsterdorf took place. The Jews were moved to the state-operated old-age home, Hamburg Oberaltenallee, on October 31, 1938. In September 1940 they were transported to the euthanasia center located at Brandenburg an der Havel, where, upon arrival, they were gassed.

The medical director at Alsterdorf was Dr. Gerhard Kreyenberg, an enthusiastic eugenicist. He and his staff had been active participants in the sterilization program authorized in 1933 by the Law for the Prevention of Genetically Impaired Progeny. Kreyenberg cast the criteria for sterilization so broadly as to include "moral debility," i.e., prostitutes and homosexuals.

Kreyenberg was also one of the creators of a register in Hamburg of misfit and outcast persons—asocials, or "Asos." The register was used for the selection of persons sent to concentration camps, and it served as a model for other communities all over Germany. In line with his eugenic principles, the medical director worked out a classification system for his Alsterdorf patients which divided them into two groups: the "worthy" ones, deserving of care and treatment, and the "unworthy" ones, who were not.

The classifications proved useful once the Aktion T-4 program was under way. It was the confident belief of the authorities at Alsterdorf that if they sacrificed only their most severe cases to the euthanasia center, they should then be able to save and protect the rest of their patients.

Of course, it did not work out that way. It started with involuntary sterilization, followed by the betrayal of the Jews; and then came the sacrifice, one by one, of the in extremis patients, until—by the end of the war in 1945—some *six hundred patients* at Alsterdorf had been transported to their deaths. Many of these persons were killed by systematic starvation or deliberate drug overdoses, after the official end of the Aktion T-4 program. Pastor Lensch thought he could shield his patients by collaborating with the Nazi authorities. He was wrong. What happened at Alsterdorf was repeated at religious institutions all over Germany.

Pastor Lensch thought he could ride the tiger, but the tiger was hungry. Neither Kreyenberg nor Lensch was prosecuted after the war; they continued in their careers.

Graf (Count) von Preysing, bishop of Berlin, was a friend of the new pope, Pius XII. The friendship had developed when the Pontiff served as papal nuncio in Berlin during the 1920s. Preysing carried on a personal correspondence with Pius throughout the war. In his letters, he informed the pope of the existence of the killing program and how it operated. Through Preysing's efforts, the Vatican issued a proclamation on December 6, 1940, condemning so-called mercy killing as "incompatible with natural and divine law." The condemnation was couched in general terms and did not single out Germany or the Nazis in any way. Nor was it widely broadcast. This behavior reflected the extreme caution with which the Vatican maneuvered between the combatants throughout World War II. The pope spoke out on euthanasia again, quite forcefully, in his 1943 pastoral letter *Mystici Corporis*. Pius XII specifically condemned the killing of "the bodily deformed, the insane, and those suffering from hereditary disease."[45] As in the first message, however, he did not specifically mention the killings in Germany of which he had been so well-informed by Preysing.

Preysing displayed a good deal of courage when, in March 1941, he gave a sermon calling attention to the killing. "With the same devotion to principles with which the Church protects matrimony, the moral focus of the people, she also protects the individual's right to life. We know that nowadays exceptions are claimed, in theory and practice, to the holy right of the innocent to life and protection. These exceptions are being justified on medical, economic, yes, even eugenic grounds. . . . The law of God proclaims that no earthly power, including the State, has the right to take the life of the innocent. This divine law is irrevocable."[46] Although brave, the sermon received little attention. The authorities took note of what he had said, but took no action against him.

In this respect Preysing's sermon was quite different from the famous, thundering sermons of the great Clemens August Graf von Galen, bishop of Münster—"The Lion of Münster."

Von Galen was the senior living member of an old and distinguished aristocratic family which had always been, as he once remarked, *"verdammt katholisch"*—incurably or irretrievably Catholic. In the seventeenth century, Christopher Bernard von Galen served as bishop-prince of Münster. At the end of the nineteenth century Ferdinand Herbert von Galen and his son held prominent positions in both Catholic and national affairs.

Bishop von Galen was born in 1878. He was sixty-three in 1941. He had served for eight years as bishop. He was both loved and respected in his diocese, and he was well-known across Germany. Von Galen's speaking voice was deep, sonorous, and authoritative; his sermons were well attended. He was a good-looking man, a powerful man, six feet four with broad shoulders and a thick chest. It is said in Münster that after he had given his three famous sermons of outrage and protest, the Gestapo was planning to arrest him. According to the story, the bishop sent word to the Gestapo that they could arrest him if they wished. They would find him standing at the door of his cathedral, arrayed in his full bishop's regalia, the miter upon his head: in his hand, the great crosier or crook—symbol of the concern and responsibility he held for the well-being of the church members in his diocese, like that of a shepherd for his flock. The powerful image of this great man, attired in the symbols of the ancient power and authority of the Roman Catholic Church, is said to have given even the Gestapo pause.

Von Galen was a conservative and a patriot. He held the full measure of support for the temporal authority, just as he did for the spiritual authority of his church. He was enthusiastically in favor of World War I, calling it no less than "a struggle for our existence."

He believed, "Each of us at his proper place in devotion to duty and readiness to sacrifice will want to implore God's mercy upon our Fatherland and God's protection for our soldiers." After the Armistice he renounced the peace policies of the Allies as "suspect from the start because they are promulgated by that Freemason Wilson and bound up with the notorious thirst for vengeance, the greed and the hunger for power that paved the way for war in the first place."[47]

Bitter about the peace, receptive to Hitler's belief that Germany had been victim to "a stab in the back," it is not surprising the bishop—like many others of his time in Germany and elsewhere—fully expected "war to break out anew."[48]

In a similar manner, it is not surprising that in the early days of the Third Reich, von Galen received special attention from the new government. The Concordat with the Vatican specified that all new bishops of the Catholic Church in Germany must take an oath of allegiance, swearing to respect the authority of the "constitutionally constituted government."[49] As it happened, von Galen was the first person to be appointed a bishop after the ratification of the Concordat. The new bishop was invited to Berlin for a ceremony of military pomp before a distinguished audience, where he was administered the oath of allegiance by no less a figure than Hermann Göring himself.

The Nazis misjudged their man. Von Galen was intensely loyal to Germany, but he was never a part or a pawn of the Nazi games. It is reported that in the early days of the Reich, the bishop was speaking from the pulpit of St. Lambert's Cathedral on the responsibilities of parenthood. He warned that the tenets and instruction of the Hitler Youth and related activities should in no way be seen as a substitute for the religious training of the young. At this point an angry party member in uniform rose from the congregation and demanded, "What right does a celibate, without wife or children, have to talk about the problems of youth and marriage?"

The bishop, a man of quick intelligence and a sense of humor, pounded the pulpit for silence and responded in a most sober tone, "*Never* will I tolerate in this cathedral any reflection upon our beloved Führer!"[50]

Von Galen had expected the outbreak of World War II. In his first wartime message he said, "War, that was openly ended by an imposed peace in 1919, has now broken out anew and has drawn our *Volk* and Fatherland into its clutches. Once again a large part of our men and youth have been called to arms, and they are engaged in bloody conflict or stand guard on the borders in firm determination to shield the Fatherland and to risk their lives to win for our *Volk* a peace of freedom and justice." [51]

Throughout the war the bishop gave strong support to Germany's war aims, and he prayed for God's blessing upon the troops at the front. He celebrated and gave thanks for the nation's "glorious victories" in France, the Low Countries, and particularly against communist Russia. He ended his every sermon with the words, "Let us pray for our *Volk*, our Fatherland, and our Führer. Our Father . . ." [52]

Von Galen was incensed by the Nazi harassment of Church institutions and properties. Such incidents persisted, to a greater or lesser extent, throughout the life of the Reich. A typical example concerned the public display of the crucifix. Efforts were made to have the crucifix removed from schoolrooms in Catholic areas. This happened in the market town of Cloppenburg in von Galen's diocese. Townsfolk were incensed. There was an actual riot; even Nazi party members who were former Catholics joined in the protest. The authorities backed down, and the crucifixes were returned to the school walls. Bishop Galen wrote a strong letter of congratulation to a Cloppenburg administrator, outlining the full story of the effort to take away the crosses and giving the details of the people's successful resistance. He published the letter in the diocesan newspaper. Copies of the letter were widely circulated throughout Germany to the intense annoyance of the Nazis. [53]

The Nazis waged a continuing propaganda campaign against Church personnel. Priests and nuns were accused of sexual perversions, of financial corruption, and of spying activities against the state. They were placed in concentration camps or under house arrest on trumped-up charges, sometimes on no charges whatever. Monasteries, nunneries, and other church institutions were seized by local authorities, without notice or compensation.

In early July 1941, the Allies began a series of massive air raids upon the city of Münster. The cathedral was damaged, the cathedral square badly hurt; block upon block of the city was laid waste, and

240

its principal street, Sonnenstrasse, destroyed. The citizens panicked and fled to the countryside for safety, even though the men were ordered to remain at their jobs by the civil authorities. The bishop's palace was hit by an incendiary bomb, which burned a part of the roof and a portion of the top floor of the building. The bishop had been out of town, celebrating the Feast of the Visitation at the ancient town of Telgte, according to his regular custom.

The bishop returned to Münster and walked about the wreckage of the city, comforting his flock. That evening he refused to leave his palace for shelter when the sirens sounded again, refusing even to go to the basement. The following day, von Galen was informed that the local Gestapo intended to seize two Jesuit institutions in the city. The bishop went at once and found the Gestapo in the very act of evicting the priests and confiscating their possessions. Here, for the first time face to face, the bishop confronted the Nazis at their work. Von Galen was outraged. This conservative aristocratic man, this German patriot, threw caution to the wind and condemned the Gestapo to their faces as thieves and robbers.

The next day the house of the Mission Sisters of the Immaculate Conception was taken. The sisters and the Jesuits were expelled from the province of Westphalia. Throughout the week, six more institutions were taken by the Gestapo, including a convent of Benedictine nuns. Bishop von Galen ordered that lodging be found for the Benedictines at a Galen family property, Castle Dinklage at Oldenburg.[54]

As von Galen was returning to the bishop's palace after his confrontation with the Gestapo, he came to a decision. He said aloud to his chaplain, but more, perhaps, to himself, *"Jetzt kann ich nicht mehr schweigen."* (Now I can no longer be silent.)

That night, in his study, at the typewriter and with his pipe at hand, the bishop began work on the first of three consecutive sermons which were to electrify Germany, infuriate Hitler, and bring von Galen lasting renown as the Lion of Münster.

According to his chaplain, the bishop was agitated and distracted at the beginning of the Sunday Mass at St. Lambert's Cathedral. The big man moved slowly, even heavily, up the steps to the pulpit. There was an unusual quaver to his voice as he read out the first sentences of his prepared sermon. Only after several minutes did he regain his composure; only then did his deep and powerful voice fill the cathedral. Chaplain Portman reported that von Galen's voice came like rolling thunder as he read forth his indictment of Nazi crimes against the Church. He listed many specific outrages. He called for justice: "Justice," he said, "is the foundation upon which the state is built."

The bishop's sermon concluded, "And, therefore, in the name of the righteous German *Volk*, in the name of the majesty of justice, in the interest of peace and solidarity on the home front, I raise my voice; as a German, as an honorable citizen, as a representative of the Christian religion, as a Catholic bishop, I publicly declare: We demand justice! If this demand remains unanswered, German *Volk* and Fatherland will perish of inner decay and rottenness despite the heroism of our soldiers and their glorious victories." [55]

A week later, the bishop again spoke out. In his second sermon he denounced the crimes which had been perpetrated against the Church and his parishioners by the Nazis. He counseled his flock to obey God's commandments. "Be strong! Stand firm! . . . it may be that obedience to God will cost you or me our life, freedom or *Heimat*. But it is better to die than to sin."

He used a powerful metaphor. "Right now we are not the hammer, but rather the anvil. Others, for the most part enemies and apostates, beat upon us seeking to bend us by force from our true relation to God and to impose a new form upon our *Volk*, ourselves and our children. But take a lesson from the forge! . . . The anvil cannot and need not strike back; it need only stand firm and strong. If it is tough enough and firm enough, the anvil outlives the hammer. And no matter how forcefully the hammer may strike, the anvil stands in quiet firmness and lives to shape that which will be forged anew." [56]

The last sermon, delivered on the third Sunday, August 3, 1941, was an unequivocal condemnation of the T-4 euthanasia program as a violation of the Commandment "Thou shall not kill."

From his pulpit Bishop Galen told his congregation in full and accurate detail about the secret government program—an offense in itself fully as serious as treason:

> . . . on orders from Berlin, mentally sick patients, who long have been under treatment and who may seem incurable, are

being forcibly removed from psychiatric clinics. Shortly afterward, as a regular practice, the family receives a notification stating that the patient is dead, that the body has been cremated and that the ashes may be collected. Broadly speaking, there is near certainty that none of the unexpected deaths of these mental cases have been due to natural causes, but were artificially induced, in accordance with the doctrine that authorizes the elimination of what are called "unworthy lives" and, consequently, the killing of innocent people, if their existence is no longer held to be productive for the nation or for the state. It is a frightful concept that seeks to justify the murder of innocents and allows the killing of invalids incapable of work, of the infirm, or incurable, and of old men and women afflicted by senility. Confronted with this doctrine the German bishops declare: No man has the right to kill an innocent person, no matter what the reason, except in case of war or in legitimate self-defense. [57]

Von Galen reminded his listeners that those being killed

. . . are our fellow men, our brothers and sisters. Poor people, sick people, unproductive people, so what? Have they somehow forfeited the right to live? Do you, do I have the right to live only as long as we are productive? . . . Some secret order could expand the . . . treatment of the mentally ill to other unproductive persons such as those suffering from incurable lung disease, the feeble elderly, disabled workers, severely wounded soldiers. Nobody would be safe any more. Who could trust his physician? . . . It is inconceivable what depraved conduct, what suspicion would enter family life if this terrible doctrine is tolerated, adopted and carried out. Woe to humanity, woe to the German people if God's holy command "thou shalt not kill" is not only transgressed but if this transgression is both tolerated and carried out without punishment. [58]

The sermon was, according to the Ministry of Propaganda, "the strongest attack made against the German political leadership in decades." [59] Von Galen had thought the Gestapo would attempt to

243

destroy the sermon manuscripts, and so he hid carbon copies of the texts in the bishop's palace. The Gestapo did, indeed, come for the sermons, but they were too late. Copies had already been made from the original, reproduced by the dozens and sent, from various mail boxes, in plain envelopes to leading church and military figures. From these copies, thousands upon thousands more were printed and passed from hand to hand, all over Germany, even to the soldiers fighting on the Russian front. The Nazi high command had a genuine crisis on its hands.

The sermon was only a part of the bishop's offensive. In addition, von Galen issued a strongly worded pastoral letter on the euthanasia program, which was distributed throughout the diocese. He sent telegrams of protest to the Reich Chancellery, to Hermann Göring, to the ministers of justice, home affairs, and public worship, and, lastly, to the supreme command of the army. He called in person to make his protest before the administrative president and the chief president of his province.

Finally, von Galen sent an official letter to the district attorney of Münster, saying that the law required citizens to report crimes to the authorities. He told the district attorney he had crimes to report: innocent persons were being murdered in clear violation of law. The bishop demanded that the attorney general protect the lives of the institutionalized patients, that he do his duty by "asking immediate protection of the *Volksgenossen* by action against their transportation and murder." The bishop could not have been more forceful.[60]

In his August 3 sermon von Galen informed his congregation that he had written this letter and told them that he was awaiting a timely reply. As he explained, "There are obligations of conscience from which no one can release us and which we must discharge even at the cost of our lives."[61]

And, indeed, his life was in danger. Friends warned him repeatedly not to move about the diocese for fear of being assaulted and murdered by the authorities. Von Galen brushed off the warnings. His brother Count Franz expressed the worry of the family: "What are we to do if you are locked up?" "Nothing at all," was the reply.[62]

In fact, Bishop von Galen was not locked up, nor was he murdered. The Nazi leaders were in a fury. Proposals were made that the bishop be put to death. Martin Bormann agreed, but Josef

Goebbels, Hitler's propaganda wizard, was strongly opposed. Goebbels understood the extraordinary popularity of the bishop. Goebbels warned that "the population of Münster could be regarded as lost during the war, if anything were done against the bishop, and in that fear one could safely include all of Westphalia."[63]

Hitler's Russian campaign was at its height. What had been expected to be a relatively easy victory was proving to be extremely costly. The fighting was fierce, and it appears that Hitler wanted no disruptions or weakening of support on the home front. The Führer ordered that no action be taken against Bishop von Galen. Further, he ordered on July 30, 1941, that seizures of church and monastic property be halted; and on August 24, 1941, in a secret, verbal order to Brandt, Hitler ordered that the T-4 killing program be halted.

Within a month of the bishop's sermons, both of the policies to which he had objected had been brought to an end.

There is no doubt whatever about Hitler's feelings concerning Bishop von Galen. The Führer, in a November 8, 1941, speech to old party members in the famed Munich beer cellar, said, "Should anyone here really be hoping to break our unity, it does not matter where he comes from or to which camp he belongs, then I will—and you know my methods—keep my eye on him for a while. This is just a time of probation. But then comes the moment when I will attack like lightning and remove the danger as quickly as possible. And then no disguise will protect him, not even the disguise of religion."[64]

In that curious book *Hitler's Table Talk* another comment of the Führer's is recorded: "I am quite sure that a man like Bishop von Galen knows full well that I shall exact retribution to the last farthing. And if he doesn't succeed in getting himself transferred in the meanwhile to the Collegium Germanicum in Rome, he may rest assured that in the balancing of our accounts, no 't' will remain uncrossed, no 'i' undotted!"[65]

The Führer despised the bishop and fully expected to exact his retribution. Even so, the bishop won and—on these two issues—the Führer was forced to back down.

We must then return to the baleful question asked at the beginning of this chapter: Why did not the churches raise their voices, rally their followers, in opposition to the other hateful Nazi

245

policies—the massacre of Jews, Gypsies, gays, and Seventh-Day Adventists; the internment of asocials; the use of terror as a tool of public policy; the bombing of civilian populations; the forced migration of millions of ethnic peoples across the face of Europe? What would have happened if the churches had condemned these hateful things as forcefully and effectively as they did euthanasia?

The question has no answer, for in fact the churches did not condemn these hateful things. The tradition of the German churches—respect for secular authority, admiration for all things German—was against their doing so.

The personnel of the Christian churches of Germany were German. There is no reason to believe their attitudes on issues were greatly different from those of the German public at large. The German public was troubled by the killing of the disabled. Thus, when the bishops condemned the practice, they had the full support of the public behind them. The persecution of Jews and asocials aroused no such outrage—neither from the public nor, it must be said, from church leaders.

Had the church leaders who *were* outraged (and there were some) spoken out, they would have received little support, either from their peers or the public. The few who did speak out had no impact and they suffered severely at the hands of the Gestapo.

12

Aktion T-4 Sequelae: 1945–88

I did do that, says my memory. I could not have done
that, says my pride. Finally memory gives in.

Friedrich Nietzsche

G ermany surrendered unconditionally on May 9, 1945. The
war had lasted five years, nine months, and nine days. The
Third Reich, the Nazi Reich of a thousand years, had lasted twelve
years, three months, and ten days.

Germany's cities lay in ruins. Its industrial structure had been
destroyed. Its society barely functioned. In madness and despair
the survivors wandered across a lunar landscape.

In 1945 every effort was required simply to sustain life—to find
food, shelter, and warmth. Before rebuilding could begin, the
rubble of the past had to be cleared away. Manpower was short—
some 3.5 million men had been killed in the armed services;
millions more were casualties, and demoralization was universal. It
was the women of Germany who began the work of reconstruction.
The women—the *Trümmerfrauen*, the rubble women—rolled up
their sleeves and with picks and shovels and makeshift wheelbar-
rows cleared the rubble, mountains of rubble. They were determined that life should begin again, that Germany should live again.
Their effort, their determination, symbolizes the extraordinary
achievement which is today's Germany. This is an achievement
which is in every way admirable.

To the Germans of the 1980s, 1945 stands as the "Year Zero," the year the building began of the modern, democratic nation which is the Germany of today.

The year zero is an appropriate term, for it denotes, at least by implication, something more than just the beginning of the physical reconstruction of German society. Zero is the beginning. There is nothing before the beginning, no history. History begins in 1945. It is commonly said that Germany experienced, and in some ways still experiences, a form of national amnesia. There is a hole where the Nazi era and World War II used to be. For decades after the war, German schoolchildren were taught nothing about the period; it simply was not there.

Adolf Hitler killed himself in his bunker, his body burned to unrecognizable ash. His Chancellery, his house at Berchtesgaden were razed to the ground. The Allied occupying powers attempted to eradicate all physical evidence of the Führer in fear that it might become a shrine to the martyred dictator at some future date. In a real sense, this was impossible; his monuments—in highways, bridges, and such—were everywhere. In a psychological sense, this was unnecessary. Hitler, the leader who was so loved and worshiped by his people, simply disappeared. His name was never mentioned. By common, if unspoken, consent, Hitler became a nonperson.

The Nazi movement, so powerful and pervasive throughout the whole of German society, disappeared with its leader. National Socialism, its Führer principle, its racial theories, its concept of society seemingly sank from sight without a trace.

Certain subjects became taboo. These subjects were not discussed, nor were they written about. Such things as anti-Semitism, racial superiority, the atrocities, the concentration camps, disappeared. And gone, too, were the principles of eugenics, the new medicine, and euthanasia for the severely disabled and the chronically insane. It was very curious. There was no defense of what had happened, no expressions of apology, hardly even acknowledgment. People just shut up.

Psychiatrists define depression as the absence of feeling; the depressed patient lives in a gray world, devoid of feeling. He uses his illness to deaden and deny the feelings he is unable to handle. If it is possible for an entire country to be depressed, Germany was that country after World War II.

Everything was denied; in the psychological sense, everything was unresolved. And this was understandable. When an individual suffers an appalling trauma—becomes a quadriplegic as the result of an accident, for example—he enters a period of denial. The mind is simply unable to comprehend, let alone deal with, the situation in which the person finds himself. It is all the person can do to deal with the minutiae of the daily nursing routine. Only gradually, over an extended period, as the rehabilitation process begins to take hold will the individual be able to deal in a realistic manner with his condition and the intense feelings it engenders. It is reasonable to believe that the people of Germany found themselves in an analogous situation.

It was impossible to deal with the enormity of the horror they had brought upon others and caused themselves; impossible to entertain such feelings and to continue, at the same time, with the desire for life.

And so the question of war guilt was left to others. The *Trümmerfrauen* hauled away the rubble. The routine of daily life began again. The men joined the women, and together they began to build a new life for themselves and their children, and for the children after them.

The essential validity of this generalization will help to understand the way that German society, the medical profession, and the disability community have behaved over the half century that has elapsed since the T-4 euthanasia program.

With the occupation of Germany, the Allied troops liberated the concentration camps. Photographs of what they found—the ghostlike survivors with their burning eyes, the piles of cadavers stacked like firewood—filled the newspapers as the world first became aware of the horrors of the Holocaust.

At first, it did not occur to the newly established Allied military governments that the hospitals, asylums, sanitoriums, and orphanages of Germany might also need liberating.

In August 1945, three months after the end of the war, Robert E. Abrams (then a junior public relations officer in the U.S. Army) was sitting at his desk in an office in Munich. A German physician came to Abrams with a troubling story. The physician had returned to his hometown of Kaufbeuren from war service at the front. Kaufbeuren

249

was, and is, the site of a psychiatric institution. The doctor told Abrams that psychiatrists at the institution were systematically killing their patients. Abrams, with the doctor, went at once to inspect the situation and found that the reports were, indeed, true. Three months after the end of the war, the psychiatrists of Kaufbeuren were still killing their patients as a matter of routine. The small institutional crematorium was still being used to dispose of the bodies. Over the previous twelve months, 25 percent of the asylum's patients had died, either by injection or starvation caused by "scientific diets." Over a hundred of these victims were children. The Americans found several corpses of patients who had died within the previous seventy-two hours waiting for cremation. [1]

All over Germany similar discoveries were being made. A month after the surrender, the public health and security officers of the American military government investigated the hospital at Eglfing-Haar, on the outskirts of Munich. They found a children's building, the Kinderhaus, with 150 patients. Within the Kinderhaus, they found a "special department"—that is, the starvation ward—with twenty children awaiting their deaths.

Eglfing-Haar was the hospital directed by the nefarious Dr. Hermann Pfannmüller. Pfannmüller had fled at the approach of the American army. In his haste, he had not tarried to destroy his secret files. He left directions that his successor, a Dr. von Braunmuhl, burn the papers. Braunmuhl did not do so. Instead, he turned them over to Major Leo Alexander of the American military government. According to von Braunmuhl, Pfannmüller was a "brutal fellow" who enjoyed killing his patients, whom he referred to as "chunks of meat." Von Braunmuhl wanted the files to be used in the prosecution of Pfannmüller as a war criminal; but he asked that it be done discreetly because he feared, as Alexander reported, "that too much publicity focused on Eglfing would interfere with the confidence of the public in the type of treatment available at Eglfing." He had a point. Considering that something like two thousand adults and at least three hundred children had been exterminated at the institution, it would not be surprising should public confidence be a bit shaken by the news of the murders.

From the evidence obtained from Pfannmüller's secret records, Alexander was able to reconstruct much of the operation of the T-4

Aktion euthanasia program and the children's program. This was evidence which would be presented at the Nuremberg trials.[2]

In 1946 the victorious allies—the U.S., the United Kingdom, the Soviet Union, and France—held war crimes trials at the Palace of Justice in Nuremberg, the city made infamous by Hitler's massive flag-waving Nazi rallies. The most renowned of the trials was the first, that of the major war criminals, including Göring, Hess, and Minister of the Interior Frick. There were twelve subsequent trials held before the International Military Tribunals at Nuremberg.

The first of these was called officially *United States of America* v. *Karl Brandt, et al.*, but it came to be known as "the Medical Case," because twenty of the twenty-three defendants were doctors. The most eminent of these was Dr. Karl Brandt, the young SS officer who had served as Hitler's personal physician and Reich commissioner for health and sanitation. He had been, of course, the man charged by the Führer with responsibility for setting up and directing the operation of Aktion T-4. A fellow defendant was Viktor Brack, chief administrative officer in the Chancellery of the Führer and the man charged with administering the T-4 euthanasia program under the supervision of Brandt and Bouhler. Brack was one of the three men on trial who were not doctors.

The proceedings lasted for close to a year: indictments were filed on October 26, 1946; arraignment was on November 26; the prosecution's opening statement was heard on the ninth of December; judgments and sentences were handed down on August 19 and 20, 1947.

The tribunal met 139 times, and the transcript of its proceedings runs to over 11,000 pages. The prosecution presented 570 written exhibits, some containing many documents; the defense introduced 901 exhibits. Oral testimony was received from thirty-two witnesses for the prosecution and thirty for the defense. Each of the twenty-three defendants testified on his own behalf, and each was subject to examination on behalf of the other defendants.

Every word of the proceedings, all of the affidavits, depositions, letters, and reports used in the preparation of the charges or presented as evidence to the court were translated into English. All of this material is available at the U.S. National Archives in Washington, D.C.

Preparation of the case against the defendants had taken months. The indictment contained four parts:

The first charged that defendants pursuant to a "common design" had "conspired" to commit "war crimes" and "crimes against humanity." These crimes had been defined by Control Council Law No. 10, as agreed by the commanding officers of the Allied occupying armies.

War crimes were specified as "atrocities or offenses against persons or property constituting violations of the laws or customs of war." This law defined crimes against civilian populations of occupied territory, prisoners of war. It outlawed plunder, wanton destruction of cities, and devastation not justified by military necessity.[3]

Crimes against humanity were more broadly defined as "atrocities or offenses including but not limited to murder, extermination, enslavement, deportation, imprisonment, torture, rape or any inhumane acts committed against any civilian population (including German citizens) or persecution on political, religious, or racial grounds."[4]

The second charge listed the specific war crimes of which the defendants were accused. There were twelve separate paragraphs, each detailing such things as inhuman medical experiments performed without consent upon unwilling victims. There was, for example, a paragraph recounting the killing of 112 Jews in the occupied territory for the purpose of building a skeleton collection for a medical school. And, lastly, there was a paragraph explaining the Aktion T-4 euthanasia program. It very carefully spelled out that among the victims were "nationals of German-occupied countries," thus putting the program within the purview of the war crimes law.

Between September 1939 and April 1945 the defendants Karl Brandt, Blome, Brack, and Hoven unlawfully, willfully, and knowingly committed war crimes, as defined by Article II of Control Council Law No. 10, in that they were principals in, accessories to, ordered, abetted, took a consenting part in, and were connected with plans and enterprises involving the execution of the so-called euthanasia program of the German Reich in the course of which the defendants herein murdered hundreds of thousands of human beings, including nationals of German-occupied countries. This program involved the systematic and secret execution of the aged, insane, incurably ill, of deformed children, and other persons, by gas, lethal injections, and diverse other means in nursing homes, hospitals, and asylums. Such persons were regarded as "useless eaters" and a burden to the German war machine. The relatives of these victims were informed that they died from natural causes, such as heart failure. German doctors involved in the "euthanasia" program were also sent to Eastern-occupied countries to assist in the mass extermination of Jews.[5]

The third charge itemized crimes against humanity for which the defendants were standing trial including the murder of their fellow German citizens over the course of the euthanasia program.

The fourth count charged Karl Brandt, Brack, and eight of the other defendants with membership in the SS, which had been "declared to be criminal by the International Military Tribunal in Case No. 1."

There was, of course, an ex post facto aspect to the indictment. The defendants were being charged with criminal acts committed before the law had been written which declared such acts to be criminal. That this made the prosecution uneasy can be seen in the concluding paragraphs of counts two and three. These sought to add dignity to Control Council Law No. 10 by listing supportive and precedent law:

The said war crimes constitute violations of international conventions particularly of Articles 4, 5, 6, 7, and 46 of the Hague Regulations, 1908, and of Articles 2, 3, and 4 of the Prisoner-of-War Convention (Geneva, 1929), the laws and customs of war, the general principles of criminal law as derived from the criminal laws of all civilized nations, the internal penal laws of the countries in which such crimes were committed and of Article II of Control Law No. 10.

It was, beyond doubt, clear to all the world that German physicians *had* committed murder and *had* perpetrated atrocities upon their patients. It was also clear to all that the world—particularly the public of the victorious nations—demanded that those who were guilty of these crimes be brought to justice. However, the Allied occupation authorities had no standing to prosecute these criminals in the German court system, which was in a state of collapse, anyway. Furthermore, there was no suitable international judicial authority to try the cases. Rather than simply let these accused criminals go free, the Allies set up a court system, with laws, procedures, and judges to try them.

In doing so, issues of justice were raised which are still discussed, forty years later. The Nuremberg trials have always aroused controversy. Troubling precedents were set concerning the rights of the victors to exact punishment of the defeated; difficult questions were raised about individual culpability. What are the responsibilities of individuals acting under orders of a valid government authority? Are they to be punished for their behavior? To what extent may a man be punished for failing to act according to the dictates of morality and conscience, *as commonly perceived* but, perhaps, not specifically outlawed?

The question of the applicability of Law No. 10 to crimes committed by German nationals *upon* German nationals was particularly difficult, as was the question whether war criminals could be prosecuted for crimes that occurred prior to the outbreak of war, September 1, 1939.

These were troubling questions, no doubt, but it would have been more troubling by far for the Allies to do nothing.

Every effort was made to have fair trials. Rules were established and published covering all aspects of the proceedings. Defendants had counsel, the right to present their defense, the right to cross-examine.

The German public has commonly attempted to dismiss the Nuremberg trials as but a part of the humiliation of defeat, little more than their vindictive conquerors seeking revenge. This system of denial has allowed them to block thoughts about the evidence presented during the trials, evidence of events which decent, law-abiding, God-fearing Germans have found very, very difficult to acknowledge as having happened in their beloved country.

Certainly the evidence presented to the court was terrible, indeed. Photographs, original documents and photostats, depositions and live testimony, all told of torture and murder in the name of science by some of the most distinguished members of the German medical and scientific community.

The opening statement for the prosecution was made by U.S. Brigadier General Telford Taylor, chief of counsel. His summary of the case to the court was sixty-two pages long.

In speaking of the euthanasia program, Taylor made the points that Aktion T-4 was not mercy killing, as the term is commonly understood, but murder; the killing had been done without the authorization of law, "not even a Nazi law."[6] Indeed, Hitler had specifically rejected the very idea of making it law. And finally, the doctors running the program had extended the killing far beyond anything ever authorized by the Führer.

In closing, he spoke of the utter perversion of medical ethics by the doctors of Germany during the Nazi years. He emphasized he was speaking not just of the defendants but of others now dead or missing or unknown: "There were many co-conspirators who are not in the dock. . . . There were many others."[7] These men, performing experiments, sterilizing and killing patients without the consent either of the patients or their families, "departed from every known standard of medical ethics."[8] He could, he said, make a long list of these violations. "But the gulf between these atrocities and serious research is so patent that such a tabulation would be cynical."[9]

And then he concluded with a most striking allusion:

> We need look no further than the law which the Nazis themselves passed on the twenty-fourth of November 1933 for the protection of animals. This law states explicitly that it is designed to prevent cruelty and indifference of man toward animals and to awaken and develop sympathy and understanding for animals as one of the highest moral values of a people. The soul of the German people should abhor the principle of mere utility without consideration of the moral aspects. The law states further that all operations or treatments which are associated with pain or injury, especially experiments involving the use of cold, heat, or infection, are prohibited, and can be permitted only under special excep-

tional circumstances. Special written authorization by the head of the department is necessary in every case, and experimenters are prohibited from performing experiments according to their own free judgment. Experiments for the purpose of teaching must be reduced to a minimum. Medico-legal tests, vaccinations, withdrawal of blood for diagnostic purposes, and trial of vaccines prepared according to well-established scientific principles are permitted, but the animals have to be killed immediately and painlessly after such experiments. Individual physicians are not permitted to use dogs to increase their surgical skill by such practices. National Socialism regards it as a sacred duty of German science to keep down the number of painful animal experiments to a minimum.

If the principles announced in this law had been followed for human beings as well, this indictment would never have been filed. It is perhaps the deepest shame of the defendants that it probably never even occurred to them that human beings should be treated with at least equal humanity.[10]

After a trial lasting close to eight months, the tribunal handed down its judgment on August 19, its sentences on August 20, 1947. Four of the defendants had been charged with war crimes and crimes against humanity in connection with the T-4 euthanasia program. Of these four, one was found not guilty and was ordered released. His name was Dr. Karl Blome. The other three were found guilty; the following day each was sentenced to death by hanging. After various appeals and requests for clemency—all of which were rejected—Dr. Karl Brandt, Dr. Waldemar Hoven, and Viktor Brack, along with four others of the twenty-three defendants, went to their deaths on June 2, 1948. The executions were carried out at Landsberg prison.

Dr. Hoven had been chief camp physician at the notorious Buchenwald concentration camp. Hoven was a pathological killer, having murdered more than a thousand prisoners by his own hand, acting on his own initiative.

Brack, who had started his career in the Nazi Party as Himmler's chauffeur, showed himself during the trial to have been little more than a bright apparatchik. Good at administrative detail and devoted to the cause, he found himself in matters which were far over his head at the Führer's Chancellery: "I was assigned duties the extent and importance of which I could not foresee. Neither my training nor my qualifications sufficed for this task."[11] He did not question what he was told to do—if the Führer wanted it, that was good enough for him.

Dr. Karl Brandt was something different. The respected Pastor Bodelschwingh, who had debated the morality of euthanasia with Brandt, had called him not a criminal but an idealist.[12] He was a thoughtful man, an intellectual, and he took his responsibilities as a physician most seriously.

So far as the euthanasia charges were concerned, Brandt presented the court with a double-barreled defense. He acknowledged his participation in Aktion T-4, made no apology for the program, and declared it to be justified—justified out of pity for the victim and out of a desire to free the family and loved ones from a lifetime of needless sacrifice. His attorney, the estimable Dr. Robert Servatius, argued that it was within the authority of a modern state to institute such a program, and he cited the actions of juries across the world which had "found offenders not guilty who freed their nearest relatives from the torment of life.

"Who would not have the desire to die while in good health rather than to be forced by all the resources of medical science to continue life degraded to an animal's existence! Only misguided civilization keeps such beings alive; in the normal struggle for existence Nature is more charitable."[13]

Servatius made the point, heard repeatedly at Nuremberg, that Brandt did no more than obey, as a patriotic German, the orders of his state, as legally constituted. It has never been a crime for a loyal citizen to obey his sovereign. The lawyer paraphrased Shakespeare: " 'My cause is just and quarrel honorable,' says the King [Henry V]. And Shakespeare's soldier answers him: 'That's more than we know.' And another soldier adds: 'Ay, or more than we should seek after; for we know enough if we know we are the king's subjects; if his cause be wrong, our obedience to the king wipes the crime of it out of us.' "[14]

Speaking in his own defense, in his final statement of July 19, 1947, Dr. Brandt said that he stood before the court as a doctor, and on my conscience lies the responsibility of being responsible for men and for life. . . . It would have no weight if friends and patients were to shield me and speak well of me, saying I had helped and I had healed. There are many examples of my actions in emergencies and my readiness to help. All that is now useless. As far as I am concerned, I shall not evade these charges; but it is my duty to attempt to vindicate myself as a man toward all these who believe in me personally, who trusted in me and who relied upon me as a man, as well as a doctor and a superior.

Brandt said he would have preferred that someone else run the program. This was not the case. It had been his responsibility, and he had done all that he could to see that the scope of the program was carefully and narrowly drawn; that economics was allowed to play no role in its operation; and that the program was under the constant review of the leading medical professors of Germany. But he said, "I assented to euthanasia. I fully realize the problem; it is as old as mankind, but it is not a crime against man or against humanity. It is pity for the incurable, literally."

And then, in conclusion: "Somewhere we must all make a stand. I am fully conscious that when I said 'yes' to euthanasia I did so with the deepest conviction, just as it is my conviction today, that it was right. Death can mean deliverance. Death is life—just as much as birth. It was never meant to be murder."[15]

The power of this argument was inescapable, but it was an argument the tribunal did not find necessary to address. In its judgment on Brandt, the court said it did not doubt the sincerity of his convictions, but

The abstract proposition about whether or not euthanasia is justified . . . is of no concern of this tribunal. Whether or not a state may validly enact legislation which imposes euthanasia . . . is likewise a question which does not enter into the issues. Assuming that it may do so, the family of nations is not obligated to give recognition to such legislation when it manifestly gives legality to plain murder and torture of defenseless human beings of other nations.

The evidence is conclusive that almost at the outset of the

program non-German nationals were selected for euthanasia and extermination.

The tribunal concluded, "We find that Karl Brandt was responsible for, aided and abetted, took a consenting part in, and was connected with plans and enterprises . . . in the course of which murders, brutalities, cruelties, tortures, and other inhumane acts were committed [against non-German nationals]. To the extent that these criminal acts did not constitute war crimes they constituted crimes against humanity." [16]

—

As Taylor told the court, many of the physicians who had participated in the killing had died, others had run away. Of the ones who had fled, an unknown number changed their names and, in time, resumed practice. The rank and file of the physicians—including many who had taken part in one way or another in the euthanasia program—simply went back to their practice or their teaching, as though nothing had happened. Instead of killing patients, they returned to treating them.

It is notorious that in a legal proceeding it is exceedingly difficult to find doctors willing to testify against a colleague. The medical profession is a close fraternity, its members loyal to one another; and this is even more true in Germany than in the United States. Over the decades since 1945, the civil authorities of West Germany have sought to track down and to prosecute the more infamous of the T-4 physicians. Their efforts have been disappointing.

This disappointment is a product of the closed-mouth policy of the medical community, the continuing high respect with which physicians are held in Germany, and the general policy of denial concerning Nazi atrocities which has marked German society since the war: Don't make waves. Why look back? What is the point of raking up the "errors and confusion during the unfortunate period of National Socialism," as Professor Peter Esch described it in a 1951 lecture on the history of the University of Münster medical faculty. [17]

Esch's position may have been typical of postwar Germany; nevertheless, it was out of touch with reality. It must be pointed out that, while the Nazi period was certainly *unfortunate,* the *errors* of the euthanasia program were few; and there was no *confusion* whatever about its purpose. This was a program in which doctors killed their patients. Aktion T-4 was a precision operation, made possible by the acquiescence and compliance of the medical profession.

Fourteen nurses were tried for murder in Munich. They were accused of killing their patients by injection at the Obrawalde-Meseritz state hospital, where over eight thousand adults and children were put to death during the years 1939–45. The nurses' defense was that "we had to bow to the orders of the physicians." One nurse testified that once when she had objected to murdering a child she had received "a big bawling out" from the female chief psychiatrist. All fourteen nurses were acquitted. [18]

In another Munich case, unrelated to the nurses' case, the court ruled that "the extermination of mental patients was not murder but manslaughter." [19]

A psychiatrist who not only killed his patients but watched them die through a peephole into the gas chamber was also acquitted. "We deal with a certain human weakness," said the court, "which does not as yet deserve moral condemnation." Still another court spoke of disabled people as "poor, miserable creatures." [20] A court in Cologne acquitted a physician who had killed many of his patients because, said the court, these persons were but "burned-out human husks." Such statements are, of course, no more than polite ways of labeling disabled people as *Untermenschen.* [21]

Werner Heyde was the physician who had served as the chief medical evaluator in the administration of the euthanasia program. A longtime member of the Nazi Party and an officer of the SS, psychiatrist Heyde had also advised the government on the development of effective torture techniques. After the war, Heyde escaped the authorities. He disappeared from view, forged his papers, and reappeared as a Dr. Sawade. Dr. Sawade practiced in the vicinity of Flensburg, Schleswig-Holstein. He became a neurological adviser for public corporations, serving from time to time as an expert witness for the state court of Schleswig. At least eighteen medical and law officials were aware of his true identity. Nevertheless, he continued in his practice until late 1959, at which time he was arrested upon the complaint of a fellow psychiatrist who had come into conflict with Heyde–Sawade over a court matter. Heyde's trial dragged on for five years, thanks to petitions, delays, and appeals, until Heyde committed suicide in his cell—it is thought at the urging of fellow physicians—in order to escape justice.[22]

Professor Werner Catel had an easier time of it. During the Nazi years, Catel served as director of a Leipzig pediatric clinic. When Hitler authorized Dr. Karl Brandt to look into the case of the disabled Knauer child—the child whose parents had asked the Führer to put it out of its misery—Brandt had consulted Catel, the child's doctor. As the result of this collaboration, Catel was appointed chairman of the three-member commission which operated the "Children's Program" that ordered the death of many thousands of infants.

After the war, Catel was appointed professor of pediatrics and director of the children's clinic at the University of Kiel. He had several brushes with the law; attempts were made to prosecute him for murder. In 1949, a court dismissed charges against him on the curious grounds that he had been a person of inexperience and goodwill, the court concluding, therefore, that Catel had believed his actions to have been legal.

Catel escaped punishment but not publicity. When the Heyde scandal broke, the euthanasia programs of the Nazi years became the subject of much excitement in the West German newspapers. The Catel case received much attention, and as a result the doctor was forced to retire from his university position. Although retired from teaching, Catel continued his practice and his writing. In 1962 he published a book, *Borderline Situations of Life*, setting forth the case for euthanasia of disabled children. In 1979 he coedited a book to be used in the training of pediatric nurses.[23]

Perhaps the last trial on T-4 euthanasia charges took place in Frankfurt in 1986. Aquilin Ullrich and Heinrich Bunke were charged with complicity in the murder of several thousand persons during the Nazi era. Both men were physicians, and both were seventy-two at the time of the trial. Ullrich was in the unhappy position of having already admitted killing 210 retarded persons with poison gas by his own hand. At a trial twenty years before, the two doctors had been found guilty: Ullrich of complicity in the killing of 1,805 mentally ill patients, Bunke of complicity in the killing of 4,950. In spite of the conviction, neither man was sentenced or fined. This was because the court found mitigating circumstances, in that while they were killing mentally ill persons "without the natural will to live"—as the court saw it—the two physicians had been unaware of the "criminality of their actions and had acted according to an unavoidable erroneous transgression."[24]

Three years later a federal court repealed the verdict. Efforts were made over the years to bring the men to justice but without success, in part because Ullrich and Bunke's medical colleagues were always willing to certify to the courts that the two men were too ill to stand trial (not so ill, however, as to drop their surgical practice). In 1986 they were again before the courts. After a year-long trial, they were convicted and, on May 18, 1987, each was sentenced to four years in prison. At the time of writing, the case is on appeal and it appears unlikely that either man will ever serve time.[25]

■

In 1946, at the express direction of the fifty-first German Doctors' Congress, the West German Physicians' Chambers appointed a special committee to monitor the Nuremberg doctors' trial. This committee asked various senior physicians to attend the trial and to prepare a report of its findings for the information of the country's medical establishment. All declined. The committee then turned to Alexander Mitscherlich, a young psychiatrist, serving as a junior university lecturer at the time.

Mitscherlich, with the assistance of medical student (later Dr.) Fred Mielke, produced a careful abstract of the trial's proceedings. The case for the prosecution and the case for the defense were summarized in an orderly fashion with important evidence, statements, and cross-examination printed in full and verbatim from the trial proceedings. It was a painfully accurate account of the trial with no editorializing, no moralizing, no lessons drawn.

The Mitscherlich report was printed in book form in 1949. Ten thousand copies were printed, a large press run for a country the size of West Germany. Copies were sent to the West German Physicians' Chambers for distribution to its members. At the Chambers the books disappeared. According to Dr. Mitscherlich, no one he met over the next ten years had ever heard of the book.[26] The book never appeared in bookstores. There were no reviews in any medical journal. Publication of the book was a nonevent.

It is not quite true that the book went unreviewed. There was one notice, written by Friedrich Hermann Rein, a physiologist and dean of faculty at the University of Göttingen. Rein was outraged: the book was "directly irresponsible"; it was "lacking . . . documentation"; an insult to German science whose "honor is inviolable." No one but a "pervert" would wish to read such a book.[27]

Two physicians in Berlin were so upset they went to court, claiming the book was libelous of German physicians, seeking to have it suppressed.[28] The two young authors of the nonbook were roundly attacked on a personal basis. As Mitscherlich remembers, "The accusations against us eventually became grotesque, and thereupon some colleagues led themselves to believe that whatever we had taken down in writing had been invented merely to humiliate our venerable medical profession."[29]

This is a curious twist on the tendency of society to blame the victim. The medical establishment of the Nazi years had devalued and destroyed those patients it could not cure. Now it was attempting to devalue and dismiss Mitscherlich's account of these years. For his pains Dr. Mitscherlich was denounced as "a traitor to his country."[30]

It is ironic that Mitscherlich's book was cited by the International Medical Association as a significant factor in its decision to readmit the German Medical Association to its organization after the war. The IMA took the book as evidence that the German medical profession was willing to examine and confront the mistakes and crimes of its past in the Nazi years![31]

For decades, virtually nothing was written or spoken in Germany about the role of medical science in the Third Reich. This was one of the forbidden subjects. According to German physician Hanauske-Abel, "Of 422 articles on medicine under National Socialism published worldwide [in medical journals] between 1966 and 1979, only two originated in the Federal Republic, and the first monograph, 'Physicians Under National Socialism,' was printed only last year [1985], fifty years after the *Machtergreifung* [Nazi seizure of power]."[32]

In 1968 a wave of student revolts swept across the Western world. In West Germany an important aspect of the movement was the demand by the more radical members of the new generation that the self-imposed national amnesia be brought to an end. The past must be examined and confronted, said the youth. It must be acknowledged. Germany must end its long denial and come to terms with its history. To the older generation, this was a frightening, even terrifying demand. As psychiatrist Mitscherlich explained to Dr. Robert Jay Lifton, in another context, " . . . most Germans of the Nazi generation were incapable of confronting their guilt because its dimensions would be too overwhelming. That is, they could not, then or now, allow themselves to feel." [33]

The young German generation which rebelled in the 1960s is now coming of age. Historians of this generation have begun to make a careful study of the Nazi years, particularly of the behavior and actions of the rank and file of the nation's citizens. They are interested in what life was like under Hitler. At last important research is being done to discover and document the extent of the killing of disabled people in the hospitals of Germany. As the early result of such studies it is now known that medical killing was far more widespread than the T-4 slaughter set forth in the evidence presented at Nuremberg. Far more research is needed on such operations as program 14 f 13 (which extended euthanasia to the concentration camps and occupied territories), the antituberculosis program in occupied Poland (in which physicians rode shotgun across the countryside, shooting peasants who "looked" tubercular), and the so-called Aktion Brandt. (During the "total war" phase, mentally ill and extended-care patients were killed so as to free their beds for short-term ill patients from hospitals destroyed by bombing.)[34]

The first major book dealing with the T-4 euthanasia program and people's reaction to it was written not by a historian but by a journalist with an interest in the disabled and their welfare. This book, *"Euthanasie" im NS-Staat; Die "Vernichtung lebensunwerten Lebens,"* by Ernst Klee, was published in Frankfurt in 1983. Klee has since published a companion volume with additional documentation on the euthanasia program. Klee has done a remarkable and difficult job of gathering information from a variety of sources to provide a reliable account of the massive killings by the German physicians during the Third Reich years. Important historians at work in this field include Goetz Aly, Karl Heinz Roth, Benno Muller-Hill, Michael H. Kater, and Rolf Winau. There are many others. The Free University of Berlin, the Institute of the History of Medicine at Mainz, and such centers as the Universities of Kiel, Bremen, and Kassel have research programs under way on various aspects of medicine under Hitler.

Research and publication of the facts of medical collaboration with the Nazis have taken a certain amount of courage. The medical establishment is not pleased with such studies. Doctoral candidates have been denied their degrees because their dissertations document matters their professors are unwilling to acknowledge. Junior professors have been rebuked, even dismissed, by their departments for stating no more than the truth: a Friedel Lapple was severely reprimanded for saying in a lecture that many of the Weimar medical officials cooperated with the Nazi regime.[35] In a particularly complex and controversial case a lecturer in medical history, said to be a member of a radical left-wing group, was dismissed, in part, for his statements concerning medical collaboration with the Nazis. One of his students wrote in protest to a local paper, "As future physicians we think it absolutely necessary that we come to terms with our National Socialist past, all the more so because it has affected medicine above everything else: experimentation on humans, euthanasia, and forced sterilization are facts of Third Reich medicine that we are all conversant with."[36]

Traditionally, the physicians of Germany have been a most conservative profession, accorded much respect by the society at large. This is as true today as it was fifty years ago. The attitude of the German medical establishment to the "facts of Third Reich medicine" has been recalcitrant and unyielding and without repentance. The establishment has acknowledged no crime, admitted no guilt, expressed no remorse, made no apology.

Typical was the behavior of the Hamburg Council of Physicians, a professional licensing board. In 1949 the council was asked to decide whether doctors who had participated in the killing of disabled children as part of the Nazi euthanasia program should be

265

denied their license to practice. After due deliberation the council ruled that the doctors should be allowed to continue their practice because "the problem of euthanasia" was an issue which remained unclear, both in law and professional ethics. The issue was raised again, twelve years later, before the Hamburg Health Authority, as well as the Council of Physicians. Again, the doctors were allowed to continue in their practice, as the ruling held that their actions during the years 1941–43 did not, in fact, constitute a "severe" transgression of medical ethics, and hence could not be the justification for the revocation of licenses, twenty years after the event.[37]

From time to time since the war, efforts have been made at meetings of German medical professionals to introduce and debate resolutions expressing regret or the wish that some sort of compensation be made to the families of the victims or to the survivors. All of these efforts have failed. In one such instance, at the Fortieth Bavarian Congress of Physicians, a motion was offered that read: "The Fortieth Bavarian Congress of Physicians requests that the appropriate authorities in the Federal Republic, after a delay of forty-two years, repeal the Law for the Prevention of Genetically Impaired Progeny of July 14, 1933. Surviving victims are to be rehabilitated morally and compensated financially." This motion was not brought to a vote, nor was it even debated on the floor.[38]

It has been the position of the Federal Council of Physicians that the Genetic Health Law should not be considered a Nazi measure, as it was proposed and discussed before the Nazi seizure of power. This is consonant with the policy of the federal government, which in 1953 passed legislation setting guidelines for compensation for persons who had been persecuted because of their opposition to Nazi ideology, their race, their faith, or philosophy. This established the principle of the *Unrechtgesetz*, which translates as the unjust law, the law that is opposite to right. Persons who had suffered as the result of illegal actions of the Nazi government or under the terms of a Nazi *Unrechtgesetz* were to be compensated. These guidelines served to deny restitution to large blocs of German citizens who had been victims of the Nazis. Homosexuals were excluded, as were the heirs of euthanasia victims and those who were forcefully sterilized or castrated. The reason for these exclusions, as the denial of compensation to the involuntarily sterilized had it, was that sterilization did not constitute persecution, since it had been done for genetic-biological reasons; and the law to prevent impaired progeny was not "contrary to lawfulness," i.e., not *Unrechtgesetz*.[39] Similarly, euthanasia was not simply a Nazi policy; it had been discussed and advocated at least since the publication of Binding and Hoche's book, back in 1920. As for homosexuals, their persecution during the Nazi years was certainly unfortunate, but the acts which had brought on their persecution were just as illegal in the Federal Republic in the 1950s as they had been during the Nazi years.

From time to time efforts have been made to expand the guidelines of the 1953 law, so as to provide for those who were victims of the sterilization and euthanasia policies. These efforts have failed. Most recently, in April 1985, the Bodelschwinghsche Institutions (of Bethel) petitioned the Committee for Petitions of the West German Parliament asking:

1. That the wrongfulness of the July 14, 1933, Law for the Prevention of Genetically Impaired Progeny be acknowledged.
2. That the judgments of the doctors' courts for genetic health be annulled.
3. That the sterilization or killing of the mentally or physically impaired during the Nazi era be declared as persecution under the terms of the 1953 law.

This petition was joined by the Alliance of Protestant Institutions for Mentally and Psychiatrically Impaired Persons, as well as by the Synod of the Protestant Church in Germany.

The West German parliament reviewed the matter of compensation for victims of Nazi persecution and on November 4, 1986, decided there was no need for new legislation. Existing compensation regulations and practices were held to be sufficient, even in disputed cases. The issue was raised yet again, in testimony presented to the Internal Committee of the West German Parliament on June 24, 1987, in which the Protestant churches of Germany expressed their conviction that compensation should be awarded to the sterilization and euthanasia victims.

Although in the postwar years the "science" of eugenics is on the list of forbidden subjects, there seems to be little reason to believe that the opinions of the German medical establishment have much changed regarding the so-called eugenic policies. Racial purity is no longer spoken of, and the concept of the *Volk* no longer carries mystical overtones. No one talks anymore of useless eaters or lives not worth living. Yet . . .

In 1987, the Federal Council of Physicians prepared guidelines for "the admissibility of sterilization of mentally retarded persons for eugenic reasons (danger of genetically impaired progeny) or social indicators (inability to meet parental duties)." The guidelines, which were published in the official medical journal *Deutsches Ärzteblatt* on October 22, 1987, were intended to authorize physicians to perform sterilization procedures on their own initiative in cases of women of child-bearing age and children adjudged to be retarded and presumed incapable of giving consent.[40]

The Bundestag is at present considering legislation which would allow such sterilization to take place. An argument advanced in favor of passage is that a legal procedure will bring an end to the illegal sterilizations—estimated to number more than a thousand a year—being performed upon retarded persons by their doctors in West Germany today.[41]

The assumptions underlying these guidelines are surely familiar: The physician *knows* whether the condition is genetically transmitted; the physician is equipped to make—and has the right to make—a judgment on the quality of parenting of which certain persons are capable; the physician is the member of society entitled to make such decisions. All of these assumptions were endorsed by the medical establishment of the Nazi years. These were assumptions which did not square with reality then—nor do they now. Doctors do not know with exactitude which conditions are genetically caused. They have no more knowledge than anyone else as to just what constitutes good parenting or who will or will not make a good parent. And there is no reason why doctors, any more than any other group in society, should have the authority to make such a decision about the life of another. In fact, these assumptions are rooted in the presumed right of a power elite to use its power to preserve the status quo and its privileged position within that status quo.

In the years since the war euthanasia has been an emotionally laden topic in West Germany. Only in the 1980s has it become possible to discuss such things as "mercy death" in a public forum, and even now the subject provokes protests and controversy. The German Society for Humane Dying was established in 1980, and its officers have been active in making speeches, issuing statements, and presenting testimony. In 1986 the society presented draft legislation which would repeal paragraph 216 of the criminal code that requires punishment for "killing on request." This proposal was debated at the Fifty-sixth Congress of Jurists in 1986. An alternative proposal of a law to authorize, in certain circumstances, assistance in dying was drafted by a group of professors of medicine and criminal law and published in 1986 by Thieme publishers.[42]

Hearings were held on such euthanasia proposals in Bonn before the judicial committee of the Bundestag in both 1985 and 1986. They received a good deal of attention in the press. In 1985 fifteen witnesses were heard. Two church representatives, a Professor Fritsche of the University of Homburg/Saar, and, interestingly enough, a representative of the Federal Council of Physicians, were opposed to any change in existing law.

The president of the German Society for Humane Dying, Hans Henning Atrott, and the well-known euthanasia exponent Dr. Julius Hackethal called for change. Atrott sought a "law for natural death," which would specifically authorize passive assistance in dying. Passive assistance is generally defined as the withholding of life-support procedures, occasionally even refusal to provide food and liquids by intravenous or gastrointestinal tube. Dr. Hackethal went further. He defined the physician's tasks as threefold: the maintenance of health, the cure of disease, and the provision of mercy killing. He saw no distinction in mercy killing between active and passive modes.[43]

Dr. Hackethal, the director of a cancer clinic, has made himself something of a celebrity on the issue of mercy killing. His words and face are often seen in the sensational press—the newspapers of Western Germany that are similar to the *National Enquirer* in the United States. It is Hackethal's practice to bring to public attention a case of the most appalling suffering—someone in great pain, totally incapacitated, without hope for improvement, begging for release. From this specific case he will argue for a general policy of euthanasia. It is interesting that under cross-examination in his testimony before the Bundestag, he did say cases of extremely sick persons asking a physician to end their lives were, in fact, quite rare. More often, he said, such requests are made by the families, unwilling to see their loved one in pain and financially strapped by the costs of the illness.

The symbolic power of the "mercy killing" issue in Germany today is very great. It is not just the issue itself but the powerful, intolerable memories stirred by it. Something of the intensity can be seen by the events which occurred at Rehab 88, the fifth international rehabilitation trade fair held at Karlsruhe in March 1988. This was a gathering of rehabilitation therapists, doctors, disabled persons, and representatives of the multibillion-dollar health products industry.

It is most extraordinary, but true, that the person asked to be the keynote speaker for the professional section of the conference was Hans Henning Atrott, president of the German Society for Humane Dying. The subject of his talk was—believe it or not—"Active Assistance for Dying: the Final Rehabilitation."

In spite of objections from organizations of disabled persons, the organizers of the program refused to cancel the presentation; the talk would go on as scheduled. In a press release the disabled said they viewed it as intolerable to have a discussion of how to assist people in dying before society has mounted a genuine effort to assist people in living. They called for dignified living conditions for all citizens including the severely disabled and ill.

The disabled then took matters into their own hands. As Atrott mounted the podium, some fifteen to twenty disabled people, twelve of them in wheelchairs, interposed themselves between the speaker and his audience. They were chanting and waving signs made of garbage bags—"lives not worth living," "useless lives," and other slogans well-known from Nazi days. They sipped straws from containers labeled "cyanide." Several of the disabled grappled the microphone away from Atrott and physically prevented him from speaking. The meeting turned into a shambles.

Atrott was forced to leave the conference. It was most unfortunate, he told the press. He had simply wanted to clear up misunder-

standings about his organization and to create better understanding—a reaching out to disabled people, as it were. The interests of the disabled as a whole had been badly served by the
actions of this splinter "radical group," he said.

A spokesman for the German Society for Social Psychiatry said
that Atrott and his society were supporting a continuation of crimes
against humanity by advocating the withdrawal of assistance to the
very sick. Atrott, for his part, said that not allowing him to speak
was a return to "terror against different thinking"—that is, a Nazi
sort of thought control. As for the social psychiatrists, Atrott said
that their "manifestation of fanaticism" was something that needed
treatment, not legal relief.

———

Pope John Paul II made a state visit to West Germany in May 1987.
On this occasion, he made a pilgrimage to Münster to pray at the
grave of Bishop—later Cardinal—von Galen and to pay tribute to
von Galen and those who stood with him against Nazi tyranny and
killing. Von Galen, said the pope in his homily, "led his diocese
courageously when darkness fell over Germany, when men in their
Godless arrogance made themselves the final judges of human life,
the result being blood, death and destruction."

> . . . Brothers and sisters, in speaking to you today about
> Cardinal von Galen I also have in mind the faithful he was
> appointed to care for. I have in mind the countless women
> and men, young and old, in Oldenburg, the Münsterland
> and on the Lower Rhine who rose up together in great
> solidarity with their bishop and stood by his side for the sake
> of their faith—and for the Cross. I also recall the numerous
> committed Protestant Christians of the Confessing Church.
> Because the faithful in their enthusiasm and love gathered
> closely around their bishop, the country's rulers could not
> afford to disregard the voice of the fearless prelate from
> Münster, let alone silence him with force. [44]

"Human life should not be divided into that which is worth living
and that which is not," the pope later told a group of disabled people
gathered to hear him at Salzburg Cathedral. [45]

The issues raised by the events outlined in this book are, as Dr. Brandt told the Nuremberg tribunal, as old as mankind. Today, they are as serious as ever and just as pressing.

AIDS

In large measure, AIDS patients are members of two population groups largely devalued and discriminated against—homosexuals and drug abusers. The position of these two groups in today's American society is, in this sense, analogous with that of the disabled in the era of Nazi Germany.

As was the case with disability in Germany, the medical establishment cannot cure AIDS, while the cost of maintenance treatment of AIDS patients is very high—both in terms of actual dollars spent and in the divergence of health resources. With AIDS as with disability, many in society have sought to blame the victims—it is said that persons with AIDS have brought their misfortune upon themselves with their deviant, asocial behavior. Such expressions only serve to strengthen the convictions of those who complain of the continuing economic drain of treating AIDS patients.

In the light of such parallels, it is perhaps not surprising that, according to *The New York Times,* increasing numbers of doctors are "helping" their terminally ill AIDS patients to die. "The public would be surprised at how helpful doctors are willing to be," Marty Jones, a Los Angeles advocate of doctor-assisted suicide, is quoted as saying in a first-page story.[46]

Genetic Engineering

Mapping of the human genome and advances in genetic engineering promise remarkable benefits to mankind. Much suffering will be avoided by the elimination of genetically transmitted disease. For the first time it will be possible—as it was not possible in Nazi Germany—to create a "master race," superb in mind and body. How will these benefits be allocated? Whose children will be perfect? Whose will not? Will the master race create a servant race to fill the service occupations? The potential benefits will be great. Great, too, will be the potential for abuse, as the experience of Germany in the 1930s makes clear.

Behavior Modification

There is nothing new about using medicine for social purposes. This is what the German physicians were doing in the 1930s. Today, the application of medical therapies to modify or restrain behavior is commonplace. "Hyperactive" children are placed on drug therapy. The enforced use of the drug Antabuse is prescribed for alcoholic offenders. Aversion therapy is used to alter sexual behavior deemed offensive. Whether such interventions are consistent with the principles of the medical profession; whether they are efficacious, let alone ethical—these are questions needing further debate. There are serious problems raised when physicians allow themselves to become instruments of social policy.

Extension of Life

Advances in technology give promise of a time when machines will be able to keep a person "alive" almost indefinitely, no matter the extent of the trauma experienced by brain or body. In such cases the moral value of preserving life—when the costs are high and there is no expectation of the return of quality life—require reassessment.

——

If the story told in this book means anything, it is that arching over all such assessments must be the principle that society may not—at its peril—abandon a person because he has become flawed in mind or body; because surely every man over the course of his life will reach such a state.

There is a fashion today that serves to aggravate this cruel dilemma: it has become a duty in today's society to work for and to idolize the perfect body, the body made fit by exercise, diet, and rest. Perhaps even more than in Nazi days, fitness, health, and beauty are worshiped. "If you stay fit, you will stay healthy" is the touchstone, and it has value. There is, however, an obverse side: if, perchance, you are not healthy, if your body is not fit but flawed, then it must be your fault. You are to blame; you did not take care of yourself properly. Soon enough this attitude leads to the old game of "blame the victim," as disabled people can tell you.

The doctors of Germany in the 1930s and 1940s sought to perfect society and its members. They tried to make the German people perfect—as they defined perfect—and to discard the imperfect. In the process, they committed gross sins of great importance to the understanding of life-and-death issues of today. These sins have never been confessed; and unconfessed, they have never been expiated.

With expiation comes understanding and with understanding comes resolution.

These are issues unresolved.

Today in many minds, there is a reluctance to accept the facts of history. This inclination or attitude is in some way similar to the fantasies which permeated the Third Reich. What happened in the years of the Third Reich remains alive in our subconscious, dangerously so. It will be fatal for us to lose touch with the truth of what happened then. We must struggle to seek out the truth of that era rather than search for improved defenses to hide us from this truth.

—Margarete and Alexander
Mitscherlich, foreword to *Die Unfähigkeit zu trauern*, 1977

Afterword: A Conversation

Else had cut her hair very short, as many Berlin women do. This gave her a boyish look. She had a terrific smile:

"That Dr. Hackethal! And his 'mercy killing'! But it is incredible. Did you see the latest article?" she asked. "He told about another one of his patients. This one was a poor woman with a broken neck. Just before Hackethal gave her the cyanide, or whatever it is he uses to kill off patients with useless lives, he said she looked deeply into his eyes and said, 'Oh, thank you, Doctor.' " Else put down her cup and laughed. "So now we are to *thank* our killers!"

Else's laugh was pure Berliner.

I thought to myself—and not for the first time—how much alike Berliners and disabled people can be. Both groups are brave, tough, rude, tolerant; both share a wry, sometimes cruel, self-deprecating wit. The "hot war" did not defeat the Berliners, and the Cold War is not about to. Berliners are survivors. So are the disabled.

I was in Berlin doing research for this book. West Berlin is a wonderful city, cynical and stubborn. It is both old and new. Destroyed in World War II, it was rebuilt from scratch, using the rubble of the old to make the bricks for the new. The buildings are new; the spirit of the place is old and enduring.

I had the name of a woman who has been active in the effort by disabled people in Germany to obtain justice and equal rights. I call this woman Else. On the phone, my lack of German and Else's halting English made conversation difficult. We agreed—I *think* we agreed—that I should come to her apartment on Sunday morning for coffee, and she would invite one or two other disability activists. She said they spoke some degree of English, and she expected that, one way or another, we might be able to communicate.

And, as it turned out, communication was no problem. It was arduous—we were discussing issues that have subtle aspects, and concepts that are difficult to express in any language. But our efforts to make very sure that we really understood what the other was saying caused us to focus and speak precisely, sometimes to express the same thought in several different ways, circling around it ever more accurately. As a result, although at times it strained the patience of us all, we ended up with a discussion which I found to be of great interest—and, certainly, of great help to me in the preparation of this book. I am very grateful to Else, and her friends Hans Peter and Anna.

Else is a short, intense woman, probably in her late thirties. A childhood attack of polio stunted her growth. Her arms and shoulder muscles are well-developed, in compensation for the weakness of her lower body. She is able to get about her flat, haltingly, by holding on to anything available. She uses a wheelchair to get about the city.

Hans Peter, a recent college graduate, uses crutches. As he has not been able to find a paying job, he lives on his state allowance and does volunteer work with a local disability-rights organization.

Anna is the only one of the three with a job—she is a graduate in psychology and works as a counselor at a clinic for mentally retarded children. She is a woman of exceedingly short stature, with stubby arms and legs. She has lovely, intelligent eyes, and her accent in English is soft and gentle.

It was a morning in mid-May, not so much cold as raw. The Berlin climate is not a gentle one. My friend Paul Waggaman and I had driven over in our tiny rental car to the modest, pleasant neighborhood, not far off the Kurfürstendamm. Else's apartment was small, but it was cozy and warm. West Berlin is an island, surrounded by East Germany. Space is at a premium, and every square inch is precious. Else is not rich—she lives, in fact, upon her welfare allowance—and she must share the little flat with two other people.

We sat around the table in the small kitchen. I was at the end of the table, and I had to back my wheelchair out into the hallway whenever Else or Paul got up to get more coffee. The room was bright, spotlessly clean in the German manner, and there were plants at the window.

The talk was polite and more than a little embarrassed at the beginning. It took awhile for us to discover that we were on the same wavelength. It was an exciting discovery. After that, the talk was intense; there was no embarrassment and nothing was held back.

They wanted to know of the progress of disability rights in the United States. It is a new idea in Germany, not more than a few years old. They said the idea that the disabled can function as a bloc and exercise real political power is a controversial one—even within the disabled community itself. The actions and demands of the activists have angered, even frightened some disabled people, who fear that if the handicapped become *too* strident in their demands for equality, they will risk losing their welfare benefits. According to Else, "The disability activists say they want jobs and dignity; the more traditional say, 'Don't rock the boat, don't risk our benefits.' "

Much education is needed, we agreed, of the disabled as well as the community at large. "The politicians don't pay attention to us," said Else. "We must get their attention."

"They patronize us," said Hans Peter. "They talk to us as though we were charity cases—all pity and concern—not like we were full citizens with a legitimate gripe."

"They need to be educated," said Anna, "one by one. But to do this we have to get their attention. That is why publicity in the newspapers is so very important. But it is difficult to get the papers to pay attention, too!"

"We are learning how," interjected Hans Peter. "Remember what Franz Christof did." Clearly they enjoyed the memory—they all smiled.

Hans Peter continued, "Christof uses crutches. He was in a receiving line, waiting to be introduced to Richard von Weizsäcker, the president of the Federal Republic. When he got up to the president he didn't shake hands. Instead, he hit Weizsäcker on the leg with his crutch—not once, but twice. If he had been able-bodied, the security police would have shot him dead on the spot. So what happened? Nothing, nothing at all. Christof was bundled out of the line, questioned, and released.

"Later, talking to the press, Christof said that was why he had hit the president—to prove that the disabled are simply not credited as being serious people. We are supposed to behave like children or, better yet, stay out of sight—the invisible people. No, the law is not equal when it comes to us.

"Christof was not invisible. And you can be sure that got the newspapers' attention!"

Anna explained to me the position of the organized disability activists in Berlin. "We are members of the A. L., the alternate list, of left-wing political organizations. We are not, per se, a part of the Green Party. In fact, they and the other leftist political groups are often uneasy with us, just like the centrist and right parties."

"Still, they feel they have to include us on their committees and invite us to their planning sessions," added Else. "I mean, they have to, don't they? They claim to represent the people and the causes ignored by the general politicians. And that means we qualify, if anyone does; but they are just as uncomfortable with our demands. You know, we ask not only that society change its attitudes about the handicapped but that our fellow leftists change theirs. Often they don't like it. Oh, they pay us lip service: they talk pretty, but they don't hear well!"

We drank our coffee as they continued: Yes, they agreed, Germany no longer approves of killing its disabled people. The government has done a lot to help us. After the war, several major rehabilitation centers were established across Germany. In recent years, curb cuts and accessible public facilities have been installed in the nation's cities. In Berlin, where parking places are rarer than rubies, there are even a few spots reserved for the cars of handicapped drivers. A quite respectable system of payments and programs has been set up to assure the long-term disabled a basic standard of living and care. Germany, they agreed, is as good as any nation, better than most, at providing care for its handicapped citizens. That, however, is not the problem.

The problem is attitude. There has been no basic change of attitude. People are still made uncomfortable by the sight of the disabled. The disabled are still the outsiders, the Other. There is no great interest in integrating disabled people into the work force; there has been only fitful attention given in some of the states to "mainstreaming" handicapped students into the public schools— and this has aroused much antagonism from the parents of able-

278

bodied children. Mrs. Weizsäcker, the wife of the president of the Republic, has made the welfare of disabled persons her interest—well-meaning as this is, it is symbolic of the position of the disabled in Germany today: objects of pity for whom good works should be performed. "That's it," said Hans Peter. "We're objects of pity."

Else added, "Jobs are scarce in Berlin for everybody; but if you are disabled, it is impossible to find work. I think able-bodied people are uncomfortable having someone crippled working beside them. Employers say to me, 'You don't need a job; you can live on your welfare.' They use that as an excuse not to deal with us."

As we were talking about this, I remembered my strong sense of being stared at on German streets, my impression that people purposely avoided contact with me and my wheelchair.

"Oh, yes," said Else. "And it is still the thing to make jokes about cripples. Comics still like to imitate the 'funny' ways we walk or talk."

Anna tried to explain something about German society to me: "Oh, we have freedom of speech and all that. But we have to be very careful. The Germans like stability. They like things the way they are. They want things to be fair, yes; but they don't want any trouble. There has been too much of that in the past. So, we can dissent, we can protest; but if we go too far, we will get thrown in prison. This is what happened to two leaders of a women's liberation group. They campaigned against amniocentesis as a medical invasion by doctors of the privacy of a woman's body. They said doctors were using it to say which women could have their babies and which women couldn't—just like Nazi days.

"And you know what happened to those women? The police came into their house and took their papers and their lists of members. And those two women were put in jail!"

Hans Peter told me about a doctor in Hamburg who had been operating a clinic for genetic counseling. He turned out to be one of the doctors who had taken part in the killing of deformed and retarded babies in the Third Reich. "And the crazy part about it is that he was using exactly the same eugenic standards today that he used then! When a disabled man named Udo Sierck wrote in the papers about all this, it caused a terrific stink. The doctor had to close his clinic, and I think he even lost his license to practice."

Anna, who counsels the parents of retarded and disabled children, began talking about German doctors. Their feelings toward disabled people, she said, have not really changed. "I see them in our clinic, talking to the parents. They do not advise. They order. After they have tested a woman and find that perhaps her baby might turn out to be deformed, they say, 'You must have an abortion!' When parents turn up with a disabled baby, they say, 'You should have been tested!' They *blame* the parents for their baby's disability. This, of course, makes the parents feel guilty. This makes them take their child from therapy to therapy—trying to assuage their guilt, trying to change or hide the *image* of their guilt, which is the child's disability. And this, of course, is impressed upon the child. The child grows up feeling there is something terribly *wrong* with him, something so terrible it makes his parents ashamed and his doctors angry."

Anna stopped. She held her hands out flat, palms out. "And here we go again. Another generation of guilty, apologetic cripples."

"This is what the disability-rights movement is all about," Else added. "We want to change these attitudes—the attitudes of the doctors, of the politicians, of the public and, yes, of our own disabled people."

Hans Peter was getting excited. "There is all this talk, today, about mercy killing and genetic counseling; all about how expensive it is to care for retarded people; about how limited health care resources are; about rationing care to those who, maybe, will use it best. Talk about quality of life, talk about economics.

"We disabled people said, 'Hey, this is *us* they are talking about.'

"We said, 'Hey, this sounds familiar. Some doctor wants to decide whether we have the right to be born, or to have kids, or how long we should live. We have been here before! Back then, they called it "lives not worth living" and "useless eaters"—but how different is it?' " Hans Peter was angry. "We should make those decisions for ourselves: it is our life, not the doctors'!"

The three of them told me of a conference they had helped organize in Berlin. The subject was the Nazi euthanasia program, and the purpose of the meeting was to emphasize to the medical community, the politicians, and the public the relevance of what had happened then to what is being talked about now. Leading historians were on the program. Berlin politicians were invited to speak. A special invitation was sent to the medical society, asking it to participate. Press releases were distributed to the media.

"We really hoped for lots of attention," said Else. "And, in fact, we had a nice crowd. There were lots of disabled people. The politicians attended. I was really pleased that medical students came. It was a good meeting. There was serious discussion and many persons participated. But not one of the papers gave us any coverage. There was a television crew at the meeting, but only because they wanted to interview a politician on another subject.

"Did the physicians take part? No. The only doctor present had been sent as an observer of the medical society. Do you know who the society sent as its representative? A former Nazi member of the SS!"

—

On the flight back to America I thought about our conversation. I was reading a remarkable article on anti-Semitism in Germany by a young journalist named Henryk M. Broder.[1] He points out how strange it is: There is anti-Semitism, but there are no Semites—very few Jews live in Germany today. Nevertheless, anti-Semitism is alive in Germany. Why? Surely the horror of Auschwitz would have exhausted or, at the least, embarrassed the bigots into silence?

Broder makes the point "that anti-Semitism in Germany today does not exist *in spite of* Auschwitz, but much rather *because of it*, because it serves as a constant reminder to people of their own misdeeds and failings."

In line with this thought, Broder quotes a character in one of Rainer Werner Fassbinder's controversial plays: "It's the Jew's fault, since he makes us feel guilty, just being there. If he had stayed where he came from or if they'd gassed him, I'd be able to sleep better tonight. I'm not joking. That's the way it thinks inside me."

It struck me that these insights work as well for the disabled as they do for the Jews.

I adjusted my paralyzed legs, leaned back in my seat, staring at the endless cloud cover below the airplane window. "You don't have to be German," I thought. "You don't have to be a Jew. It thinks the same inside us all."

Appendix A

With diligence and great courage, Pastor P. Braune prepared a report in the summer of 1940 providing specific details on the extent and operation of the T-4 killing operation. In his report Braune presented a powerful case for ending the killing. He submitted his report to the highest officers of the Nazi government in hopes they would end the killing. Hitler himself is said to have read Braune's words.

The complete text of the historic Braune document is presented here in English for the first time. It was translated at Nuremberg by Dorothy Plummer.

Report of Pastor P. Braune

TRANSLATION OF DOCUMENT NO.631-PS
OFFICE OF CHIEF OF COUNSEL FOR WAR CRIMES

[handwritten] Confidential!

Memorandum

Re: Systematic transfer of inmates of nursing homes and asylums.

In the course of these last months it has been observed in various regions of the Reich that a host of institution and asylum inmates have been transferred continually according to a systematic and economic plan. Some of them have even been transferred several times, until after a few weeks their next of kin are informed about their death. The similarity of the measures taken, as well as the similarity of the accompanying circumstances, leaves no doubt that this is a large-scale measure designed to remove somehow from this world thousands of people who are not worthy to live. The opinion is held that it is necessary to remove useless mouths for the sake of the defense of the Reich. The opinion is also held that it is an absolute necessity for the process of regeneration of the German nation to do away as quickly as possible with insane or otherwise hopeless cases as well as with the abnormal antisocial and with those who cannot adapt themselves to life in a collectivity. It is estimated that one hundred thousand or more people may be involved. In an article published by Professor KRANZ in the April issue of the *NS-Volksdienst*, the number of those whose extermination seems to be considered desirable was quoted at an even one million. Thus thousands of German nationals are probably already concerned who have been removed without any legal foundation or whose death is imminent. It is urgently necessary to put an end to these measures as quickly as possible, as they are shaking the ethical foundations of our national being to the roots. The inviolability of human life is one of the main supports of any national order. If killing has to be ordered, valid laws must be the basis of such a measure. It is unbearable that sick people should continually be done away with for strictly utilitarian reasons without either careful medical examination or any legal protection, and without hearing the desire of their next of kin and of their legal guardians.

The following facts have been observed continually:

First of all in October 1939, in many institutions and asylums as well as in a series of privately owned nursing homes, which took in cases of insanity epilepsy, and others, there appeared a circular letter from the Reich Minister of the Interior, of which I enclose a copy as *Enclosure 5*. This letter said that in view of the necessity for a systematic listing of institutions and asylums, the attached questionnaires were to be filled out. On December 1 at the latest they were to be sent in directly to the Minister of the Interior.

Signature Dr. CONTI.

What struck one immediately about the way this investigation was carried out was that it came straight from the Reich Minister of the Interior, without the competent offices of the District Presidents (Regierungspräsidenten) and the Health Offices (Gesundheitsämter) being entrusted with it. Already this fact aroused bewilderment. To a direct inquiry addressed to the competent official (Sachbearbeiter) in the Reich Ministry of the Interior, the information was given that it was a question of a merely statistical investigation. Upon this, all the homes which had received the request—homes which I knew—without thinking gave the names of a mass of inmates who apparently came under the regulations in the attached leaflet, which says that all patients have to be reported who:

1. suffer from the following diseases and cannot be employed in the workshops of the institution or can only be occupied there with mechanical work (picking and similar jobs):
   Schizophrenia,
   Epilepsy (if exogenetic, state whether from injury received in military service, or from other causes),
   Senile diseases,
   Paralysis refractory to treatment and other metic diseases,
   Insanity of whatever origin,
   Encephalitis,
   Huntington or other neurological fatal fits;
   or
2. have been for at least five years permanently in institutions;
   or
3. are kept as criminally insane;
   or
4. do not possess German citizenship or are not of German or ethnically related blood. State race and citizenship.

In many cases the institutions believed these to be preparatory measures for a law concerning custody.

Dated January 20, 1940, there suddenly appeared a letter from the Reich Defense Commissioner (Reichsverteidigungs Kommissar) addressed to the same institutions, a copy of which I attach as *Enclosure 2*. In accordance with this letter, the transfer of inmates of institutions and asylums was made imminent. It was laid down that the sick should be transferred in large collective shipments. The notification of their next of kin was not desired. This peculiar information again aroused misgivings, as there was no comprehensible reason why the sick should be transferred.

As far as is known, these measures have been carried out wholesale in the following districts:

Pomerania,
Brandenburg-Berlin,
Saxony,
Württemberg, and
Hamburg,

and since June they have been introduced in most of the Reich territories.

In the second half of April, the institutions received nearly identical letters of which I attach a specimen as *Enclosure 3*. In these letters dates were fixed for the transfer of the inmates. An enclosed list for shipment specified the names of the inmates to be transferred. But it now became clear that these data were taken from the lists which had been requested allegedly for statistical purposes in October and November.

Then in March 1940, there came unexpected news from Württemberg that of a shipment of thirteen epileptics, who had been removed from the institution in Pfingstweide to the one in Grafeneck, four patients had already died after about three weeks. Relatives were usually informed eight to fourteen days after the deaths and the notification always had a similar wording: the patients were said to have died suddenly from influenza, pneumonia, apoplexy of the brain and similar causes. In accordance with police directives relative to contagious disease the bodies were cremated immediately, it was said, and the clothes burnt as well. The urns were said to be at the relatives' disposal. Emanating from this Grafeneck institution, now styled "Landespflegeanstalt Grafeneck" (district nursing home), the same notifications appeared in different regions of Germany. Patients who were physically healthy and suffered merely from mental disorders died there within a short time. That this also happened to persons who had previously worked successfully in their lives may be shown in the following case. Herr H., the former director of a power station in the Kreuznach Institutions, fell sick with typhus a few years ago and remained a carrier of the germ. As a result of the physical disease he showed signs of mental depression. Accordingly he was put into the nursing home of Bedburg-Hau in the Rhineland. Before Christmas 1939 his son went to see him. The father was perfectly clear in the head, but suffered from depression. On March 7, 1940, his transfer to Grafeneck was carried out in a collective shipment without any notification of his family, which had to pay the costs. Only upon their inquiry as to his state of health was his transfer from Bedburg-Hau to Grafeneck noted. An inquiry addressed to Grafeneck remained without reply. About four weeks later word came that the patient had died from a circulatory disease and that the body had had to be cremated immediately. The urn was said to be held at the family's disposal. Both the urn and the correspondence already bore the number A 498. Herr H. died at Grafeneck on April 10.

Also from Berlin-Buch many patients were brought to Grafeneck after some of them had been brought temporarily to the former penitentiary Waldheim in Saxony. Among them was the opera singer Charlotte BOBBE, whose urn was offered to her relatives on May 16, 1940, Fräulein BURGNITZ from Berlin-Pankow, whose urn was declared available at the end of June 1940, Fräulein Helene MÜLLER from Berlin, whose urn was buried in Berlin on June 28, 1940, and a few other persons from Berlin-Hermsdorf and Köpenick.

In order to ascertain the probable number of persons who died at Grafeneck, I draw attention to the fact that Herr HEIMER's urn—he died on April 10, 1940—bears the number A 498, whereas Max DREISOW's urn—he too died at Grafeneck on May 12, 1940—is already numbered A 1092. As the whole institution normally contains only one hundred beds, it can only be a question here of the consecutive number of deaths. Consequently, 594 people seem to have died within thirty-three days. This could mean eighteen deaths per day in an institution with about one hundred beds. This conclusion does not seem excluded, as reports say that during a period of one to two months three hundred patients were transferred from Bedburg-Hau to Grafeneck, likewise a few hundred from Buch, about 150 from Kückenmühle, and also a large number, unknown to me, from Württemberg homes.

Another region where these observations have been made on a larger scale is Saxony. First, the national nursing homes there were struck by these measures. This concerns the following institutions: Hohenweitzschen near Westerwitz, Grosschweidnitz near Löbau, Arnsdorf and Hubertusburg, and Zadrasch. In the first-mentioned institution, for instance, the number of deaths

in the year 1938 amounted to about   80
in the year 1939   "   "   "   102
until 15 May 1940   "   "   "   124.

In the home at Grosschweidnitz, the number of deaths amounted to

	1938	50
	1939	141
until 25 May	1940	228.

Whereas normally about twelve patients died in a quarter of a year, in 1940 as many as 125 died in a quarter of a year. The higher death figure for 1939 originates exclusively from the last quarter of the year. The cause of death stated in most of the cases is general inanition. A similar situation prevailed in the Arnsdorf home, where death figures amounted to

	1938	101
	1939	200
until 25 May	1940	101.

This means that the number of deaths was tripled. As to the Saxon institutions it has been ascertained through visits beyond any doubt, that mortality is increased through deprivation of food. Food is reduced, as has been reported by a reliable person, to a daily amount of twenty-two to twenty-four Reichpfennigs' worth. As it is impossible for the patients to live on so little, they are given a medicine (Paralyth) by force which puts them in a state of apathy. Through verbal and written reports it is made clear in a pathetic manner how the patients always repeat their cry of "Hungry, hungry!" Employees and attendants who could not stand it any longer have now and then helped to stay their hunger out of their private funds, but there is no doubt about the truth of the matter. These past months, hundreds of people have been brought to a quick death through these measures.

But it is not only a question of sick people who are absolutely dull-witted, but on the contrary of sick people who recognize what is going on quite well and who observe how often per day burials take place. A report depicted the mortal terror of one of the patients who surmised clearly the fate that was to be prepared for him and his fellow patients.

In Saxony, in pursuance of these measures, the former penitentiary of Waldheim has changed its name to District Nursing Home. Also from this so-called nursing home notifications of death always written in the same form suddenly reach the relatives who know nothing of the transfer, and they are informed that the patient has died from influenza, heart disease, or some other disease. The body is said to have been cremated immediately for fear of epidemics, and the clothes are said to have been burned, too, or handed over to the NSV (National Socialist Public Welfare Association).

A female visitor reports that patients at Waldheim get a slice of bread in the morning, a plateful of food at noon, and a plate of soup in the evening. A similar report comes from Zadrasch. But only those patients who work are said to be fed in that way. Those who are not able to work are said to get only half a slice of bread, a quarter of a plateful of food, and half a goblet of soup. If somebody is confined to his bed, still less is given him; in a cell nothing is given at all. If in such a case working patients share their meager ration with their hungry companions, their next meal is curtailed in order to punish them, as it is supposed that they had too much. All the patients are said to look appallingly pale, emaciated, and wretched. The accommodation of the patients is said to be catastrophic. They lie on thin mattresses on the floor, fifty-one in one room. Also, they no longer receive official garments, but must wear their own clothes. With all that, those responsible still have to pay RM3.50 per patient.

The impressions reported are shocking and simply not worthy of a "nursing institution." As a consequence of the frequent transfers no attendants and no doctors know the patients any longer, and it is reported that patients wear their names on adhesive tapes fixed to their shoulders, so that in case of death their bodies may at least be identified.

The same observations have also been made in the province of Brandenburg and in Berlin. Here it seems that it is especially the city of Brandenburg where this so-called *Sterbehilfe* (euthanasia) is carried out. The former penitentiary in Brandenburg is now called "District Nursing Home" of Brandenburg, 90a Neuendorfer Strasse. The penitentiary is no longer under judicial authority, but has been sold to the city of Brandenburg. From this institution various letters have reached relatives. I include copies of three of them. Occurrences in the so-called nursing home of Brandenburg are kept a strict secret. It is reported that the attempt of a relative to see a patient was flatly refused. In this case it was a bride, who wanted to see her husband, a dentist. Very soon afterwards the notification of his death arrived. The building of the former penitentiary in which this mysterious District Nursing Home is located contains about 120 single cells and several dormitories. It has been said that during the night cries are not infrequently heard coming from this house. In any case, it is not clear why this nursing home should be so completely secluded from the outer world if it were not because things happen there which are not meant to come into the light of publicity.

The patients deceased according to the enclosed letter were probably not even insane, but were inmates of the above-mentioned Waldheim penitentiary in Saxony on whose behalf in one case steps were already supposed to have been taken for their release from the institution. At all events the relatives did not know that the member of their family who died suffered from an incurable disease. The "letters of condolence" thus seem to be drawn up according to a general scheme which might be pertinent in the case of the mentally deranged and epileptics. But it is shocking when the sentence, "Despite all medical efforts it was not possible to keep your husband———alive" appears again and again in the letters. Since the city of Brandenburg has its own crematorium the cremation of the dead is possible without any difficulty, especially as Neuendorfer Strasse has a separate exit.

All patients who were transferred from Brandenburg homes kept up by free welfare work, for instance, from the Samaritan institutions in Ketschendorf near Fürstenwalde Spree, and from the Nämi-Wilcko convent in Guben, were apparently first brought to the district nursing home Brandenburg-Görden. In no case were the relatives, trustees, and so on asked for their prior consent. They merely learned one day that their children, brothers and sisters, wards, etc., had been transferred. In the case of the shipment from the Samaritan institutions the first notification of death was already delivered after five weeks (Emmi HEBERLEIN). In another case the parents did everything in their power to find out where their child was and discovered it finally in Brandenburg-Görden. On their second visit already they found the child filthy and miserable. In reply to their request to transfer the child back to the Samaritan institutions again they were told that that was out of the question. They were no longer allowed to bring any further means of relief and joy to the child; this was absolutely impossible now. It seems as if those patients who were ripe for death were in many cases slowly transferred from Brandenburg-Görden to the former penitentiary in Brandenburg where they met their fate in the so-called nursing home.

In any case, repeated observations show that patients who are transferred together in collective shipments from institutions are already so completely mixed up in the big nursing homes after only a few days that no one knows anything about the others anymore. So nobody ever learns anything about another person's fate. The remaining mass of people remain unknown to them. They slowly pine away and die in complete despair.

From the Berlin-Buch institution it is reported that the lawyer Günther ROTTMANN, born on June 12, 1906, the son of Oberregierungsrat ROTTMANN, a party member since 1927, and at Buch since 1939 through overwork and a nervous breakdown, was transferred from Buch on June 10 of this year to the district home of Hartheim near Linz. This was done without the knowledge of his parents, who visited him regularly. After many efforts the parents learned from acquaintances, a member of whose family had also been transferred, that their son, too had been transferred to the district home of Hartheim near Linz. When they made inquiries by telephone on June 27, 1940, they received the news that their son had died there on June 23, 1940, from mastoiditis. The letter in which they were notified of the death contains the same statements as all similar letters, cremation of the body because of the danger of epidemics, etc. Various other Berlin families also received notification of the deaths of their relatives in Hartheim.

Further, it is reported from Buch that besides the transfers mentioned above, the death rate within the house itself has increased considerably. At least six hundred patients have been transferred by collective shipments. But it is strange that all visiting of Berlin-Buch was prohibited on April 12, 1940, by the placing of a sign outside the institution "Closed because of dysentery." And yet on April 14 a large shipment took place despite the fact that any transfer of patients is usually prohibited in case of contagious diseases such as dysentery. On April 14 Max DREISOW, already mentioned above, was transferred among others from Buch to Grafeneck and on May 12 he unexpectedly died, also from concussion of the brain. It has already been mentioned above that patients from Buch were transferred to Waldheim, Grafeneck, and Hartheim near Linz. The death notices were promptly delivered to the relatives.

If within such a short time more than ten notifications of death became known to me accidentally, how many more may have died in reality, since I have no means of determining through an official examination what the real number of deaths is.

From Pomerania the same shocking incidents became known. The provincial nursing homes of Lauenburg and Stralsund with approximately one thousand beds each were first emptied out, and the inmates allegedly brought to Obrawalde near Meseritz, a nursing home with about one thousand beds. At the end of May this year the well-known Kückenmühler institutions near Stettin with a total of about fifteen hundred mentally deficients, epileptics, psychopathic cases, and imbeciles were requisitioned by the Gauleiter of Pomerania. The executive committee was dissolved and immediately after that the forcible transfer of the patients was undertaken. Within fourteen days about 750 patients were shipped away in big buses; up to today about 1,300 have already been transferred. A part of them had to be kept in readiness between three and four o'clock at night on a remote railway station near Stettin. They were supposed to be shipped to the East, to the Warthegau, to Meseritz, but also to Grafeneck. The relatives were not consulted at all. The competent social welfare organizations were not listened to. Until now it is not possible in any way to estimate how many patients from Kückenmühle died in the meantime. Soon there were rumors that forty-two deaths were known already. But here like everywhere else the number of deaths will be hard to ascertain since many inmates have no relatives or do not receive many visits from their relatives. Often it will become known only after weeks or months, quite by accident only, that this or that person died somewhere. An official investigation can find out here the real number of deaths. The patients from Obrawalde are supposed to have already been transferred again to an institution near Posen, and certainly to Kosten.

As is confirmed by the individual letters enclosed, it appears that in the above-mentioned regions of the Reich incidents occur continually in the same way: transfer by force in collective shipments, the mixing-up of patients so that they do not know each other, the deprivation of food, the introduction of conditions to induce weakness, the administering of medicine by force—the people talk about injection, meaning deadly injections—then in almost every case the cremation of the body and burning of the clothes to prevent any possibility of investigation, the tardy informing of relatives through letters which are nearly always formulated in a similar way.

So it is a question here of a conscious action carried out according to plan in order to suppress all those who are insane or otherwise unable to live within the community. But among the latter there are people who are not complete idiots, incapable of knowing and understanding what is going on around them and incapable of any further occupation, but—as is shown by many individual observations—they are often people who worked in a definite profession for years and in whom mental disturbances appeared only later on.

If one considers that official leaflet which explains how the questionnaire should be filled out, illnesses caused by senility are also included, and there is no doubt at all that every person who has grown old and who with age suffers from some hopeless mental disease or perhaps only from a physical one may meet the same fate. Of course, people begin to talk about these facts since the relatives of the patients in nursing homes become acquainted with each other on their visits and exchange their observations. Thereby the confidence in such institutions is deeply shaken, especially confidence in the physicians and authorities. But if the trust in physicians is lost the great danger arises that all measures taken by the health and welfare services will meet with complete mistrust and that thereby the great good work accomplished by all institutions and by many valuable medical measures will be made illusory. It was the very fact of their being gathered together in institutions which made it possible to separate the sick elements in the people from the healthy ones and which took thereby an enormous burden off the families and public life. The increase and the reproduction of such persons was likewise prevented by keeping them in the institutions. On the other hand, when the sick member of the family, mother, brother, or child, was looked after with kindness in a good institution this was always a great relief to the healthy members of the family. How favorably Germany distinguished herself in this field from other countries where misery lived in the streets. Besides this the medical profession has learned a tremendous amount in the institutions for the benefit of the healthy. Nearly every physician has been through such a school. The personnel of such homes has been trained to such unselfish readiness that it has become a matter of course for them. How much cheerful devoted work has been accomplished even where, humanly speaking, there is no hope anymore. Are these definitely constructive factors within the life of the people to die slowly away? The highest school of unselfish service is no longer to exist? How many thousands or millions of sick people have become healthy again through such loyal, competent service? But once the mistrust in such institutions becomes general among the people, this means the heaviest setback for public health organizations. Only through trust is the physician able to heal and only through trust can the authorities help.

But another serious question also appears. How far is the destruction of so-called worthless lives intended to go? The procedure to date has shown that many people have been included who are still serene and of sound mind. In a case particularly well-known to me six girls who were about to be released from the institution in order to be employed as domestics were to be transferred with the others. Are only the absolutely hopeless—for instance, idiots and imbeciles—to be concerned? As already mentioned above, the leaflet enumerates the maladies due to age also. The latest regulation issued by the same authority requests the inclusion of children with serious congenital maladies and deformities of any kind, and their concentration in special institutions. What serious apprehensions must arise there! Are those suffering from tuberculosis going to be excluded? Apparently euthanasia measures have already been started for those who have been transferred for safety. Are other abnormal and antisocial cases also going to be included? Where is the limit? Who is abnormal, antisocial, who is hopelessly sick? Who unable to live within the community? What is going to happen to soldiers who contract on incurable malady in their fight for the fatherland? Such questions have emerged already in certain circles.

The most serious questions and anxieties arise here. It is a dangerous undertaking to give up the inviolability of the individual without any legal basis. Legal protection is granted to anyone who violates the law. Shall only the helpless be left unprotected? Will it not endanger the morals of the whole nation if human life is worth so little? How far will the strength to withstand difficulties be weakened if one cannot even bear one's sick anymore? It belongs to the true spirit of a national community and of unity in the best sense if healthy people take care of the sick ones, if families bear willingly and gladly the burden imposed upon them. And how much joy does it mean for many to devote themselves to an "unworthy" life? Just during the last few days certain well-known parents took their hopelessly sick son out of our institution and brought him back home in order that he should take the place of another son who had fallen in action as an officer.

If it is stated in order to justify these measures that the food situation of our people makes it necessary to eliminate these superfluous eaters, I must reply to this that for one thousand healthy people only one sick person is removed and this does not mean anything for the food situation. It cannot be a reason either that the use of the existing buildings and premises is considered a waste from the point of view of national economy. After all, these houses were built in the first place for the sick, and when the war started these very institutions provided tens of thousands of hospital beds without the service for the sick being limited beyond a tolerable extent. Sick people, of course, must take part in the burdens imposed by the war but that is still a far cry from systematic annihilation.

Thus it is a question here of a critical state of affairs which profoundly grieves all those who are informed about it, and which destroys the peace of many families and above all, threatens to develop into a menace the consequences of which cannot even be foreseen yet.

May the responsible authorities see to it that these harmful measures are suspended and that the whole question is carefully examined with respect to the legal, medical, moral, and state political aspects before the fate of thousands and tens of thousands is decided. *Videant consules, ne quid detrimenti res publia capiat.*

Hoffnungstaler Institutions

P. Braune, Pastor

Lobetal via Bernau near Berlin

Tel. Bernau 451

Lobetal, 9 July 1940

BRAUNE, Pastor

Chief of the Hoffnungstaler Institutions, vice president of the central committee for the internal mission of the German Protestant church.

Appendix B

Clemens August Cardinal Graf von Galen was a man of dignity, honor, and unquestioned integrity. Hitler despised him. In a series of three sermons, delivered in the summer of 1941, the then Bishop von Galen attacked the Nazi authorities for harassing church personnel, seizing church property, oppressing the citizenry, and killing the chronically disabled and insane. Von Galen's words were reproduced in secret and passed from hand to hand throughout the whole of Germany. The full text of the last of the three sermons, the one denouncing euthanasia, is printed here in English for the first time. The text was translated by Helga Roth.

Sermon of Clemens August Graf von Galen, Bishop of Münster
August 3, 1941

Source: Dokumente zur Euthanasie, ed. Ernst Klee, Fischer Tagebuch Verlag, 1985.

Devout Christians! A pastoral message of the German bishops of June 26, 1941, which was read in all Catholic churches on July 6, says: "According to the Catholic moral code there are some commandments which need not be kept if their observance would involve great difficulties. But there are others, holy obligations of our moral consciousness which we have to fulfill even at the cost of our lives. Never, under any circumstances, may a human being kill an innocent person outside of war or in just self-defense." On July 6 I already had occasion to add to the words of this universal pastoral message the following explanation: For the past months we have heard reports from care and residential institutions for mental patients that patients who had been ill for a long time and who appear to be incurable have been removed forcibly on orders from Berlin. Relatives are being notified a short time afterwards that the corpse has been cremated and that they can claim the ashes. There is a suspicion bordering on definite knowledge that these numerous unexpected deaths among psychiatric patients are not due to natural causes but have been intentionally brought about. The philosophy behind this is the assumption that so-called unworthy lives can be terminated, innocent human beings killed if their lives have no value for the nation and the state. This is a terrible doctrine that seeks to justify the murder of innocent people and allows the killing of invalids who can no longer work, cripples, incurable patients, and the feeble elderly.

We have heard from reliable sources that lists have been made of such patients who will be removed from the care and residential institutions in the province of Westphalia and shortly afterwards killed. The first transport left the Marienthal institution near Münster in the course of the past week.

German men and women! Paragraph 211 of the criminal code is still in force. It states, "Whosoever intentionally kills a person will be punished for murder by death if he has done it with premeditation."

To protect those who intentionally kill those poor people, members of our families, from legal punishment, patients who have been designated to die are being removed from their home institutions to far-away facilities. Some illness is given as a cause of death. Since the corpse is immediately cremated neither relatives nor the criminal police can ascertain what the cause of death was. But I have been assured that neither the Ministry of the Interior nor the agency of Dr. Conti, the surgeon general, denies that a large number of psychiatric patients have been intentionally killed in Germany and will be killed in the future.

Paragraph 139 of the criminal code states, "Whosoever becomes aware of the plan for a capital offense and does not bring it to the attention of the authorities or the threatened person will be punished." When I heard of the plan to remove patients from Marienthal and to kill them, I filed the following charges by letter with the prosecutor of the court in Münster and the president of police in Münster: "According to reports a large number of patients, so-called unproductive citizens, of the provincial care institution of Marienthal near Münster have been transferred in the course of this week to the Eichberg institution to be intentionally killed as has happened in other institutions according to general belief. Since such a procedure is not only contrary to the divine and natural moral code but has to be punished by death according to paragraph 211, I herewith dutifully raise charges according to paragraph 139 of the criminal code and ask that the threatened citizens be immediately protected through prosecution of the agencies which organize the transport and the murder and that I be notified of whatever has been done." I have not received any information on intervention by the state prosecutor or the police.

I had previously lodged a protest on July 26 with the provincial administration of Westphalia which is responsible for the institutions to which patients have been entrusted for care and cure. It was in vain. I have heard that three hundred persons have been removed from the residential care Wartstein institution.

Now we have to expect that these poor defenseless patients will be murdered in due time. Why? Not because they have committed a heinous crime, not because they attacked the caregiver in a way which would have forced him to defend his own life in justified self-defense. Are these cases in which killing is allowed and even necessary, besides killing of the enemy in a just war? No, these hapless patients have to die not for any of these reasons but because they have become unworthy to live according to the judgment of some agency or the expert opinion of some commission and because according to these opinions they are "unproductive citizens." The judgment holds that they cannot produce any goods; they are like an old machine which does not run anymore, they are like an old horse which has become lame and cannot be cured, they are like a cow which has ceased to give milk. What does one do with such an old machine? One wrecks it. What does one do with a lame horse, with unproductive cattle? No, I do not want to labor the comparison, justified and illuminating as it would be. We are not dealing with machines, or horses, or cows, whose only destiny is to serve people, to produce goods for human beings. They can be wrecked, they can be slaughtered when they can no longer serve their purpose. No, these are human beings, our fellow citizens, our brothers and sisters. Poor people, sick people, unproductive people, so what. But have they forfeited their right to live? Do you, do I have a right to live only as long as we are productive, as long as others recognize us as being productive? If the principle is established and applied that "unproductive fellow citizens" can be killed, woe to all of us when we get old and feeble. If it becomes permissible to kill unproductive people, woe to the invalids who invested and sacrificed and lost their energies and sound bones during their working careers. If unproductive fellow citizens can be eliminated by force, woe to our brave soldiers who return to their homeland severely injured, as cripples, as invalids. Once it becomes legal for people to kill "unproductive" fellow citizens—even if at present only our poor defenseless mentally ill are concerned—then the basis is laid for murder of all unproductive people, the incurable, the invalids of war and work, of all of us when we become old and feeble.

All that is necessary is another secret decree that the procedure tested with mental patients is to include other "unproductive persons," is to be applied to patients with incurable lung disease, to the feeble elderly, the disabled workers, to severely injured veterans. Nobody would be safe anymore. Some commission can put him on the list of the "unproductive." And no police will protect him and no court prosecute his murder and punish the murderer. Who could still trust his physician? Maybe he would report the patient as "unproductive" and would be ordered to kill him? It is inconceivable what depraved conduct, what suspicion will enter family life if this terrible doctrine is tolerated, adopted and carried out. Woe to humanity, woe to the German people if God's holy command "Thou shalt not kill" is not only transgressed but if this transgression is both tolerated and carried out without punishment.

I will give you an example of what happened today. In Marienthal there was a man about fifty-five years old, a farmer in a village in the area of Münster—I know his name—who had been suffering from episodes of mental derangement for some years and who had been brought to the Marienthal care and residential institution. He was not really a psychiatric case; he was able to receive visitors and was always happy when his relatives came. Just two weeks ago he was visited by his wife and one of his sons who was home on leave from the front. The son dotes on his father. Saying farewell was difficult, since nobody knows if the son will return and see his father again because he may be killed fighting for his fellow citizens. The son, the soldier, will certainly not see his father again, who has meanwhile been placed on the list of "unproductive" people. A relative who wanted to visit the father this week in Marienthal was sent away with the information that the patient had been transferred on orders of the Ministry for Defense. The destination was unknown but the relatives would be informed in a few days. What will this information contain? The same as in other cases? That the person died, was cremated, and that the ashes could be claimed after payment of a fee? The soldier who fights and risks his life for fellow German citizens will not see his father again on this earth because fellow German citizens in his own country have killed him.

Appendix C

Dr. Robert Servatius was Karl Brandt's attorney at Nuremberg. In his final plea for Brandt, Servatius summed up the argument presented to the court in defense of the euthanasia program and Dr. Brandt's role therein. The following is Servatius's argument:

Final Plea for Defendant Karl Brandt by Dr. Servatius July 14, 1947

Mr. President, your Honors:

I shall deal here with euthanasia only to the extent that it is officially dealt with under the ordinance of September 1, 1939. Concerning the "Reich committee," I refer to my closing brief. . . .

What did the defendant Karl Brandt know about the procedure?

He knew that the authorization which was issued was not an order given to the doctor, but only conferred on him the right to act on his own responsibility after the most careful consideration of the patient's condition. This was a clause inserted in the ordinance of September 1, 1939, on Karl Brandt's initiative.

The defendant Karl Brandt knew that the specialists, whom he did not know, were chosen by the Ministry of the Interior, and that the experts were eminent men in their special spheres.

The defendant Karl Brandt also knew that the authorities concerned saw no reason to object to the execution of the measure, and that even the chief jurists of the Reich declared the legal foundations to be irreproachable, after having been informed of the facts.

Within this framework the defendant Karl Brandt approved of official euthanasia and supported it.

But the prosecution even calls euthanasia a thousand-fold murder. In their opinion there was no formal law, and it is alleged that the expert Dr. Lammers confirmed this.

Yes, but he also stated that even an informal ordinance was valid. Even an order issued by the Führer had the force of law, as can be clearly seen from the indisputable effects of such orders, in particular in relation to foreigners.

But for the defendant Karl Brandt it is of no importance whether the ordinance of September 1, 1939, was actually valid or not; the only important thing is that he had reason to believe it was valid and that he could rely on their opinion.

German courts have already dealt with cases of the practice of euthanasia; but these cases occurred after the official procedure had been stopped, as at Hadamar, or after persons had been killed who could never have come under the powers conferred by the ordinance, or other crimes were committed.

It should be observed that these sentences always confirm the base motives of the offenders. On the other hand, these courts were concerned with the question of public law only to the extent that they confirm that no formal law was available. In one case the court restricted itself to information given by a member of the prosecution staff in the trial before the International Military Tribunal.

The real objections to euthanasia are not based on a formal point of view, but rather on the same reasons which are advanced against the admissibility of the medical experiments.

Even an insane person of the lowest grade may not be killed, it is said. No human being may presume to kill another human being.

But the right to kill in war is accepted in international law, and public law allows the suppression of a revolt by violence.

What prevents the state from ordering killing in the sphere of euthanasia, too?

The answer is that there is no motive which might justify an action of this kind.

The economic motive of eliminating "useless eaters" is certainly not sufficient for such measures. Such a motive was never upheld by the defendant Karl Brandt; it was apparently mentioned by others as an accompanying contingency and later taken up by counter propaganda.

The defendant Karl Brandt considered the motive of pity for the patient to be the decisive one. This motive is tacitly accepted for euthanasia on the deathbed, and doctors in all countries increasingly acknowledge it.

In former times the courts were repeatedly concerned with killings committed out of pity, and in sensational trials, juries found offenders not guilty who freed their nearest relatives from the torment of life.

Who would not have the desire to die while in good health rather than to be forced by all the resources of medical science to continue life degraded to an animal's existence! Only misguided civilization keeps such beings alive; in the normal struggle for existence Nature is more charitable.

But the legislator has hitherto refrained from giving authority to kill in such cases. But he can solve the problem if he wants to. The reasons for his restraint are exactly those which led in this case to the disguising of those measures and to the secrecy observed. There is the fear of base intrigues concerning inheritance, the mental burden of the relatives, and so on. The individual does not want to bear this burden, nor is he able to do so. It can be taken over only by the state, which is independent of the desires of those concerned.

That such is the will of the great majority of those who really come into touch with these problems was shown by the result of the inquiry conducted by Professor Meltzer, which has been offered in evidence. It was carried out by him many years ago in order to obtain an argument against euthanasia and its principal supporters, Binding and Hoche. He obtained the reverse of what he had himself expected as an expert.

But I see a third motive which unconsciously plays an important part; it is the idea of sacrifice.

A lunatic may cause the mental and economic decay of a family and also ruin it morally.

If healthy human beings make great sacrifices for the community and lay down their lives by order of the state, the insane person, if he could arouse himself mentally and make a decision, would choose a similar sacrifice for himself.

Why should not the state be allowed to enact this sacrifice in his case and impose on him what he would want to do himself?

Is the state to be forbidden to carry out such euthanasia until the whole world is a hospital, while the creatures of nature keep unblemished through what is believed to be the brutality of Nature?

The decision as to whether such an order given by the state is admissible or not depends on the conception of the social life of mankind and is, therefore, a political decision.

Neither the defendant Karl Brandt nor anyone else who participated in legalized euthanasia would ever have killed a human being on his own authority, and in the German sentences passed the blameless former life of the persons stigmatized as mass murderers is always emphasized.

This is a warning to be cautious. Did they really commit brutalities, or were they sentenced only because they were not in a position to swim against the tide of the times and to oppose it with their own judgment?

A Christian believing in dogma will turn away in pity from this way of thinking. But if the order to use euthanasia to the desired limited extent was really in such contradiction to the commandment of God that everyone could realize it, then it is incomprehensible why Hitler, who never withdrew from the Church, was not excommunicated.

This must remove the burden of guilt which one now wants to pile up. Then humanity would have clearly realized at the time that in this devilish struggle man cannot prevail, for God stands for Justice.

If there are offenders there are many co-offenders, and one understands Pastor Niemoeller saying, "We are all guilty."

This is a moral or a political guilt, but cannot be shifted to a single person as criminal guilt.

Appendix D

Dr. Karl F. Brandt was Hitler's personal physician. The Führer appointed him as the chief physician and co-director of the T-4 euthanasia program. Brandt claimed, right up to his death by hanging as a war criminal, "that when I said 'Yes' to euthanasia I did so with the deepest conviction . . . that it was right." Brandt's moving final statement to the court is printed here in its entirety.

Final Statement of Defendant Karl Brandt
July 19, 1947

There is a word which seems so simple—order; and how colossal are its implications. How immeasurable are the conflicts which hide behind the world "obey." Both affected me, obey and order, and both imply responsibility. I am a doctor and on my conscience lies the responsibility of being responsible for men and for life. Quite dispassionately the prosecution has brought the charge of crime and murder and they have raised the question of my guilt. It would have no weight if friends and patients were to shield me and speak well of me, saying I had helped and I had healed. There would be many examples of my actions during danger and my readiness to help. All that is now useless. As far as I am concerned I shall not evade these charges. But the attempt to vindicate myself as a man is my duty toward all who believe in me personally, who trusted in me and who relied upon me as a man as well as a doctor and a superior.

No matter how I was faced with the problem, I have never regarded human experiments as a matter of course, not even when no danger was entailed. But I affirm the necessity for them on grounds of reason. I know that opposition will arise. I know things that disturb the conscience of a medical man, and I know the inner distress that afflicts one when ethics of every form are decided by an order or obedience.

It is immaterial for the experiment whether it is done with or against the will of the person concerned. For the individual the event seems senseless, just as senseless as my actions as a doctor seem when isolated. The sense lies much deeper than that. Can I, as an individual, detach myself from the community? Can I remain outside and do without it? Could I, as part of this community, evade it by saying I want to live in this community, but I don't want to make any sacrifices for it, either of body or soul? I want to keep a clear conscience. Let them see how they can get along. And yet we, that community and I, are somehow identical.

Thus I must suffer these contradictions and bear the consequences, even if they remain incomprehensible. I must bear them as my lot in life, which allocates to me its tasks. The meaning is the motive—devotion to the community. If on its account I am guilty, then on its account I will be answerable.

There was war. In war, efforts are all alike. Its sacrifices affect us all. They were incumbent upon me. But are those sacrifices my crime? Did I tread on the precepts of humanity and despise them? Did I pass over human beings and their lives as if they were nothing? Men will point at me and cry "euthanasia," and falsely, "the useless," "the incapable," "the worthless." But what actually happened? Did not Pastor Bodelschwingh, in the middle of his work at Bethel last year, say that I was an idealist and not a criminal? How could he say that?

Here I am, subject of the most frightful charges, as if I had not only been a doctor, but also a man without heart or conscience. Do you think that it was a pleasure to me to receive the order to permit euthanasia? For fifteen years I had toiled at the sickbed and every patient was to me like a brother. I worried about every sick child as if it had been my own. My personal lot was a heavy one. Is that guilt?

Was it not my first thought to limit the scope of euthanasia? Did I not, the moment I was included, try to find a limit and demand a most searching report on the incurables? Were not the appointed professors of the universities there? Who could there be who was better qualified? But I do not want to speak of these questions and of their execution. I am defending myself against the charge of inhuman conduct and base intentions. In the face of these charges I fight for my right to humane treatment! I know how complicated this problem is. With the utmost fervor I have tortured myself again and again, but no philosophy or other wisdom helped me here. There was the decree and on it there was my name. It is no good saying that I could have feigned sickness. I do not live this life of mine in order to evade fate if I meet it. And thus I assented to euthanasia. I fully realize the problem; it is as old as mankind, but it is not a crime against man or against humanity. It is pity for the incurable, literally. Here I cannot believe like a clergyman or think as a jurist. I am a doctor and I see the law of nature as being the law of reason. In my heart there is love of mankind, and so it is in my conscience. That is why I am a doctor!

When I talked at the time to Pastor Bodelschwingh, the only serious admonisher I knew personally, it seemed at first as if our thoughts were far apart; but the longer we talked and the more we came into the open, the closer and the greater became our mutual understanding. At that time we were not concerned with words. It was a struggle and a search far beyond the human sphere. When the old Pastor Bodelschwingh left me after many hours and we shook hands, his last words were: "That was the hardest struggle of my life." For him as well as for me that struggle remained; and the problem remained, too.

If I were to say today that I wish this problem had never come upon me with its convulsive drama, that would be nothing but superficiality in order to make me feel more comfortable in myself. But I am living in these times and I see that they are full of antitheses. Somewhere we all must make a stand. I am fully conscious that when I said "Yes" to euthanasia I did so with the deepest conviction, just as it is my conviction today, that it was right. Death can mean deliverance. Death is life—just as much as birth. It was never meant to be murder. I bear a burden, but it is not the burden of crime. I bear this burden of mine, though with a heavy heart, as my responsibility. I stand before it, and before my conscience, as a man and as a doctor.

Notes

Introduction

1. Hugh Gregory Gallagher, *FDR's Splendid Deception* (New York: Dodd, Mead, 1985).
2. Goetz Aly and Heinz Roth, "The Legalization of Mercy Killings in Medical and Nursing Institutions in Nazi Germany from 1938 Until 1941," *International Journal of Law and Psychiatry* (1984), 7:163.

Chapter 1

1. Leon Jaworski, *After Fifteen Years* (Houston: Gulf Books, 1963), 107.
2. Robert Jay Lifton, *The Nazi Doctors—Medical Killing and the Psychology of Genocide* (New York: Basic Books, Inc., 1986), 71.
3. *Trials of War Criminals Before the Nuremberg Military Tribunals Under Control Council Law No. 10*, Nuremberg, October 1946–April 1947 (Washington, D.C.: U.S. Government Printing Office) I: 877.
4. Alexander Mitscherlich, *The Death Doctors*, trans. James Cleugh (London: Elek Books, 1962), 21.
5. *Trials of War Criminals*, I: 886.
6. *Trials of War Criminals*, I: 877.
7. *Trials of War Criminals*, I: 883–84.
8. Mitscherlich, *The Death Doctors*, 256.
9. Mitscherlich, *The Death Doctors*, xxvii.
10. *Mensch-achte den Menschen Furhe Texte über die Euthanasieverbrechen der Nationalsozialisten in Hessen* (Kassel: Landeswohlfahrts verbandes, 1985).
11. Jaworski, *After Fifteen Years*, 119.

12. *Mensch-achte den Menschen.*
13. Earl W. Kintner, ed., *The Hadamar Trial: Trial of Alfons Klein, Defendant* (Edinburgh: William Hodge, 1949), 93.
14. Ernst Klee, *"Euthanasie" im NS-Staat, Die "Vernichtung lebensun-werten Lebens"* (Frankfurt: S. Fisher, 1983), 336.
15. Klee, *"Euthanasie" im NS-Staat*, 336.
16. *Mensch-achte den Menschen.*
17. Klee, *"Euthanasie" im NS-Staat*, 336.
18. *Mensch-achte den Menschen.*
19. Kintner, ed., *Hadamar Trial*, 95.
20. Jaworski, *After Fifteen Years*, 121.
21. Kintner, ed., *Hadamar Trial*, 109.
22. Kintner, ed., *Hadamar Trial*, 121.
23. Kintner, ed., *Hadamar Trial*, 130.

Chapter 2

1. Shearer quotes from *Disability: Whose Handicap?* (London: Basil Blackwell, 1981) and Kemp adaptation from remarks of Commissioner Evan J. Kemp, Jr., before the 1988 Labor Law and Labor Relations Seminar, Degray State Park, Arkadelphia, Arkansas, April 8, 1988.
2. Beatrice A. Wright, *Physical Disability—a Psychosocial Approach* (New York: Harper & Row, 1983), 442, 443.
3. Wright, *Physical Disability*, 443.
4. Wright, *Physical Disability*, 444–46.
5. Hentig, "Physical Disability, Mental Conflict, and Social Crisis," *Journal of Social Issues* (1948 b): 4 (4).
6. Wright, *Physical Disability*, 64.
7. Henry E. Sigerist, *A History of Medicine* (New York: Oxford University Press, 1951), 21–27.
8. Dominique Le Disert, "Entre la Peur et la Pitié: Quelques Aspects Sociohistoriques de l'infirmité," trans. Vivien Reubin. *International Journal of Rehabilitation Research* 10 (no. 3, 1987): 253–65.
9. Hugh Gregory Gallagher, *FDR's Splendid Deception* (New York: Dodd, Mead, 1985).
10. Le Disert, "Entre la Peur et al Pitié," 253–65.
11. Ibid.
12. P. H. Mussen and R. G. Barker, "Attitudes Toward Cripples," *Journal of Abnormal Social Psychology* 39 (1944): 351–55.
13. E. K. Strong, Jr., *Change of Interests with Age* (Palo Alto: Stanford University Press, 1931).

14. L. M. Shears & C. J. Jensema, "Social Acceptability of Anomalous Persons," *Exceptional Child* 36 (1969): 91–96.

15. P. Schoggen, "Environmental Forces on Physically Handicapped Children" (1978), 144–45, as quoted in Wright, *Physical Disability*, 75.

16. Hentig, *"Physical Disability,"* 4 (4).

17. John Gliedman and William Roth, *The Unexpected Minority* (New York: Harcourt Brace Jovanovich, 1980), 430n.

18. Wright, *Physical Disability*, 33.

19. As told to the author.

20. Gliedman and Roth, *Unexpected Minority*.

21. Wright and Muth, as quoted in Wright, *Physical Disability*, 34.

22. Gliedman and Roth, *Unexpected Minority*, 254.

23. E. Becker, *The Denial of Death* (New York: Free Press, 1973), 26–27.

24. Jay Katz, *The World of Doctor and Patient* (New York: Free Press, 1984), 219.

25. Erving Goffman, *Stigma, Notes on the Management of Spoiled Identity* (Englewood Cliffs, N.J.: Simon and Schuster, 1963), 3.

26. Katz, *World of Doctor*, 209.

27. "A Study of the Mental and Emotional Development of the Thalidomide Child," ed. Brian M. Foss, *Determinants of Infant Behavior* (London: Methuen, 1969), 4.

28. Fred Davis, *Passage Through Darkness: Polio Victims and Their Families* (Indianapolis: Bobbs-Merrill, 1963).

Chapter 3

1. Fredric Wertham, M.D., *A Sign for Cain: An Exploration of Human Violence* (London: Robert Hale Ltd., 1968), 153.

2. Alexander Mitscherlich, *The Death Doctors*, trans. James Cleugh (London: Elek Books, 1962), 234.

3. Mitscherlich, *Death Doctors*, 239.

4. U.S. Nuremberg War Crimes Trials, November 21, 1946–August 20, 1947 (National Archives Microfilm Publications), M887, Tape 17, Doc. 630–PS.

5. Mitscherlich, *Death Doctors*, 265.

6. Mitscherlich, *Death Doctors*, 234.

7. Mitscherlich, *Death Doctors*, 235.

8. Mitscherlich, *Death Doctors*, 234.

9. Ibid.

10. Wertham, *Sign for Cain*, 186.

11. John Toland, *Adolf Hitler* (Garden City, N.Y.: Doubleday and Co., Inc., 1976), 595.
12. Toland, *Adolf Hitler*, 388.
13. Toland, *Adolf Hitler*, 595.
14. Adolf Hitler, *Mein Kampf* (New York: Stackpole Sons Publishers, 1939), 391.
15. Hitler, *Mein Kampf*, 445.
16. Hitler, *Mein Kampf*, 391.
17. Hitler, *Mein Kampf*, 392.
18. Guenter Lewy, *The Catholic Church and Nazi Germany* (New York, Toronto: McGraw-Hill, 1964), 258.
19. Wallace R. Deuel, *People Under Hitler* (New York: Harcourt Brace and Co., 1942), 222.
20. Deuel, *People Under Hitler*, 226.
21. Mitscherlich, *Death Doctors*, 236.
22. Ibid.
23. Ibid.
24. Gerald Reitlinger, *The Final Solution: The Attempt to Eliminate the Jews from Europe, 1939–1945* (New York: A. S. Barnes and Co., 1961), 9, 128.
25. Amnon Amir, "Euthanasia in Nazi Germany" (Ph.D. diss., State University of New York at Albany, 1977), 183.
26. Gitta Sereny, *Into That Darkness: From Mercy Killing to Mass Murder* (New York: McGraw Hill, 1974), 80.
27. Hartmut M. Hanauske-Able, "Politics and Medicine: From Nazi Holocaust to Nuclear Holocaust—a Lesson to Learn?" *The Lancet*, August 22, 1986, 272.
28. Goetz Aly and Heinz Roth, "The Legalization of Mercy Killings in Medical and Nursing Institutions in Nazi Germany from 1938 Until 1941," *International Journal of Law and Psychiatry* (1984), 7: 148.
29. Mitscherlich, *Death Doctors*, 235.
30. Mitscherlich, *Death Doctors*, 238.
31. Gitta Sereny, *Into That Darkness, from Mercy Killing to Mass Murder* (New York: McGraw-Hill, 1974), 56.
32. Mitscherlich, *Death Doctors*, 238.
33. Peter Roger Breggin, M.D., "The Psychiatric Holocaust," *Penthouse*, January 1979, 81–84.
34. *Deutsches Ärzteblatt* 80 (1983): 23–26, as quoted in Hanauske-Able, "Politics and Medicine," 272.
35. Benno Muller-Hill, *Murderous Science* (Oxford: Oxford University Press, 1988), 42.

36. Geoffrey Cocks, *Psychotherapy in the Third Reich* (New York: Oxford University Press, 1985), 99.
37. Wertham, *Sign for Cain*, 168, 169.
38. *Trials of War Criminals Before the Nuremberg Military Tribunals Under Control Council Law No. 10*, Nuremberg, October 1946–April 1947 (Washington, D.C.: U.S. Government Printing Office), I: 849, 850.
39. Mitscherlich, *Death Doctors*, 239.
40. *Trials of War Criminals*, I: 880.
41. Amir, "Euthanasia," 198.
42. Leo Alexander, Major, MC, AUS, *Public Mental Health Practices in Germany: Sterilization and Execution of Patients Suffering from Nervous or Mental Disease.* Combined Intelligence Objectives Subcommittee, G2 Division, SHAEF (Rear), APO 413 (National Archives), 13.
43. Ernst Klee, ed., *Documentation of Euthanasia* (Frankfurt: Fischer Taschenbuch Verlag 4327, 1988), IIIA.
44. U.S. Nuremberg War Crimes Trials, November 21, 1946–August 20, 1947 (National Archives Microfilm Publications), M887, Tape 4, Doc. No. 2420.
45. Amir, "Euthanasia," 202.
46. U.S. Nuremberg War Crimes Trials, M887, Tape 17, Doc. No. 617.
47. U.S. Nuremberg War Crimes Trials, M887, Tape 17, Doc. No. 189.

Chapter 4

1. Charles Darwin, *The Descent of Man and Selection in Relation to Sex* (New York: Appleton, 1922), 136 and 632.
2. Charles Davenport, *Heredity in Relation to Eugenics* (New York: Henry Holt & Co., 1911), 1.
3. Haller, *Eugenics: Hereditarian Attitudes in American Thought* (New Brunswick, N.J.: Rutgers University Press, 1963), 79, 81.
4. Haller, *Eugenics*, 147.
5. Bertrand Russell to the author, 1951.
6. Haller, *Eugenics*, 33, 34.
7. Haller, *Eugenics*, 106–109.
8. Haller, *Eugenics*, 42.
9. Haller, *Eugenics*, 135.
10. Haller, *Eugenics*, 131.
11. *Buck* v. *Bell*, 274 U.S. 200 (1927).
12. Haller, *Eugenics*, 126.
13. Daniel Gasman, *The Scientific Origins of National Socialism: Social*

Darwinism in Ernst Haeckel and the German Monist League (New York: American Elsevier Publishing Co., 1971), 14.

14. Gasman, *Scientific Origins*, 95.
15. Gasman, *Scientific Origins*, 96.
16. Gasman, *Scientific Origins*, 98.
17. Ibid.
18. Gasman, *Scientific Origins*, 96.
19. Gasman, *Scientific Origins*, 96–97.
20. Peter Roger Breggin, M.D. "The Psychiatric Holocaust," *Penthouse*, January 1979, 81–84.
21. James M. Gardner, "Contribution of the German Cinema to the Nazi Euthanasia Program," *Mental Retardation*, August 1982, 174–75.
22. Alexander Mitscherlich, *The Death Doctors*, trans. James Cleugh (London: Elek Books, 1962), 234; Leo Alexander, M.D., "Medical Science Under Dictatorship," *New England Journal of Medicine* 241:2 (July 14, 1949): 39.
23. Breggin, "Psychiatric Holocaust," 81–84.
24. *New York Times*, October 8, 1933, 1.
25. Ibid.
26. Breggin, "Psychiatric Holocaust," 81–84.
27. Foster Kennedy, M.D., "Brutalities of Nazi Physicians, the Problem of Social Control of the Congenital Defective: Education, Sterilization, Euthanasia," *American Journal of Psychiatry*, July 1942, 142.
28. Kennedy, "Brutalities of Nazi Physicians," 143.

Chapter 5

1. *Trials of War Criminals Before the Nuremberg Military Tribunals Under Control Council Law No. 10*, Nuremberg, October 1946–April 1947 (Washington, D.C.: U.S. Government Printing Office), I: 800.
2. Benno Muller-Hill, *Murderous Science* (Oxford: Oxford University Press, 1988), 13.
3. Leon Poliakov, *Harvest of Hate: the Nazi Program for the Destruction of the Jews in Europe* (Westport: Greenwood Press, 1975), 185.
4. Robert Jay Lifton, *The Nazi Doctors—Medical Killing and the Psychology of Genocide* (New York: Basic Books, Inc., 1986), 71.
5. *Trials of War Criminals*, I: 877.
6. Ibid.
7. Amnon Amir, "Euthanasia in Nazi Germany" (Ph.D. diss., State University of New York at Albany, 1977), 218.
8. Ibid.
9. Lifton, *Nazi Doctors*, 73.

10. Amir, "Euthanasia," 216.
11. Gitta Sereny, *Into That Darkness: From Mercy Killing to Mass Murder* (New York: McGraw-Hill, 1974), 53.
12. Amir, "Euthanasia," 182.
13. Ernst Klee, *"Euthanasie" im NS-Staat, Die "Vernichtung lebensunwerten Lebens"* (Frankfurt: S. Fisher, 1983), 180–81.
14. Sereny, *Into That Darkness*, 39, 55.
15. Leo Alexander, Major, MC, AUS, *Public Mental Health Practices in Germany: Sterilization and Execution of Patients Suffering from Nervous or Mental Disease*, Combined Intelligence Objective Subcommittee, G2 Division, SHAEF (Rear) APO 413 (National Archives), 9.
16. Fredric Wertham, M.D., *A Sign for Cain: an Exploration of Human Violence* (London: Robert Hale Ltd., 1968), 182.
17. Alexander, *Public Mental Health*, 15.
18. *Trial of War Criminals*, I: 852.
19. Lifton, *Nazi Doctors*, 60.
20. Alexander Mitscherlich, *The Death Doctors*, trans. James Cleugh (London: Elek Books, 1962), 252.
21. Wertham, *Sign for Cain*, 181.
22. U.S. Nuremberg War Crimes Trials, November 21, 1946–August 20, 1947 (National Archives Microfilm Publications), M887, Tape 17, Doc. No. 1144.
23. Ibid.
24. Alexander, *Public Mental Health*, 26.
25. U.S. Nuremberg War Crimes Trials, M887, Tape 17, Doc. No. 1144.
26. Ibid.
27. Ibid.
28. Ibid.
29. Ibid., Doc. No. 842.
30. Lifton, *Nazi Doctors*, quoting Heyde trial, 74.
31. U.S. Nuremberg War Crimes Trials, M887, Tape 17, Doc. No. 842.
32. *Trials of War Criminals*, I: 848.
33. Ibid.
34. *Trials of War Criminals*, I: 852.
35. Muller-Hill, *Murderous Science*, 47.
36. Klaus Dörner, "Nationalsozialismus und Lebensvernichtung," *Vierteljahrshefte für Zeitgeschicte*, 5: 2 (April 1967) 151.
37. Goetz Aly and Heinz Roth, "The Legalization of Mercy Killings in Medical and Nursing Institutions in Nazi Germany from 1938 Until 1941," *International Journal of Law and Psychiatry* (1984), 7: 162.

38. Alexander as quoted in Peter Breggin, "The Psychiatrist Holocaust," 84.
39. Muller-Hill, *Murderous Science*, 20.

Chapter 6

1. Alexander Mitscherlich, *The Death Doctors*, trans., James Cleugh (London: Elek Books, 1962), 272.
2. Arlene Fischer, "Babies in Pain," *Redbook*, October 1987, 124.
3. E. Kuby, "Rot . . . Stopp . . . Grun . . . Anfahren . . . Scharf Bremsen," *Der Spiegel*, 15:19 (1965).
4. Ralf Dahrendorf, *Society and Democracy in Germany* (London: Weidenfeld and Nicolson Ltd., 1961), 358–59.
5. Dahrendorf, *Society and Democracy*, 362.
6. Dahrendorf, *Society and Democracy*, 355.
7. Ibid.
8. Dahrendorf, *Society and Democracy*, 354.
9. Mary Tedeschi, "Infanticide and Its Apologists," *Commentary*, November 1984, 31–35.
10. Ibid.
11. Nat Hentoff, "The Awful Privacy of Baby Doe," *The Atlantic Monthly*, January 1985, 54–58.
12. *Trials of War Criminals Before the Nuremberg Military Tribunals Under Control Council Law No. 10*, Nuremberg, October 1946–April 1947 (Washington, D.C.: U.S. Government Printing Office), I: 894.
13. Robert Jay Lifton, *The Nazi Doctors—Medical Killing and the Psychology of Genocide* (New York: Basic Books, Inc., 1986), 47.
14. Amnon Amir, "Euthanasia in Nazi Germany" (Ph.D. diss., State University of New York at Albany, 1977), 278.
15. Goetz Aly and Heinz Roth, "The Legalization of Mercy Killings in Medical and Nursing Institutions in Nazi Germany from 1938 Until 1941," *International Journal of Law and Psychiatry* (1984), 7: 151.
16. U.S. Nuremberg War Crimes Trials, November 21, 1946–August 20, 1947 (National Archives Microfilm Publications), M887, Tape 17, Doc. No. 883.
17. Referred to in Chapter 3.
18. *Trials of War Criminals*, I: 894.
19. Aly and Roth, "Legalization of Mercy Killings," 151.
20. Ernst Klee, *"Euthanasie" im NS-Staat. Die "Vernichtung lebensunwerten Lebens"* (Frankfurt: S. Fischer, 1983), 80.
21. Robert N. Proctor, *Racial Hygiene: Medicine Under the Nazis* (Cambridge: Harvard University Press, 1988), 187–88.

22. Leo Alexander, Major, MC, AUS, *Public Mental Health Practices in Germany: Sterilization and Execution of Patients Suffering from Nervous or Mental Disease*, Combined Intelligence Objectives Subcommittee, G2 Division, SHAEF (Rear) APO 413 (National Archives): 17.
23. Mitscherlich, *Death Doctors*, 272.
24. Alexander, *Public Mental Health*, 19–20.
25. Lifton, *Nazi Doctors*, 120.
26. Alexander, *Public Mental Health*, 16–21 (Pfannmüller's correspondence).
27. Alexander, *Public Mental Health*, 21.
28. Ibid.
29. Alexander, *Public Mental Health*, 19.
30. *Trials of War Criminals*, I: 801.
31. Klee, *"Euthnasie,"* 311.
32. Klee, *"Euthnasie,"* 294–317.
33. Klee, *"Euthnasie,"* 304.
34. Amir, "Euthanasia," 286.
35. George Brand, ed., *The Velpke Baby Home Trials: Trial of Heinrich Gerike, Defendant* (London: William Hodge and Co., Ltd., 1950), 7.
36. Warren G. Kinzey, ed., *The Evolution of Human Behavior: The Primate Models* (New York: State University of New York Press, 1987), 130–32.

Chapter 7

1. Ernst Klee, *"Euthanasie" im NS-Staat, Die "Vernichtung lebensunwerten Lebens"* (Frankfurt: S. Fischer, 1983), 188–89.
2. Ibid.
3. Ibid.
4. Ibid.
5. Ibid.
6. U.S. Nuremberg War Crimes Trials, M887, Tape 17, Doc. No. 18.

Chapter 8

1. Heinz Hohne, *The Order of the Death's Head: the Story of Hitler's SS* (New York: Coward-McCann, 1970), 8.
2. Hohne, *Order of the Death's Head*, 10.
3. Hohne, *Order of the Death's Head*, 8–11.
4. U.S. Nuremberg War Crimes Trials, M887, Tape 17, Doc. No. 906. 24–25.
5. *Trials of War Criminals Before the Nuremberg Military Tribunals Under Control Council Law No. 10*, Nuremberg, October 1946–April

1947 (Washington, D.C.: U.S. Government Printing Office), I: 855–56.

6. *Trials of War Criminals*, I: 857.

7. U.S. Nuremberg War Crimes Trials, M887, Tape 17, Doc. No. 1312.

8. U.S. Nuremberg War Crimes Trials, M887, Tape 17, Doc. No. 906, 23.

9. U.S. Nuremberg War Crimes Trials, M887, Tape 17, Doc. No. 906, 24.

10. U.S. Nuremberg War Crimes Trials, M887, Tape 17, Doc. No. 906, 25.

11. Leo Alexander, Major, MC, AUS, *Public Mental Health Practices in Germany: Sterilization and Execution of Patients Suffering from Nervous or Mental Disease*, Combined Intelligence Objectives Subcommittee, G2 Division, SHAEF (Rear) APO 413 (National Archives), 14, 15.

12. Alexander Mitscherlich, *The Death Doctors*, trans. James Cleugh (London: Elek Books, 1962), 268.

13. Robert N. Proctor, *Racial Hygiene: Medicine Under the Nazis* (Cambridge: Harvard University Press, 1988), 194.

14. U.S. Nuremberg War Crimes Trials, M887, Tape 17, Doc. No. 906.

15. U.S. Nuremberg War Crimes Trials, M887, Tape 17, Doc. No. 2.

16. Leon Poliakov, *Harvest of Hate: the Nazi Program for the Destruction of the Jews in Europe* (Westport: Greenwood Press, 1975), 188–89.

17. Mitscherlich, *The Death Doctors*, 107.

18. U.S. Nuremberg War Crimes Trials, M887, Tape 17, Doc. No. 206, 24.

19. Ernst Klee, *"Euthanasie" im NS-Staat, Die "Vernichtung lebensunwerten Lebens"* (Frankfurt: S. Fischer, 1983), 54.

20. Klee, *"Euthanasie,"* 184.

21. Klee, *"Euthanasie,"* 190.

22. Amnon Amir, "Euthanasia in Nazi Germany" (Ph.D. diss., State University of New York at Albany, 1977), 227.

23. Alexander, *Public Mental Health*, 14.

24. Proctor, *Racial Hygiene*, 194.

25. Klee, *"Euthanasie,"* 131.

26. U.S. Nuremberg War Crimes Trials, M887, Tape 17, Doc. No. 288.

27. U.S. Nuremberg War Crimes Trials, M887, Tape 17, Doc. No. 288–89.

28. Alexander, *Public Mental Health*, 35.

29. Klee, *"Euthanasie,"* 184–85.

Chapter 9

1. Hartmut M. Hanauske-Able, "Politics and Medicine: From Nazi Holocaust to Nuclear Holocaust: a Lesson to Learn?", *The Lancet* (August 22, 1986): 272.
2. Alexander Mitscherlich, *The Death Doctors*, trans. James Cleugh (London: Elek Books, 1962), 17.
3. Ernst Klee, ed., *Documentation of Euthanasia* (Frankfurt: Fischer Taschenbuch Verlag 4327, 1988), 28.
4. Renate Jaeckle, *The Physicians and Politics: 1930 Until Today* (Frankfurt: Beck'sche Reihe 361, 1988), 9.
5. Benno Muller-Hill, *Murderous Science* (Oxford: Oxford University Press, 1988), 71.
6. Leo Alexander, Major, MC, AUS, *Public Mental Health Practices in Germany: Sterilization and Execution of Patients Suffering from Nervous or Mental Disease*, Combined Intelligence Objectives Subcommittee, G2 Division, SHAEF (Rear) APO 413 (National Archives), 330.
7. Mitscherlich, *Death Doctors*, 265.
8. Amnon Amir, "Euthanasia in Nazi Germany" (Ph.D. diss., State University of New York at Albany, 1977), 235–36.
9. Mitscherlich, *Death Doctors*, 263.
10. Amir, "Euthanasia in Nazi Germany," 237.
11. Ernst Klee, *"Euthanasie" in NS-Staat, Die "Vernichtung lebensunwerten Lebens"* (Frankfurt: S. Fischer, 1983), 216.
12. Robert Jay Lifton, *The Nazi Doctors—Medical Killing and the Psychology of Genocide* (New York: Basic Books, Inc., 1986), 81.
13. Klee, ed., *Documentation of Euthanasia*, 28.
14. Lifton, *Nazi Doctors*, 86.
15. Klee, *"Euthanasie,"* 223.
16. Muller-Hill, *Murderous Science*, 36.
17. U.S. Nuremberg War Crimes Trials, November 21, 1946–August 20, 1947 (National Archives Microfilm Publications), M887, Tape 17, Doc. PS 3067.
18. Mitscherlich, *Death Doctors*, 254.
19. Klee, *"Euthanasie,"* 194–95.
20. Joseph Tenenbaum, *Race and Reich: the Story of an Epoch.* (New York: Twayne Publishers, 1956), 86.
21. Muller-Hill, *Murderous Science*, 107.
22. Michael Kater, "The Burden of the Past: Problems of a Modern Historiography of Physicians and Medicine in Nazi Germany," *German Studies Review*, X:1 (February 1987), 32.

23. Hanauske-Abel, "Politics and Medicine," 271.
24. Robert N. Proctor, *Racial Hygiene: Medicine Under the Nazis* (Cambridge: Harvard University Press, 1988), 90 (quoting Ramm).
25. *Trials of War Criminals Before the Nuremberg Military Tribunals Under Control Council Law No. 10,* Nuremberg, October 1946–April 1947 (Washington, D.C.: U.S. Government Printing Office), II: 58.
26. Proctor, *Racial Hygiene,* 157.
27. Proctor, *Racial Hygiene,* 62.
28. Proctor, *Racial Hygiene,* 287.
29. Proctor, *Racial Hygiene,* 102.
30. Muller-Hill, *Murderous Science,* 29.
31. Proctor, *Racial Hygiene,* 161.
32. Ibid.
33. Proctor, *Racial Hygiene,* 154.
34. Mitscherlich, *Death Doctors,* 265.
35. Proctor, *Racial Hygiene,* 193.
36. U.S. Nuremberg War Crimes Trials, M887, Tape 17, Doc. No. 2.
37. Alexander, *Public Mental Health,* 42.
38. Muller-Hill, *Murderous Science;* Fredric Wertham, M.D., *A Sign for Cain: an Exploration of Human Violence* (London: Robert Hale Ltd., 1968); Hanauske-Able, "Politics and Medicine."
39. Leo Alexander, M.D., "Medical Science Under Dictatorship," *New England Journal of Medicine* 241 (2) (July 14, 1949): 39–47.
40. Letter on pages 183–84.
41. Mitscherlich, *Death Doctors,* 302.
42. Goetz Aly and Heinz Roth, "The Legalization of Mercy Killings in Medical and Nursing Institutions in Nazi Germany from 1938 until 1941." *International Journal of Law and Psychiatry* (1984), 7:145–63.
43. Mitscherlich, *Death Doctors,* 293.
44. Wertham, *Sign for Cain,* 160.
45. Mitscherlich, *Death Doctors,* 266.
46. Wertham, *Sign for Cain,* 160.
47. Wertham, *Sign for Cain,* 169.
48. Mitscherlich, *Death Doctors,* 238.
49. Wertham, *Sign for Cain,* 160.
50. Alexander, "Medical Science Under Dictatorship," 29–47.

Chapter 10

1. Detlev J. K. Peukert, *Nazi Germany: Conformity, Opposition, and Racism in Everyday Life,* trans. Richard Deveson (New Haven: Yale University Press, 1988), 198.

2. Peukert, *Nazi Germany*, 220.
3. Peukert, *Nazi Germany*, 198.
4. Peukert, *Nazi Germany*, 199.
5. Fritz Stern, *Dreams and Delusions* (New York: Knopf, 1987), 119.
6. Amnon Amir, "Euthanasia in Nazi Germany" (Ph.D. diss., State University of New York at Albany, 1977), 119.
7. William L. Shirer, *The Rise and Fall of the Third Reich: a History of Nazi Germany* (New York: Simon and Schuster, 1960), 250.
8. Amir, "Euthanasia," 126.
9. Amir, "Euthanasia," 128.
10. Amir, "Euthanasia," 124.
11. Heinz Hohne, *The Order of the Death's Head: the Story of Hitler's SS* (New York: Coward-McCann, 1970), 9.
12. U.S. Nuremberg War Crimes Trials, November 21, 1946–August 20, 1947 (National Archives Microfilm Publications), M887, Tape 17, Doc. No. 622-PS.
13. U.S. Nuremberg War Crimes Trials, M887, Tape 17, Doc. No. 681-PS.
14. Alexander Mitscherlich, *The Death Doctors*, trans. James Cleugh (London: Elek Books, 1962), 253–54.
15. Amir, "Euthanasia," 157.
16. Mitscherlich, *Death Doctors*, 261.
17. U.S. Nuremberg War Crimes Trials, M887, Tape 17, Doc. No. 832.
18. U.S. Nuremberg War Crimes Trials, M887, Tape 17, Doc. No. 836.
19. Amir, "Euthanasia," 154.
20. Amir, "Euthanasia," 158.
21. U.S. Nuremberg War Crimes Trials, M887, Tape 17, Doc. No. 832.
22. Mitscherlich, *Death Doctors*, 257.
23. Goetz Aly and Heinz Roth, "The Legalization of Mercy Killings in Medical and Nursing Institutions in Nazi Germany from 1938 until 1941," *International Journal of Law and Psychiatry* (1984), 7:145–63.
24. *Trials of War Criminals Before the Nuremberg Military Tribunals Under Control Council Law No. 10*, Nuremberg, October 1946–April 1947 (Washington, D.C.: U.S. Government Printing Office), II: 61.
25. Mitscherlich, *Death Doctors*, 240.
26. Mitscherlich, *Death Doctors*, 234.
27. Amir, "Euthanasia," 138.
28. Amir, "Euthanasia," 152.
29. Amir, "Euthanasia," 147.
30. Ibid.

31. U.S. Nuremberg War Crimes Trials, M887, Tape 17, Doc. No. 84.
32. Amir, "Euthanasia," 159.

Chapter 11

1. John S. Conway, *The Nazi Persecution of the Churches, 1933–1945* (New York: Basic Books, Inc., 1968), 232.
2. Richard J. Evans, *Rethinking German History, Nineteenth-Century Germany and the Origins of the Third Reich* (London: Allen and Unwin, 1987), 150.
3. Mary Alice Gallin, *Ethical and Religious Factors in the German Resistance to Hitler* (Washington, D.C.: The Catholic University of America Press, 1955), 33.
4. Gallin, *Ethical and Religious Factors*, 34.
5. Gallin, *Ethical and Religious Factors*, 35.
6. Evans, *Rethinking German History*, 147.
7. Michael Wunder, *There Is No Stopping on This Slope* (Hamburg: Rauhes Haus, 1988).
8. John S. Conway, "The Silence of Pope Pius XII," *The Review of Politics* 27 (1967): 105–31.
9. Conway, *Nazi Persecution*, 30.
10. Conway, "Silence of Pope," 105.
11. Conway, *Nazi Persecution*, 61.
12. Conway, *Nazi Persecution*, 445.
13. Conway, *Nazi Persecution*, 54.
14. Ernst Klee, ed., *Documentation of Euthanasia* (Frankfurt: Fischer Taschenbuch Verlag 4327, 1988), 46–47.
15. Klee, ed., *Documentation of Euthanasia*, 54–55.
16. Klee, ed., *Documentation of Euthanasia*, 38.
17. *Vergessene Opfer*, EKD Texte.
18. Klee, ed., *Documentation of Euthanasia*, 38.
19. Ibid.
20. Ernst Christian Helmreich, *The German Churches Under Hitler* (Detroit: Wayne State University Press, 1979), 254.
21. Helmreich, *German Churches*, 260.
22. Klee, ed., *Documentation of Euthanasia*, 39.
23. Klee, ed., *Documentation of Euthanasia*, 43.
24. Gitta Sereny, *Into That Darkness: From Mercy Killing to Mass Murder* (New York: McGraw-Hill, 1974), 66–68.
25. Sereny, *Into That Darkness*, 71.
26. Höllen, in Aktion T-4.
27. Helmreich, *German Churches*, 312.

28. Amnon Amir, "Euthanasia in Nazi Germany" (Ph.D. diss., State University of New York at Albany, 1977), 263.
29. Amir, "Euthanasia," 267.
30. Amir, "Euthanasia," 262.
31. Helmreich, *German Churches*, 311, 312.
32. Klee, ed., *Documentation of Euthanasia*, 151–62.
33. Helmreich, *German Churches*, 311.
34. Klee, ed., *Documentation of Euthanasia*, 151.
35. Helmreich, *German Churches*, 311.
36. Klee, ed., *Documentation of Euthanasia*, 151.
37. Conway, *Nazi Persecution*, 35.
38. Helmreich, *German Churches*, 313.
39. Ibid.
40. Bodelschwingh letter printed in Klee, ed., *Documentation of Euthanasia*.
41. Helmreich, *German Churches*, 314.
42. Amir, "Euthanasia," 261.
43. Amir, "Euthanasia," 260.
44. Klee, ed., *Documentation of Euthanasia*, 300.
45. Amir, "Euthanasia," 266.
46. Sereny, *Into That Darkness*, 75.
47. Gordon C. Zahn, *German Catholics and Hitler's Wars* (New York: E. P. Dutton and Co., 1969), 88, 89.
48. Zahn, *German Catholics*, 88.
49. Helmreich, *German Churches*, 246.
50. *The Nation*, November 1, 1941, 99.
51. Zahn, *German Catholics*, 93.
52. "German Bishop Warns That Gestapo Menaces Reich," *Catholic Mind* 39 (December 8, 1941): 11.
53. "Bishop von Galen Defies Hitler," *Catholic Mind* 40 (December 22, 1942): 4.
54. Heinrich Portmann, *Cardinal von Galen* (London: Jarolds, 1958), 107.
55. Zahn, *German Catholics*, 84.
56. Ibid.
57. Amir, "Euthanasia," 270.
58. Klee, ed., *Documentation of Euthanasia*, 197.
59. Conway, *Nazi Persecution*, 281.
60. Amir, "Euthanasia," 270.
61. Ibid.
62. Portmann, *Cardinal von Galen*, 109.

63. Guenter Lewy, *The Catholic Church and Nazi Germany* (New York, Toronto: McGraw-Hill, 1964), 265.
64. Conway, *Nazi Persecution*, 282.
65. Adolf Hitler, *Hitler's Table Talk*, A. Bullock, ed. (London: Odhams Press, 1953), as quoted in Conway, *Nazi Persecution*, 283.

Chapter 12

1. Peter Roger Breggin, M.D., "The Psychiatric Holocaust," *Penthouse*, January 1979, 81.
2. Leo Alexander Major, MC, AUS, *Public Mental Health Practices in Germany: Sterilization and Execution of Patients Suffering from Nervous or Mental Disease*. Combined Intelligence Objectives Subcommittee, G2 Division, SHAEF (Rear) APO 413, National Archives.
3. *Trials of War Criminals Before the Nuremberg Military Tribunals Under Control Council Law No. 10*, Nuremberg, October 1946–April 1947 (Washington, D.C.: U.S. Government Printing Office, Article II, section 1, paragraph (b), I: xvii.
4. *Trials of War Criminals*, paragraph (c), I: xvii.
5. *Trials of War Criminals*, I: 15.
6. *Trials of War Criminals*, I: 66.
7. *Trials of War Criminals*, I: 68.
8. Ibid.
9. Ibid.
10. *Trials of War Criminals*, I: 71.
11. *Trials of War Criminals*, II: 164.
12. *Trials of War Criminals*, II: 139.
13. *Trials of War Criminals*, II: 135.
14. *Trials of War Criminals*, II: 127.
15. *Trials of War Criminals*, II: 138–40.
16. *Trials of War Criminals*, II: 196–98.
17. Michael H. Kater, "The Burden of the Past: Problems of a Modern Historiography of Physicians and Medicine in Nazi Germany," *German Studies Review* X: 1 (February 1987), 31–56.
18. Frederic Wertham, M.D., *A Sign for Cain: an Exploration of Human Violence* (London: Robert Hale Ltd., 1968), 191.
19. Wertham, *A Sign for Cain*, 189.
20. Ibid.
21. Ibid.
22. Ernst Klee, *"Euthanasie" im NS-Staat. Die "Vernichtung lebensunwerten Lebens"* (Frankfurt: S. Fischer, 1983), 414, and Kater, "Burden of the Past," 43.

23. Robert N. Proctor, *Racial Hygiene: Medicine Under the Nazis* (Cambridge: Harvard University Press, 1988), 300, and Amnon Amir, "Euthanasia in Nazi Germany" (Ph.D. diss., State University of New York at Albany, 1977), 281.

24. Renate Jaeckle, *The Physicians and Politics, 1930 Until Today* (Frankfurt: Beck'sche Reihe 361, 1988), 79.

25. Jaeckle, *Physicians and Politics*, 83.

26. Robert N. Proctor, *Racial Hygiene: Medicine Under the Nazis* (Cambridge: Harvard University Press, 1988), 309.

27. Hartmut M. Hanauske-Able, "Politics and Medicine: From Nazi Holocaust to Nuclear Holocaust: a Lesson to Learn?", *The Lancet*, August 22, 1986, 272.

28. Kater, "Burden of the Past," 38.

29. Ibid.

30. Hanauske-Able, "Politics and Medicine," 272.

31. Proctor, *Racial Hygiene*, 310.

32. Hanauske-Able, "Politics and Medicine," 271.

33. Robert Jay Lifton, *The Nazi Doctors—Medical Killing and the Psychology of Genocide* (New York: Basic Books, Inc., 1986), 447.

34. Goetz Aly, "Die Aktion Brandt," *Aktion T-4, 1939–1945* (Berlin: Hentrich G.m.b.H., 1987), 168–78.

35. Kater, "Burden of the Past," 39.

36. Ibid.

37. Jaeckle, *Physicians and Politics*, 152, 153.

38. Jaeckle, *Physicians and Politics*, 167.

39. Ibid.

40. Jaeckle, *Physicians and Politics*, 169.

41. "All Things Considered," National Public Radio, February 27, 1989.

42. Jaeckle, *Physicians and Politics*, 169.

43. Michael Wunder, "Sterbehilfe—Tötung auf wessen Verlangen?" *Dokumente* (September 1987), 19–22.

44. *L'Osservatore Romano*, May 25, 1989, N. 21, 2.

45. "Pope Condemns World War II Treatment of Handicapped," New York *Daily News*, June 27, 1988, 2.

46. "Doctors Debate Helping the Terminally Ill Die," *New York Times*, May 24, 1989, 1.

Afterword

1. Henryk M. Broder, " 'It Thinks Inside Me . . .' Fassbinder, Germans and Jews," *Encounter*, March 1986, 64–68.

Bibliography

Books

Albrecht, Gary. *The Sociology of Physical Disability and Rehabilitation*. Pittsburgh: University of Pittsburgh Press, 1976.

Alexander, Leo, Major, MC, AUS. *Public Mental Health Practices in Germany: Sterilization and Execution of Patients Suffering from Nervous or Mental Disease*. Combined Intelligence Objectives Subcommittee, G2 Division, SHAEF (Rear) APO 413. National Archives.

Aly, Goetz. "Die Aktion Brandt," in *Aktion T-4, 1939–1945*. Berlin: Hentrich G.m.b.H., 1987.

Amir, Amnon. "Euthanasia in Nazi Germany." Ph.D. diss., State University of New York at Albany, 1977.

Arendt, Hannah. *Eichmann in Jerusalem: A Report on the Banality of Evil*. New York: Penguin Books, 1963.

Becker, E. *The Denial of Death*. New York: Free Press, 1973.

Bleuel, Hans Peter. *Sex and Society in Nazi Germany*, trans. J. Maxwell Brownjohn. Philadelphia: J. P. Lippincott and Co., 1973.

Boorstein, S. W. *Orthopedics for the Teachers' Crippled Children*. New York: Arden, 1935.

Bowe, Frank. *Handicapped in America*. New York: Harper and Row, 1978.

Brand, George, ed. *The Velpke Baby Home Trial: Trial of Heinrich Gerike, Defendant*. London: William Hodge and Co., Ltd., 1950.

Brennan, William. *Medical Holocausts: The Exterminative Medicine in Nazi Germany and Contemporary America*. Volume I in Nordland Series in Contemporary American Social Problems. Boston: Nordland Publishing International, 1980.

Brief *Amici Curiae* of the American Coalition of Citizens with Disabilities, et al., *in re Heckler* v. *American Hospital Association, et al.*, in the Supreme Court of the United States, October term, 1985, #84–1529.

Bromberger, Barbara. *Medizin, Faschismus und Widerstand*. Köln: Pahl-Rugenstein, 1985.

Broszat, Martin. *The Hitler State: The Foundation and Development of the Internal Structure of the Third Reich*, trans. John W. Hiden. London and New York: Longmans, 1981.

Buck v. *Bell,*. 274 U.S. 200. 1927.

Cocks, Geoffrey. *Psychotherapy in the Third Reich*. The Göring Institute. New York and Oxford: Oxford University Press, 1985.

Conway, John S. *The Nazi Persecution of the Churches, 1933–1945*. New York: Basic Books, Inc., 1968.

Dahrendorf, Ralf. *Society and Democracy in Germany*. London: Weidenfeld and Nicolson Ltd., 1961.

Danimann, Franz, et al., *Wien 1938* (illustrated catalogue of an exhibit), 1988.

Darwin, Charles. *The Descent of Man and Selection in Relation to Sex*. New York: Appleton, 1922.

Davenport, Charles. *Heredity in Relation to Eugenics*. New York: Henry Holt and Co., 1911.

Davidson, Eugene. *The Trial of the Germans*. New York: Macmillan, 1966.

Davis, Fred. *Passage Through Darkness: Polio Victims and Their Families*. Indianapolis: Bobbs-Merrill, 1963.

Deuel, Wallace R. *People Under Hitler*. New York: Harcourt Brace and Co., 1942.

Ehrardt, Helmut. *"Euthanasie" und Vernichtung "Lebensunwerten" Lebens*. Stuttgart: Ferdinand Enke, 1965.

Evans, Richard J. *Rethinking German History: Nineteenth-Century Germany and the Origins of the Third Reich*. London: Allen and Unwin, 1987.

Fest, Joachim C. *Face of the Third Reich—Portraits of the Nazi Leadership*, trans. Michael Bullock. New York: Pantheon Books, 1970.

Foss, Brian M., ed. "A Study of the Mental and Emotional Development of the Thalidomide Child." *Determinants of Infant Behavior*. London: Methuen, 1969.

Foucault, Michel. *Madness and Civilization: A History of Insanity in the Age of Reason*. New York: Vantage Books, Random House, 1965.

Fouquet, Christiane. *"Euthanasie" und Vernichtung "Lebensunwerten" Lebens unter Berucksichtigung des behinderten Menschen*. Jarick: Oberbiel, 1978.

Gallagher, Hugh Gregory. *FDR's Splendid Deception*. New York: Dodd, Mead, 1985.

Gallin, Mary Alice. *Ethical and Religious Factors in the German Resistance to Hitler*. Washington, D.C.: The Catholic University of America Press, 1955.

Gasman, Daniel. *The Scientific Origins of National Socialism: Social Darwinism in Ernst Haeckel and the German Monist League*. London: Macdonald; New York: American Elsevier Publishing Co., 1972.

Gliedman, John and William Roth. *The Unexpected Minority*. New York: Harcourt Brace Jovanovich, 1980.

Goffman, Erving. *Stigma, Notes on the Management of Spoiled Identity*. Englewood Cliffs, New Jersey: Simon and Schuster, 1963.

Grunberger, Richard. *The Twelve-Year Reich: A Social History of Nazi Germany, 1933–45*. New York: Holt, Rinehart and Winston, 1971.

Grunfeld, Frederic V. *The Hitler File, 1918–1945*. New York: Bonanza Books, 1979.

Guillebaud, C. W. *The Social Policy of Nazi Germany*. New York: Howard Fertig, 1971.

Gunther, John. *Inside Europe*. New York: Harper and Brothers, 1938.

Haller, Mark H. *Eugenics: Hereditarian Attitudes in American Thought*. New Brunswick, N.J.: Rutgers University Press, 1963.

Heger, Heinz. *The Men with the Pink Triangles*, trans. David Fernback. Boston: Alyson Publications, Inc., 1980.

Helmreich, Ernst Christian. *The German Churches Under Hitler*. Detroit: Wayne State University Press, 1979.

Heston, Leonard H., and Renate Heston. *The Medical Casebook of Adolf Hitler*. London: William Kimber, 1979.

Heyde Trial. Trial of Werner Heyde, Gerhard Bohne, and Hans Heflemann. Generalstaats-anwalt Frankfurt, Js 17/59 (G St A), 4 VU 3/61, Strafkammer des Landgerichts Limburg/Lahn.

Heydecker, Joe and Johanes Leeb. *The Nuremberg Trials*. London: Heinemann, 1962.

Hildebrand, K. *The Third Reich*, trans. P. S. Falla. London: Allen and Unwin, 1984.

Hitler, Adolf. *Mein Kampf*. New York: Stackpole Sons Publishers, 1939.

Hoffman, Peter. *German Resistance to Hitler*. Cambridge: Harvard University Press, 1988.

Hofstadter, Richard. *Social Darwinism and American Thought*. Boston: Beacon Press, 1971.

Hohne, Heinz. *The Order of the Death's Head: the Story of Hitler's SS*. New York: Coward-McCann, 1970.

Ivy, Andrew Conway. *Report on War Crimes of a Medical Nature*

Committed in Germany and Elsewhere on German Nationals and the Nationals of Occupied Countries by the Nazi Regime During World War II. National Archives, 1945.

Jackel, Eberhard. *Hitler in History.* Hanover and London: University Press of New England for Brandeis University Press, 1984.

Jaeckle, Renate. *The Physicians and Politics: 1930 Until Today.* Frankfurt: Beck'sche Reihe 361, 1988.

Jaworski, Leon. *After Fifteen Years.* Houston: Gulf Books, 1963.

Katz, Jay. *The World of Doctor and Patient.* New York: Free Press, 1984.

Kaul, F. K. *Die Psychiatrie im Strudel der "Euthanasie."* Frankfurt: Europäische Verlagsanstalt, 1979.

Kintner, Earl W., ed. *The Hadamar Trial: Trial of Alfons Klein, Defendant.* Edinburgh: William Hodge, 1949.

Kinzey, Warren G., ed. *The Evolution of Human Behavior: Primate Models.* New York: State University of New York Press, 1987.

Klee, Ernst, ed. *Documentation of Euthanasia.* Frankfurt: Fischer Taschenbuch Verlag 4327, 1988.

Klee, Ernst. *"Euthanasie" im NS-Statt, Die "Vernichtung lebensunwerten Lebens."* Frankfurt: S. Fisher, 1983.

Langer, Walter C. *The Mind of Adolf Hitler: The Secret Wartime Report.* New York and London: Basic Books, Inc., 1972.

Lewy, Guenter. *The Catholic Church and Nazi Germany.* New York, Toronto: McGraw-Hill, 1964.

Lifton, Robert Jay. *The Nazi Doctors—Medical Killing and the Psychology of Genocide.* New York: Basic Books, Inc., 1986.

Mensch-achte den Menschen Furhe Texte über die Euthanasieverbrechen der Nationalsozialisten in Hessen. Kassel: Landeswohlfahrts verbandes, 1985.

Mitscherlich, Alexander. *The Death Doctors*, trans. James Cleugh. London: Elek Books, 1962.

Motion and Brief *Amici Curiae* of the Association for Retarded Citizens/ U.S.A., et al., *in re City of Cleburne, Texas, et al.* v. *Cleburne Living Center, et al.*, before the Supreme Court of the United States, October term, 1984, #84–468.

Muller-Hill, Benno. *Murderous Science.* Oxford: Oxford University Press, 1988.

Peukert, Detlev J. K. *Nazi Germany: Conformity, Opposition, and Racism in Everyday Life*, trans. Richard Deveson. New Haven: Yale University Press, 1988.

Poliakov, Leon. *Harvest of Hate: The Nazi Program for the Destruction of the Jews in Europe.* Westport: Greenwood Press, 1975.

Porter, Jack Nusan. *Genocide and Human Rights: a Global Anthology.* Lanham, Md., New York, and London: University Press of America, 1982.

Portmann, Heinrich. *Cardinal von Galen.* London: Jarolds, 1958.

Proctor, Robert N. *Racial Hygiene: Medicine Under the Nazis.* Cambridge: Harvard University Press, 1988.

Rapport, Samuel, and Helen Wright, eds. *Great Adventures in Medicine.* New York: The Dial Press, 1952.

Reitlinger, Gerald. *The Final Solution: The Attempt to Eliminate the Jews from Europe. 1939–1945.* New York: A. S. Barnes and Co., 1961.

Safilios-Rothschild, Constantina. *Sociology and Social Psychology of Disability and Rehabilitation.* New York: Random House, 1981.

Sassone, S. M. and R. L. Sassone. *Handbook on Euthanasia.* R. L. Sassone, 1975.

Schmidt, Gerhard. *Selektion in der Heilanstalt 1939–45.* Stuttgart: Evangelisches Verlagswerk, 1965.

Schoenbaum, David. *Hitler's Social Revolution: Class and Status in Nazi Germany 1933–1939.* Garden City, N. Y.: Doubleday and Co., 1968.

Sereny, Gitta. *Into That Darkness: From Mercy Killing to Mass Murder.* New York: McGraw-Hill, 1974.

Shearer, Ann. *Disability, Whose Handicap?* London: Basil Blackwell, 1981.

Shirer, William L. *The Rise and Fall of the Third Reich: A History of Nazi Germany.* New York: Simon and Schuster, 1960.

Sichrovsky, Peter. *Born Guilty. Children of Nazi Families*, trans. Jean Steinberg. New York: Basic Books, Inc., 1988.

Sigerist, Henry E. *A History of Medicine* (Volume II). New York: Oxford University Press, 1961.

Snyder, Louis L. *Encyclopedia of the Third Reich.* New York: McGraw-Hill Book Company, 1976.

Sontag, Susan. *Illness as Metaphor.* New York: Farrar Straus Giroux, 1977.

Stern, Bernhard J., *Society and Medical Progress.* Princeton: Princeton University Press, 1941.

Stern, Fritz. *Dreams and Delusions.* New York: Knopf, 1987.

Strong, E. K., Jr. *Change of Interests with Age.* Stanford University Press, 1931.

Taylor, A. J. P. *The Course of German History, a Survey of the Development of Germany Since 1815.* London: Hamish Hamilton, 1946.

Taylor, Telford. *Final Report to the Secretary of the Army on the Nuremberg War Crimes Trials Under Control of Council Law #10.* Washington, D.C.: U.S. Government Printing Office, August 15, 1949.

Tenenbaum, Joseph. *Race and Reich: The Story of an Epoch.* Westport, Connecticut: Greenwood Press, 1976.

Toland, John. *Adolf Hitler.* Garden City, N.Y.: Doubleday and Co., Inc., 1976.

Trials of War Ciminals Before the Nuremberg Military Tribunals Under Control Council Law No. 10, Nuremberg, October 1946–April 1947. Washington, D.C.: U.S. Government Printing Office, Volumes I and II.

U.S. Nuremberg War Crimes Trials, November 21, 1946–August 20, 1947. National Archives Microfilm Publications, M887.

Vash, Carolyn. *Psychology of Disability.* New York: Springer, 1980.

Wagner, Albrecht. *Die Umgestaltung der Gerichtsverfassung und des Verfahrens- und Richterrechts im nationalsozialistischen Staat.* Stuttgart: Deutsche Verlags-Anstalt, 1968.

Wertham, Fredric, M.D. *A Sign for Cain: An Exploration of Human Violence.* London: Robert Hale Ltd., 1968.

Whalen, Robert Weldon. *Bitter Wounds: German Victims of the Great War 1914–1939.* Ithaca and London: Cornell University Press, 1984.

Wistrich, Robert. *Who's Who in Nazi Germany.* New York: Macmillan, 1982.

Wright, Beatrice A. *Physical Disability–A Psychological Approach.* New York: Harper and Brothers, 1960.

Wunder, Michael. *There Is No Stopping on This Slope.* Hamburg: Rauhes Haus, 1988.

Zahn, Gordon C. *German Catholics and Hitler's Wars.* New York: E. P. Dutton and Co., 1969.

Zola, Irving Kenneth. *Missing Pieces.* Philadelphia: Temple University Press, 1982.

———. *Ordinary Lives.* Cambridge, Mass.: Applewood Books, 1982.

Articles

"Bishop of Münster." *Tablet* 178 (October 18, 1941): 248.

"Bishop von Galen and the Reich." *Catholic World* 154 (Nov 22, 1941): 235–6.

"Bishop von Galen Defies Hitler." *Catholic Mind* 40 (December 22, 1942): 1–5.

"Bishop von Galen Protests." *Ave Maria* 54 (October 25, 1941): 514.

"Bishop Worries Hitler." *Ave Maria* 54 (November 15, 1941): 613.

"Brutalities of Nazi Physicians." *Journal of the American Medical Association* (December 28, 1946): 1104.

"Catholic Bishop Speaks Out." *Ave Maria* 54 (November 1, 1941): 549.

"Defending the Retarded." *Newsweek* (July 4, 1988).

"Euthanasia in Naziland." *Catholic Digest* 6 (March 1943): 51–3.

"Extermination of Disabled People in Nazi Germany." *Disabled U.S.A.* 4(2) 1980: 23–24.

"Fertility of Patients with Mental Diseases." *Journal of the American Medical Association* 118(4): 1941.

"German Bishop Speaks." *America* 66 (November 1, 1941): 99.

"German Bishop Warns that Gestapo Menaces Reich." *Catholic Mind*, 39 (December 8, 1941): 1–11.

"Hefelmann Trial," *New York Times*, February 20, 1964, p. 2, col. 5.

"Hefelmann Trial Opens . . . Reportedly Sought Mercy Death for His Own Mother," *New York Times*, February 19, 1964, p. 5, col. 2.

"Hefelmann Trial Postponed Indefinitely," *New York Times*, August 29, 1964, p. 5, col. 6.

"Hefelmann Trial, Recessed Because of His Health, to Resume," *New York Times*, July 26, 1964, p. 3, col. 1.

"Hesse State to Try Drs. W. Heyde, G. Bohne and H. Hefelmann for Mercy Killing," *New York Times*, July 24, 1962, p. 2, col. 4.

"Heyde Pleads Innocent," *New York Times*, November 15, 1959, p. 42, col. 6.

"New Decisions on Sterilization and Castration." *Journal of the American Medical Association* 104(23): 2109–10.

"Pope Condemns World War II Treatment of Handicapped," New York *Daily News*, June 27, 1988.

"Religious War Heroes." *Ave Maria* 55 (May 30, 1942): 674–5.

"Sentence on Daubers of Swastikas." *The Times* (London), October 5, 1966, 1.

"Special Eugenics Courts." *Journal of the American Medical Association* 103(11): 849–50.

"Swedish Health Board Sanctions Euthanasia by M.D." *Medical World News*, November 20, 1964, 56–60.

"Systematic Killing by Germans of the Mentally Deranged." *Journal of the American Medical Association* 128(1): 47.

"The Brutalities of Nazi Physicians." Editorial. *Journal of the American Medical Association*, 132(12): 714.

"Useless Petitions for Sterilization." *Journal of the American Medical Association* 104(13): 1183.

Abicht, Ludo. "The Holocaust as Suicidal Enterprise." *New German Critique* 20 (Spring 1980): 177–86.

Adamek, Raymond J. "It Has Happened Here," *Human Life Review* 3 (Fall 1977): 74–83.

Alexander, Leo, M.D. "Medical Science Under Dictatorship."

New England Journal of Medicine 241 (2) (July 14, 1949): 39–47.

Aly, Goetz, and Heinz Roth. "The Legalization of Mercy Killings in Medical and Nursing Institutions in Nazi Germany from 1938 Until 1941." *International Journal of Law and Psychiatry* 7 (1984): 145–63.

Boozer, Jack S. "Children of Hippocrates: Doctors in Nazi Germany." *Annals of the AAPSS* (July 1980): 83–95.

Breggin, Peter Roger, M.D. "The Psychiatric Holocaust." *Penthouse*, January 1979, 81–84.

Broder, Henryk M. " 'It Thinks Inside Me . . .': Fassbinder, Germans and Jews." *Encounter*, March 1986, 64–68.

Cohen, Cynthia B. " 'Quality of Life' and the Analogy with the Nazis." *The Journal of Medicine and Philosophy* 3 (May 1983), 113–36.

Conway, John S. "The Silence of Pope Pius XII." *The Review of Politics* 27 (1967): 105–31.

Dörner, Klaus. "Nationalsozialismus und Lebensvernichtung." *Vierteljahrshefte für Zeitgeschicte*, 15: 2 (April 1967), 122–152.

Ebon, Martin. "Why Did Hitler Hate the Jews?" *Midstream*, October 1979, 19–24.

Fischer, Arlene. "Babies in Pain." *Redbook*, October 1987, 124–25.

Fisher, Eugene J. "The Holocaust and Christian Responsibility." *America*, February 14, 1981, 119–21.

Gallagher, Hugh Gregory. "The Body Silent." *The Fessenden Review*, 12:1.

Gallin, Mary Alice. "The Cardinal and the State: Faulhaber and the Third Reich." *The Journal of Church and State* 12 (1970): 385–420.

Gardner, James M. "Contribution of the German Cinema to the Nazi Euthanasia Program." *Mental Retardation*, August 1982, 174–75.

Graham, Robert A., S.J. "The 'Right to Kill' in the Third Reich. Prelude to Genocide." *Catholic Historical Review* 62 (1976): 56–76.

Griggens, Cynthia. "The Disabled Face a Schizophrenic Society."

Hanauske-Able, Hartmut M. "Politics and Medicine: From Nazi Holocaust to Nuclear Holocaust: a Lesson to Learn?" *The Lancet*, August 22, 1986, 271–73.

Helmreich, Ernst C. "The Nature and Structure of the Confessing Church in Germany Under Hitler." *Journal of Church and State* 12 (1970): 405–20.

Hentig, H. von. "Physical Disability, Mental Conflict, and Social Crisis." *Journal of Social Issues* 4 (1948 B): 4.

Hentoff, Nat. "The Awful Privacy of Baby Doe." *The Atlantic Monthly*, January 1985, 54–58.

Holt, Niles R. "Monists and Nazis: a Question of Scientific Responsibility." Hastings Center Report, April 1975, 37–42.

Hughes, John Jay. "The Pope's 'Pact With Hitler': Betrayal or Self-Defense?" *Journal of Church and State* 17 (1975): 63–80.

Ivy, Andrew. "Report on War Crimes of a Medical Nature in Germany and Elsewhere." National Archives, 1945.

Kater, Michael H. "The Burden of the Past: Problems of a Modern Historiography of Physicians and Medicine in Nazi Germany." *German Studies Review* X:1 (February 1987): 31–56.

Kennedy, Foster, M.D. "Brutalities of Nazi Physicians, the Problem of Social Control of the Congenital Defective: Education, Sterilization, Euthanasia," *American Journal of Psychiatry* 99 (July 1942): 13–16.

Koop, Everett G. "The Slide to Auschwitz." *Human Life Review* 3: 109–113.

Kuby, E. "Rot . . . Stopp . . . Grun . . . Anfahren . . . Scharf Bremsen." *Der Spiegel* 15: 19 (1965).

LaChat, Michael R. "Utilitarian Reasoning in Nazi Medical Policy: Some Preliminary Investigations." *Linacre Quarterly*, February 1975.

Lauder, H., and J. E. Meyer. "Mercy Killing Without Consent. Historical Comments on the Controversial Issue." *Acta Psychiatrica Scandinavica* 65, (1982): 134–41.

Le Disert, Dominique. "Entre la Peur et la Pitié: Quelques Aspects Sociohistoriques de l'infirmité," trans. Vivien Rubin. *International Journal of Rehabilitation Research* 10:3 (1987): 253–65.

Lenox, William G. "Should They Live? Certain Economic Aspects of Medicine." *American Scholar*, 7:4 (October 1938): 454–66.

McGuire, T. "Nazis, Reds, and Religious." *Sign* 21 (November 1941): 195.

Mussen, P. H., and R. G. Barker. "Attitudes Toward Cripples." *Journal of Abnormal Social Psychology* 39 (1944): 351–55.

Peeling, William. "Reconditioning the Maimed." *The Listener*, November 10, 1937, 1003.

Shirer, William L. " 'Mercy Deaths' in Germany" (condensed from *Berlin Diary*). *Reader's Digest*, June 1941, 55–58.

Tedeschi, Mary, "Infanticide and Its Apologists." *Commentary*, November 1984, 31–35.

Wolfensberger, Wolf. "The Extermination of Handicapped People in World War II Germany." *Ethics*, February 1981.

Wunder, Michael. "Sterbehilfe—Tötung auf wessen Verlangen?" *Dokumente*, September 1987, 19–22.

Sound Recordings

"For What It's Worth." Buffalo Springfield. Arco Record Company, 1967.

Index

Aboriginal hunting society, 25
Abortion, 108
Abrams, Robert E., 249–50
Absberg, 137–38
    and Aktion T-4 program, 138–44,
        146, 172, 173
Academy of German Law, 208
Africans, 79
    See also Western Africa
Age of Reason, 24
AIDS, 25, 32, 272
Aktion Brandt, 264
Aktion T-4 euthanasia program, 126,
        255, 256, 257, 280
    at Absberg, 138–44, 146, 172, 173
    administrative procedures for, 65–69,
        71–72, 100–102, 114–17, 146–
        47, 233–34
    beginning of, 45–73
    Central Accounting Office, 105
    and the church, 219–46
    condemnation of, 242–44
    correspondence with families of de-
        ceased, 108–14
    estimates of killings, 118–19
    exemptions from, 70–71
    explanation of, 252–53
    at Hadamar, 9, 11–23

halted, 245
institutions for, 97–98
killing procedures, 98–105
last trial on, 261–62
and lawyers, 205–18
official central killings, 118
operation of, 57–59, 96–119
origins of, 74–95
personal tragedies under, 173–76
and physicians, 178–204
and public opinion, 148–56, 165–73,
        176–77
and research, 106–8
sequelae, 247–74
Alaska, north, 27–28
Alberta (Canadian province), 84
Alexander, Dr. Leo, 105–6, 109–10,
        119, 132, 195, 198, 250–51
    notes of, 173–74
    writings of, 203–4
Allers, Dietrich, 179
Alliance of Protestant Institutions for
        Mentally and Psychiatrically Im-
        paired Persons, 267
Allied Boards of the Bodelschwingh In-
        stitutions of Bethel, 235–36
Allied powers, 223, 239, 240, 249
    occupying forces of, 248, 252, 254

331

Alsterdorf (Protestant facility), 236–37
Aly, Goetz, 7, 119, 126, 172, 214, 265
Amazon, North West, 29
America, 11, 25, 48, 86, 105, 220, 272
  Bill of Rights in, 206
  disability insurance in, 33
  disease in, 40
  South in, 201
  See also United States
American Academy of Pediatrics, 124
American Neurological Association, 93
American Psychiatric Association, 94
Americans, vs. Germans, 1, 24, 34–35
Amir, Amnon, 126, 187, 216, 218
Anglo-Saxons, 80
  aristocracy in U.S., 78
  Nordic European states, 85
Anti-Semitism, 86, 165, 189, 191, 281
Arctic, 28
Arendt, Hannah, 22, 146, 209
Aryans, 69, 70, 89
Athens (Greece), 33
Atrott, Hans Henning, 269, 270–71
Auschwitz, 281
Australia, 29
Azande tribe, 28

Baby Doe case, 123, 131
Badische Heil- und Pflegeanstalt (hospital), 180
Balinese, the, 30
Baumann (priest), 230
Baumhardt, Dr., 185, 186–87
Bavaria, 135
  See also Kaufbeuren
Bavarian State Ministry of the Interior, 69–70
Behavior modification, 273
Belgium, 188
Berlin, 17, 130, 275, 278, 279
  politicians, 280–81
  See also West Berlin
Berlin-Buch (institution), 119
Berlin Diary (Shirer), 95

Bernberg (euthanasia institution), 98, 117, 118
Bertram, Cardinal, 228, 230
Bethel Mission, 226, 233–36, 267
Binding, Karl, 91–92, 94, 126, 218, 267
Bismarck, Otto von, 189, 208, 221
Blacks, attitudes toward, 37
Blome, Dr. Karl, 201, 252, 256
Blum, Philipp, 15–16
Blutkitt, 198
Bodelschwingh, Pastor Friedrich von, 48, 233–35, 257
Bodelschwinghsche Institutions (Bethel), 267
Book of Common Prayer, 37
Borderline Situations of Life (Catel), 196, 261
Bormann, Martin, 55–56, 149, 244
Borneo, 6
Bouhler, Philip, 46, 48, 55–57, 64, 98–99, 100, 104, 144, 217, 251
Brace, Charles Loring, 80
Brack, Viktor, 14, 48, 60, 64, 68, 69, 98, 99, 100, 113, 148, 215, 217, 251, 252, 253
  duties of, 56–57
  letter to, 144–45
  trial of, 256–57
Brandenburg on the Havel prison (euthanasia institution), 97, 98, 99, 118, 132, 176, 236
  letter from, 112–13
Brandenburg province, 119
Brandt, Dr. Karl, 46–48, 56–57, 99, 117, 118, 119, 216, 235, 245
  charges against, at Nuremberg, 252, 253
  death of, 256
  eminence of, 251
  final statement at Nuremberg, 257–58
  judgment on, 258–59
  and Knauer case, 261
  testimony at Nuremberg, 55, 70, 71–72, 103, 126, 127–28, 129, 152, 180, 194, 202, 272
Braune, Paul Gerhard, 168, 230–33

Braunmuhl, Dr. von, 250
Brenner, Dr., 21
Britain, 86, 88, 136, 224
  See also English blood; Great Britain;
    United Kingdom
Broder, Henryk M., 281
Bruckberg Institution, 172–73
Buch, Frau, 165
  letter to, 152–56
Buch, Walter
  letter from, 165–66
  letter to, 167, 194–95
Buchenwald concentration camp, 56,
  256
Bumke, Erwin, 217
Bumke, Professor, 63
Bundestag, 268, 269, 270
Bunke, Heinrich, 261–62

Caesar, Julius, 62
California, 82
Calvin, John, 220
Calvinists, 219, 221
Campbell, Dr. A. G. M., 123–24
Canada, 84
Caritas Institute of Science, 225, 226,
  229
Carnegie Foundation, 93
Carolines
  East Central, 29
  Eastern, 29
Casti Conubii (encyclical), 226
Catel, Dr. Werner, 128, 129, 196, 261
Catholic Center Party, 222
Catholics. *See* Roman Catholic Church
Caucasian world, 39
Cavaliers (Va.), 78
Central Committee of the Inner Mission,
  225, 234
Chagga, the, 29
Children
  brutality toward, in Germany, 122–23
  cruelty toward, in U.S., 120–21,
    123–25
Children's program, 118, 121, 125,
  126–36, 251, 261

administrative confusion in, 134–35
authorization of, 126
decision making in, 129
numbers killed in, 131–33
passive vs. active killing in, 130–31
Christianity, 24, 31, 32–33
Christof, Franz, 277, 278
Cold War, 275
Collegium Germanicum (Rome), 245
Columbus, Christopher, 62
Committee for Petitions of the West Ger-
  man Parliament, 267
Concordat, with Germany, 223–24, 227,
  239
Congress (U.S.), 25, 85
Constitution (U.S.), 83
Conti, Dr. Leonardo, 55, 99, 182, 229,
  234
  letter from 64–65, 68
Control Council Law No. 10, 252, 253,
  254
Council of Physicians (Hamburg), 265–
  66
Cox, Dr. Alan, 124
Creek Indians, 29
Creutz, Walter, 181
Criminals, 82
  and sterilization, 83
Crinis, Dr. Max de, 63, 196–97
Custodial-care institutions, in U.S.,
  85

Dahomeans, the, 29
Dahrendorf, Ralf, 122
Danzig, 118
Darwin, Charles, 74
  followers of, 81, 88
  theories of, 27, 75–76, 86, 90
  See also Social Darwinists
Davenport, Charles, 77, 79
Death, physicians' attitudes toward, 42–
  43
Descent of Man, The (Darwin), 76
Detoxification, 59
Deuel, Wallace, 53
"Devaluation," 38

Dibelius, Friedrich, sermon of, 205–6
Dibelius, Otto, 223
Dickmann, Friedrich, 16
Dieri, the, 29
Disability
  in aboriginal world, 27–30
  in animal kingdom, 27
  attitudes toward, 38–39
  and discrimination, 2–3
  and doctor-patient relationship, 39–40, 42–43
  and genetic inferiority, 80–82
  and learned inferiority, 40–42
  meaning of, 25–26
  and money, 43–44
  and nineteenth-century advances, 74–75
  psychological studies of, 34–38
  and status, 43–44
  in Western society, 30–34
Disability: Whose Handicap? (Shearer), 25–26
Disney, Walt, 30
Division of Nursing Homes of the Interior Ministry, 147
Doctor-patient relationship, 39–40, 42–43, 199–200
Doctors. *See* German physicians
Dörner, Klaus, 118
Draper, G. I. D., 136
Duff, Dr. Raymond, 123–24
Dugdale, Richard, 80
Duoch, Alex von, 166
Duoch, Else von. *See* Löwis, Else von
Duoch, Grete von, 165
Du Pont, Coleman, 84
Düsseldorf court, 61, 181
Dutch blood, 79

Eastern Europe, 85
East Germany, 276
Eglfing-Haar hospital, 70, 106, 109, 111, 116, 127, 130, 132–35, 171, 183, 195, 199, 250
Egypt, 32
Enabling Act, 207–8

Endruweit, Dr. Klaus ("Dr. Bader"), 196
English blood, 79
  See also Britain; Great Britain; United Kingdom
Esch, Peter, 259
Ethiopia, 180
Eugenics movement, in U.S., 77–86, 87, 88
Europe, 5, 53, 74, 82, 85, 89, 246
  Black Death of, 6
  See also Eastern Europe; Nordic European states; Northern Europeans; Southern Europe; Western Europe
Euthanasia, defined, 59n
  See also Aktion T-4 euthanasia program
"Euthanasie" im NS-Staat, Die "Vernichtung lebensunwerten Lebens" (Klee), 118, 264
Evangelical Church of Prussia, 233
Ewald, Gottfried, 60, 179, 182, 183
Exodus, 33

Falthauser, Dr., 106, 117
Fassbinder, Rainer Werner, 281
Faulhaber, Cardinal, 224, 227–28, 230
FDR's Splendid Deception (Gallagher), 2
Federal Council of Physicians, 266, 268, 269
Feis, Oswald, 109
Fifty-sixth Congress of Jurists, 269
Fischer, Dr. E., daughter of, 188
Fortieth Bavarian Congress of Physicians, 266
Foundation for the Care of Institutions in the Public Interest, 57
14 f 13 program, 9, 118, 264
France, 33, 48, 240, 251
Franco-Prussia, 137
Frank, Hans, 208–9
Frankfurt County Court, letter from, 104, 105
Frankfurt am Main Provincial Court of Appeal, communication from, 210–11
Frederick the Great, King of Prussia, 223

Freisler, Dr., 217, 218
Frick, Pastor Constantin, 232, 234
Frick, Henry Clay, 84
Frick, Minister of the Interior, 56, 227, 229, 251
Fritsche, Professor, 269
Führer principle, 233

Ganzer, Ernst, 184–85
Gardner, James M., 92
General Patient Transport Company, 11, 58, 97, 106, 107, 116
Genetic engineering, 272–73
Genetic Health Law, 266
Genkel, Ingrid, 223
German Doctors' Congress, 262
German Evangelical Church, 233
Germania, 94
German Medical Association, 189, 190, 263
German physicians
    as agents, 18–19
    atrocities of, 253–54
    authority of, 64, 218
    and children's program, 125, 126, 129–34
    decision making of, 117–18, 129
    defensiveness of, 265–66
    and disease, 40
    incentives and imperatives of, 96–97, 187–94
    and inferior citizens, 44, 55
    killing methods of, 98–99, 131
    and mental patients, 72–73
    motivation of, 194–95, 197–204
    as participants, 62–63, 103–4, 196–97
    perversion of medical ethics, 255
    and "refractory cases," 2–7
    research of, 106–8
    resistance of, 178–85
    and secret meetings, 59–61
    and "spread," 38
    violence by, 185–87
Germans
    vs. Americans, 1, 24, 34–35

blood, 79
    denial of, 264
    religious practice of, 219–20
German Society for Humane Dying, 269, 270
German Society for Social Psychiatry, 271
Germany, 108, 271, 281
    abolition of freedom in, 207
    army, 117
    and authority, 19
    biological prowess of, 51–52
    bombing of, 118
    castration in, 54
    children in, 122–23
    churches of, 45, 46, 219–46
    citizens of, 69
    Concordat with, 223–24, 227, 239
    court system in, 254
    death notices in, 177
    depressed state after World War II, 248–49
    disability rights in, 275, 277–79
    emergency decree in, 207
    establishment of, 223
    gallows humor in, 100
    and Great Depression, 191
    as jungle state, 136
    and lawyers, 205–18
    learned inferiority in, 40–41
    madness of, 4
    medical delivery system of, 146–47
    medical excellence in, 187–89
    monism in, 86–92
    Nazi revolution in, 49–53, 190
    in 1930s, 47–49, 105
    penal code in, 93
    population of, 219
    postwar, 259
    racism in, 38, 60, 86–87
    rebuilding of, 247–48
    during Second Reich, 206
    social progress in, 50
    sterilization in, 52–55, 84, 89, 93–95, 126, 192, 266–68
    stress in, 179–80

Germany (cont'd)
  traffic accidents in, 122
  unconditional surrender of, 247
  unique contributions of, 24
  war posture of, 104
  young people in, 50–51
  See also Aktion T-4 euthanasia program; Children's program; East Germany; Nazis; West Germany; Wilhelmine state
Gerry, Martin, 125
Gerstner (Nazi official), 143–44, 152
Gestapo, 104, 135, 146, 165, 228, 232, 235, 238, 241, 246
  and von Galen sermon, 243–44
Glass Menagerie, The, 34
Gliedman, John, 37, 40
Goebbels, Josef, 39, 49, 244–45
Göring, Hermann, 56, 182, 232, 234, 239, 244, 251
Göring, Karin, 165
Göring, Matthias, 182
Grafeneck (euthanasia institution), 97, 98, 112, 117, 118, 144, 154, 167, 172, 174, 175, 180, 185, 186
Graz, district attorney of, 212–13
Great Britain, 84
  See also Britain; English blood; United Kingdom
Greeks, ancient, 31, 32, 52, 200
Gröber, Archbishop, 227, 229–30
Gross, Dr. Richard, 124
Gugenberg (mother superior), 139–40
Gürtner (Reich Minister of Justice), 216, 217, 230, 232
Gypsies, 51, 69, 168, 191, 205, 206, 246

Hackethal, Dr. Julius, 269, 275
Hadamar Psychiatric Institute, 10
  Aktion T-4 program at, 9, 11–23, 98, 104, 105, 114, 118, 169, 202, 210
Haeckel, Ernst, 87–88, 89–90, 91
Hague Regulations, 253
Hallervorden, Dr. Julius, 107–8, 196
Hamburg Council of Physicians, 265–66

Hamburg Health Authority, 266
Hamburg Oberaltenallee, 236
Hamburg report, 53, 54–55
Hanauske-Abel, 263
Hanover, 181
Harriman, Mrs. E. H., 84
Hartheim (euthanasia institution), 97, 98, 102–3, 104, 117, 118
Hartl, Albert, 228, 229
Hartmann Bund, 189
"Health in marriage" law of 1935, 192
Hebrews, ancient, 31
Hefelmann, Dr. Hans, 143, 194
Hegener, Dr. von, 133
Heinze, Hans, 128, 129
Henry V (Shakespeare), 257
Hentig, H. von, 30, 37
Herbron (sanitorium), 101
Heredity in Human Progress (McKim), 81
Herrlinger, Dr. R., 196
Hess, Rudolf, 191, 251
Heyde, Dr. Werner ("Dr. Sawade"), 13, 57, 182, 197, 202, 217–18, 260–61
  letter to, 150–51
Heydrich, Reinhard, 228, 232
Himmler, Heinrich, 56, 57, 179, 208, 256
  letter from, 144–45, 167, 194–95
  letter to, 165–66
Himmler, Mrs. Heinrich, 57
Hindenburg, Paul von, 205, 207, 223
Hippocrates, 43, 190, 202
Hippocratic Oath, 6, 180, 193, 197, 200
Hitler, Adolf, 12, 20, 39, 71, 74, 86, 92, 93, 99, 117, 129, 146, 152, 153, 165, 172, 182, 194, 198, 205, 218, 232, 234, 235, 239, 241, 251, 264, 265
  achievements of, 50–51
  adulation of, 49–50, 155–56
  Chancellery of, 48, 57, 58–59, 60, 128, 143, 228, 229, 248
  and church power, 149, 219, 224–25, 227–28, 233
  complexity of, 51

dictatorial authority of, 207–8
and disability, 52
on "eternal struggle," 136
euthanasia order of, 5, 44, 45–47, 48, 49, 51, 55, 56, 59, 61, 64, 96, 142, 166, 167, 208, 209, 213, 216, 217
and formal law, 214–15, 255
halts program, 245
and Knauer affair, 127–28, 261
madness of, 4
personal failures of, 48–49
rise to power, 188–91, 206, 207, 220
Russian campaign of, 245
and social unrest, 222–23
suicide of, 248
Hitler Cut, 53–54
Hitler's Table Talk, 245
Hitler Youth, 239
Hobbes, Thomas, 27
Hoche, Alfred, 91–92, 94, 126, 218, 267
Hoellen, Martin, 229
Hofelmann, Dr., 151
Hohenzollern kings, 223
Hohne, Heinz, 146
Holmes, Oliver Wendell, 83
Holocaust, the, 6, 55, 62, 98, 104, 195, 216, 249
Holy Roman Empire, 221
Holzel, Dr. F., 199
    letter from 183–84
Holzhäuer, Public Prosecutor, 212
Homer, 34, 77
Homosexuals, 266–67
Hottentots, 79
Hoven, Dr. Waldemar, 252, 256
Huber, Irmgard, 13, 14, 16, 21–23
Hubsch, Lothar, mother of, 133–34

I Accuse, 92
I. G. Farben (company), 99
Iliad (Homer), 34
Indiana, 82
Infanticide, 123
Inner Mission, 226, 231, 232–33

Central Committee of, 225, 234
Internal Committee of the German Parliament, 267
International Medical Association (IMA), 263
International Military Tribunals (Nuremberg), 251, 253
International Red Cross, 127, 201
Inuits, 25, 28
Ivy, Dr. Andrew, 62

Japan, 121
Jasperson, H., 181
Jaworski, Leon, 21–22
Jennewein, Mr., 70
Jensema, C. J., 36
Jesuits, 222, 241
Jesus, 32
Jews, 14, 31, 37, 51, 69–71, 106, 118, 127, 135, 179, 189, 190, 193, 205, 218, 219, 223, 235–37, 246, 252, 253, 281
John Paul II, Pope, 271
Johnson, Hiram, 82
Jones, Marty, 272
Jordans, Dr. Joseph, 168
Jukeses, the, 80, 81, 82
Jukes, Max, 80
Jukun, the, 29
Jung, Dr. Herbert, 133
Justinian, Code of, 33

Kallikak, Martin, 81
Kallikaks, the, 80, 81, 82
Kallmeyer, Dr., 99
Kater, Michael H., 188, 265
Katz, Jay, 42
Kaufbeuren (institution), 104, 106, 117, 119, 249–50
    letters to, 65, 115
Kehr, Maria, 151
    letter from, 149–50
Kehr family, 151–52
Keitel, Wilhelm, 71
Keller, Dr. Franz, 225
Kemp, Evan, 26

Kennedy, Dr. Foster, 94, 95
Kerrl, Minister, 232
Khan, Genghis, 198
Kirchof (Nazi official), 139–41, 143
Kite, Elizabeth S., 81
Klee, Ernst, 118, 135, 181, 264–65
Klein, Alfons, 13, 15, 16, 20, 21, 22
Klein, Dr. F., 60
Knauer affair, 127–28, 214, 261
Koch (epileptic), 168
Koch, Karl, 56
Koller, Dr., letter from, 112
Kopper, Herr, 115
Kreyenberg, Dr. Gerhard, 236, 237
Kreyssig, Dr., 216–17
Kristallnacht, 165
Krupp works, 91
Kuhn, Dr., 183
Ku Klux Klan, 201
Kulturkampf, 221, 225

Lambroso, Cesare, 82
Lammers, Dr., 215, 216, 230, 232
    letters to, 211–12, 213
Lapple, Friedel, 265
"Law on Mercy Killing," 215
"Law for the Prevention of Genetically
    Impaired Progeny," 168, 192, 214,
    236, 266, 267
Lawyers, in Germany, 205–18
Le Desert, Dominique, 34
Legal Sterilization of Mental Patients
    (Mayer), 226–27, 228
Lehner, Ludwig, 127
Leinisch, Dr. M., letter to, 106
Lensch, Friedrich, 236, 237
Lewis, Jerry, 38, 85
Lichtenberg, Bernhard, 230
Liebenau, 175
Life extension, 273
Lifton, Dr. Robert Jay, 107, 132, 179,
    264
Limburg, Bishop of, 230
    letter from, 15
Lincoln, Abraham, 51
Lindemann, Hans, 150

Lindemann, Ottilie (née Ortmann), 150
Linden, Dr. Herbert, 57, 97
Lohnauer, Dr., 102–3
Louis XIV, King of France, 51
Löwis, Else von (von Duoch), 165–67
    letter from, 152–56
Luther, Martin, 32, 220–21
Lutherans, 94, 219, 221
Lysias, 33

Mackensen, Field Marshal von, 223
McKim, W. Duncan, 81
McMahon, Ed, 38
Mader, Mrs. Anna, 170–71
Mader, Maria, 170–71
Maisel, E., 27, 28
Malay Peninsula, 29
Manifesto of the Ninety-three, 188
Mann, Ernst, 91
Maori, the, 30
Marin, Rubell, 110
Masai, the, 29
Mathematics in the Service of National
    Political Education, 93
Mauthe, Otto, 186
Mayer, Dr. Joseph, 226–27, 228–29
Medicare, 33
Mediterranean types, 79
Mein Kampf (Hitler), 52, 92
Mendelian laws, 76, 77
Meng, H., 30
Mennecke, Dr. Fritz, 60–61, 169, 202
Mental patients, 69–73, 116, 119, 227
Merkle, Adolf, 16–17, 21
Meyer, Dr., letter from, 112–13
Middle Ages, plague in, 30–31
Mielke, Dr. Fred, 262
Ministry of the Interior, 57, 97, 172, 212
    Division of Nursing Homes, 147
    letter from, 64–65
Ministry of Justice, 93, 185, 209, 213,
    216, 231
    Division Four of, 214
    letter from, 211–12
    letter to, 15, 104
    official communication to, 210–11

Ministry of Propaganda, 243
Mission Sisters of the Immaculate Conception, 241
Missouri, 83
Mitscherlich, Dr. Alexander, 179, 262–64, 274
Mitscherlich, Margarete, 274
Mockel, Dr. Wilhelm, 174, 180
Monism, in Germany, 86–92
Moral der Kraft (Mann), 91
Moritz, Mrs. Johanna Sara, letter to, 110
Muckermann, Dr. Hermann, 225–26
Muller, Director, 169
Muller-Hill, Benno, 179, 184, 265
Münster, 181, 240–41, 244, 245, 271
Mystici Corporis, 237

Nacht und Nebel, 216
National Institute of Immigration, 79
National Socialist German Physicians' League, 190
Natural selection, 75–77
Naumburg an der Saale, 212
Navajo Indians, 28
Nazi Doctors, The (Lifton), 107
Nazis (National Socialists), 31, 144, 192, 248, 279
  and animal experiments, 255–56
  behavior under, 197–200
  and bureaucracy, 146
  denial of atrocities, 259, 263
  and disability, 92–93
  killing program of, 93–95
  and legal system, 207–9
  medical laws under, 192–93
  and physicians, 5, 193
  problems of, 235–37, 239–46
  and public health, 191–92
  and public opinion, 148–49, 152–56, 177
  racism of, 179, 191, 222
  revolution of, 49–53, 190
  and Roman Catholic Church, 224–27
  terror of, 205
  and *Untermenschen*, 38
  victims of, 265–68

See also Aktion T-4 euthanasia program; Children's program; German physicians; Germany; Third Reich
Neumeister, Heddy, 122–23
New England Journal of Medicine, 123–24
  article, quoted, 203–4
New Guinea, 29
New Jersey, 82
New York Times, The, 93, 272
New Zealand, 30
Niedernhart, 116, 171
Nitsche, Dr. Paul, 57, 196, 202
Nordic European states, 85
Northern Europeans, 79, 80
Nuremberg
  International Military Tribunals, 251, 253
  party convention at, 52
  trials at, 5, 11, 15, 46, 55, 60, 62, 69–72, 97, 103, 114, 126–29, 134, 152, 180, 202, 203, 208, 215, 235, 254, 257, 262, 264, 272
  See also United States of America v. *Karl Brandt, et al.*

Obrawalde-Meseritz hospital, 260
Odyssey (Homer), 77
Old Testament, 31
Order of the Death's Head (Hohne), 146
Organ system, in West, 39–40
Orientals, 85, 89
Origin of Species (Darwin), 74, 75
Orthopedic medicine, 199
Ortmann, Christine, 150
Ottilienheim Abbey, 137, 139

Pacelli, Cardinal, 223, 224
  See also Pius XII, Pope
Paderborn, bishop of, 73
Panse, Professor, 181
Paracelsus, 190
"Passing," 39, 43
Paul, Saint, 220
Peace of Augsburg, 221

People Under Hitler (Deuel), 53
Permission to Destroy Life Unworthy of Life, The (Binding/Hoche), 91–92, 126
Peukert, Detlev, 205
Pfalz, I. D., 110
Pfannmüller, Dr. Hermann, 70, 96, 106, 110, 127, 130, 131, 132, 133, 134, 250
  letter from, 111
Pfingstweide-bei-Tettnang, 172
Pfister (constable), 143, 144
"Physicians Under National Socialism," 263
Pius XII, Pope, 223, 237
  See also Pacelli, Cardinal
Planck, Max, 188
Pohlisch, Professor, 181
Poland, 9, 14, 20, 45, 47, 104, 106, 118, 201, 235, 264
Pollay, Dr. Michael, 124
Pomerania, 118
Ponape, the, 29
Popenoe, Paul, 94
Portman, Chaplain, 242
Potsdam Day, 223
Preysing, Count Graf von, 237–38
Prisoner-of-War Convention, 253
Proctor, Robert, 191
Protestant Church, 219–23, 225, 226, 228, 231, 233, 236, 271
  Synod of, 267
  See also Calvinists; Lutherans
Prussia, 223
  See also West Prussia
Psychology of Schizophrenia, The (Schneider), 197
Puritans (Mass.), 78

Race Policy Office, 54
Reagan, Ronald, 51
Rechtsstaat, 206
Reformation, 24
Rehab 88, 270
Reich Association of Medical and Care Institutions, 59

Reich Association of Sanitoriums and Nursing Homes, 57–58, 116
Reich Chancellery, 231, 233, 244
Reich Committee for Scientific Research of Serious Illness of Hereditary and Protonic Origin, 58, 60, 64, 128–31, 133, 214, 215
Reichsbank, 105
Reichstag, 93, 189, 207, 208, 222, 223
Rein, Friedrich Hermann, 263
Renaissance, 24
Renno, Dr., 102–3
Reuter, Dr., 170
Riddle of the Universe, The (Haeckel), 87
Roentgen, Wilhelm, 188
Roman Catholic Church, 31, 94, 137, 140, 155, 177, 219–30, 237–40, 242, 246
Romans, the, 31
Romantic movement, 24, 86
Rome, 32, 222
  See also Collegium Germanicum
Roosevelt, Franklin D. (FDR), 2, 25, 39, 50, 51
Roosevelt, Teddy, 79
Roth, Karl Heinz, 7, 119, 126, 214, 265
Roth, William, 37, 40
Rüdin, Dr. Ernst, 202
Ruoff (male nurse), 14
Russell, Bertrand, 79
Russia, 20, 71, 117, 240, 244, 245, 251
  Stalinist, 212–13

Schallmayer, Dr. Wilhelm, 89
Schlaich, Pastor, letter from, 213–14
Schlegelberger, Dr. Franz, 113, 217
  letters from 211–12, 213
Schmidt, Dr. Walter, 61, 68
Schmiedel, Ernst, 209
Schneider, Karl, 63, 197, 202
Schumann, Dr., letter from, 150–51
Schweitzer, Dr. Albert, 48
Schwellenbach, Dr., 20
Scotch-Irish blood, 79
SD (Security Service), 143
Seip, Transport Director, 169

Sellmer (Nazi official), 143, 173
  letter from, 147–48
Semang, the, 29–30
Servatius, Dr. Robert, 257
Shakespeare, William, 257
Shaw, Anthony, 124
Shearer, Ann, 25–26
Shears, L. M., 36
Shirer, William L., 95
Sierck, Udo, 279
Sigerist, Henry, 31
Siriono Indians, 28
Social Darwinists, 5, 74, 77, 79, 86, 91, 191
Socialist League of Doctors, 190
Social Security disability insurance, 33
Sonder, Gertrud, 108–9
Sonder, Hans, letter from, 108–9
Sonnenstein (killing institution), 98, 117, 118, 134
  letter from, 150–51
  letter to, 149–50
Southern Europe, 85
Soviet Union. See Russia
Sparta, 52
Spencer, Herbert, 75
"Spread," 38
SS, 11, 12, 19, 55, 143, 144, 146, 155, 166, 167, 174, 186, 194–95, 198, 253
Stangl, Franz, 104
State Ministry of the Interior, 116
Steinhof (institution), 132
Stellbrink (pastor), 230
Sterilization
  in Germany, 52–55, 84, 89, 93–95, 126, 192, 266–68
  and Roman Catholic Church, 226–27
  in U.S., 82–84, 126
Sterilization Act, 93
Stetten (sanitorium), 142, 213
Stieberitz, Karl, 209
Strohmaier, Elise, letter from, 110–11
Sudan, 29
Sumner, William Graham, 79
Supreme Court (U.S.), 83

Survival of the fittest, 75–77
Swabia, 115, 117
Sweden, 84, 121

Taylor, Telford, 255, 259
T-4 program. See Aktion T-4 euthanasia program
Thalidomide, 44
Third Reich, 59, 247
  See also Nazis
Treasure Island, 34
Tribunals of Hereditary Health, 192
Trojan War, 34
Truk peoples, 29
Tulsa case, 124–25, 129, 131

Ullrich, Dr. Aquilin, 261–62
Unfähigkeit zu trauern, Die (Mitscherlich/Mitscherlich), 274
Unger, Helmet, 128
United Kingdom, 50, 251
  See also Britain; English blood; Great Britain
United States, 5, 53, 55, 74, 89, 93, 95, 108, 203, 206, 251, 259
  children in, 120–21, 123–25
  disability rights in, 277
  eugenics movement in, 77–86, 87, 88
  immigration to, 85
  infant mortality in, 121
  sensational press in, 269
  sterilization in, 82–84, 126
  study of disabilities in, 34–35
  traffic accidents in, 122
  See also America; Americans
United States of America v. Karl Brandt, et al., 251–59
  details of proceedings, 251
  evidence presented, 254–55
  indictment, 252–53
  issues of, 254
  prosecution's opening statement, 255–56
  sentences at, 256–59
  See also Nuremberg
Unrechtgesetz, 266–67

Untermenschen, 38, 40, 260
U.S. Army, 21, 22, 118, 130, 249–50

Vatican, 224, 237, 239
Velpke baby home, 136
Victorian England, 201
Villinger, Dr. Werner, 197
Volksgenossen, 244
Von Galen, Christopher Bernard, 238
Von Galen, Count Clemens August Graf
    (Lion of Münster), 238–45, 271
Von Galen, Ferdinand Herbert, 238
Von Galen, Count Franz, 244
Voss, Dr. Hermann, 196

Waggaman, Paul, 276
Wagner, Albrecht, 209
Wagner, Dr. Gerhardt, 46, 92
Wagner, Robert, 166
Wahlmann, Dr. Adolf, 12–16
WASPs, in U.S., 78
Wassermann, August von, 188
Wehrmacht, 231
Weimar Republic, 49, 51, 93, 191, 193,
    206, 208, 217, 220, 222, 265
Weizsäcker, Richard von, 277
Weizsäcker, Mrs., 279
Wentzler, Dr. Ernst, 128, 129, 132, 133
Wertham, Fredric, 119
West Berlin, 275, 276
Western Africa, 29
Western Europe, 24, 86
West German Parliament
    Committee for Petitions of, 267
    Internal Committee of, 267
West German Physicians' Chambers,
    262

West Germany, 259, 262, 264, 268, 271
    press in, 261, 269
    See also Germany
Westphalia, 233, 241, 245
West Prussia, 118
Widmann, Amalie, 173–74
Wienken, Heinrich, 229
Wieslech Clinic, 169–70, 173–74
Wild, Anny, 110–11
Wilhelm, Crown Prince of Germany, 223
Wilhelm II, Emperor of Germany, 208
Wilhelmine state, 86, 220
Wilm, Ernst, 230
Wilson, Woodrow, 82, 239
Winau, Rolf, 265
Wirth, Christian, 61, 98, 100
Witoto Indians, 29
Wogeo, the, 29
Wolf (official), 173
World War I, 49, 51, 71, 86, 137, 169,
    182, 188, 220, 223, 238–39
World War II, 5, 11, 45, 53, 71, 84, 137,
    138, 237, 239–40, 248, 275
    aftermath of, 208
Woth, Professor, 63
Wright, Beatrice, 27, 35, 38, 41
Wurm, Theophil, 229
Württemberg, 172, 173
Württemberg, bishop of, 230
Würzburg hospital, 217–18

Yale-New Haven case, 123–24, 131
Yerkes, Robert, 27

Zell, Lotte, 116
Ziegler, Dr. Heinrich, 88–89, 90–91
Zottmann, Father Joseph, 140–41